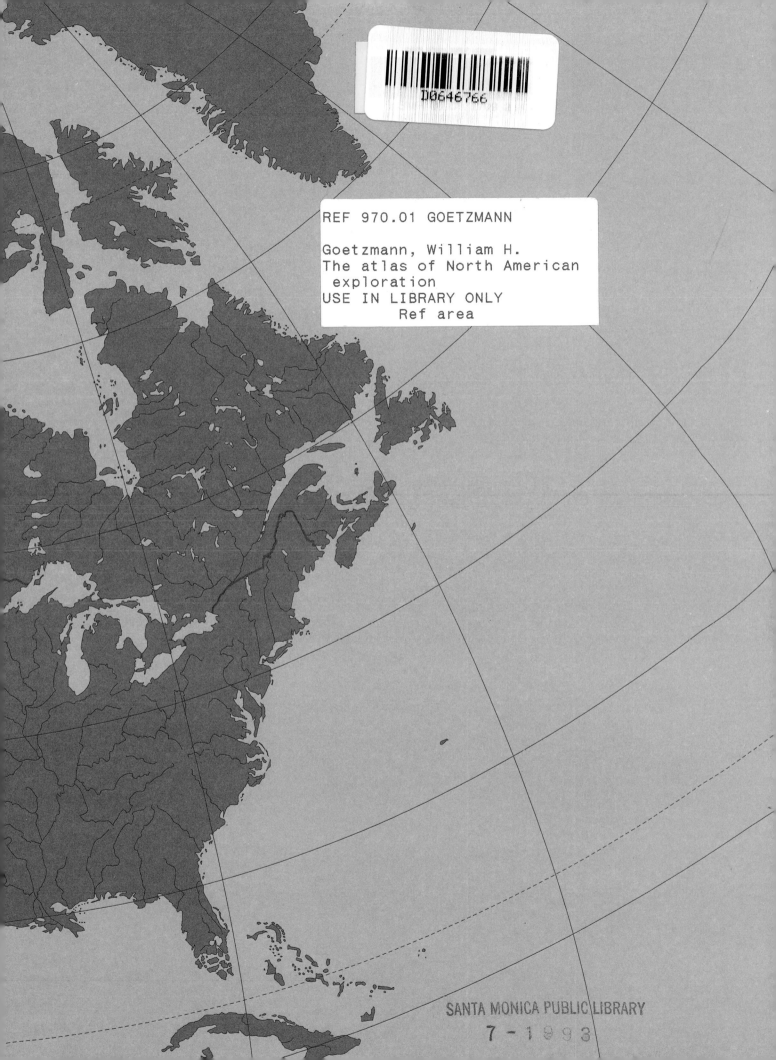

# The Atlas of
# North American Exploration

# The Atlas of
# North American Exploration

## From the Norse Voyages to the Race to the Pole

## William H. Goetzmann
## Glyndwr Williams

Prentice Hall General Reference

New York ● London ● Toronto ● Sydney ● Tokyo ● Singapore

Prentice Hall General Reference
15 Columbus Circle
New York, New York, 10023

Library of Congress Cataloging-in-Publication Data

Goetzmann, William H.
    The atlas of North American exploration / William Goetzmann and
Glyndwr Williams.

        p.    cm.
    Includes index.
    ISBN 0-13-297128-3
    1. North America — Discovery and exploration — Maps.  2. Explorers —
North America — History — Maps.   I. Williams, Glyndwr.   II. Title.
    G1106.S12G6    1992   <G&M>
    911.7 — dc20                                                92-8573
                                                               CIP
                                                               MAP

Artwork: Swanston Graphics Limited,
Vernon House, Vernon Street, Derby DE1 1FR

Cartographic director: Malcolm Swanston
Maps created by: Isabelle Lewis and Jacqueline Land
Assisted by: Pamela Hopkinson and Andrew Bright

Editorial: Swanston Publishing Limited,
The Fitzpatrick Building, 188-194 York Way,
Kings Cross, London N7 9AX

Editorial director: Anne Benewick
Editor: Chris Schüler
Assisted by: Cathy Jones, Elizabeth Wyse,
George Wilkes, Alex de Berry
Picture research: Suzanne O'Farrell
Additional design: Albert Kueh, Ian Cockburn

Consultant: G. Malcolm Lewis,
Amerindian and Inuit Maps and Mapping Programme,
University of Sheffield

Printed and bound in Hong Kong
Produced by Mandarin Offset Ltd.

10   9   8   7   6   5   4   3   2   1

First Edition

# Contents

# Preface

The story of the explorers of North America begins many thousand years before Columbus, with the crossing by Mongoloid hunters of the land bridge from Asia. In the intervening millennia before the coming of the Europeans the trickle of migration from the north broadened until it spread a thin layer of settlement over much of the continent. As they adapted to their new environments, the migrants settled into what the European arrivals would find a bewildering variety of culture types: the Inuit of the far north, the elusive Beothuk of Newfoundland, the farming Algonquians of the northeast, the elaborate temple-mound cultures of the southeast, the fishing communities of the west coast, the buffalo hunters of the plains, the pueblo-dwellers of the southwest.

These societies developed in almost unbroken isolation from Europe. Despite the forays westward across the Atlantic of the pre-Columbian area, notably by the Norsemen, whose sagas, reports to the Vatican and even maps alerted few beyond fisherman and the Hanseatic League. Despite the mighty voyages of Columbus and Magellan, America did not exist as a separate entity until Amerigo Vespucci gave it a name and gold poured into Europe as a result of Cortés's conquest followed by those of many other Spaniards. North America remained relatively neglected in the light of these glittering finds and did not bulk large in the European consciousness until the 16th century. To the end of his life Columbus himself assumed that his discoveries were part of Asia, and only after his death was there general acceptance of the existence of a previously unsuspected continent.

From that exciting period of realization, four hundred years were to pass before Europeans completed their exploration and mapping of the main features of North America. It is their endeavors which are represented in this volume. As far as possible we tell the story through their own maps and drawings, their journals and letters, to capture some of the immediacy of their reaction to the new lands. But what was new to the first Europeans was old to the existing inhabitants, and we have tried to set the narrative of European exploration against the Amerindian response. The clash of cultures which followed the European arrival in North America has been told many times, usually in the context of Indian hostility to white settlement. Here, we have stressed the importance of the Indian in influencing the course of European exploration. Indian friendship could pull the new arrivals in one direction, Indian hostility push them in another. As carriers, guides and hunters the Indians were essential to the newcomers once they moved away from their ships. Indian methods of travel became standard for the Europeans – the snowshoe in winter, the birchbark canoe or dugout boat in summer. Where the evidence exists, we show how the mysterious land beyond the river or over the hills was often familiar terrain to the Indians who made crucial maps for explorers like Lewis and Clark or Jedediah Smith. We would not wish to understate the courage and endurance of the explorers from Europe, but it needs to be remembered that their "discoveries" were often the formalization and recording of knowledge already held by the indigenous inhabitants.

The spreads in this atlas follow a common pattern. They include an analysis of the particular exploration; a modern map; one or more historical maps or illustrations; and an extract from the explorer's own record. The modern maps show the explorers' routes in relation to Indian and European settlements at the time. Important modern boundaries and cities are shown in grey.

A word of caution is needed here. By its very nature a map implies certainty, but often the explorers' routes can only be plotted by informed guesswork. Some of the earlier explorers in particular had only rudimentary navigational and surveying instruments, and their journals have sometimes disappeared or survived in mangled form. Indian tribal boundaries were rarely formal or precise, and in any case fluctuated with migration and dispersal. European forts, missions and trading posts also shifted, and quite often an old name would be reused in a new location.

The bibliography is both a guide to further reading and an acknowledgement of our debt to the work of many fine scholars. We specifically wish to acknowledge the help of G. Malcolm Lewis, who advised on the names and locations of Indian and Inuit peoples; Professor Charles Hudson, whose recent researches have greatly advanced our knowledge of the route taken by de Soto; Professor Louis De Vorsey; Mary Marmon; Ann Gaines; Chris Schüler; John Morris; and William Pugsley. The latter two are in large measure responsible for the Arctic maps at the end of this book, while Morris also located the routes eastwards from Santa Fé across the Llano Estacado of Texas.

W.H.G.
G.W.

# America: Found, Lost, and Found Again

BY
DAVID BEERS QUINN

America was far from being a "new country" when seafarers from Europe reached its shores in the 15th century. The continent was discovered not once, but several times. Firstly, by nomadic hunters crossing from Siberia in prehistoric times; then by Norse seafarers from Greenland who established a fragile colony on Newfoundland; and only much later, by Columbus and his successors.

For each new set of arrivals, the continent represented something different. For the first pioneers who made the icy crossing from Asia, it was an extension of their hunting grounds. For the Norse seafarers, it was Vinland. For Columbus, it was the Asian mainland. Only after his death did the idea of America – the continent – materialize on European maps.

The land-bridge with northeast Asia that existed some 50,000 years ago allowed human emigrants to reach America for the first time. Joined by successive waves of reinforcements, they spread over the two halves of the continent and developed into many widely differentiated cultures. Native American society had developed a long way before Europe had consolidated to any meaningful degree. Consequently, European notions about the "primitive" condition of the indigenous peoples in eastern North America were very wide of the mark. Most of these societies had highly developed agriculture or horticulture; specialized hunting areas and group divisions; and lived a satisfactory social life, in places with highly developed and widespread religious practices.

## MYTHS AND LEGENDS

Europe and America developed in ignorance of one another for millennia. The westward expansion of Europe came only after centuries of epic myths, legends and tentative explorations of the vast ocean which fringed its western lands.

The oldest of these legends was probably that of the Seven Cities. When the Moors invaded Portugal in the 8th century, it claimed, seven bishops and their flocks fled across the ocean to establish Seven Islands (or Cities) far to the west. The story, which seems to have flourished orally in Portugal, surfaced in the sea charts of the 15th century, and was current at the time Columbus sailed. When Spanish conquistadors in the early 16th century heard reports of the pueblos of New Mexico, the Seven Cities shifted their location and began to appear on maps of this region.

*A reconstruction of an Irish curragh of the 6th century, of the type St Brendan may have used.*

## THE LEGEND OF ST BRENDAN

The second legend was that of St Brendan, bishop of Clonfert in Ireland, who died in 577. His reputation as a traveler took shape about 900 in a "Life" which circulated widely

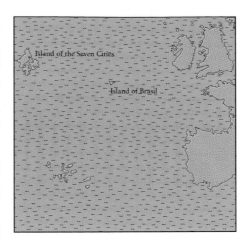

in manuscript from then onward. This credited him with making voyages into the ocean to islands later identified as, in particular, the Fortunate Islands (the Canaries). About 1000, this was followed by the "Navigatio," a fine tale of his voyages to the ultimate western limits of the known world. The lands Brendan was supposed to have visited have been identified in modern times as the Faröes, Iceland and America; and in the 1970s Tim Severin made a successful attempt to cross to Newfoundland by the same route in a replica of an Irish ship of the period. Later charts placed St Brendan's Isle on varying parts of the northern Atlantic. No serious scholars now consider that Brendan did any of these things apart from probably cruising up the western Scottish islands; but Irish monks did reach Iceland well before the Norse invasion of the later 9th century.

## THE LEGEND OF MADOC

The last legend to obtain widespread publicity was that of the Welsh Madoc (Madog ab Owain Gwynedd). Late medieval Welsh poets had characterized Madoc as a sea rover; but between 1578 and 1584, Queen Elizabeth's astrologer John Dee and the writer on exploration Richard Hakluyt resurrected this mythical figure and concocted a story that he had discovered America long before Columbus. At a time when Francis Drake and Walter Raleigh were staking a claim to North America, the story lent an air of legitimacy to English territorial ambitions. The authenticity of this claim was not finally exploded until the mid-19th century.

Throughout the late 14th and 15th centuries, sea charts (portolan charts) incorporated these and other legends. From 1424 a great rectangular island, named Antilia, far to the west, was equated with the mythical Seven Cities. Columbus himself believed in its existence, and was amazed he did not encounter it in 1492.

*Above left: Several imaginary islands were located in the Atlantic by 15th-century cartographers. The Paris Map of c.1490 (redrawn) shows the Island of Brasil and the Seven Cities to the west of Ireland. Above: Martin Behaim's 1492 globe (detail redrawn above) shows the rectangular island of Antilia midway between Europe and Japan (Cipangu).*

## THE NORSE SETTLEMENTS

Late in the 9th century, Norse adventurers discovered Iceland, and by AD 900 they had established a substantial colony there. It soon outgrew the island's limited resources. When Eirik the Red was temporarily exiled for a crime there, he sailed southward and westward and discovered Greenland in 983. The climate was milder than in modern times, and he returned to Iceland with tales of fine open lands. In 986 he succeeded in bringing out a colony there, founding the Eastern Settlement (Julianehåb). A little later the Western Settlement (Godthåb) developed, and soon thrived by exploiting the rich fishing and sea-mammal resources of the area, together with a limited range of grazing for livestock.

Bjarni Herjolfsson, on his way to Greenland in 985, had sighted further land to the west and south of Greenland, so that about 1000, Leif Eiriksson undertook a voyage from Eirik's home at Brattahlid in the Eastern Settlement. He traveled first to the northwest, finding a rocky land he called Helluland (Baffin Island), and farther south another he named Markland (Labrador) and finally a land (Newfoundland, or some other farther south) he called Vinland, where he wintered. All we have as a record of his voyage are the sagas, oral accounts which were not written until the 13th century. They state that Vinland was the residence of a sequence of would-be colonists from Eirik's extended family, some with women and children, over the next twenty years or so. They all moved back to Greenland or came to a tragic end, and if other settlements were

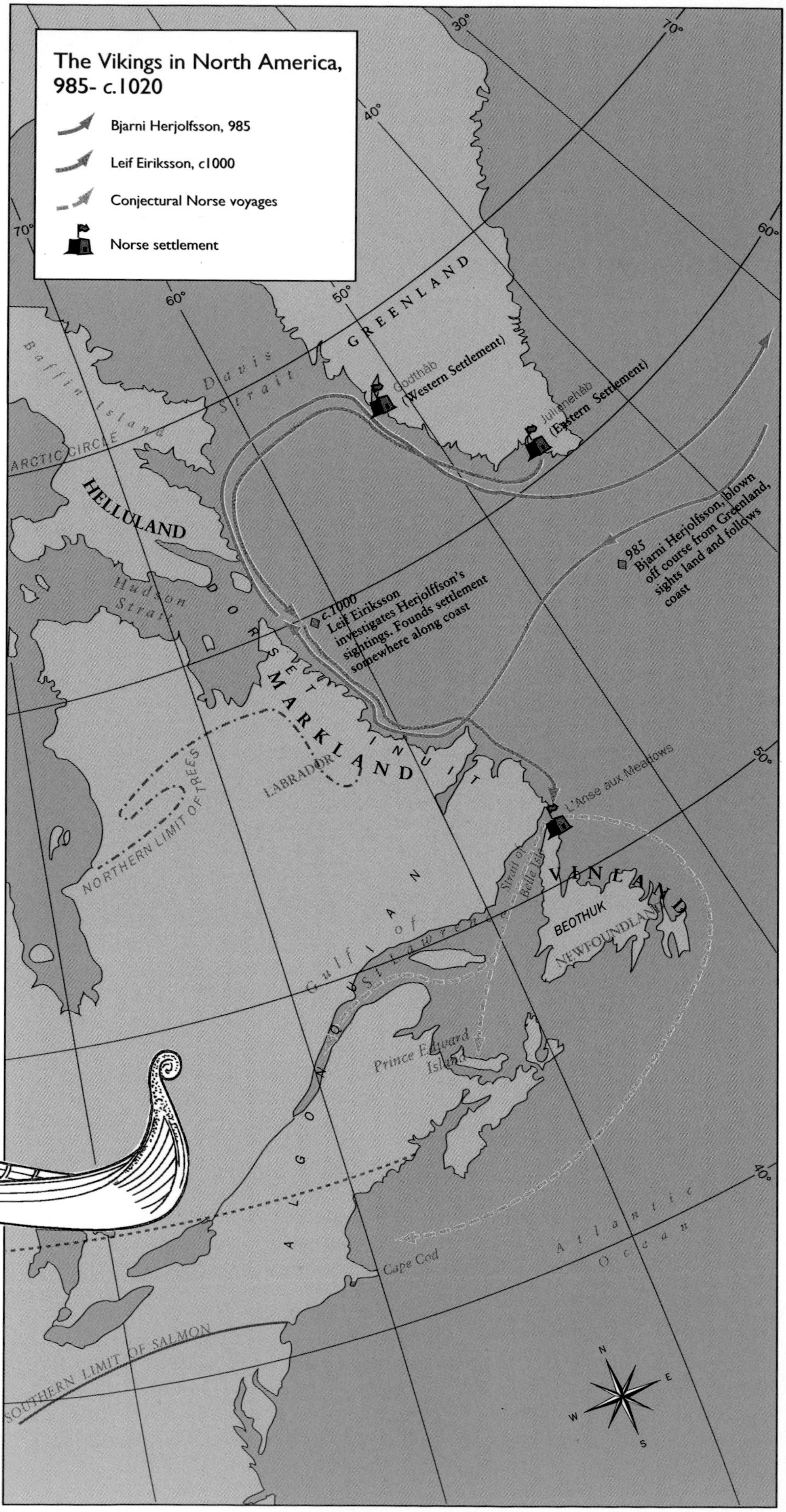

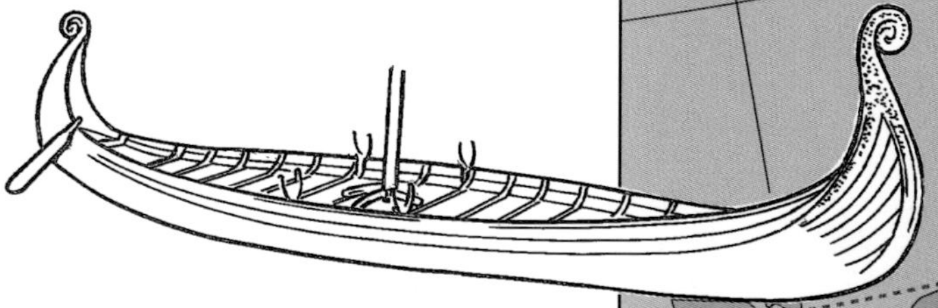

## The Vikings in North America, 985- c.1020

Bjarni Herjolfsson, 985

Leif Eiriksson, c1000

Conjectural Norse voyages

Norse settlement

GREENLAND

Godthåb (Western Settlement)

Julianehåb (Eastern Settlement)

985 Bjarni Herjolfsson, blown off course from Greenland, sights land and follows coast

BAFFIN ISLAND

Davis Strait

ARCTIC CIRCLE

HELLULAND

Hudson Strait

c.1000 Leif Eiriksson investigates Herjolffson's sightings. Founds settlement somewhere along coast

MARKLAND

LABRADOR

INUIT

NORTHERN LIMIT OF TREES

L'Anse aux Meadows

Strait of Belle Isle

VINLAND

BEOTHUK

NEWFOUNDLAND

Gulf of St Lawrence

Prince Edward Island

Cape Cod

Atlantic Ocean

SOUTHERN LIMIT OF SALMON

*Above: A reconstruction of a Viking ship of the 9th century, based on the Oseberg ship, found in Norway in 1905. Leif Eiriksson would perhaps have made his voyage in a similar craft.*

made they have not yet been located. By 1020, or a little later, the Vinland voyages were discontinued, except for occasional expeditions to Markland for timber.

The Vinland of the sagas cannot be identified as such. The grapes brought with their green branches by Leif in the spring sound unlikely. Finally, after much search, a Norse site was found at L'Anse aux Meadows, on the Newfoundland side of the Strait of Belle Isle. It was excavated between 1961 and 1968 by Anne Stine Ingstad and her husband, Helge, and subsequently by Parks Canada. The archaeologists found house sites which could have accommodated about 80 persons, evidence of iron-smelting and, more recently, indications of ships being repaired. The absence of cattle byres and of a substantial midden has called in question the wintering of cattle there and of over-winter residence by colonists, but Inuit looting of the site may well explain these anomalies.

There is little doubt that expeditions were made from the site to Prince Edward Island, possibly up the St Lawrence, and even the long haul to New England, where summer grapes can be freely found. Yet history and legend have not yet been wholly reconciled. The climate deteriorated, and after Greenland became subject to Norway in the late 13th century, the Norse outposts became more and more isolated. The Western Settlement succumbed to the advance of the Inuit, while the Eastern Settlement eventually withered through isolation and attrition. By the time John Cabot coasted the area in 1497, the forgotten Norse settlements had dwindled away.

## PORTUGUESE EXPLORATION

The second European venture to pave the way to the Americas was the Portuguese maritime exploration of the western Atlantic in the 15th century. First Madeira was discovered and colonized between 1419 and 1435. Then the far-flung chain of the Azores was found in three groups between 1427 and 1452, and all colonized by about 1460. The farthest of these islands, Flores, was 1000 miles west of Portugal. A vigorous fishery centered on Terceira led to many attempts to discover islands or mainland farther west, but no clear evidence that the Corte Réal family, which dominated the island, discovered land before Columbus has been found.

## THE INFLUENCE OF MAP-MAKERS

Material, technical and academic developments in the 15th century not only improved the capacity of seamen to make long voyages, they also encouraged visionary theorists and

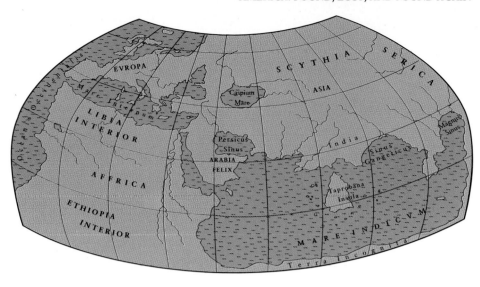

even practical sailors to make fresh calculations about the accessibility of distant parts of the globe. Asia was the subject of much speculation, even if it was Guinea gold which promoted most economically-motivated ventures in the 1470s and 1480s.

At the academic level, the circulation of Ptolemy's "Geographia" in manuscript, and later in print, set out a clear, if antiquated, picture of the world. The 2nd-century Alexandrian geographer's maps were sectionalized by a grid of latitude and longitude. Ptolemy thought there was an equal distribution of land and water eastward and westward round the globe; but his map of furthest Asia was obligingly left unterminated, which permitted those with interests in reaching out from Europe to the East by the Atlantic Ocean free reign for their theories. Pierre d'Ailly's "Imago Mundi" (c.1415) was also widely copied, and raised doubts in its readership about the potential distance westward of Asia from Europe. It, too, circulated widely in print during the 1470s.

The third influence was the vivid narrative of Marco Polo on eastern Asia (Cathay in particular) in the late 13th century, which also circulated in manuscript and was printed shortly after 1480. He gave the impression that Cipangu (Japan) was 1500 miles to the east of Quinsay (Hangchou) and so a milestone on the way to Europe, even though conservative academic theory correctly placed Cathay at least 10,000 miles from Europe. It was on such material that Columbus, John Cabot and others such as the Florentine doctor Toscanelli, were to build theories which seemed to bring Asia much nearer to Europe than had ever been considered.

The influence of these works on Portuguese scholars and administrators, and probably even on a few seamen such as Columbus, was

*Above: The geographer Claudius Ptolemy produced his "Geographia" in Alexandria around AD150. In the early 15th century a Byzantine copy found its way to western Europe, where it was widely reproduced (the version redrawn above was printed in Ulm in 1486). It stimulated much discussion about what lay beyond the point where Asia runs off the edge off the map.*

considerable. It contributed to the almost unending search, aided by trade in gold and slaves, for a sea route southward and then eastward to Asia, until the final turning of the southern tip of Africa by Dias in 1488.

## THE REVOLUTION IN SHIPPING

Such feats could not have been accomplished without much improved shipping. During the 15th century there was a Europe-wide movement away from the round ship towards longer, narrower and higher vessels. In some respects the Portuguese led the way. Their adoption of light, narrow caravels powered by two, three or more lateen sails, enabled them to penetrate coastal inlets and to cover considerable distances at greater speed than hitherto. For longer voyages they built larger ships which combined the traditional mainmast with its great square sail with the lateen which added maneuverability to the driving power of the older types of sailing vessel. This type of ship, with local variations, was also being used in other parts of western Europe, including England, well before 1500.

Navigation also improved. To the compass was added the astrolabe (adapted from the astronomer's instrument), and the quadrant, which enabled noon sun-sights to be taken with some approach to accuracy in calm weather. These could be checked by the observation of the Pole Star (a routine known as "the Regiment of the North Star" was in

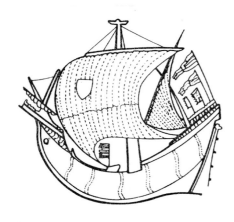

*During the 15th century, the essentially Mediterranean round ship (top) gave way to more oceanworthy craft such as the carrack (above). In such vessels, the Portuguese reached out into the Atlantic as far as Madeira and the Azores.*

vogue before the end of the century), and latitude tables were also beginning to appear. Speed could, in most cases, still only be calculated by expert observation by skilled navigators (though the log and line, with half-hour glasses, is thought to have been available before 1500).

But sailors still had no way of estimating the distance they had traveled from east to west except by dead reckoning: sailing along a specific latitude and roughly calculating their speed. Despite its limitations, the method enabled European sailors to reach the southern tip of Africa and to reach out into the Atlantic to discover the Caribbean islands and, eventually, America.

## THE EARLY VOYAGES OF COLUMBUS

In 1574 Paolo Toscanelli of Florence wrote to an influential friend in Portugal to propose that the distance westwards from Europe to Asia was much less than had previously been proposed. He communicated this to King Manuel who had an expedition sent westward in 1474 to locate Antilia, at least, if not Cipangu. The expedition came back without result, but it paved the way for Christopher Columbus a few years later.

Columbus indeed may have had some ideas about exploration in the north or west before he left Genoa for Portugal or the north in 1476. After being shipwrecked in southern Portugal he was picked up by a Genoese fleet and brought to England early in 1477.

The English had been the pioneer venturers into the northwest Atlantic, both for fishing and trading off Iceland, since before 1400. Bristol had joined east coast ports in trading in air-dried cod (*bacalhau*) and train oil, for English foodstuffs and cloth, from 1424 onwards. Columbus made his way to Bristol, where he joined a ship bound for Iceland. If one is to believe his own muddled account given near the end of his life, he must have transfered to a fishing vessel to round the westward end of Iceland and sail some way along the north coast, finding the water open but being warned of long months of icebound waters. If Columbus had any notion of exploring over the North Pole it was ended then. He returned by way of Galway, where he saw two strange bodies cast up by waves in the remains of a boat, which he afterwards decided were orientals from Cathay.

By 1479 at the latest, Columbus was back in Portugal and had settled in Lisbon. He then moved to the Madeiras, and took part in at least one voyage to West Africa. But he was also learning navigation and studying books and manuscripts relevant to westward exploration. By 1481 he had learned about the Toscanelli letter. He wrote direct to its author and when he may have received an encouraging reply, prepared his grand design of sailing westward to Asia.

## BRISTOL MARINERS

Meanwhile in England, Bristol merchants, frustrated in the Iceland trade by Danish competition, were searching for new fishing grounds. If, as seems highly probable, Columbus used Bristol vessels to make his first voyage of exploration to Iceland in 1477, it is probable that he also conveyed to them up-to-date portolan sea charts, which showed many islands in the Western Ocean. We know that the Bristol merchants had such charts by 1480 at the latest. In that year, Thomas Lloyd set out to search for the Isle of Brasil, which was, confusingly, shown twice on some charts, one version close to Kerry, the other far in the west.

Lloyd failed to find the island, and had to put back to Ireland. He was probably the agent of a syndicate which had received permission from Edward IV to make unusual voyages into the ocean. One member of this group was Thomas Croft. As collector of customs in Bristol, he was not allowed to trade. The government commissioners suspected him of breaking this prohibition and, on 24 September 1481, they questioned him about his activities. He was alleged to have owned shares (one-eighth) in two ships which sailed earlier in that year, and to have supplied salt towards their lading. His defense (which was accepted) was that the *George* and the *Trinity* had gone to " 'search' and find the Isle of Brasile" and were not engaged in trading. The phrase, the only reference we have, is ambiguous, but it could mean that land across the ocean was at least sighted. If so, this could have been Newfoundland.

As we do not have any evidence of further Bristol maritime activity in the Atlantic before 1490 or 1491, this vague suggestion that land was found has been treated with considerable scepticism. However, in 1955, the late L. A. Vigneras found in Spain a letter of December 1497 or January 1498 from the Bristol merchant, John Day, to Columbus. It gave a detailed account of John Cabot's successful voyage to eastern North America, adding the mysterious comment that they had found this land before "in times past" (*en otros tiempos*), "as your Lordship knows." This raised the question whether the 1481 expedition, or some intermediate voyage, had found land in the west, had indeed found land before 1492. This has been argued back and forward ever since. No conclusive evidence has yet appeared, but there is at least a possibility that Bristol may have been the starting point of a pre-Columbian discovery of America.

## THE GRAND DESIGN

By 1484 Columbus had his grand design worked out. He had convinced himself that from the western Canary Islands he could reach Marco Polo's Cipangu (Japan) by a voyage of 2400 miles, which was within the capacity of sailing ships by this time. From there he believed he could reach Quinsay (Hangchou) after another voyage of 1150 miles. We now know these distances to be 10,600 and 11,766 miles respectively.

Columbus attempted to sell this scheme to John II of Portugal in 1484, but without success, and in 1486 he turned to Ferdinand and Isabella of Spain. They gave him some slight encouragement, but postponed their decision indefinitely. In 1488 Columbus returned to Portugal in time to observe the return of Bartholomew Dias from his triumphant rounding of southern Africa. This achievement irrevocably committed Portugal to planning ocean voyages round Africa to the eastern Indies, and led to a final rejection from Spain.

In despair of getting Iberian support for his project, Columbus sent a modified version to his brother Bartholomew, a cartographer in Lisbon, in the hope of selling the project to Henry VII of England. His plan was to construct a sea chart which would place the Island of the Seven Cities, not opposite Morocco or the Iberian lands as on other sea charts, but in the low 50s of north latitude opposite Ireland, approximately where Newfoundland was to be defined not so long after, and with a convenient stopping place in mid-Atlantic, named as the Isle of Brasil. Henry VII rejected the scheme in 1489; Bartholomew then attempted to sell the

project to France, but was again unsuccessful. He returned to England in 1492, where it appears (though evidence is far from conclusive) that Henry VII eventually accepted the plan. If Henry did so, he may have been influenced by the knowledge that from about 1490 Bristol ships were known to be making western voyages once more, either for exploration or trade.

Returning by way of France in 1493, Bartholomew learned that not only had his brother won the support of Spain at last, but had set out and returned with news of his discovery of the western Indies. Yet Bartholomew, on returning to Spain, was chagrined to learn that Christopher, now honoured as Admiral of the Ocean Sea, had already set out once again with a large fleet for the new islands and, it was expected, the Asiatic mainland.

Christopher Columbus had returned to Spain in 1490, only to learn the details of the long inquiry into his project which had ended unfavorably for him. He was, however, informed by the Queen that when the war with the Moors of the Kingdom of Granada was over he might apply again. This he did by appearing at court, then established outside the city of Granada, the last besieged remnant of the Moorish kingdom. After the fall of the city in January 1491 he was finally refused by King Ferdinand, but, through the intercession of an official, Isabella recalled him and at last agreed to his project in principle. In the enthusiasm of the conquest she felt generous enough to gamble.

Columbus made hard terms, demanding and obtaining the prospective title of admiral and governor of any lands he found, with a share of their revenues, together with the fitting out of his squadron by the crown. He had made maritime friends at Palos in 1486, so it was there that he went for his ships and

their crews. The Pinzon family furnished him with two small Portuguese-type caravels – the *Niña* and *Pinta* – and agreed to provide officers for them. A larger Galician ship – the *Santa Maria* – then in port at Palos, was hired. The three ships were fitted out for a long voyage.

They set out from Palos for the Canaries on 1 August 1492. Columbus believed that Antilia lay on the parallel of 28°N (which would have brought him to Florida), so he decided to sail down that latitude, setting out from Gomera on 6 September. He expected to reach Antilia after some 12 or 13 days' sailing, and expressed some surprise when he did not. On the 19th he said he was certain that to the north or south there were some islands, though they never appeared, but he sailed ahead on his westward course, with some minor variations, until 7 October (by which time his men were very restive), when, attracted by a flight of birds to the southwest, he changed course in that direction.

## COLUMBUS'S FIRST LANDFALL

On the night of 11 October, lookouts reported what they regarded as clear signs of land ahead and the ships made a landfall at the island the natives called Guanahani on the 12th. They solemnly annexed it to the king and queen of Spain. Columbus believed that it lay off the coast of Cipangu (Japan) as it was close to his estimate of the distance of that country from the Canaries.

The land which Columbus reached on 12 October 1492 is generally reckoned to have been Watlings Island in the Bahamas. So firmly established has this attribution become that since 1926 the island has been called San Salvador, the name Columbus gave to his landfall. It formed the centerpiece of the 1992 quincentenary, but the attribution has not satisfied everyone. In scholarly circles, minute

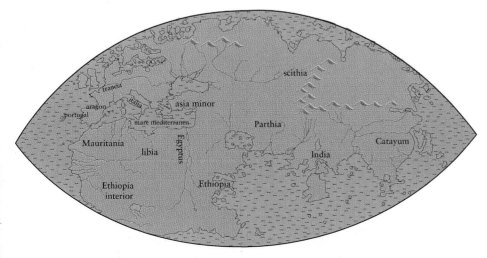

*The 1457 Florence "Mappemonde" (redrawn left) anticipated Columbus's views on the proportions of the globe and the distance westwards from Europe to Asia. Such maps, which placed Asia much closer to Europe than had previously been thought, encouraged mariners such as Columbus and Cabot to seek a westward route to Cathay.*

*Martin Waldseemüller's globe of 1507 (redrawn right) correctly identified the lands found by Columbus, Cabot and Vespucci as part of one continent. From the first name – Amerigo – of the latter explorer, the German cartographer named the entire southern part of the landmass "America." The name stuck and by 1520 applied to North America also.*

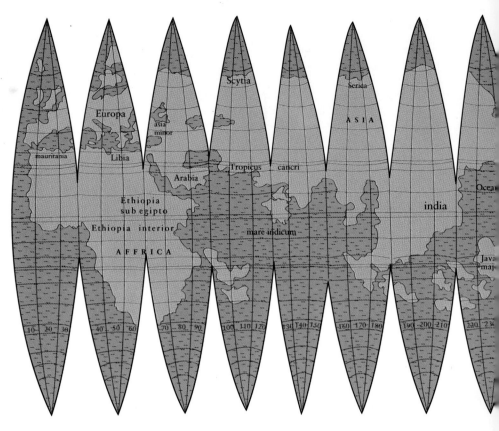

examination of the surviving materials on the voyage has produced a number of alternative landfalls, although none of them has ousted San Salvador from popular esteem. The closest studies, however, have concluded that while Columbus's first landfall was in the Bahamas, or not very far south of them, the evidence is insufficient to make an entirely positive identification with any particular island.

Columbus passed a further series of islands before making a crucial landfall on what he regarded as an outpost of Asia. He named the island Hispaniola. His opinion was confirmed by the discovery of the north coast of Cuba which must, in his view, be part of Asia itself. He turned back, ran the *Santa Maria* aground on the north of Hispaniola, and left her crew to set up the first Spanish colony in the West. They were never seen again.

Columbus was fortunate in his return voyage in the *Pinta*. When he entered Seville on 31 March 1493 he found he had to follow the Spanish sovereigns to Barcelona. There, on 20 April 1493, he presented his version of his discovery of the Indies, describing the Tainos (male and female) whom he had captured as "Indians." This letter to the king's treasurer, which he had sent ahead of him,

was printed for the information of courtiers and officials before the end of April. He was ennobled and regranted all and more of the privileges and powers which he obtained on paper at Granada. His sovereigns and he were soon to receive from Pope Alexander VI the Bull Inter Caetera confirming his "conquests" to Spain and enshrining for all time the description of the land and people as the "Indies" and the people as "Indians."

### THE "NEW" AMERICAN CONTINENT

What was to follow was a more complex and very different story. Columbus died in 1506, still believing he had found Asia. But the events of 1492 and those which followed produced the most remarkable shift in European, and indeed world, perceptions of the layout of the globe; and in 1507 the American continent appeared as such on a German map.

In the year that Columbus set out, Ferdinand and Isabella had completed the reconquest of Spain from the Muslims. This, and the techniques of colonial administration developed in the Canary Islands between 1479 and 1492, enabled the Spanish to begin the exploitation of the new islands at once. A great expedition was dispatched to the

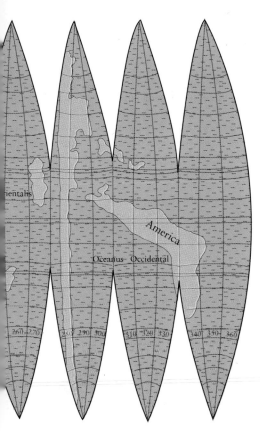

Caribbean in 1493; the conquests of Mexico and Peru followed in 1521 and 1533. Within a few decades Spain had acquired a colonial empire that astounded 16th-century Europe, and helped to dominate large parts of it. It was not until the 17th century that Spain began to run out of impetus, and countries like England, France and the Netherlands were able to challenge its monopoly position in the New World.

All this was brought about at great cost to the peoples Columbus took to be "Indians." The complexity and sophistication of the indigenous societies was to be only slowly, in fact much too slowly, appreciated by the European intruders, and in much of North America, European interventions, far from bringing "civilization" to backward peoples, destroyed highly organized, if simply equipped, societies.

*A three-masted ocean-going caravel of around 1480. The front and middle masts are square-rigged, while the rear carries a lateen sail. Columbus and Cabot's ships, the* Santa Maria *and the* Matthew, *would have been very similar.*

# Part I : A Continent on the Edge of the World

In search of a new route to the East, European seafarers were hindered and often confused by the unknown lands which stood in their way. At first these lands appeared disconnected, but by the second decade of the 16th century it was generally accepted that there existed a vast new continent, previously unsuspected and still shrouded by ignorance: North America. European explorers clung to their dream of finding a route to the riches of Cathay. Only gradually, as they searched the rivers, bays and frozen northern straits for a navigable route to the Pacific, and the Spaniards probed deep into the southern interior, did they begin to grasp the size of the continent they had stumbled upon.

While Cabot and the Corte-Réals skirted the coastlines of Newfoundland and Nova Scotia, Spanish exploration of the Caribbean north of Cuba led to the gradual appearance on the maps of the Florida peninsula. Between these two areas lay a huge gap of 1500 miles. This was bridged by Verrazano's expedition in 1524, which showed that the Atlantic coast of North America extended from Florida to Nova Scotia.

The more of the new shoreline was revealed, the more urgent to Europeans became the need to find a way through this barrier to the lands of the East. By the 1530s the French were searching for such a route in the region just beyond Verrazano's farthest north. Sailing into the St Lawrence River, Cartier reached a thousand miles into the continent, only to be informed by Indians that he was still three months' travel from the western ocean.

For the first time some comprehension emerged of the massive dimensions of the North American continent, and efforts grew to find a way around rather than through the great landmass. Repeated voyages to northern waters explored the complex maze of the Arctic archipelago. The endeavor was heroic as small sailing vessels battled, and failed, to find a way through its ice-choked channels.

To the south, the Spaniards had roughly charted the outline of the Gulf of Mexico. They now attempted to conquer the interior, launching a series of expeditions on a scale not to be repeated for another two centuries. Cabeza de Vaca covered a large area west of the Mississippi with a handful of companions. De Soto, with mailed soldiers and chained Indian bearers laid a bloody trail across 3000 miles of what is now the southern United States. Coronado led a great and ambitious expedition in search of fabulous cities which lay, according to a potent mix of legend, folklore and Indian information, somewhere north of Mexico. Spanish ships, meanwhile, set out from their Mexican ports to explore the west coast as far north as Oregon.

The amount of knowledge gained by the early European explorers was vast, but much of it was half-remembered, carelessly recorded, and distorted. Nowhere was this more so than in the response to the native peoples encountered. These had emerged in a bewildering variety of culture types, from the Inuit of the far north to the pueblo-dwellers of the upper Rio Grande. Although the nature of contact differed, collaboration was as usual as violence. At this stage settlement was not a preoccupation of the European newcomers, so a major cause of later tension rarely arose. The dominant European motives were the search for a route to the East through the continental barrier, and the hopes of finding gold and silver on the scale found by the Spaniards in Mexico and Peru. Neither route nor riches was found and an air of frustration and failure hangs over early European explorations.

# The Country of the Grand Khan

## THE VOYAGE OF JOHN CABOT, 1497

*As Columbus explores the Caribbean and its shores, far to the north John Cabot seeks a different route to Asia.*

In 1496 the Spanish ambassador in London reported home that "uno como Colón" ("one like Columbus") was trying to interest the English king, Henry VII, in a voyage across the Atlantic. The seafarer was John Cabot, a Venetian who had settled in Bristol some time between 1493 and 1495. He sailed from Bristol in May 1497 in a single small vessel, the *Matthew,* and sighted land within a month. No maps or latitudes survive to identify his landfall, which may have been anywhere between southern Nova Scotia and northern Newfoundland; most scholars favor the midway point around Cape Breton. Cabot ventured inland only a bowshot's distance, and saw no inhabitants; but snares, a fire-site, and a painted stick convinced him that they were not far off.

Like Columbus, Cabot thought that he had reached Asia, the land of the Great Khan. The king's modest award of £10 was simply and more realistically, "to hym that founde the new Isle." A larger expedition set out the following year, but ended in disaster: one ship turned back, the other four vanished, and with them John Cabot. "He is believed," wrote a contemporary some years later, "to have found the new lands nowhere but on the very bottom of the ocean."

News of Cabot's discovery reached Portugal, where preparations were being made for voyages to the same region. In 1500, Gaspar Corte-Réal probably sighted the southern tip of Greenland at Cape Farewell. In 1501 he seems to have reached Labrador, Newfoundland, and possibly as far south as Maine. Gaspar and his ship were lost, but his brother Miguel, in another vessel, kidnapped 50 Micmac or Beothuk and sold them as slaves in Lisbon.

Further expeditions from Bristol are shrouded in even more obscurity. John Cabot's son Sebastian may have been involved; in 1505 he was rewarded by Henry VII for "the fyndinge of the newe founde landes." Three North American "savages" were presented to the English court in 1502. But the cod banks John Cabot had crossed in 1497 were soon attracting more interest (▶ *page 50)* than a mainland which, it was slowly being realized, was not a part of Asia.

*Right: An ocean-going caravel of the same period and type as Cabot's ship, the* Matthew. *A relief from Tiverton church, Devon, dated 1489.*

All that is known about John Cabot's 1497 voyage comes from these two contemporary accounts.

That Venetian of ours who went with a small ship from Bristol to find new islands has come back and says he has discovered mainland 700 leagues away, which is the country of the Grand Khan, and that he coasted it for 300 leagues and landed and did not see any person; but he has brought here to the king [Henry VII] certain snares which, were spread to take game and a needle for making nets, and he found certain notched trees so that by this he judges there are inhabitants.

Letter from Lorenzo Pasqualigo, August 1497

He [John Cabot] landed at one spot of the mainland, near the place where land was first sighted... they found tall trees of the kind masts are made, and other smaller trees, and the country is very rich in grass... they found a trail that went inland, a site where a fire had been made, manure which they thought to be of farm animals, and a stick half a yard long pierced at both ends, carved and painted with brazil, and by such signs they believed the land to be inhabited. Since he was with just a few people, he did not dare advance inland beyond the shooting distance of a crossbow, and after taking fresh water he returned to his ship.

John Day's letter to the Grand Admiral (Christopher Columbus), 1497-98

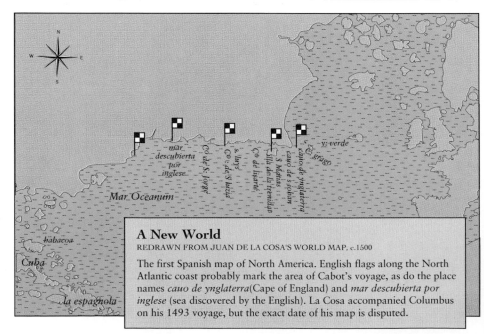

### A New World

REDRAWN FROM JUAN DE LA COSA'S WORLD MAP, c.1500

The first Spanish map of North America. English flags along the North Atlantic coast probably mark the area of Cabot's voyage, as do the place names *cauo de ynglaterra*(Cape of England) and *mar descubierta por inglese* (sea discovered by the English). La Cosa accompanied Columbus on his 1493 voyage, but the exact date of his map is disputed.

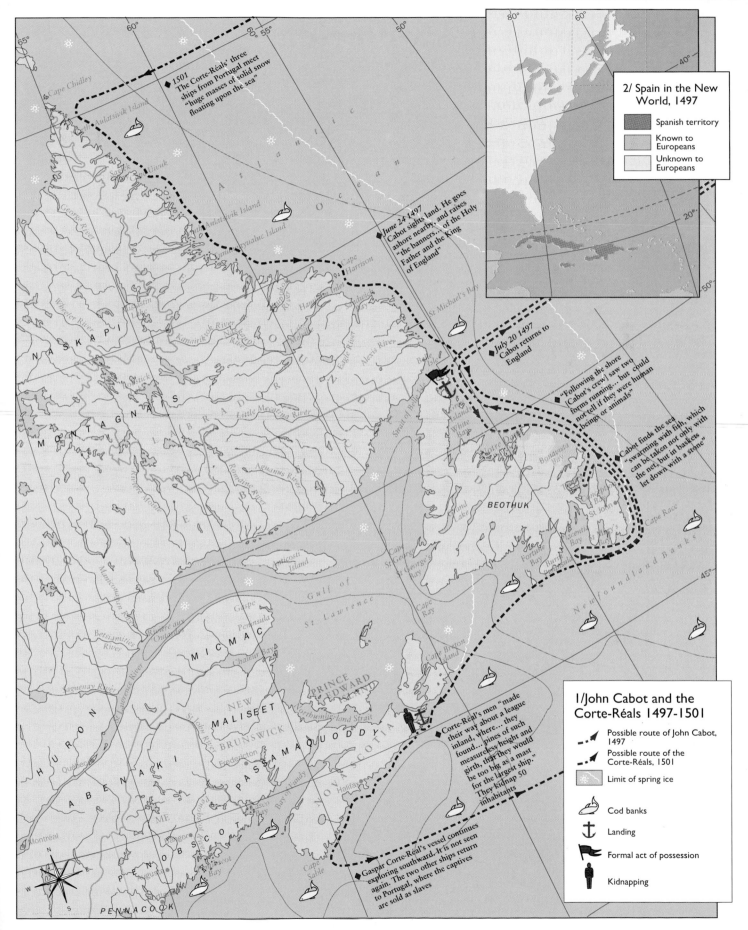

1501
The Corte-Réals' three ships from Portugal meet "huge masses of solid snow floating upon the sea"

June 24 1497 Cabot sights land. He goes ashore nearby, and raises "the banners... of the Holy Father and the King of England"

July 20 1497 Cabot returns to England

"Following the shore [Cabot's crew] saw two forms running... but could not tell if they were human beings or animals"

"Cabot finds the sea "swarming with fish, which can be taken not only with the net, but in baskets let down with a stone"

2/ Spain in the New World, 1497

Spanish territory
Known to Europeans
Unknown to Europeans

Corte-Réal's men "made their way about a league inland, where... they found... pines of such measureless height and girth, that they would be too big as a mast for the largest ship." They kidnap 50 inhabitants

Gaspar Corte-Réal's vessel continues exploring southward. It is not seen again. The two other ships return to Portugal, where the captives are sold as slaves

1/John Cabot and the Corte-Réals 1497-1501

Possible route of John Cabot, 1497
Possible route of the Corte-Réals, 1501
Limit of spring ice
Cod banks
Landing
Formal act of possession
Kidnapping

# They Named It La Florida

## PONCE DE LEÓN TO AYLLÓN, 1513-26

*The Spanish explore the Florida coast and found their first, short-lived settlement on the North American mainland.*

In the two decades that followed Columbus's first voyage, the Spanish strengthened their hold on Hispaniola and conquered and settled Cuba, Puerto Rico and Jamaica. To the north, near Cuba and the homeward track of Spanish ships, lay further undiscovered lands, and, from 1502, the projecting snout of the Florida peninsula began to appear on maps.

In 1512, Juan Ponce de León, the conqueror of Puerto Rico who had sailed with Columbus on his second voyage, was granted a royal licence "to discover and settle the island of Bimini," one of the "marvelous countries" to the north. In 1513 León set sail from Puerto Rico and landed on the east coast of the peninsula. It was Easter Week – "Pasqua Florida" – and the name soon became attached to an area of the southeast considerably larger than the modern state of Florida.

The inhabitants of the region attacked the Spanish, wounding two of them. The expedition then sailed south against the Gulf Stream, which bore against them so strongly as they rounded Cape Canaveral, that León named the spit *Cabo de las Corrientes.*

> Of the 500 men who set off on this mission, only 150 returned. Oh Captains, you who preach of those lands you are going to settle or to attack and destroy, preaching conversion and baptism, destroying the land wherein you go and the natives with it, taking the Christians, who were deceived and misled by the promises you gave them, to their deaths... May God forgive you!
>
> from Oviedo's *History of the Indies,* 1535

Skirting the Florida keys, León finally landed on the west coast at a natural harbor he called San Carlos Bay – almost certainly Charlotte Harbor or Tampa Bay. Here too the inhabitants attacked, launching fleets of canoes against the Spanish ships.

The expedition then returned to Puerto Rico. León had traced the southeast corner of the North American mainland, although he may not have realized it; in 1521 he wrote to the king of Spain that he had discovered "the island of Florida and others in its district." He returned to San Carlos Bay that year with a colonizing venture of 250 men, but was driven off by the fierce resistance of the inhabitants and died of his wounds a few days later.

But another colonizing expedition was already under way, sponsored by Lucas Vásquez de Ayllón, a judge on Hispaniola. The expedition's commander, Francisco Gordillo, teamed up with the slave-hunter

*Above: A suit of armor of the type worn by the early Spanish conquistadors. The kettle hat, bevor (chin plate) and leg-guards are Spanish, the breast and back plates German.*

Pedro de Quexos, and landed around Winyah Bay. They explored the region, took formal possession of it for Spain and, disobeying Ayllón's orders, enslaved 50 native people.

One of them, baptized Francisco de Chicora, accompanied Ayllón to Spain, and gave glowing descriptions of his homeland. Ayllón was granted a licence to settle between the latitudes 35°N and 37°N, and in 1526 left Hispaniola with six vessels and 500 men, women and children, including a number of African slaves. The ships reached the area of Winyah Bay before turning south to find a more promising site, probably at the mouth of the Savannah River. Here Ayllón founded San Miguel de Gualdape, the first Spanish municipality in North America. But the settlement came under repeated attack from the native people of the region, the slaves revolted, and the settlers were racked by hunger and disease. Ayllón died of fever, the survivors returned to Hispaniola, and the east coast of Florida was left to its inhabitants for another 40 years. Only the maps recorded the ambitions of these frustrated conquistadors.

## The Florida Peninsula

REDRAWN FROM JUAN VESPUCCI'S WORLD MAP, 1526

For the first time, Florida is shown correctly as a peninsula, not an island as had previously been thought. The coast on either side is also mapped in detail, and *Trá. nueva de Ayllón* (New land of Ayllón) marked with a Spanish flag. From there, no further land is shown until *Trá. de los bacallaos* (Land of Cod, or Newfoundland).

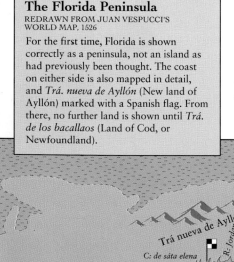

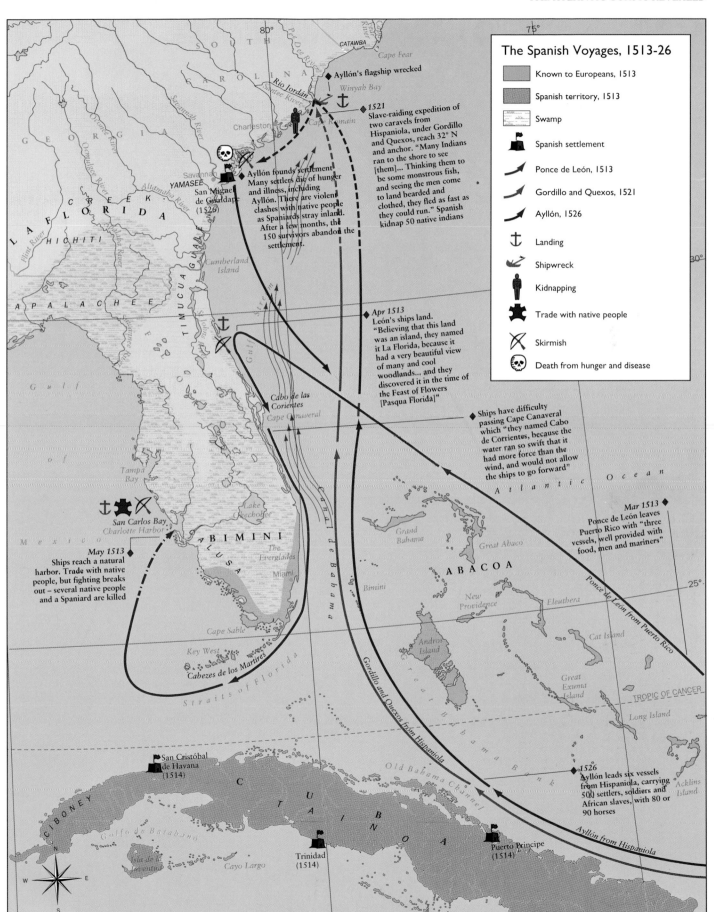

**The Spanish Voyages, 1513-26**

- Known to Europeans, 1513
- Spanish territory, 1513
- Swamp
- Spanish settlement
- Ponce de León, 1513
- Gordillo and Quexos, 1521
- Ayllón, 1526
- Landing
- Shipwreck
- Kidnapping
- Trade with native people
- Skirmish
- Death from hunger and disease

Ayllón's flagship wrecked

*1521*
Slave-raiding expedition of two caravels from Hispaniola, under Gordillo and Quexos, reach 32° N and anchor. "Many Indians ran to the shore to see [them]... Thinking them to be some monstrous fish, and seeing the men come to land bearded and clothed, they fled as fast as they could run." Spanish kidnap 50 native indians

Ayllón founds settlement. Many settlers die of hunger and illness, including Ayllón. There are violent clashes with native people as Spaniards stray inland. After a few months, the 150 survivors abandon the settlement.

*Apr 1513*
León's ships land. "Believing that this land was an island, they named it La Florida, because it had a very beautiful view of many and cool woodlands... and they discovered it in the time of the Feast of Flowers [Pasqua Florida]"

Ships have difficulty passing Cape Canaveral which "they named Cabo de Corrientes, because the water ran so swift that it had more force than the wind, and would not allow the ships to go forward"

*Mar 1513*
Ponce de León leaves Puerto Rico with "three vessels, well provided with food, men and mariners"

*May 1513*
Ships reach a natural harbor. Trade with native people, but fighting breaks out – several native people and a Spaniard are killed

*1526*
Ayllón leads six vessels from Hispaniola, carrying 500 settlers, soldiers and African slaves, with 80 or 90 horses

San Miguel de Gualdape (1526)

San Cristóbal de Havana (1514)

Trinidad (1514)

Puerto Principe (1514)

San Carlos Bay
Charlotte Harbor

Cabezes de los Martires

Ponce de León from Puerto Rico

Gordillo and Quexos from Hispaniola

Ayllón from Hispaniola

Old Bahama Channel

TROPIC OF CANCER

# A New Land Never Seen Before

## THE VOYAGE OF GIOVANNI DA VERRAZANO, 1524

*In his search for the "eastern sea," the Italian navigator Giovanni da Verrazano traces the 1500-mile eastern coastline of North America.*

Balboa's sighting of the Pacific from a peak in Darien in 1513 and Magellan's voyage of 1519-22, the first round the world, had established that America was a separate continent. Coastal explorers now began to seek a way through the landmass which blocked the way to the Pacific and Asia. Magellan had found one such route far to the south through the strait named after him, but a northern passage would be quicker. In 1524 Giovanni da Verrazano led a French expedition to the Atlantic coast of North America in hope of finding such a route.

*Above: Probably Verrazano's ship,* La Dauphine. *This 100-ton vessel of the French navy was built in Le Havre in 1519 and carried a crew of 50. Detail from Gerolamo da Verrazano's world map, 1529.*

Making his landfall probably somewhere to the south of Cape Fear, Verrazano sailed for about 150 miles along the coast of South Carolina before turning back north. His ship coasted along the Outer or Carolina Banks which enclose Pamlico and Albemarle sounds. From the masthead a wide expanse of water could be seen across the sandy spit of land with no hint of a farther shore. Probably because of the shoal water he made no attempt to reach this "sea," but it was to appear in all its illusory glory on maps and globes of the period.

After keeping north, too far offshore to spot the entrances to Chesapeake and Delaware bays, Verrazano turned back towards the coast where he anchored near the Narrows of what became New York Bay, the first European to do so. But, with the wind blowing onshore, the expedition stayed there only a day. It was not until the ship reached Narragansett Bay, where it anchored in Newport Harbor, that Verrazano stayed long enough – 15 days – to see much of the country and its inhabitants. Men from the ship went some miles inland, and found wide clearings "adapted to every branch of cultivation – grain, wine, oil... of such fertility that a seed in them would produce the best crops." Verrazano's description of the inhabitants of this region – the Narragansett and Pokanoket – provide the earliest detailed account of the

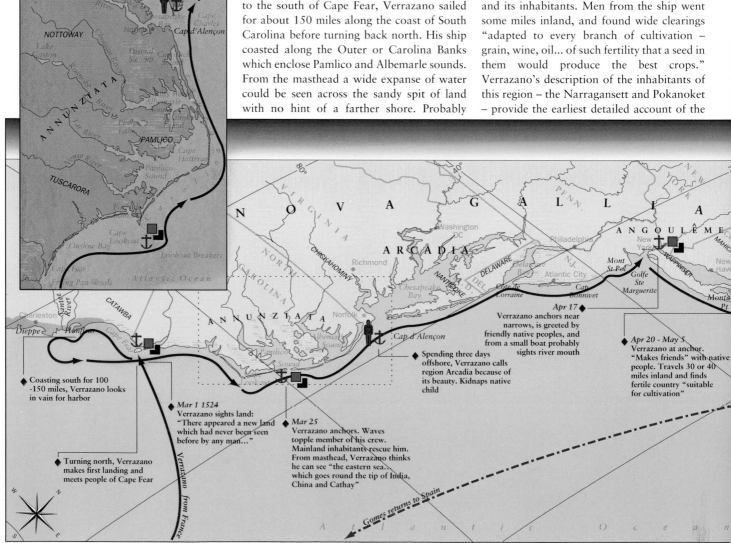

native peoples of the northeast.

Farther north, the Indians – probably Eastern Abenaki or Penobscot – were much warier, evidence perhaps of contact with European fishing vessels. Verrazano then sailed on past Cape Breton and New-foundland before returning to France.

Verrazano's voyage was followed by a Spanish expedition in 1525 commanded by a Portuguese pilot, Estevão Gomes, who paid particular attention to the coast of southern

New England, and by an English ship under John Rut which in 1527 ran down the Atlantic coast from north to south. What little is known of these voyages confirmed Verrazano's report that North America extended from Florida to Cape Breton without any obvious break in the coastline. Verrazano also realized that the new continent had potential of its own, but at the time this was overshadowed by the fact that it barred the way to the Pacific.

The people of Cape Fear "go completely naked except that around their loins they wear skins of small animals like martens, with a narrow belt of grass around the body, to which they tie various tails of other animals which hang down to the knees; the rest of the body is bare, and so is the head. Some of them wear garlands of birds' feathers. They are dark in color, not unlike the Ethiopians, with thin black hair, not very long, tied back behind the head like a small tail. As for the physique of these men, they are well proportioned, of medium height, a little taller than we are."

The Narragansett "are the most beautiful and have the most civil customs that we found on this voyage... we made great friends with them... When we were lying at anchor one league out to sea because of unfavourable weather, they came out to the ship with a great number of their boats; they had painted and decorated their faces with various colors, showing us that it was a sign of happiness. They brought us some of their food, and showed us by signs where we should anchor in the port for the ship's safety, and accompanied us all the way until we dropped anchor."

Two extracts from Verrazano's letter to King Francis I of France, 1524

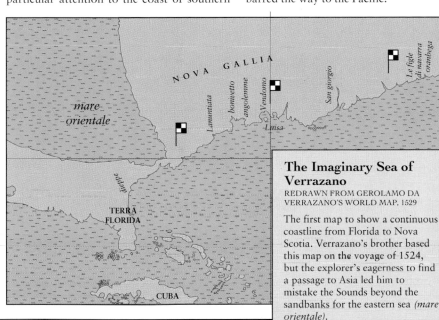

**The Imaginary Sea of Verrazano**
REDRAWN FROM GEROLAMO DA VERRAZANO'S WORLD MAP, 1529

The first map to show a continuous coastline from Florida to Nova Scotia. Verrazano's brother based this map on the voyage of 1524, but the explorer's eagerness to find a passage to Asia led him to mistake the Sounds beyond the sandbanks for the eastern sea (mare orientale).

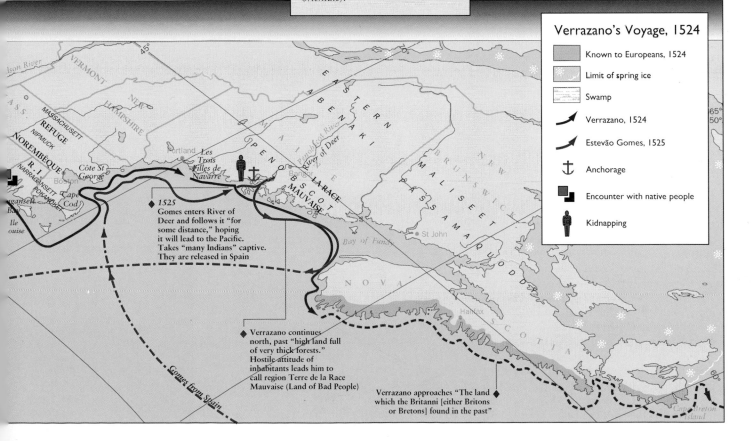

# St Lawrence, the River of Canada

## THE EXPLORATIONS OF JACQUES CARTIER, 1534-36

*The Breton seafarer Jacques Cartier finds one of North America's great rivers and travels a thousand miles into the interior of the continent.*

Verrazano had shown that the lands discovered by Cabot and the Spanish were linked by a continuous coastline, but explorers did not give up hope of finding a westward passage further north. One possibility was an opening known to French fishermen in Newfoundland-Labrador waters as the "Baye des Chasteaux" (the Strait of Belle Isle).

Cartier left St-Malo in 1534 with two ships and a commission from King Francis I to investigate the area. Ice floes made the going difficult, but they entered the strait and landed on its northern shore. The region was so desolate that Cartier dismissed it as "the land God gave to Cain." He continued in a clockwise course around what seemed to be a great inland sea, missing the entrance to the St Lawrence River. On the Gaspé Peninsula he met 300 Iroquois from the St Lawrence valley, and took two of them back to France, together with descriptions of birch-bark canoes, and the first recorded references to fur trading.

Cartier returned the following year with three ships. On the northern shore, Cartier named a bay after St Laurens on that saint's day, August 10. The name would soon apply to the whole gulf and eventually to the river, which he discovered and entered on this journey. He took his ships to the spot on the river's north shore where the Iroquois village of Stadacona huddled underneath the great rock ramparts where Québec would later be built. From there Cartier followed the river farther west, in the last stages by boat, until he reached the fortified Iroquois village of Hochelaga, with its long-houses sheltering as many as a thousand inhabitants. From a nearby hill, Mont Réal (the future Montréal), Cartier could see the Laurentian Highlands to the north, the Adirondacks to the south, and in between "the most beautiful land, arable, smooth and plain." Unable to pass the Lachine Rapids, Cartier retraced his route and wintered near Stadacona, where his men suffered from scurvy and the intense cold. When the ice broke up in the spring, the expedition left the gulf through a new southern route, later named Cabot Strait after an explorer who never set eyes on it.

In 1541 Cartier returned with an advance guard of settlers, but after enduring another winter near Stadacona and failing to get his boats through the rapids above Hochelaga, he returned to France. In 1543 the last settlers were evacuated.

Cartier had staked France's claim to a huge expanse of North America far removed from Spanish activities. His findings became an established feature on European maps, as did the names he gave them: New France, the St Lawrence and, most prophetically, the Iroquois name which Cartier had heard in 1535 on his second voyage, then refering simply to the region farther west along the great river – Canada.

> From the middle of November until the fifteenth of April we lay frozen up in the ice, which was more than two fathoms in thickness, while on shore there were more than four feet of snow, so that it was higher than the bulwarks of our ships... All our beverages froze in their casks... and the whole river was frozen where the water was fresh up to beyond Hochelaga.
>
> Winter on the St Lawrence, from the journal of Cartier's second voyage

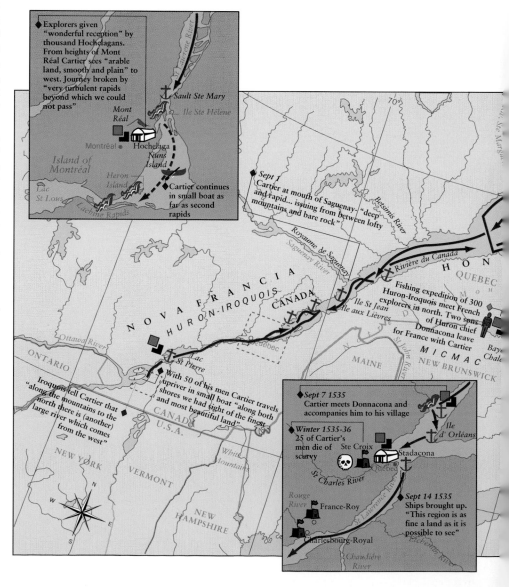

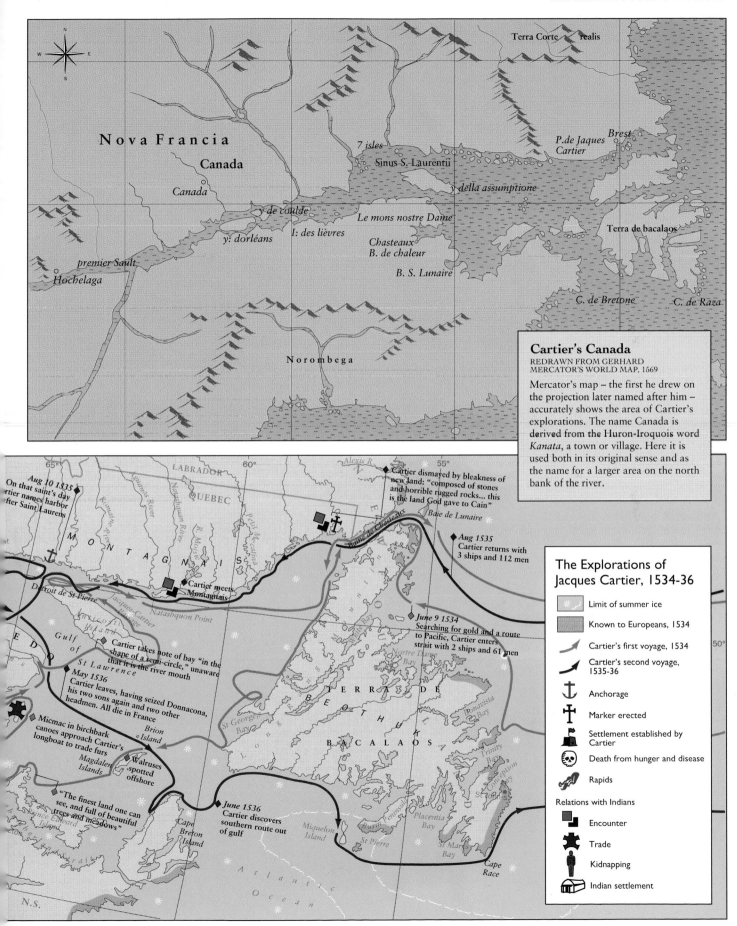

Nova Francia

Canada

Canada

*premier Sault*
Hochelaga

*y? dorléans*   I: des lièvres

*y de coulde*

Norombega

7 isles
Sinus S. Laurentii

*y della assumptione*

Le mons nostre Dame

*Chasteaux*
B. de chaleur

B. S. Lunaire

Terra Corte   realis

P. de Jaques
Cartier   *Brest*

Terra de bacalaos

C. de Bretone   C. de Raza

## Cartier's Canada
REDRAWN FROM GERHARD
MERCATOR'S WORLD MAP, 1569

Mercator's map – the first he drew on the projection later named after him – accurately shows the area of Cartier's explorations. The name Canada is derived from the Huron-Iroquois word *Kanata*, a town or village. Here it is used both in its original sense and as the name for a larger area on the north bank of the river.

Aug 10 1535
On that saint's day
Cartier names harbor
after Saint Laurens

Cartier meets
Montagnais

Cartier dismayed by bleakness of new land; "composed of stones and horrible rugged rocks... this is the land God gave to Cain"

Baie de Lunaire

Aug 1535
Cartier returns with
3 ships and 112 men

Cartier takes note of bay "in the shape of a semi-circle," unaware that it is the river mouth

May 1536
Cartier leaves, having seized Donnacona, his two sons again and two other headmen. All die in France

Micmac in birchbark canoes approach Cartier's longboat to trade furs

Magdalen
Islands

Walruses
spotted offshore

"The finest land one can see, and full of beautiful trees and meadows"

Cape
Breton
Island

June 1536
Cartier discovers
southern route out
of gulf

Miquelon
Island

June 9 1534
Searching for gold and a route to Pacific, Cartier enters strait with 2 ships and 61 men

## The Explorations of Jacques Cartier, 1534-36

- Limit of summer ice
- Known to Europeans, 1534
- Cartier's first voyage, 1534
- Cartier's second voyage, 1535-36
- Anchorage
- Marker erected
- Settlement established by Cartier
- Death from hunger and disease
- Rapids

**Relations with Indians**
- Encounter
- Trade
- Kidnapping
- Indian settlement

# First Searches for a Northwest Passage

## THE VOYAGES OF FROBISHER AND DAVIS, 1576-87

*English adventurers place the great opening of Davis Strait on the map and bring back the first descriptions of Baffin Island. The existence of the Hudson Strait eludes them.*

All attempts to find an opening in the eastern coastline had failed, leading explorers to look for a navigable route to the north, around the continent. This was probably an objective of the Corte-Réals' voyages in the early 16th century (▶ *page 20*) and there is evidence that in 1508 and 1509 John Cabot's son, Sebastian, may have ventured as far as what is now known as the Hudson Strait. But it was another 70 years before London's financial, court and mercantile circles became interested in the route which the English called the Northwest Passage.

In 1576 Martin Frobisher set out northwest in the tiny ship *Gabriel* with a crew of 18. After battling with tremendous seas off Greenland, he reached the southeast coast of Baffin Island, where he found an opening which seemed to divide "two maynelands or continents asunder." The strong tides led Frobisher to believe that this was "the West Sea, whereby to pass to Cathay." Back in England, interest in this prospect faded when news circulated that ore picked up by Frobisher's men contained gold.

Frobisher's expeditions of 1577 and 1578 were therefore directed more towards mining than exploration. In 1578 Frobisher's 15 ships, facing fog and snow, in error entered an

### Passage to the Pacific
REDRAWN FROM MICHAEL LOK'S MAP OF THE NORTHERN HEMISPHERE, 1582

This map (*right*) reflects European hopes of finding a sea passage through the North American landmass to Asia. It shows Verrazano's imaginary sea (▶ *page 23*), and interprets Frobisher Bay as a strait leading to the Pacific between Queen Elizabeth's Foreland (R. ELIZABETH) and Lok's Land (LOK). The mapmaker was one of Frobisher's sponsors, and the explorer duly named an island after him.

opening to the south. This was the opening to the great waterway of the Canadian north but after 20 days Frobisher turned back, ruefully naming Hudson Strait "Mistaken Strait." Nor was the expedition's mining successful for the minerals they found proved to be iron pyrites or "fool's gold." The Company of Cathay, which had promoted the enterprise, collapsed amid financial loss and mutual recrimination.

The next decade saw three more voyages, under the master mariner John Davis. In 1585 Davis found Cumberland Sound, a mighty opening which he thought might lead to the Pacific. On his return he insisted that "The northwest passage is a matter nothing

doubtful, but at any tyme almost to be passed, the sea navigable, void of use, the air tolerable, and the waters very deep."

During his next voyage, in 1586, Davis explored the west coast of Greenland, crossed the strait which would bear his name to Baffin Island, and worked later his way south to the Labrador coast. On his final voyage, Davis explored Cumberland Sound to its head. He then failed to identify Frobisher Bay, naming it Lord Lumley's Inlet, and to the south crossed "a very great gulfe." This was the entrance of Hudson Strait, but it was yet again to be ignored.

T hey are men of a large corporature and good proportion: their colour is not much unlike the Sunne burnte Countrie man... They weare their haire somethinge long and cut before, either with stone or knife, very disorderly... They eate their meate all rawe, both fleshe, fishe, and foule, or something perboyled with bloud & a little water, whiche they drinke. For lacke of water, they will eate yce, that is hard frosen, as pleasantly as we doe Sugar Candie.

Description of Baffin Island Inuit on Frobisher's second voyage

*Left: On Frobisher's 1577 journey, fighting broke out between his men and the Inuit at Bloody Point in Frobisher Bay. The scene was captured by the artist John White, who may have been an eye-witness. His painting accurately shows the clothes, kayaks and skin tents of the Inuit.*

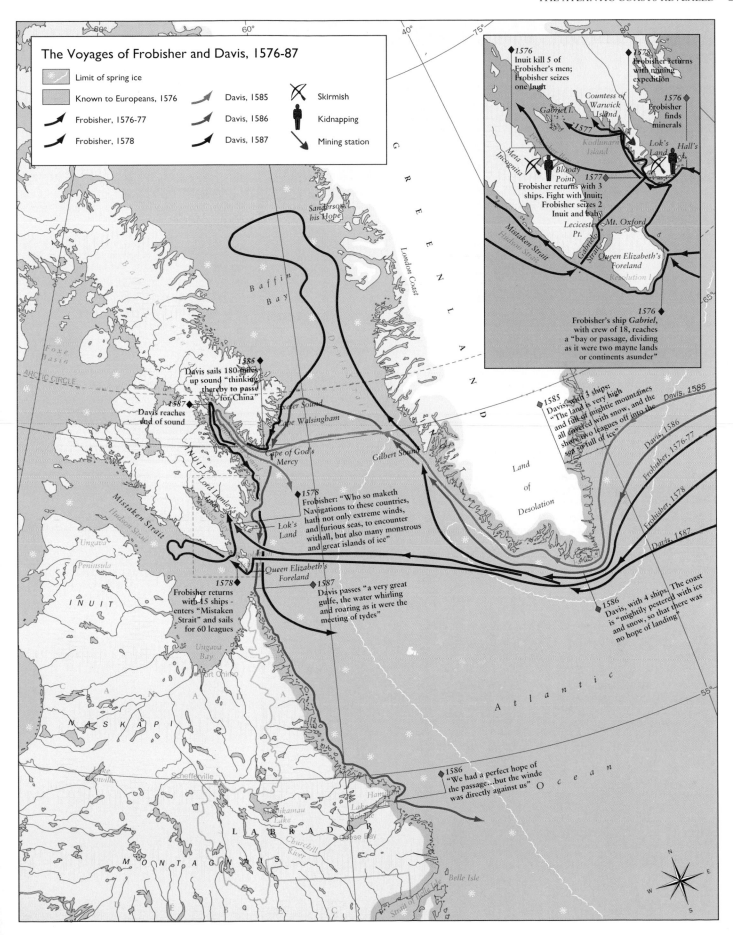

## The Voyages of Frobisher and Davis, 1576-87

Limit of spring ice

Known to Europeans, 1576

Frobisher, 1576-77

Frobisher, 1578

Davis, 1585

Davis, 1586

Davis, 1587

Skirmish

Kidnapping

Mining station

**1576** Inuit kill 5 of Frobisher's men; Frobisher seizes one Inuit

**1578** Frobisher returns with mining expedition

**1576** Frobisher finds minerals

Countess of Warwick Island

Gabriel I.

Kodlunarn Island

Lok's Land

Hall's I.

Meta Incognita

**1577** Frobisher returns with 3 ships. Fight with Inuit; Frobisher seizes 2 Inuit and baby

Bloody Point

Leicester Pt.

Mt. Oxford

Gabriel Strait

Queen Elizabeth's Foreland

Mistaken Strait

Hudson Strait

Resolution I.

**1576** Frobisher's ship *Gabriel*, with crew of 18, reaches a "bay or passage, dividing as it were two mayne lands or continents asunder"

Sanderson his Hope

London Coast

Baffin Bay

Davis Strait

Foxe Basin

ARCTIC CIRCLE

**1585** Davis sails 180 miles up sound "thinking thereby to passe for China"

Exeter Sound

Cape Walsingham

Cape of God's Mercy

Gilbert Sound

**1587** Davis reaches end of sound

INUIT

Lord Lumley's Inlet

Lok's Land

**1578** Frobisher: "Who so maketh Navigations to these countries, hath not only extreme winds, and furious seas, to encounter withall, but also many monstrous and great islands of ice"

Mistaken Strait

Hudson Strait

Ungava

Ungava Peninsula

INUIT

Queen Elizabeth's Foreland

**1578** Frobisher returns with 15 ships - enters "Mistaken Strait" and sails for 60 leagues

**1587** Davis passes "a very great gulfe, the water whirling and roaring as it were the meeting of tydes"

**1585** Davis, with 3 ships: "The land is very high and full of mightie mountaines all covered with snow, and the shore two leagues off into the sea so full of ice"

Land of Desolation

Davis, 1585

Davis, 1586

Frobisher, 1576-77

Frobisher, 1578

Davis, 1587

**1586** Davis, with 4 ships. The coast is "mightily pestered with ice and snow, so that there was no hope of landing"

Port Chimo

Ungava Bay

CANADA

NASKAPI

Schefferville

Lake Menville

MONTAGNAIS

Ashikamau Lake

Churchill River

Goose Bay

LABRADOR

Hamilton Lake

**1586** "We had a perfect hope of the passage...but the winde was directly against us"

Atlantic

Ocean

Belle Isle

Strait of Belle Isle

QUEBEC

# The Great Bays of the North

## THE VOYAGES OF HUDSON AND BAFFIN, 1610-16

*The English explore Arctic waters in search of a Northwest Passage to Asia. They find no passage but become skilled in the art and science of navigating these dangerous waters.*

At the turn of the 17th century the route to Asia lay around the Cape of Good Hope and was dominated by the Portuguese and the Dutch. In 1602, in search of a new route to Asia, the East India Company of London organized and financed a voyage to the northwest by George Waymouth. Neither Waymouth nor his immediate successors made any real progress.

In 1609 Henry Hudson explored what was to become the Hudson River. Then in 1610 he set out on a new and dramatic voyage. Early in August he arrived at the great bay that would also take his name and was described by one of his crew as "a spacious sea." Hudson wintered in the south at today's James Bay. The following summer his crew mutinied and Hudson was cast adrift, along with his son and seven crew members. They all died.

A new company was set up in search of the supposed new route to Asia, "The Governor and Company of the Merchants of London, Dicoverers of the North-West Passage." Almost 300 investors sponsored, among others, the voyages of Thomas Button, 1612-13 and William Baffin in 1616. Button explored 600 miles of the unknown west and

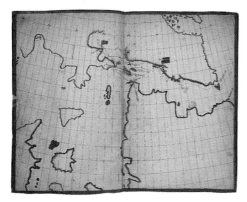

*Baffin's own chart from his logbook, of his journey through Hudson Strait in 1615. The red dotted line shows his route; the flags mark his landings; while the coasts outlined in green are those he saw himself.*

north shores of Hudson Bay, including the estuaries of the Churchill and Port Nelson rivers, later important in the European fur trade. He found no sign of a passage west; nor did Robert Bylot, a survivor of Hudson's final voyage, who was sent out in 1615 with Baffin as his pilot.

The search shifted farther north. In 1616 Bylot and Baffin sailed again, pushing through heavy ice in Davis Strait to open water, the "North Water" of Baffin Bay as

whalers later knew it. At their farthest north they reached Smith Sound, not entered until the mid-19th century, and on the west side of Baffin Bay "another great Sound," which Baffin named Lancaster Sound. In the 19th century it proved to be the entrance to the Northwest Passage, but Baffin noted a "ledge of ice" along the coast, and later that "there is no passage in the north of Davis Straights."

The search was virtually over. In 1619-20 Jens Munk led a Danish expedition but when he wintered at Churchill River only three men survived. There were further English attempts by Luke Foxe in 1631 and Thomas James, 1631-32.

Off the shore of Hudson Bay, east of Port Nelson, Foxe and James actually met. A disagreement occurred over protocol. Foxe wrote: "I did not thinke much for his keeping out his flagg... To this was replide, that hee was going to the Emperour of Japon, with letters from his Majestie...'Keep it up then', quoth I, 'but you are out of the way to Japon, for this is not it'."

All their searches for a strait to the Pacific from Hudson Bay were futile and their voyages provided little new geographical information. But a tradition of English Arctic navigation was established. English explorers had learned how to deal with problems of navigating through ice, compass variations and the phenomenal rise and fall of the tides. These skills would prove profitable in future days, as the great trade of cod, whales and furs developed in northern waters.

*Left: Munk's expedition at Churchill, where most of his crew died of scurvy on board the ships. "As I could not now any more stand the bad smell and stench from the dead bodies," Munk wrote, "I spent that night on deck, using the clothes of the dead." Woodcut taken from Munk's 1624 account of his voyage.*

In the evening, we were inclosed amongst great pieces; as high as our Poope, and some of the sharpe blue corners of them did reach quite under us. All these great pieces...did heave and set, and so beat us that it was wonderful how the ship could indure one blow of it.

Thomas James, 1631

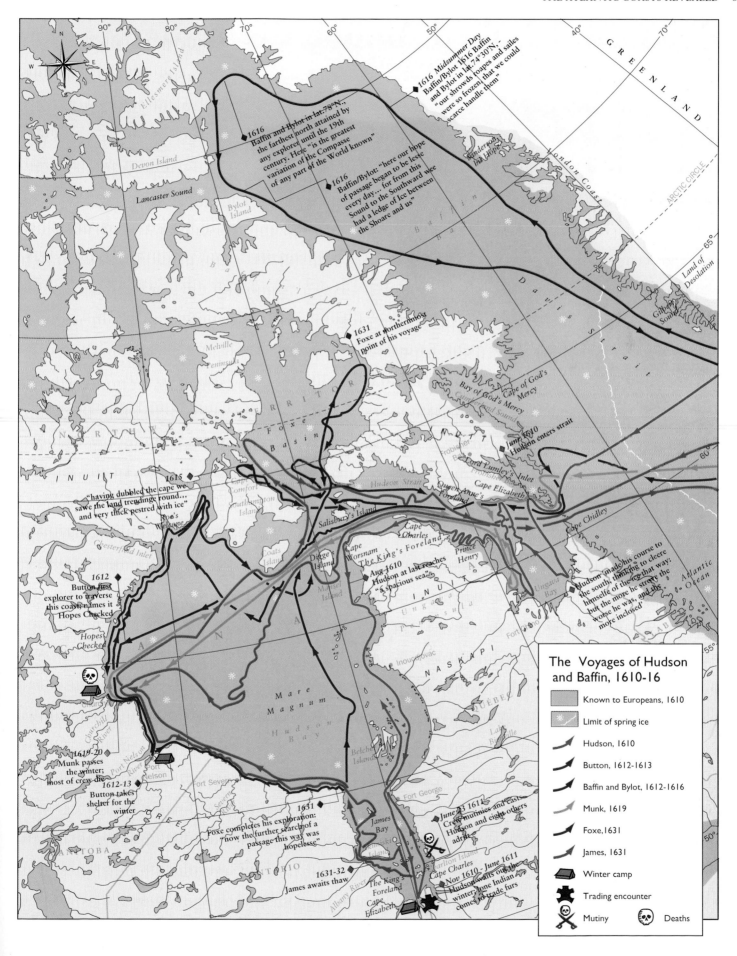

*1616 Midsummer Day* Baffin/Bylot 1616 Baffin and Bylot in lat 74°30'N... "our shrowds roapes and sailes were so frozen, that we could scarce handle them"

1616 Baffin and Bylot in lat 78°N, the farthest north attained by any explorer until the 19th century. Here "is the greatest variation of the Compasse of any part of the World known"

1616 Baffin/Bylot: "here our hope of passage began to be lesse every day... for from this Sound to the Southward wee had a ledge of Ice between the Shoare and us"

GREENLAND

Sanderson his Hope

London Coast

ARCTIC CIRCLE

Ellesmere Island

Devon Island

Lancaster Sound

Bylot Island

Baffin Island

Baffin Bay

Davis Strait

Land of Desolation

Gilbert Sound

1631 Foxe at northernmost point of his voyage

Melville Peninsula

NORTH WE       TERRITOR

Foxe Basin

Bay of God's Mercy   Cape of God's Mercy

Cumberland Sound

Frobisher

Lord Lumley's Inlet

June 1610 Hudson enters strait

1615 "having dubbled the cape we sawe the land trendinge round... and very thick pestred with ice"

INUIT

Cape Comfort

Southampton Island

Roe's Welcome

Salisbury's Island

Coats Island

Digges Island

Cape Worsnam

The King's Foreland

Aug 1610 Hudson at last reaches "a spacious sea"

Hudson Strait

Queen Anne's Foreland

Cape Charles

Prince Henry

Cape Chidley

Cape Elizabeth

Ungava Bay

INUIT

Ungava Peninsula

Fort Chimo

'Hudson made his course to the south, thinking to cleere himselfe of the ice that way: but the more he strove the worse he was, and the more inclosed'

Atlantic Ocean

Chesterfield Inlet

1612 Button first explorer to traverse this coast; names it Hopes Checked

Hopes Checked

N       A

Mare Magnum

Hudson Bay

Inoucdjouac

NASKAPI

QUÉBEC

LAB

Churchill River

1619-20 Munk passes the winter; most of crew die

Port Nelson

Port Nelson

Nelson River

1612-13 Button takes shelter for the winter

Fort Severn

Severn River

CREE

MANITOBA

Belcher Island

Fort George

Fort Albany

Lake Bienville

1631 Foxe completes his exploration: "now the further search of a passage this way was hopelesse"

ONTARIO

Akimiski Island

Albany River

James Bay

Charlton Island

Cape Charles

June 23 1611 Crew mutinies and casts Hudson and eight others adrift

Nov 1610 – June 1611 Hudson waits out the winter; June Indian comes to trade furs

1631-32 James awaits thaw

The King's Foreland Cape Elizabeth

### The Voyages of Hudson and Baffin, 1610-16

- Known to Europeans, 1610
- Limit of spring ice
- Hudson, 1610
- Button, 1612-1613
- Baffin and Bylot, 1612-1616
- Munk, 1619
- Foxe, 1631
- James, 1631
- Winter camp
- Trading encounter
- Mutiny
- Deaths

# Alone and Naked Among the Indians

## THE WANDERINGS OF CABEZA DE VACA, 1528-36

*Four survivors of a doomed army of conquistadors walk 1600 miles across North America and bring back reports of the land to the north of Spain's American possessions.*

The conquest of Mexico by Hernan Cortés in 1519 had given the Spanish their first base on the American mainland. Cortés believed that the most promising area for expansion lay to the south and west; but rival conquistadors hoped to make their fortunes in the north. As early as 1519, Alonzo Alvaro de Pineda had coasted from Florida to Mexico, proving that they were parts of a continuous mainland. In 1528, Pánfilo de Narváez landed at Tampa Bay in Florida with an army of 400 men.

After allowing his ships to depart with only vague plans for a rendezvous, he led his army inland. They had brought little food, and as they ransacked the corn supplies of villages they found, the inhabitants became increasingly hostile. By the time the expedition reached the gulf, its numbers had been halved

> Throughout all this country we went naked, and as we were unaccustomed to being so, twice a year we cast our skins like serpents. The sun and air produced great sores on our breasts and shoulders, giving us sharp pain; and the large load we had... caused the cords to cut into our arms... The country is so broken and thickly set, that... thorns and shrubs tore our flesh wherever we went.
>
> Cabeza de Vaca, *La Relacion*, 1542

by illness and attack. The survivors built five ramshackle boats and tried to sail back along the coast to Mexico. Three of the boats sank, and two were driven ashore around Galveston Island, where the expedition disintegrated.

There were four survivors: Narváez's second-in-command, Alvar Núñez Cabeza de Vaca, a nobleman whose grandfather had conquered Gran Canaria; Captain Alfonso de Castillo; Andrés Dorantes; and Estevan, a black slave from Morocco. In his account of his experiences, printed in 1542, Cabeza de Vaca recalled how "I was in this country nearly six years, alone among the Indians, and naked like them." The four were separated for a while, living among the tribes who eked out an existence in the harsh Texas coastlands. "The famine," de Vaca recalled, "is so great that they eat spiders and the eggs of ants, worms, lizards...the dung of deer... Were there stones in that land they would eat them."

In a state of semi-slavery, the three Spaniards and the Moroccan survived on their

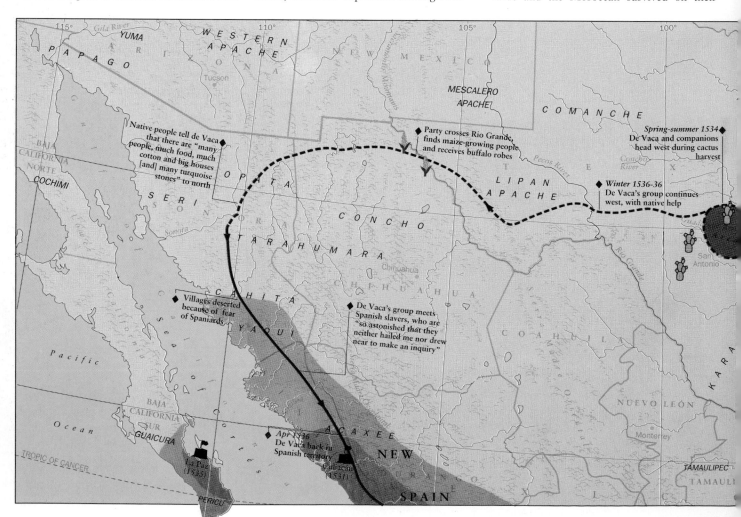

wits, their bartering skills and their willingness to learn. In 1534, they met up again, and decided to use the summer gathering of tribes at the annual cactus harvest to depart for Mexico. Their route was circuitous, and distances, directions and dates are understandably missing from de Vaca's account. But as they traveled across the (Texan) Colorado and Pecos rivers, the land became more fertile, and they found people living in "fixed dwellings." Using their rudimentary medical knowledge, they gained a reputation as faith-healers and were welcomed with great festivities wherever they went.

After crossing a "sterile and difficult" region to the Sonora valley, Cabeza de Vaca spotted an Indian wearing a Spanish horseshoe nail as an amulet. In the spring of 1536, the four travelers were picked up by Spanish slave raiders. By July they were in Mexico City, where they were questioned by Cortés and the viceroy, Antonio de Mendoza. Their reports stressed the factors that had dominated their eight years of survival: the country and its food supplies, the Indians, the hardships. They had seen the importance of cactus fruit and heard about buffalo herds

and "populous towns and very large houses." It was not much, but it encouraged the view that the next stage of expansion should be northward.

Cabeza de Vaca, meanwhile, went on to lead a 1000-mile walk across Brazil in 1540. His experiences had given him an understanding of the culture and values of the native people rare among his European contemporaries. The slave-raiders who found him told the Indians that "we were persons of mean condition and small force. The Indians... said [they] lied: that we healed the sick, they killed the sound; that we had come naked and barefoot, while they had arrived in clothing and on horses with lances; that we were not covetous of anything...[while] the others had the only purpose to rob whomsoever they found."

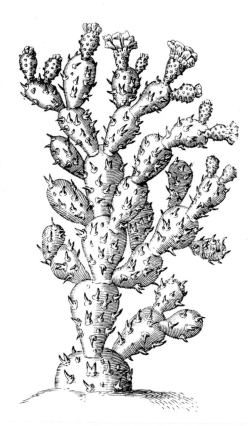

*Right:The prickly pear (Opuntia ficus indica) was an essential source of food for the tribes of southern Texas. "The happiest part of the year," de Vaca wrote, "is the season of eating prickly pears; they have hunger then no longer, pass all the time in dancing, and eat day and night. While these last, they... set them to dry, and... put [them] in hampers like figs. These they kept to eat on the way back."*
*An engraving of 1641 by J. T. de Bry.*

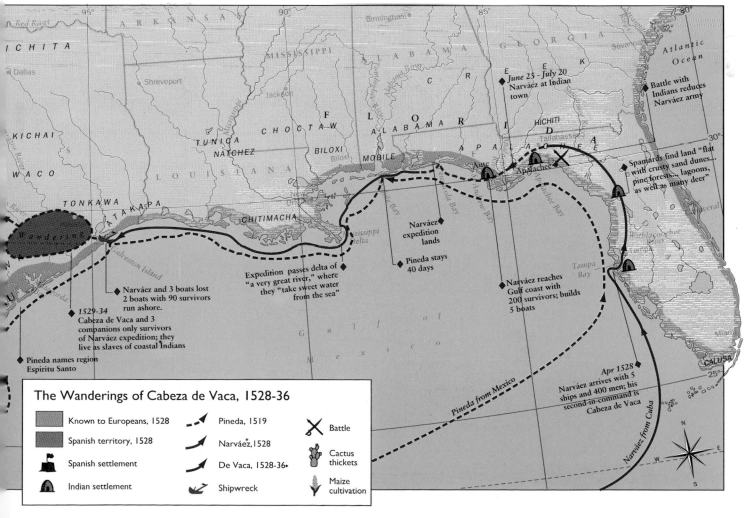

The Wanderings of Cabeza de Vaca, 1528-36

- Known to Europeans, 1528
- Spanish territory, 1528
- Spanish settlement
- Indian settlement
- Pineda, 1519
- Narváez, 1528
- De Vaca, 1528-36
- Shipwreck
- Battle
- Cactus thickets
- Maize cultivation

June 25 - July 20 Narváez at Indian town

Battle with Indians reduces Narváez army

Spaniards find land "flat with crusty sand dunes... pine forests... lagoons, as well as many deer"

Narváez expedition lands

Pineda stays 40 days

Narváez reaches Gulf coast with 200 survivors; builds 5 boats

Expedition passes delta of "a very great river," where they "take sweet water from the sea"

Narváez and 3 boats lost 2 boats with 90 survivors run ashore.

1529-34 Cabeza de Vaca and 3 companions only survivors of Narváez expedition; they live as slaves of coastal Indians

Pineda names region Espiritu Santo

Apr 1528 Narváez arrives with 5 ships and 400 men; his second-in-command is Cabeza de Vaca

Pineda from Mexico

Narváez from Cuba

# Blade and Buckler

## THE EXPEDITION OF HERNANDO DE SOTO, 1539-43

*A Spanish conquistador leads and army of mailed soldiers across 3000 miles of what is now the southern United States.*

When Cabeza de Vaca returned to Spain in 1537, he found an ambitious expedition being prepared for Florida. Its commander was Hernando de Soto. One of Pizarro's lieutenants in the conquest of Peru, he had gone there with "nothing more than blade and buckler" and come home a rich man. Now he was to lead his own expedition farther north than any Spaniard had ventured.

De Soto landed at Tampa Bay in May 1539 with a well-organized force of about 200 horsemen, 400 foot-soldiers, some fighting dogs and a small herd of hogs for food. Once away from the coast he hoped to find gold or other treasure, and his gubernatorial powers from the crown became in effect a licence to plunder the peoples of the interior. He soon revealed his methods: local chiefs were seized and held for a ransom of bearers, women and corn. Usually captives would be released once the next tribe was reached and the process would begin again. Inevitably, such tactics provoked resistance, and turned the expedition into a series of running skirmishes.

As de Soto marched westwards, the expedition's chroniclers noted many different peoples, from the warlike Timucua of Florida to the elaborate, temple-mound cultures of the Creek and Choctaw Indians. The Spanish

soldiers were the first Europeans to see the Mississippi. (At first, they called it "the great river," then Rio del Spirito Santo.) They crossed it in clumsy dugout canoes in June 1541 somewhere below present-day Memphis, where it was one-and-a-half miles wide. "A man standing on the shore could not be told, whether he were a man or something else from the other side." In eastern Arkansas, de Soto's outriders encountered Plains Indians, and heard reports of the great buffalo herds, and also of another sea. De Soto assumed this was the Pacific, and even considered trying to reach it.

No gold was found, though rumors of it explain many of the twists and turns of the expedition's route. One of the survivors recalled that "neither the governor nor anyone else knew where they were headed other than to find a land so rich as to satisfy their desires."

Depressed and repentant, de Soto died of a "flux of blood" in May 1542, and was buried in the Mississippi. After an abortive attempt

to reach Mexico overland, the survivors, led by Luis de Moscoso, headed back to the river. There they built crude boats which they sailed downstream, through the tangle of the delta channels, and along the coast to Mexico.

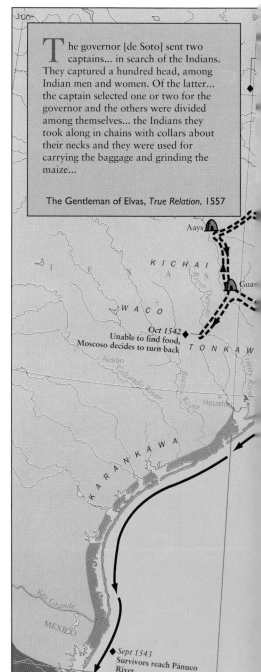

> The governor [de Soto] sent two captains... in search of the Indians. They captured a hundred head, among Indian men and women. Of the latter... the captain selected one or two for the governor and the others were divided among themselves... the Indians they took along in chains with collars about their necks and they were used for carrying the baggage and grinding the maize...
>
> The Gentleman of Elvas, *True Relation*, 1557

### The Interior of Florida
REDRAWN FROM ABRAHAM ORTELIUS'S ATLAS, 1584

This map draws on de Soto's explorations in the vast region then known as Florida. It shows many native settlements, the southern Appalachians, and the Mississippi (*Rio del Spirito Santo*), incorrectly mapped as a short river flowing from inland mountains.

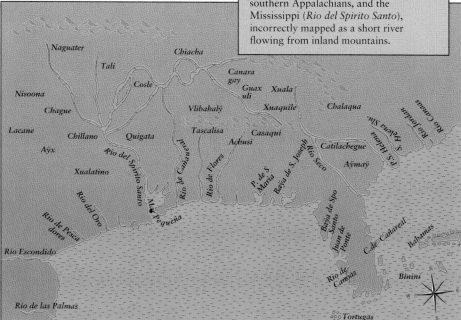

That 311 men survived says much for their fortitude, and for de Soto's qualities of leadership. But the cost of his methods was the mutilation, torture and killing of hundreds and thousands of native people. "Never resting anywhere," the historian Oviedo wrote, "they made neither settlement nor conquest, but caused desolation of the land and loss of liberty of the people."

*In his* History of the New World, *published 1565, Italian traveler Girolamo Benzoni, who had witnessed many such atrocities in the Americas, tells of de Soto's cruelties. De Soto seized a number of native people demanding that they lead him to gold. When they did not find any, "the governor becoming bitterly enraged, cut off their hands."*
*From an engraving by Theodore de Bry.*

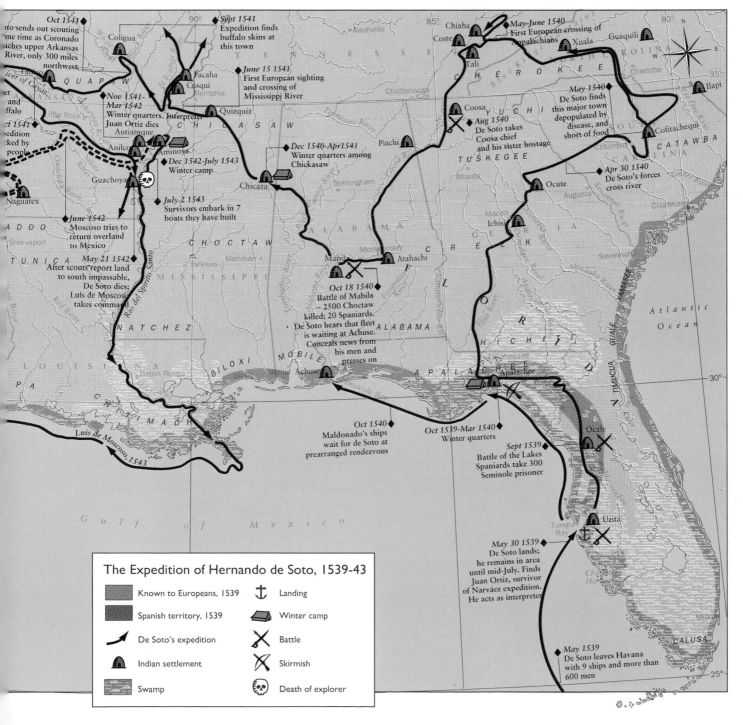

## The Expedition of Hernando de Soto, 1539-43

- Known to Europeans, 1539
- Spanish territory, 1539
- De Soto's expedition
- Indian settlement
- Swamp
- Landing
- Winter camp
- Battle
- Skirmish
- Death of explorer

# The Quest for Cibola

## THE EXPEDITION OF VÁSQUEZ DE CORONADO, 1540-42

*The Spanish expedition headed by Coronado fails in its quest for fabulous cities to rival Aztec Mexico; but it discovers a vast swathe of the North American interior.*

By the late 1530s Antonio de Mendoza, recently appointed viceroy of New Spain, was ready to mount a full-scale expedition to explore the unknown lands to the north. Cabeza de Vaca's reports of populous towns to the north, rumors of precious metals, and fears that De Soto's planned expedition from Florida would stake out a rival claim, all lent urgency to the matter.

In 1539 a reconnaissance party, including Estevān (a north African slave who had been with Cabeza de Vaca), a Franciscan friar Marcos de Niza and several hundred native peoples followed the Indian road to Sinaloa. There Marcos heard tales of the "Seven Cities" further north in Cibola. Estevān crossed the desert with an advance party to reach the Cibola pueblos where he was killed by the apprehensive Zuñi inhabitants. Marcos almost certainly did not get even within distant sight of the place, which nevertheless he described as "a very beautiful city...bigger than the city of Mexico."

Encouraged by this report, the 30-year old governor of the frontier province of New Galicia, Francisco Vásquez de Coronado, left for the north in February 1540. He was accompanied by 330 Spaniards (two-thirds of them mounted), more than a thousand native allies and servants, and a baggage and provision train. So large a force was slow on the move, and difficult to feed; Coronado soon split the expedition into different groups. Hernando de Alarcón took three vessels along the coast with supplies, while the main force headed for the Seven Cities. These proved a sad disappointment. There were

*Above: Indians defending their pueblo against Coronado's forces, drawn by a Spanish-Tlaxcalan mestizo, Diego Muñoz Camargo, within living memory of the event. Part of a manuscript presented to King Philip II of Spain by a Tlaxcalan embassy in 1585. The caption says that during Coronado's expedition "the Tlaxcalans were in the service of Your Majesty." This central Mexican people had also assisted Cortés in his conquest of the Aztecs.*

only six (to which the collective name Cibola applied) and they were villages rather than cities.

Exploring parties sent out to east and west of the main force had varying fortunes. One led by López de Cárdenas in search of a river route to the Pacific, came to the Grand Canyon, the first Europeans to see it, and also the last for more than two hundred years. It was an awesome but frustrating sight, since for the Spaniards on its southern rim there was no way down or across the mighty chasm. Another group under Melchor Díaz reached the Lower Colorado River at Yuma, and crossed into California for a few days – pathfinders on the overland route from Mexico to Lower California. Yet another party under Hernando de Alvarado went east to the Upper Rio Grande, the Canadian River,

and the edge of the Great Plains. They brought back a Plains Indian, "the Turk," who described a country to the northeast, Quivira, rich in gold with lordly rulers. Excited by this news, Coronado, who had wintered among the pueblos of Tiguex on the Upper Rio Grande, set out for Quivira in 1541. After bridging the Pecos River he reached the plains: hundreds of miles of "land as level as the sea," where men became hopelessly lost, and the only trails were those made by the buffalo. It was on Coronado's expedition that Europeans for the first time saw the great buffalo herds, and the Plains Indians who lived off them.

On the plains Coronado headed north to the Arkansas River, and into the country of the Wichita Indians between the Arkansas and Kansas rivers. Meanwhile, 300 miles to the southeast, de Soto had crossed the Mississippi into eastern Arkansas – the nearest the two expeditions came to each other. Coronado had reached Quivira – a fertile land, but with no dwellings more impressive than thatched beehive-like huts, and no signs of great cities or great riches. Coronado decided to turn for home; it was a tattered and despondent party which reached Mexico City in the early fall of 1542.

*Below: Pueblo Indians encountered by Coronado had inherited a long tradition of ceramic art. This storage jar from Arizona shows the design and spatter technique used in the 15th and 16th centuries.*

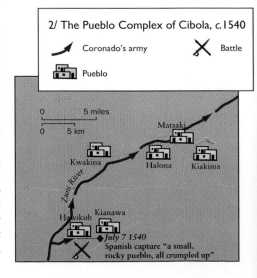

2/ The Pueblo Complex of Cibola, *c.*1540

Coronado's army     Battle

Pueblo

0   5 miles

0   5 km

109°

Matsaki

Kwakina

Halona

Kiakima

Zuni River

35°

Hawikuh     Kianawa

Kianawa

*July 7 1540*

Spanish capture "a small, rocky pueblo, all crumpled up"

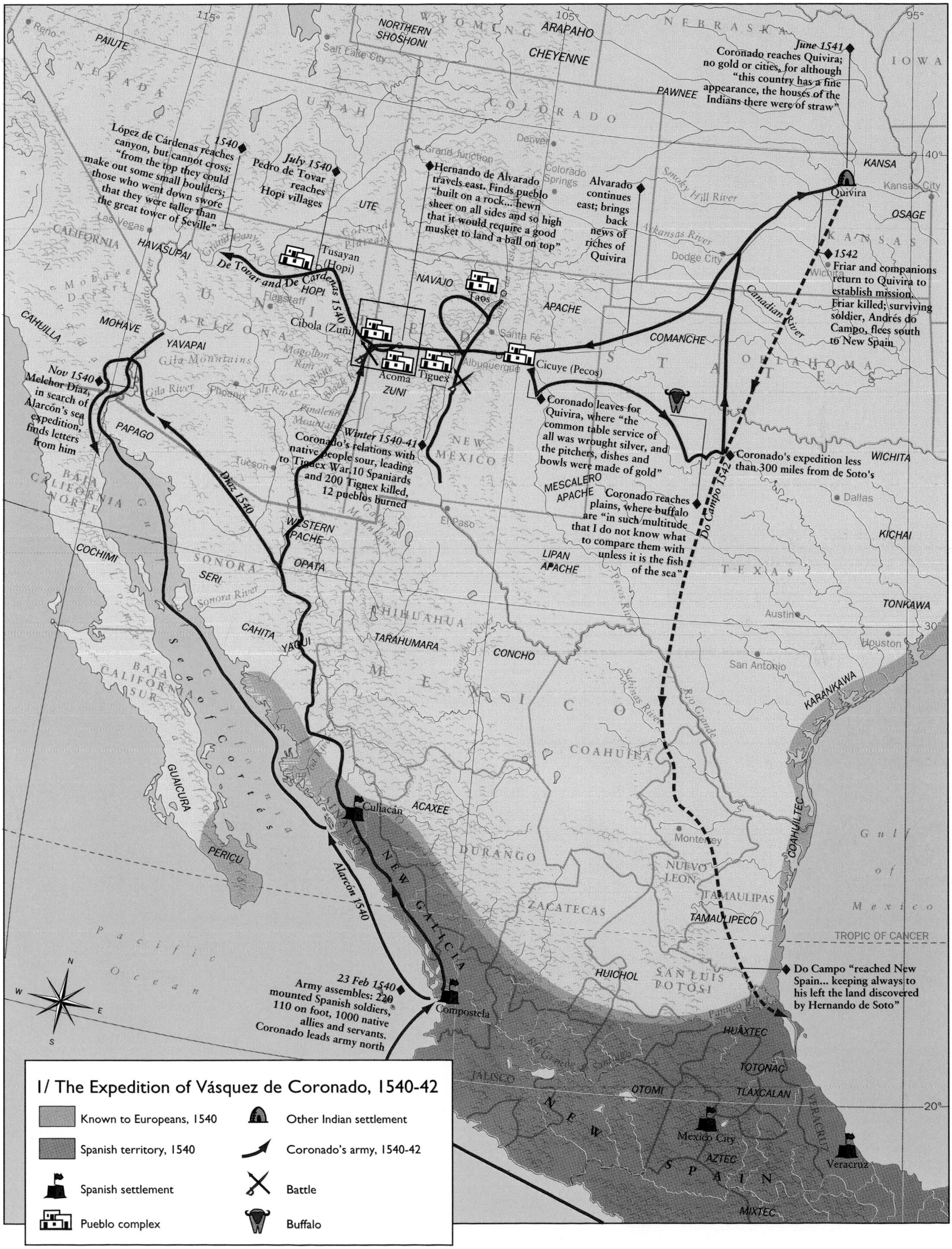

I/ The Expedition of Vásquez de Coronado, 1540-42
Known to Europeans, 1540
Spanish territory, 1540
Spanish settlement
Pueblo complex
Other Indian settlement
Coronado's army, 1540-42
Battle
Buffalo
June 1541 Coronado reaches Quivira; no gold or cities, for although "this country has a fine appearance, the houses of the Indians there were of straw"
1540 López de Cárdenas reaches canyon, but cannot cross: "from the top they could make out some small boulders; those who went down swore that they were taller than the great tower of Seville"
July 1540 Pedro de Tovar reaches Hopi villages
Hernando de Alvarado travels east. Finds pueblo "built on a rock... hewn sheer on all sides and so high that it would require a good musket to land a ball on top"
Alvarado continues east; brings back news of riches of Quivira
1542 Friar and companions return to Quivira to establish mission. Friar killed; surviving soldier, Andrés do Campo, flees south to New Spain
Nov 1540 Melchor Díaz, in search of Alarcón's sea expedition, finds letters from him
Winter 1540-41 Coronado's relations with native people sour, leading to Tiguex War. 10 Spaniards and 200 Tiguex killed, 12 pueblos burned
Coronado leaves for Quivira, where "the common table service of all was wrought silver, and the pitchers, dishes and bowls were made of gold"
Coronado's expedition less than 300 miles from de Soto's
Coronado reaches plains, where buffalo are "in such multitude that I do not know what to compare them with unless it is the fish of the sea"
23 Feb 1540 Army assembles: 220 mounted Spanish soldiers, 110 on foot, 1000 native allies and servants. Coronado leads army north
Do Campo "reached New Spain... keeping always to his left the land discovered by Hernando de Soto"
De Tovar and De Cárdenas 1540
Díaz 1540
Alarcón 1540
Do Campo 1542
Quivira
Tusayan (Hopi)
Cibola (Zuñi)
Acoma
Tiguex
Taos
Cicuye (Pecos)
Culiacán
Compostela
Mexico City
Veracruz
NORTHERN SHOSHONI
ARAPAHO
CHEYENNE
PAWNEE
PAIUTE
KANSA
OSAGE
UTE
HAVASUPAI
HOPI
NAVAJO
APACHE
COMANCHE
MOHAVE
CAHUILLA
YAVAPAI
ZUNI
PAPAGO
WICHITA
MESCALERO APACHE
WESTERN APACHE
LIPAN APACHE
KICHAI
COCHIMI
SERI
OPATA
TONKAWA
CAHITA
YAQUI
TARAHUMARA
CONCHO
KARANKAWA
GUAICURA
ACAXEE
COAHUILTEC
PERICU
TAMAULIPECO
HUICHOL
HUAXTEC
TOTONAC
OTOMI
TLAXCALAN
AZTEC
MIXTEC
NEBRASKA
IOWA
WYOMING
NEVADA
UTAH
COLORADO
KANSAS
CALIFORNIA
ARIZONA
NEW MEXICO
OKLAHOMA
TEXAS
UNITED STATES
BAJA CALIFORNIA NORTE
BAJA CALIFORNIA SUR
SONORA
CHIHUAHUA
MEXICO
COAHUILA
DURANGO
NUEVO LEON
TAMAULIPAS
ZACATECAS
SAN LUIS POTOSI
NUEVA GALICIA
JALISCO
VERACRUZ
NEW SPAIN
Sea of Cortés
Pacific Ocean
Gulf of Mexico
TROPIC OF CANCER
Reno
Salt Lake City
Grand Junction
Denver
Colorado Springs
Kansas City
Dodge City
Wichita
Las Vegas
Flagstaff
Santa Fe
Albuquerque
Phoenix
Tucson
El Paso
Dallas
Austin
Houston
San Antonio
Monterrey
Smoky Hill River
Arkansas River
Canadian River
Colorado River
Gila River
Salt River
Pecos River
Rio Grande
Sonora River
Grand Canyon
Colorado Plateau
Gila Mountains
Mogollon Rim
115°
105°
95°
40°
30°
20°
N
S
E
W

# North to California

## SPANISH COASTAL VOYAGES, 1539-43

*The Spanish turn their ambitions northward. They sail up the west coast in search of a northeast strait through the continent to the Atlantic Ocean.*

After conquering central Mexico, Hernando Cortés wanted to establish Spanish control to the north and find the rumored strait to the Atlantic, later known as the Strait of Anian. In 1524 he informed Charles V, "The voyage from the spice region to your kingdom would be very easy and very short...without any risk to the vessels... because they would always come and go through your dominions."

Progress was slow. In 1535 Cortés led an expedition which confused the "island of Santa Cruz" with the peninsula of Baja California and failed to colonize it. New reports then emerged, some from Cabeza de Vaca's travels (▶ *page 32*), of rich and populous regions to the north. In 1539 Cortés sent Francisco de Ulloa with three vessels northward to explore the coast beyond his own discovery of La Paz. Within a few months Ulloa reached the Gulf of California, naming it the Sea of Cortés, sensed the presence of the Colorado River and proved Baja California to be a peninsula. He then sailed north along its Pacific shore at least to the Isla de Cedros.

In 1540 the Spanish viceroy sent Alarcón on a voyage with supplies for Coronado (▶ *page 36*). Alarcón sailed into the Gulf of

California and entered the Colorado River. By boat he followed it some 90 miles inland to its junction with the Gila. Yuma Indians told Alarcón of the death of a black man, Estevaán, and Coronado's attack, on Cibola. Alarcón, deciding it was too far and too dangerous to reach Coronado, turned back.

In 1542 the viceroy sent further ships north, under Juan Rodríguez Cabrillo, who had heard that the Portuguese had discovered a northern strait between the two oceans. Cabrillo reached the harbor San Miguel, now San Diego, becoming the first European to land in Upper California. Sailing north, away from the coast because of winds, Cabrillo glimpsed neither Monterey nor San Francisco harbors. He turned back and probably did sight Drake's Bay but died in January 1543. Bartolomé Ferrelo, the chief pilot, courageously returned north along the coast.

The expedition explored 900 miles of unknown coast but found neither riches nor any great strait leading east. Further exploration north from New Spain had to wait to near the end of the century.

*Below: Map by Juan de Martinez (1578) showing the seven cities of Cibola.*

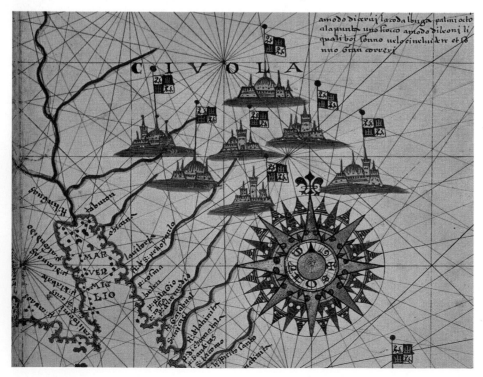

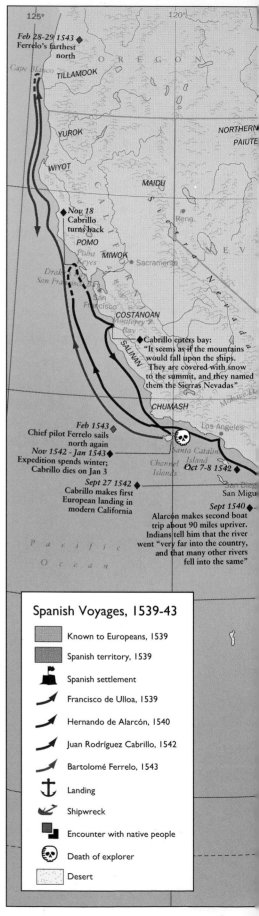

### Spanish Voyages, 1539-43

- Known to Europeans, 1539
- Spanish territory, 1539
- Spanish settlement
- Francisco de Ulloa, 1539
- Hernando de Alarcón, 1540
- Juan Rodríguez Cabrillo, 1542
- Bartolomé Ferrelo, 1543
- Landing
- Shipwreck
- Encounter with native people
- Death of explorer
- Desert

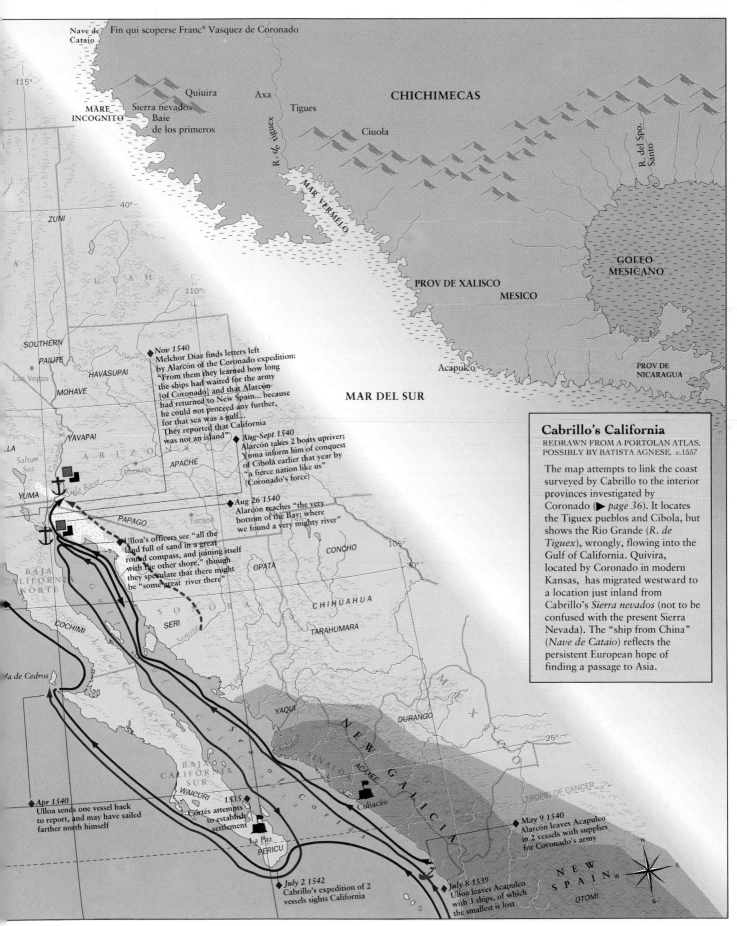

Nave de Cataio    Fin qui scoperse Franc° Vasquez de Coronado

115°

MARE
INCOGNITO

Quiuira    Axa    CHICHIMECAS

Sierra nevados    Tigues
Baie
de los primeros    Ciuola    R. del Spo. Santo

40°    ZUNI    R. de tiguex

MAR VERMELO

UTAH

GOLFO
MESICANO

110°

PROV DE XALISCO

MESICO

SOUTHERN
PAIUTE    HAVASUPAI

Los Vegas    MOHAVE    **Nov 1540**
Melchor Diaz finds letters left
by Alarcón of the Coronado expedition:
"From them they learned how long
the ships had waited for the army
[of Coronado] and that Alarcón
had returned to New Spain... because
he could not proceed any further,
for that sea was a gulf...
They reported that California
was not an island"    Acapulco    PROV DE
NICARAGUA

MAR DEL SUR

YAVAPAI    **Aug–Sept 1540**
Alarcón takes 2 boats upriver;
Yuma inform him of conquest
of Cibola earlier that year by
"a fierce nation like us"
(Coronado's force)

Salton
Sea    ARIZONA    APACHE

Phoenix

YUMA    Gila River    **Aug 26 1540**
Alarcón reaches "the very
bottom of the Bay; where
we found a very mighty river"

PAPAGO    Tucson

Ulloa's officers see "all the
land full of sand in a great
round compass, and joining itself
with the other shore," though
they speculate that there might
be "some great river there"    CONCHO    105°

30°

BAJA
CALIFORNIA
NORTE    SERI    OPATA

CHIHUAHUA

COCHIMI    Sonora    TARAHUMARA

la de Cedros

### Cabrillo's California
REDRAWN FROM A PORTOLAN ATLAS,
POSSIBLY BY BATISTA AGNESE, c.1557

The map attempts to link the coast
surveyed by Cabrillo to the interior
provinces investigated by
Coronado (▶ page 36). It locates
the Tiguex pueblos and Cibola, but
shows the Rio Grande (R. de
Tiguex), wrongly, flowing into the
Gulf of California. Quivira,
located by Coronado in modern
Kansas, has migrated westward to
a location just inland from
Cabrillo's Sierra nevados (not to be
confused with the present Sierra
Nevada). The "ship from China"
(Nave de Cataio) reflects the
persistent European hope of
finding a passage to Asia.

YAQUI    MEXICO

DURANGO

25°

BAJA
CALIFORNIA
SUR    NEW
GALICIA

WAICURI    1535
Cortés attempts
to establish
settlement    Culiacán

**Apr 1540**
Ulloa sends one vessel back
to report, and may have sailed
farther north himself

La Paz
PERICU    TROPIC OF CANCER

**May 9 1540**
Alarcón leaves Acapulco
in 2 vessels with supplies
for Coronado's army

**July 2 1542**
Cabrillo's expedition of 2
vessels sights California    **July 8 1539**
Ulloa leaves Acapulco
with 3 ships, of which
the smallest is lost    NEW
SPAIN    N
W    E
S

OTOMI

# English Incursions, Spanish Responses

## DRAKE, VIZCAÍNO AND OÑATE, 1579-1609

*The English arrive unexpectedly on the Californian coast. Their activities prompt further Spanish ventures beyond the northern frontiers of New Spain.*

After the disappointments of Coronado and Cabrillo (▶ *pages 36, 38*), official interest in New Spain's northern frontiers faded. The annual galleon from Manila to Acapulco might sight the northern Californian coast, but it rarely landed. It was the arrival of English seaman Francis Drake which jolted Spanish officialdom out of the assumption that the north Pacific was closed to foreigners.

In the spring of 1579, after raiding along the Pacific coasts of Spanish America, Drake approached the northwest coast somewhere near the present California-Oregon border. Turning south again he stayed at a bay for five weeks, though its identity remains the subject of controversy. Drake took possession of the land, allegedly invited by local Miwok Indians, and named it New Albion. In 1587 another English expedition, led by Thomas Cavendish, captured the Manila galleon off Cape San Lucas.

Spanish concern increased but reaction was leisurely. No Spanish ship reached Drake's area until one of the Manila galleons, commanded by Sebastián Rodriguez Cermeño, did so in 1595. He made a landfall near Cape Mendocino and sailed south of present-day Drake's Bay. But laden cargo vessels are unsuitable for coastal exploration and his galleon was wrecked.

Seven years later Sebastián Vizcaíno, in a more professional foray, sailed north from Acapulco, following Cabrillo's course of 60 years earlier. Beating against headwinds and with crews suffering from scurvy, Vizcaíno's ships reached Cape Mendocino after nine months. Vizcaíno himself turned back but one of his vessels reached Cape Blanco, from where "the coast ran northeast, and the cold was so great that they thought they should be frozen." Inland expeditions were even less successful. In 1582 Antonio de Espejo

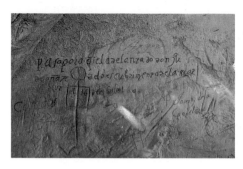

*Above: Oñate, governor of New Mexico, rode south along the Colorado River with 30 men in 1604. He reached the Gulf of California and inaccurately claimed to be the first Spaniard to do so. A translation of the inscription he made at El Morro reads: "Passed by here the Governor Don Juan de Oñate, from the discovery of the Sea of the South on the 16th of April, 1605."*

journeyed along the Rio Grande as far as Zuñi and Hopi territory, reviving dreams of Coronado's day. In 1598, Juan de Oñate, governor of New Mexico, led 500 soldiers and settlers north to conquer and settle pueblo country. Oñate's grand design of a northern empire based on mines, ranches and missions was afflicted by desertions, sickness and Indian resistance. But he carried out useful exploration and established a mission settlement at Santa Fé in 1609. On paper a royal province, New Mexico was in fact a thinly-held salient, north of the main line of Spanish frontier posts.

Oñate's expeditions were the final stage of a northward ambition which had begun with Coronado. But apart from the pearl fisheries of the Gulf of California the Spanish had found little of immediate value. They were becoming convinced that if there were a Strait of Anian somewhere to the north it had better remain unfound. As one viceroy reflected, with backward glances at Drake and Cavendish, such a finding could "awaken someone who was asleep." New Spain's northern frontiers were protected by their inaccessibility.

*Left: Since Coronado's day, the Spaniards had continued to speculate about fabulous kingdoms and a navigable strait through the North American landmass. Cornelius de Jode's 1593 map of "The Kingdom of Quivira" combines these fantasies with geographical knowledge of the day. The Californian coast is fairly accurately shown as far north as Cape Mendocino, where it takes an abrupt turn to the east into the mythical Strait of Anian, believed to lead to the Atlantic. The map shows the many buffalo seen by Coronado and Oñate.*

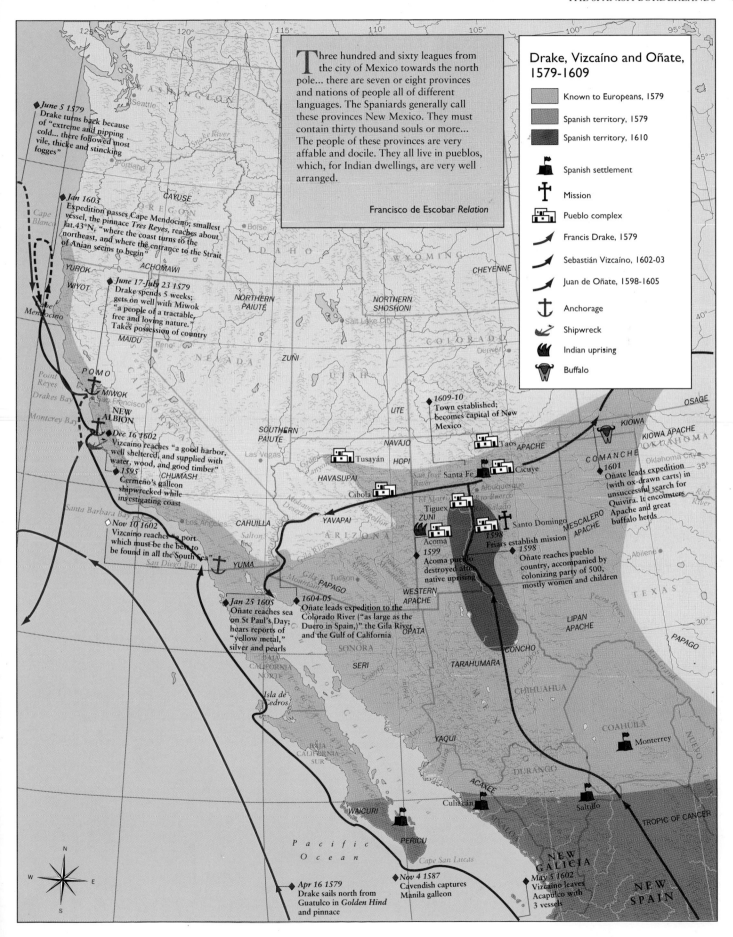

## Drake, Vizcaíno and Oñate, 1579–1609

- Known to Europeans, 1579
- Spanish territory, 1579
- Spanish territory, 1610
- Spanish settlement
- Mission
- Pueblo complex
- Francis Drake, 1579
- Sebastián Vizcaíno, 1602–03
- Juan de Oñate, 1598–1605
- Anchorage
- Shipwreck
- Indian uprising
- Buffalo

Three hundred and sixty leagues from the city of Mexico towards the north pole... there are seven or eight provinces and nations of people all of different languages. The Spaniards generally call these provinces New Mexico. They must contain thirty thousand souls or more... The people of these provinces are very affable and docile. They all live in pueblos, which, for Indian dwellings, are very well arranged.

Francisco de Escobar *Relation*

**June 5 1579** Drake turns back because of "extreme and nipping cold... there followed most vile, thicke and stincking fogges"

**Jan 1603** Expedition passes Cape Mendocino; smallest vessel, the pinnace *Tres Reyes*, reaches about lat.43°N, "where the coast turns to the northeast, and where the entrance to the Strait of Anian seems to begin"

**June 17–July 23 1579** Drake spends 5 weeks; gets on well with Miwok "a people of a tractable, free and loving nature." Takes possession of country

**Dec 16 1602** Vizcaíno reaches "a good harbor, well sheltered, and supplied with water, wood, and good timber"

**1595** Cermeño's galleon shipwrecked while investigating coast

**Nov 10 1602** Vizcaíno reaches a port which must be the best to be found in all the "South Sea"

**Jan 25 1605** Oñate reaches sea on St Paul's Day; hears reports of "yellow metal," silver and pearls

**1604–05** Oñate leads expedition to the Colorado River ("as large as the Duero in Spain,") the Gila River and the Gulf of California

**1609–10** Town established; becomes capital of New Mexico

**1601** Oñate leads expedition (with ox-drawn carts) in unsuccessful search for Quivira. It encounters Apache and great buffalo herds

**1599** Acoma pueblo destroyed after native uprising

**1598** Friars establish mission

**1598** Oñate reaches pueblo country, accompanied by colonizing party of 500, mostly women and children

**Apr 16 1579** Drake sails north from Guatulco in *Golden Hind* and pinnace

**Nov 4 1587** Cavendish captures Manila galleon

**May 5 1602** Vizcaíno leaves Acapulco with 3 vessels

Taos
Cicuye
Santa Fe
Albuquerque
Tusayán
Hopi
Cibola
Tiguex
ZUNI
Acoma
Santo Domingo
San José River
San Pedro River
El Morro
Rio Puerco
Rio Grande

Seattle
Portland
Boise
Salt Lake City
Reno
Las Vegas
Los Angeles
San Diego Bay
Tucson
Denver
Oklahoma City
Abilene
Monterrey
Saltillo
Culiacán

WASHINGTON
OREGON
IDAHO
WYOMING
NEVADA
UTAH
COLORADO
CALIFORNIA
ARIZONA
OKLAHOMA
TEXAS
SONORA
DURANGO
CHIHUAHUA
COAHUILA
NUEVO
BAJA CALIFORNIA NORTE
BAJA CALIFORNIA SUR
NEW GALICIA
NEW SPAIN

CAYUSE
YUROK
WIYOT
POMO
MIWOK
MAIDU
CHUMASH
CAHUILLA
YUMA
YAVAPAI
PAPAGO
HAVASUPAI
ACHOMAWI
NORTHERN PAIUTE
NORTHERN SHOSHONI
SOUTHERN PAIUTE
UTE
NAVAJO
ZUNI
APACHE
COMANCHE
KIOWA
KIOWA APACHE
OSAGE
MESCALERO APACHE
LIPAN APACHE
PAPAGO
WESTERN APACHE
OPATA
SERI
CONCHO
TARAHUMARA
YAQUI
ACAXEE
WAICURI
PERICU

Cape Blanco
Cape Mendocino
Point Reyes
Drakes Bay
Monterey Bay
NEW ALBION
Santa Barbara Bay
Isla de Cedros
Salton
Gila River
Colorado River
Mohave Desert
Grand Canyon
Cape San Lucas
Rio Grande
Red River
Pecos River
Arkansas River

Pacific Ocean

TROPIC OF CANCER

N
S
E
W

# Fantasies and Fabrications

## THE APOCRYPHAL VOYAGES, 1592-1640

*The imaginary discoveries of hoaxers, fantasists and charlatans find their way into the geography of northwest America.*

Spanish expeditions had tracked the coast and penetrated inland far north from Mexico (▶ *pages 38-41*) but they did not find what they expected: the Strait of Anian, gold and silver mines, or populous towns and cities. Such were ambitions, however, that fact sometimes became confused with fiction.

Lorenzo Ferrer Maldonado alleged that in 1588 he sailed from the Atlantic across the top of North America to the Strait of Anian and then into the Pacific. He claimed to achieve this, and back again, in a single summer. By the time his account was published in the late 18th century it was clear that the Strait of Anian did not exist.

More puzzling was Juan de Fuca's voyage in command of a Spanish expedition of 1592. Greek-born pilot Fuca claimed that the land north of the California coast turned north-east, where he discovered a great inlet whose entrance was marked by an "exceeding high Pinacle" on its northern side. Through the inlet they came to the "North Sea," and countries rich in gold.

Fuca's story, related to English promoter Michael Lok in 1596, has been surrounded by controversy ever since. There was indeed a Greek pilot in Spanish service on the northwest coast between 1588 and 1594. And there is a strait at a similar latitude (now named after Juan de Fuca) with a pillar of rock at its *southern* entrance. Fuca or Lok may have embellished the account to sustain interest in the Northwest Passage.

A more preposterous story was published in 1708, and reprinted in England and France in the mid-18th century, of a supposed voyage by Admiral Bartholomew de Fonte. He was said to have sailed north from Lima in 1640, in search of a Northwest Passage. On the northwest coast, Fonte claimed to have explored an extensive network of straits and rivers, and met a Boston ship trading furs. This supposedly proved that a Northwest Passage must exist. The Spanish archives contained no reference to Fonte, but this was ignored. Even so judicious a reader as Benjamin Franklin thought Fonte's account was genuine. The narratives of Fuca and Fonte, however spurious, were to influence the course of later exploration as much as many genuine expeditions.

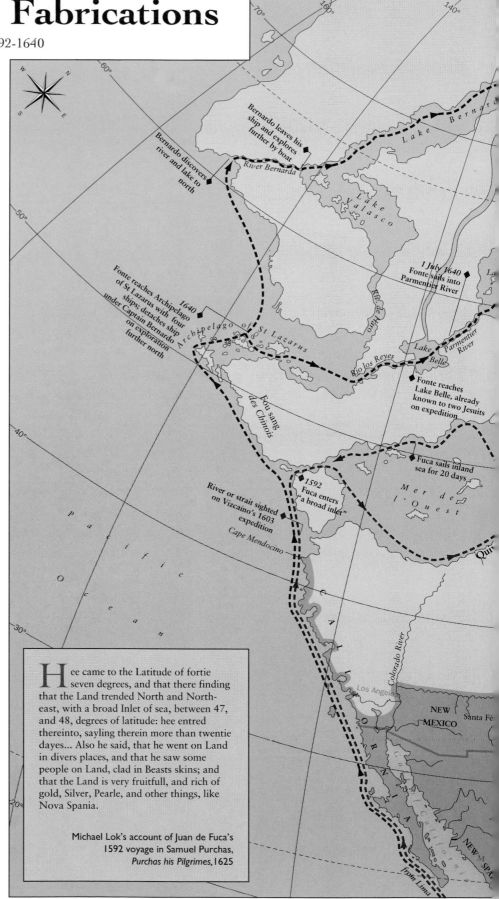

Hee came to the Latitude of fortie seven degrees, and that there finding that the Land trended North and North-east, with a broad Inlet of sea, between 47, and 48, degrees of latitude: hee entred thereinto, sayling therein more than twentie dayes... Also he said, that he went on Land in divers places, and that he saw some people on Land, clad in Beasts skins; and that the Land is very fruitfull, and rich of gold, Silver, Pearle, and other things, like Nova Spania.

Michael Lok's account of Juan de Fuca's 1592 voyage in Samuel Purchas, *Purchas his Pilgrimes,* 1625

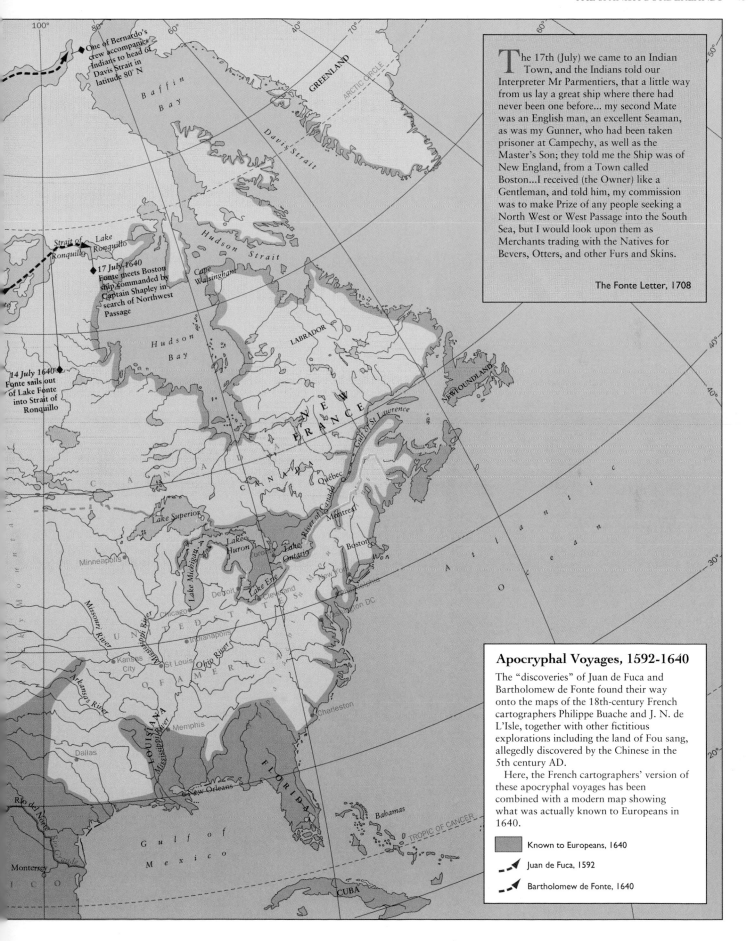

The 17th (July) we came to an Indian Town, and the Indians told our Interpreter Mr Parmentiers, that a little way from us lay a great ship where there had never been one before... my second Mate was an English man, an excellent Seaman, as was my Gunner, who had been taken prisoner at Campechy, as well as the Master's Son; they told me the Ship was of New England, from a Town called Boston...I received (the Owner) like a Gentleman, and told him, my commission was to make Prize of any people seeking a North West or West Passage into the South Sea, but I would look upon them as Merchants trading with the Natives for Bevers, Otters, and other Furs and Skins.

The Fonte Letter, 1708

## Apocryphal Voyages, 1592-1640

The "discoveries" of Juan de Fuca and Bartholomew de Fonte found their way onto the maps of the 18th-century French cartographers Philippe Buache and J. N. de L'Isle, together with other fictitious explorations including the land of Fou sang, allegedly discovered by the Chinese in the 5th century AD.

Here, the French cartographers' version of these apocryphal voyages has been combined with a modern map showing what was actually known to Europeans in 1640.

Known to Europeans, 1640

Juan de Fuca, 1592

Bartholomew de Fonte, 1640

# Part II : The Opening of a Continent

The early decades of the 17th century saw the first sustained European effort to colonize North America. With settlement came more detailed local exploration of the eastern coastal regions, a better understanding of the land, and more precise maps. But while tiny Spanish garrisons guarded the northern outposts of their vast American empire and the English clung to their precarious coastal settlements, French fur traders and missionaries pushed deep into the heart of the continent and down the Mississippi to the Gulf of Mexico.

In 1600, there was little to mark the European presence in North America: a handful of Spaniards in Florida, and a few summer fishing camps in the north. But in the decades that followed, settlements – mostly English – were established along the coast from Newfoundland to Virginia. The initial cost was high in terms of people and money, but by the third decade of the century the little clusters of European occupation were taking on a more permanent appearance.

There was some exploration inland, although acquired knowledge was mainly local. Exploration was secondary to the need to plant, to grow and to survive. Behind the coast the terrain was often rugged and unpromising, with no easy routes into the interior, and an array of Indian peoples to bar the way.

The pioneer French settlements on the St Lawrence served as a springboard for a different kind of expansion. The succession of rivers and lakes drew the French westward. They had three main motives: the quest for a route to the Pacific; the search for furs; and the missionary impulse to convert the Indians. The traders, or *coureurs du bois* as they were called, pushed deep into the interior in their never-ending quest for beaver skins. Although the English tried to outflank them in the north by setting up trading posts on Hudson Bay, the French set the pace. The *coureurs du bois* came nearer to living on easy terms with the Indians than any other group of Europeans. They were quick to pick up Indian wilderness skills, and the birchbark canoe in summer and the snowshoe in winter became indispensable to Europeans traveling across the roadless terrain of Canada.

If the rough, often illiterate *coureurs du bois* were the outriders of European discovery in the north, it is to the missionaries that we owe reliable narratives of the course of exploration. Their writings give a detailed picture of the land and its inhabitants, with the Indian far removed from the crude stereotype which often appeared in other accounts.

As the French pushed westward, opening to view the immense inland waters of the Great Lakes, they heard Indian reports of a great river, the Mississippi. By the 1680s they had reached its outlet to the sea. At first, the French were disappointed that this was not the western or Pacific Ocean but the Gulf of Mexico; but they soon realized that from this vantage point they could dominate the North American heartland, threatening the silver mines of New Spain in one direction and the cramped coastal colonies of the English in another.

At the end of the 17th century, however, the French empire in North America was an outline rather than a reality. Impressive though the French advance had been, it was buttressed by little in the way of settlement – no more than a scattering of trading posts, mission stations and military forts. In both exploring and trading the French depended on Indian help, and the necessities of the fur trade required the preservation rather than the elimination of wilderness. The fine thread of the explorers' tracks on the map tells its own story.

# The Beginnings of Spanish Florida

## FRANCO-SPANISH RIVALRY, 1562-74

*In the second half of the 16th century the murderous national and religious antagonisms of contemporary Europe reach North America.*

By the mid-16th century the Spanish recognized that Florida, lying close to the homeward route of the treasure fleets, had become strategically very important. One plan was for a base on the roadstead of Port Royal (Santa Elena), just north of Ayllón's short-lived settlement of 1526 on the Savannah River (▶ *page 22*). Such projects were thrown into disarray, however, by the unexpected arrival of the French.

In 1562 three French ships took possession of St Johns River before sailing on to establish the settlement of Charlesfort at Port Royal. This fort was soon abandoned but two years later a larger French force built another fort on St Johns River, Fort Caroline, in alliance with local Indians, the Timucua. Exploring parties were sent into the interior, both along the river and more directly west, in search of the preciousmetals reported inthe "Apalatci" mountain. Cibola (▶ *page 36*) was thought to be "towards the southe sea" and an oddly precise Indian report claimed it was only 22 days' paddling distance away. But weak leadership, internal quarrels and disputes with the Indians meant that this French venture was also abandoned, and when a rescue expedition of seven ships arrived in August 1565 it was the prelude to a bloodbath.

Spanish anxieties had been roused by reports of these French settlements, and close behind the French force came a Spanish armada under Pedro Menéndez de Avilés. Within a few weeks it had wiped out the settlers. They were killed, Menéndez explained, not merely as Frenchmen but as heretics.

As Governor of Florida, Menéndez pursued an energetic policy of exploration, conquest and settlement. In the tradition of Cortés and de Soto, he conjured up a grand design of an empire based on peninsular Florida which would extend west to Mexico and north along the coast as far as he could reach. Along Florida's Atlantic coast he set up a string of forts, while on its Gulf coast he established posts at Tampa Bay and Charlotte Harbor.

To the north, Menéndez encouraged a Jesuit mission to Chesapeake Bay in 1570 and significantly expanded his empire through the inland expeditions of Captain Juan Pardo from Santa Elena. In 1566 Pardo and 125 men followed the Savannah River for 250 miles northwest. They established the small fort of San Juan in Cheraw country, near what is now the border between South Carolina and Georgia. The following year Pardo returned to San Juan, following Indian roads west over the Appalachians and into the Tennessee Valley, and approaching de Soto's path of more than a quarter-century earlier.

The way seemed open for a direct if distant land route to Mexico; but men at the small posts Pardo left behind were either attacked by Indians or died of starvation. In the north, the few Jesuits at Chesapeake Bay had already died by 1571, presumably at the hands of the Indians. From Santa Elena to the south, settlements faltered, from disillusionment, Indian suspicion and European hostility.

Soon the only Spanish garrisons left were those at San Pedro and San Agustín, the latter being *presidio* of the colony. The northern areas were left to the missionaries, whose efforts to change indigenous customs led to unrest among the Guale and Cusabo Indians. San Agustín was subject to much rebuilding and resiting, and was destroyed by an English expedition under Francis Drake in 1586. Nevertheless it showed the tenacity of the Spanish presence in Florida and it was the first permanent European colonial settlement in what was to become the United States. Today it is St Augustine, with a history of continuous occupation of well over 400 years. In the late 16th century it was a reminder to other European nations that Spain's claims of imperial dominion extended to North America.

> The two promontories of Florida and Yucatan form the Gulf of Mexico, or Gulf of Florida. A great current pours without ebb between Cuba and Yucatan into this gulf, to emerge between Cuba and Florida. This is one of the reasons that ships going to the Indies cannot go back as they have come, for the current is constant and there is no wind blowing along the route of entrance, so that the mariners go north to search for one. Thus it is a matter of great moment in the preservation of the Indies, and for its trade and commerce, that Florida remain Spanish and be strongly guarded.
>
> **Report by Bartolomé Barrientos, 1565**

*Below: "The French select a place for building a fort." This engraving of either Fort Caroline or Fort Charles was done by the artist Jacques Le Moyne de Morgues when he accompanied Laudonnière's expedition to Florida in 1564. Although built of wood, its outline is that of a typical European fort of the period.*

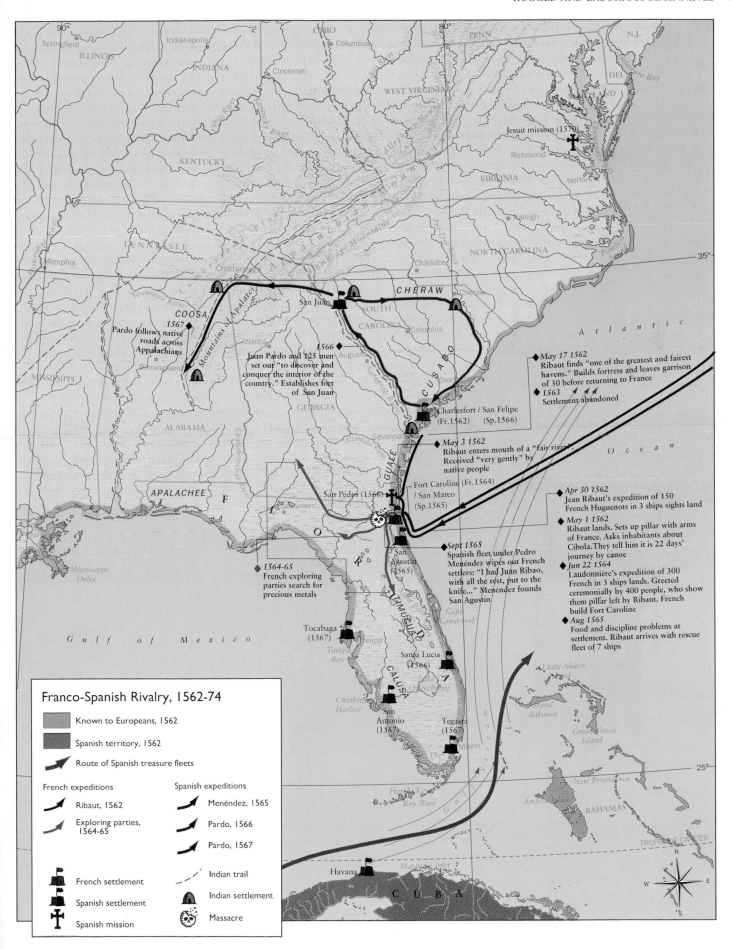

Jesuit mission (1570)

May 17 1562
Ribaut finds "one of the greatest and fairest havens." Builds fortress and leaves garrison of 30 before returning to France

1563
Settlement abandoned

CHERAW

San Juan

COOSA

1567
Pardo follows native roads across Appalachians

1566
Juan Pardo and 125 men set out "to discover and conquer the interior of the country." Establishes fort of San Juan

Charlesfort / San Felipe
(Fr.1562) (Sp.1566)

May 3 1562
Ribaut enters mouth of a "fair river." Received "very gently" by native people

Apr 30 1562
Jean Ribaut's expedition of 150 French Huguenots in 3 ships sights land

May 1 1562
Ribaut lands. Sets up pillar with arms of France. Asks inhabitants about Cibola. They tell him it is 22 days' journey by canoe

Jun 22 1564
Laudonnière's expedition of 300 French in 3 ships lands. Greeted ceremonially by 400 people, who show them pillar left by Ribaut. French build Fort Caroline

Aug 1565
Food and discipline problems at settlement. Ribaut arrives with rescue fleet of 7 ships

Fort Caroline (Fr.1564) / San Mateo (Sp.1565)

San Pedro (1566)

APALACHEE

1564-65
French exploring parties search for precious metals

Mississippi Delta

Sept 1565
Spanish fleet under Pedro Menéndez wipes out French settlers: "I had Juan Ribao, with all the rest, put to the knife..." Menéndez founds San Agustín

San Agustín (1565)

Tocabaga (1567)

Santa Lucia (1566)

CALUSA

San Antonio (1567)

Tegasta (1567)

Gulf of Mexico

Havana

CUBA

## Franco-Spanish Rivalry, 1562-74

Known to Europeans, 1562

Spanish territory, 1562

Route of Spanish treasure fleets

French expeditions

Ribaut, 1562

Exploring parties, 1564-65

Spanish expeditions

Menéndez, 1565

Pardo, 1566

Pardo, 1567

Indian trail

French settlement

Spanish settlement

Spanish mission

Indian settlement

Massacre

# The Lost Colony of Roanoke

## ENGLISH COLONIZING ATTEMPTS IN "VIRGINIA," 1584-90

*The first serious English effort to establish a colony in North America brings first-hand knowledge of New World conditions, but ends in tragedy.*

By the 1580s, the English court was becoming interested in establishing settlements in North America. The region soon to be called Virginia had the advantage of a temperate climate, which could produce a whole range of "Mediterranean" products, and was a safe distance from the Spanish bases. The fate of the French colony in Florida (▶ *page 46*) was a grim reminder of the risks, but worsening relations between England and Spain strengthened the argument for a base from which to attack the Spanish Indies.

In 1584 Walter Raleigh obtained a royal grant to settle "lands and territories not actually possessed by any Christian prince," and sent out two ships under Philip Amadas and Arthur Barlowe. They entered an inlet on the Outer Banks (of modern North Carolina) which the Indians called Hatarask, and which the explorers renamed Port Ferdinando after their Portuguese pilot; they established good

*Above: This watercolor of a Virginia Indian in body paint is the work of John White, official artist on Grenville's 1585 expedition, and governor of the 1587 colony at Roanoke. White had accompanied Frobisher on his 1577 voyage to Baffin Island (▶ page 28). His paintings of the people, plants and animals of North America, helped to shape European images of the new continent.*

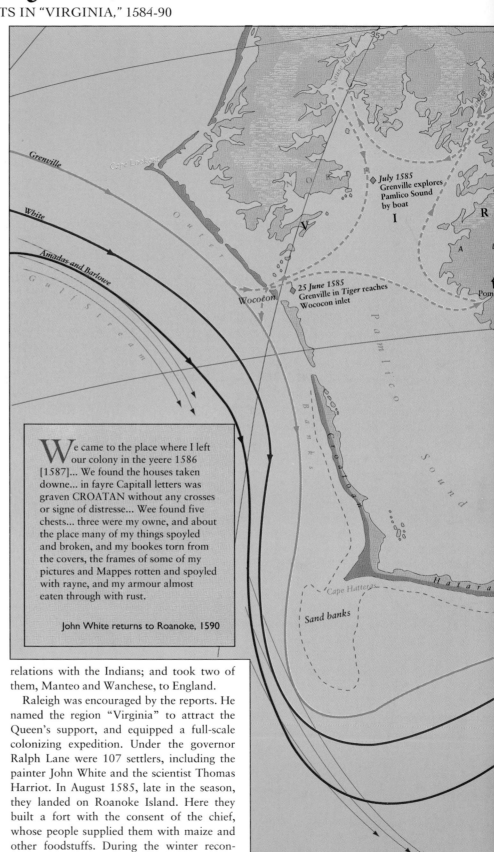

> We came to the place where I left our colony in the yeere 1586 [1587]... We found the houses taken downe... in fayre Capitall letters was graven CROATAN without any crosses or signe of distresse... Wee found five chests... three were my owne, and about the place many of my things spoyled and broken, and my bookes torn from the covers, the frames of some of my pictures and Mappes rotten and spoyled with rayne, and my armour almost eaten through with rust.
>
> **John White returns to Roanoke, 1590**

relations with the Indians; and took two of them, Manteo and Wanchese, to England.

Raleigh was encouraged by the reports. He named the region "Virginia" to attract the Queen's support, and equipped a full-scale colonizing expedition. Under the governor Ralph Lane were 107 settlers, including the painter John White and the scientist Thomas Harriot. In August 1585, late in the season, they landed on Roanoke Island. Here they built a fort with the consent of the chief, whose people supplied them with maize and other foodstuffs. During the winter reconnaissance parties explored Albemarle and

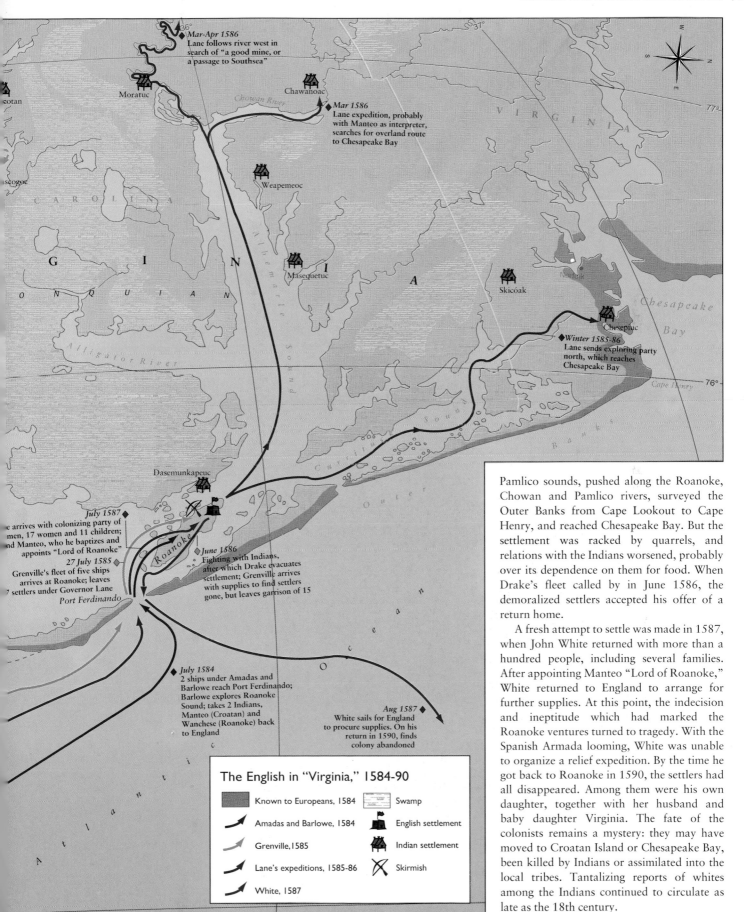

Mar-Apr 1586
Lane follows river west in
search of "a good mine, or
a passage to Southsea"

Moratuc

Chawanoac

Mar 1586
Lane expedition, probably
with Manteo as interpreter,
searches for overland route
to Chesapeake Bay

Weapemeoc

Masequetuc

Skicóak

Norfolk

Chesepiuc

Winter 1585-86
Lane sends exploring party
north, which reaches
Chesapeake Bay

Cape Henry

V I R G I N I A

C A R O L I N A

G I N I A

O N Q U I A N

Alligator River

Albemarle Sound

Chowan River

Currituck Sound

Outer

Banks

Dasemunkapeuc

July 1587
e arrives with colonizing party of
men, 17 women and 11 children;
nd Manteo, who he baptizes and
appoints "Lord of Roanoke"

27 July 1585
Grenville's fleet of five ships
arrives at Roanoke; leaves
7 settlers under Governor Lane
Port Ferdinando

June 1586
Fighting with Indians,
after which Drake evacuates
settlement; Grenville arrives
with supplies to find settlers
gone, but leaves garrison of 15

Roanoke

July 1584
2 ships under Amadas and
Barlowe reach Port Ferdinando;
Barlowe explores Roanoke
Sound; takes 2 Indians,
Manteo (Croatan) and
Wanchese (Roanoke) back
to England

Aug 1587
White sails for England
to procure supplies. On his
return in 1590, finds
colony abandoned

Atlantic

Ocean

The English in "Virginia," 1584-90

Known to Europeans, 1584          Swamp

Amadas and Barlowe, 1584          English settlement

Grenville, 1585                    Indian settlement

Lane's expeditions, 1585-86        Skirmish

White, 1587

Pamlico sounds, pushed along the Roanoke, Chowan and Pamlico rivers, surveyed the Outer Banks from Cape Lookout to Cape Henry, and reached Chesapeake Bay. But the settlement was racked by quarrels, and relations with the Indians worsened, probably over its dependence on them for food. When Drake's fleet called by in June 1586, the demoralized settlers accepted his offer of a return home.

A fresh attempt to settle was made in 1587, when John White returned with more than a hundred people, including several families. After appointing Manteo "Lord of Roanoke," White returned to England to arrange for further supplies. At this point, the indecision and ineptitude which had marked the Roanoke ventures turned to tragedy. With the Spanish Armada looming, White was unable to organize a relief expedition. By the time he got back to Roanoke in 1590, the settlers had all disappeared. Among them were his own daughter, together with her husband and baby daughter Virginia. The fate of the colonists remains a mystery: they may have moved to Croatan Island or Chesapeake Bay, been killed by Indians or assimilated into the local tribes. Tantalizing reports of whites among the Indians continued to circulate as late as the 18th century.

# The Golden Fleece

## NEWFOUNDLAND FISHERY AND SETTLEMENT, 1500-1763

*Newfoundland's fisheries yield great wealth and in the 16th century attract more Europeans than any other part of North America.*

From the time of Cabot and the Corte-Réals (▶ *page 20*) the shores of Newfoundland were a familiar landfall for European seamen. Each year the island's coasts and offshore fishing banks provided cargoes for hundreds of vessels from Portugal, Spain, France and England. Newfoundland cod, a limitless source of cheap protein, became a staple of the European diet. Yet the growth of fisheries excited little interest in the geography of the region. Throughout the 16th century it was assumed that Newfoundland was at least two islands, perhaps even a group.

The English concentrated on inshore fishing, involving only the light salting of the fish before laying it out to dry on "flakes" or stages. The French and others fished further out on the banks and carried the fish back to Europe after heavily salting it at sea.

The English, with their presence onshore, made the decisive move towards settlement and claiming possession. The Newfoundland Company was founded in 1610, with a charter claiming rights over the southeast coast from Cape Bonavista to Cape St Mary's. It immediately sent out a small colonizing venture under John Guy, who established the first permanent settlement at Cuperts (or Cupids) Cove. Settlers ashore helped to supply and repair the fishing fleets and in winter they would protect the fishermen's flimsy buildings, stages and boats from the Beothuk Indians, their rivals, or the ravages of the elements.

By the latter half of the 17th century there were 30 or so establishments along the "English Shore" between Cape Bonavista and Cape Race, though most had only a dozen residents, not all of them permanent. The French also set up small settlements along the "South Shore" from Plaisance westward. The English still concentrated on inshore fishery, while the French fished along the Gulf. But in 1713 the Treaty of Utrecht recognized British sovereignty over Newfoundland and the French withdrew.

A prominent English settler of the 17th century, William Vaughan, claimed that the Newfoundland fisheries, together with their trading and shipping activities, were a Golden Fleece yielding more wealth to England than the treasure of the Indies to Spain.

### New Found Land
REDRAWN FROM A MAP BY JOHN MASON, 1625

Mason was governor of the tiny English colony in Newfoundland from 1616 to 1621. His surveys resulted in the first English map of the island. The main settlement at Cuperts (Cupids) Cove is clearly marked.

*Left: This illustration from the original manuscript of Herman Moll's 1720 map of North America shows the inshore dressing and drying of cod, as practised by the English in Newfoundland. The stages were for curing the fish, and the casks were used to catch the cod-liver oil.*

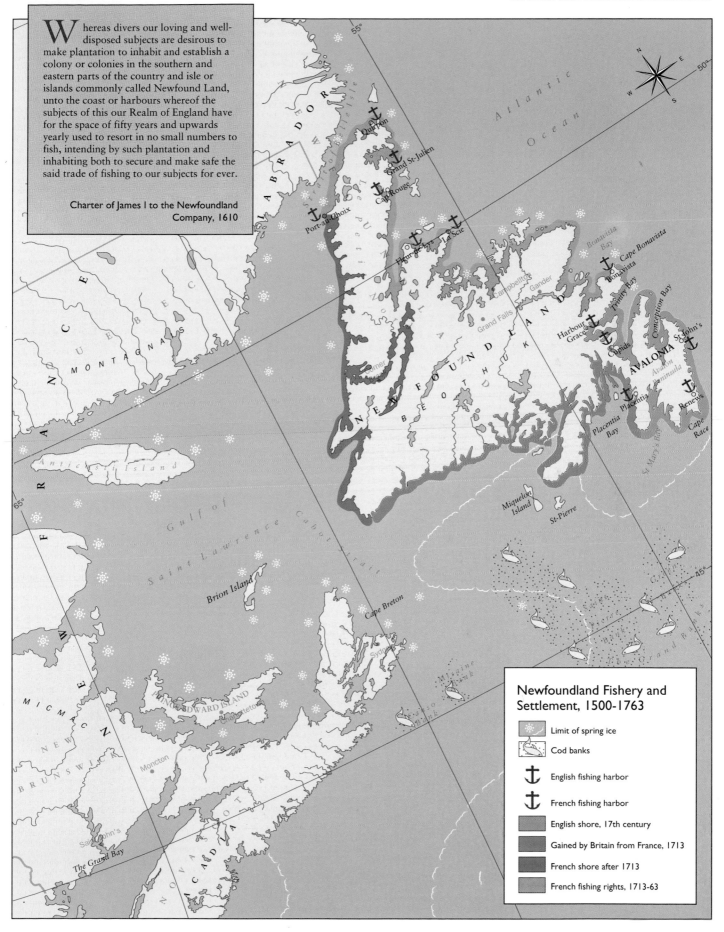

Whereas divers our loving and well-disposed subjects are desirous to make plantation to inhabit and establish a colony or colonies in the southern and eastern parts of the country and isle or islands commonly called Newfound Land, unto the coast or harbours whereof the subjects of this our Realm of England have for the space of fifty years and upwards yearly used to resort in no small numbers to fish, intending by such plantation and inhabiting both to secure and make safe the said trade of fishing to our subjects for ever.

Charter of James I to the Newfoundland
Company, 1610

## Newfoundland Fishery and Settlement, 1500-1763

- Limit of spring ice
- Cod banks
- English fishing harbor
- French fishing harbor
- English shore, 17th century
- Gained by Britain from France, 1713
- French shore after 1713
- French fishing rights, 1713-63

# The Founding of New France

## FRENCH SETTLEMENT IN CANADA, 1600-08

*Champlain explores the St Lawrence and the Atlantic coast. The French begin to develop two areas of trade and settlement, one on the St Lawrence, the other in Acadia.*

After the failure of the Québec colony of 1541-43 (▶ *page 26*) Breton and Basque vessels continued to visit the Gulf of St Lawrence for fishing and trading. But it was not until the 1580s that the French again reached Cartier's great "River of Canada." Tadoussac, at the junction of the St Lawrence and Saguenay rivers, then became a regular summer rendezvous for French ships and the Montagnais Indians of the interior.

In 1600, an all-year trading post was built there, but because of severe weather it was abandoned before the winter was out, leaving two-thirds of the small garrison dead from scurvy. The French complained that winter lasted more than six months there and they again questioned whether Europeans could survive such hostile conditions.

Samuel de Champlain took a different view. The French explorer had already accompanied a Spanish expedition to their American dominions. Appointed royal geographer by Henri IV on his return, he went on to lay the foundation for France's own empire on the continent. But royal backing for

> S now fell first on the sixth of October... This we had to a depth of three or four feet up to the end of the month of April... Our beverages all froze except the Spanish wine. Cider was given out by the pound... It was difficult to know this country without having wintered there; for on arriving in summer everything is very pleasant on account of the woods, the beautiful landscapes, and the fine fishing.
>
> **Champlain describes the winter at Sainte-Croix, 1604-05**

Champlain did not extend to the provision of ships, and when he first visited the northeast in 1603, it was as an observer aboard a fur-trading ship, the *Bonne-Renommée*, commanded by François Gravé.

Champlain was the first European to venture up the Saguenay River, forty or fifty miles from Tadoussac. Indians told him about a salt sea to the north and, six years before the English reached Hudson Bay, Champlain

argued that this must be a gulf of the Atlantic. He then journeyed with Gravé to Hochelaga where they were stopped, as Cartier had been, by the Lachine Rapids. Unlike Cartier, they had Indian interpreters with them who knew of three huge lakes to the west. These were presumably Lakes Ontario, Erie and Huron and Champlain considered the latter to be the western ocean.

After they detoured a few miles into the Richelieu River, the Indians told them about a waterway, eventually known as the Hudson, which flowed down to the Atlantic coast. In his first few months of exploration, Champlain had gained an extensive if still sketchy knowledge of the lands bordering the St Lawrence.

In 1604 Champlain switched his attention to the Atlantic coast, where he accompanied the colonizing expedition led by Sieur de Monts to explore the Bay of Fundy and to set up a post on the Maine coast at the Sainte-Croix River. After a miserable winter in which the garrison suffered from cold and scurvy, the little settlement was moved to Port

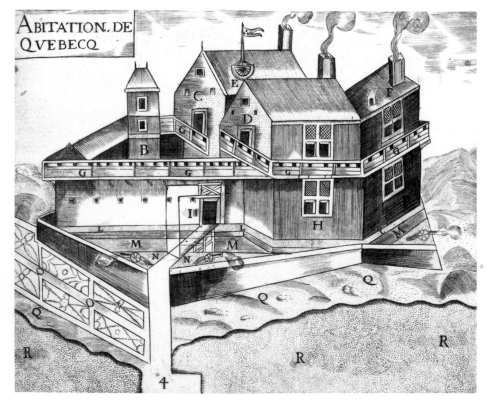

*Left: Champlain's first fort at Québec, the* Habitation, *resembled a late medieval European Castle and was clearly built with defense in mind. The engraving was first published in the* Voyage due Sieur de Champlain *(1613).*

*Above: In 1623 Champlain replaced his original fort with a larger, stronger building. The clay pipe (left) and lead inkwell (right) were found in the surrounding ditches, and are believed to date from this second period of occupation.*

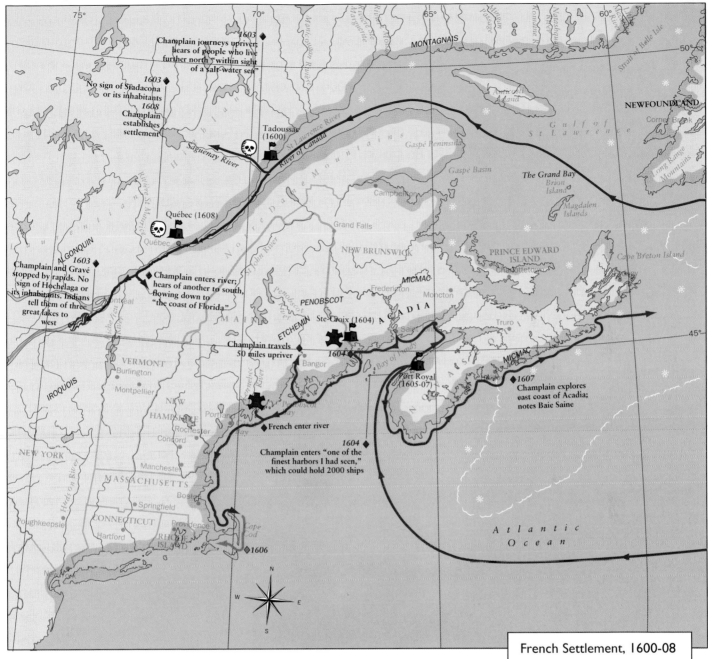

1603
Champlain journeys upriver;
hears of people who live
further north "within sight
of a salt-water sea"

1603
No sign of Stadacona
or its inhabitants.
1608
Champlain
establishes
settlement

Tadoussac
(1600)

MONTAGNAIS

NEWFOUNDLAND

Corner Brook

Gulf of
St Lawrence

Anticosti
Island

Gaspé Peninsula

Gaspé Basin

The Grand Bay
Brion
Island

Magdalen
Islands

Québec (1608)

Québec

ALGONQUIN

1603
Champlain and Gravé
stopped by rapids. No
sign of Hochelaga or
its inhabitants. Indians
tell them of three
great lakes to
west

Montréal

Champlain enters river;
hears of another to south,
flowing down to
"the coast of Florida"

NEW BRUNSWICK

Grand Falls

Fredericton

Moncton

PRINCE EDWARD
ISLAND

Charlottetown

Cape Breton Island

PENOBSCOT

ETCHEMIN

Ste-Croix (1604)

ACADIA

Saint

Truro

MICMAC

IROQUOIS

VERMONT

Burlington

Montpelier

Champlain travels
50 miles upriver

Bangor

1604

MICMAC

Port Royal
(1605-07)

1607
Champlain explores
east coast of Acadia;
notes Baie Saine

NEW
HAMPSHIRE

Rochester

Concord

Portland

French enter river

1604
Champlain enters "one of the
finest harbors I had seen,"
which could hold 2000 ships

Bay of Fundy

NEW YORK

Manchester

MASSACHUSETTS

Boston

Springfield

Poughkeepsie

CONNECTICUT

Providence

Hartford

RHODE
ISLAND

Cape
Cod

1606

Atlantic
Ocean

N
W    E
S

## French Settlement, 1600-08

| | |
|---|---|
| (symbol) | Limit of spring ice |
| (symbol) | Known to Europeans, 1603 |
| (symbol) | French settlement |
| (symbol) | Gravé and Champlain, 1603 |
| (symbol) | De Monts and Champlain, 1604-05 |
| (symbol) | Champlain, 1606 |
| (symbol) | Champlain, 1607 |
| (symbol) | Trading encounter |
| (symbol) | Death of settlers |
| (symbol) | Rapids |

Royal in the Bay of Fundy. It survived there until 1607. These faltering ventures at settlement were accompanied by alliances with the Micmac and Etchemin Indians and further exploration. Champlain and de Monts coasted the shores of Maine, entered the Penobscot River and sailed south along the New England coast as far as Cape Cod. The great peninsula of Acadia and the Bay of Fundy would soon appear on the maps for the first time.

Disappointments at Sainte-Croix and Port Royal turned the French back to the St Lawrence, and in 1608 Champlain established a settlement at Québec, near the deserted Indian site of Stadacona. Here,

where the river narrowed, the French built a small, fortress-like establishment, complete with moat and drawbridge. Only eight out of the garrison of 28 survived the first winter, but the French were slowly learning the techniques of cold-weather survival.

It would be long before this and other tiny French settlements could in any sense be regarded as permanent. Even so, the shape of 17th-century New France could now be glimpsed in embryo.

# Norembèque Becomes New England

## EXPLORATIONS ON THE NORTHEAST COAST, 1602-16

*The English explore the little-known coast
from New York to Maine, with a view to
settlement as well as trade.*

After the voyages of Verrazano in 1524 and
Gomes in 1525, along the shores of what
Verrazano called "Norembèque" (▶ *page
24*), there was little further exploration of the
region for the rest of the century. It could be
hazardous, for along the coast there were
reefs and shoals and the area was subject to
summer storms. However there was some
European fishing and trading, an overspill
from further north, and occasionally
Europeans landed and made contact with the
Indians who were living there.

It was not until the early 17th century that
sporadic interest in the region became more

> osnold meets Micmac Indians off the
> Maine coast, May 1602:
> They came boldly aboord us being all
> naked, saving about their shoulders certaine
> loose Deere-skinnes, and neere their wastes
> Seale-skinnes [but] one that seemed to be
> their Commander wore a Wastecoate of
> blacke worke, a paire of Breeches, cloth
> Stockings, Shooes, Hat, and Band, one or
> two more had also a few things made by
> some Christians, these with a piece of
> Chalke described the Coast thereabouts,
> and could name Placentia of the New-
> found-land, they spake divers Christian
> words, and seemed to understand much
> more than we.
>
> Samuel Purchas, *Pilgrimes*, 1625

systematic. The French looked to the coast
between the Penobscot River and Cape
Breton, now becoming known as Acadie or
Acadia. The English were more active along
the coast running south from the Penobscot to
about latitude 40°N, an area which they
called North Virginia. English reconnaissance
voyages surveyed much of this coastline,
looking for possible areas for settlement as
well as trade; for somewhere along that coast
was Verrazano's "Refugio," with its good
harbor, friendly Indians and fertile soil.

In 1602 an expedition under Bartholomew
Gosnold reached and named such features of
the coast as Cape Cod and Martha's Vine-
yard. Three years later George Waymouth
sailed up the St George River, where he was
impressed, perhaps over-impressed, by the
fertility of the region. He seized five Indians

(probably Eastern Abenaki of the Etchemin
tribe) and took them back to England. One of
them returned to his own country in 1607,
with a hundred English colonists sent out by
the Virginia Company. They established a
settlement, Fort St George, near the mouth of
Sagadahoc, now the Kennebec River. After
suffering the same severe winter conditions
and casualties that were experienced by the
French further north at Sainte-Croix and Port
Royal (▶ *page 52*), the settlement was
abandoned. Summer landings, mistaken
assumptions about a Mediterranean-style
climate, and the sight of land cleared and

planted by Indians, meant that the European
settlers were surprised by the harsh winter of
the "Little Ice Age."

The most important exploration was made
by an English navigator leading a Dutch
expedition. The initial objective was to search
for a polar passage to the Pacific. Sailing in
the *Half Moon*, thwarted by early summer ice
in the Barents Sea, Henry Hudson turned west
across the Atlantic to the American coast. He
was probably prompted by information from
John Smith in Virginia (▶ *page 56*). In
September 1609 Hudson sailed, as Verrazano
had already done, through the narrows and

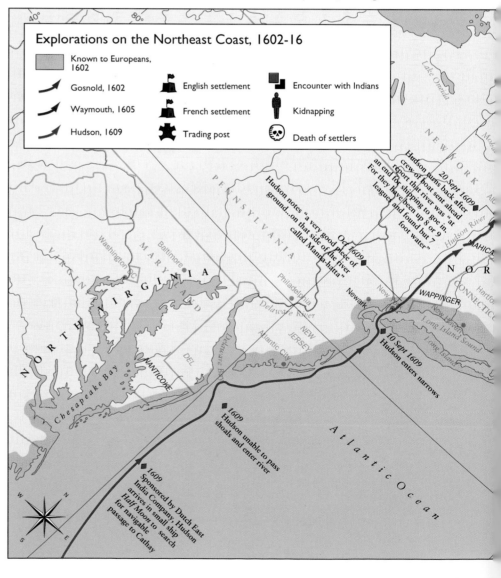

## Explorations on the Northeast Coast, 1602-16

| | |
|---|---|
| ▨ | Known to Europeans, 1602 |
| ↗ | Gosnold, 1602 |
| ↗ | Waymouth, 1605 |
| ↗ | Hudson, 1609 |
| 🏰 | English settlement |
| 🏰 | French settlement |
| ⚜ | Trading post |
| ◼ | Encounter with Indians |
| 🧍 | Kidnapping |
| ☠ | Death of settlers |

into New York Harbor. He then entered the river now known as the Hudson and sailed up it as far as present-day Albany. As the water shoaled it was soon realized that he had not found a strait to the Pacific. Nevertheless, Hudson had confirmed the existence of a great harbor and had journeyed up the most important waterway on the east coast. When he turned back, somewhere near the Mohawk River, he was less than a hundred miles from the spot reached a few weeks earlier by Samuel de Champlain, pushing south from the St Lawrence (▶ page 58).

Hudson's explorations formed the basis for a Dutch claim to an area soon to be known as New Netherland. To the north John Smith, who in 1614 mapped the coast from Cape Cod to the Penobscot, gave a new and prophetic name to the region where English settlers would soon arrive: New England.

*Right: Part of the "Velasco map" c.1610, sent to Spain in 1611 by the Spanish ambassador in London, Don Alonso de Velasco. This English manuscript map, which stretches from Cape Fear to Newfoundland, shows a surprisingly full knowledge of the recent exploration of the English, French and Dutch. Probably put together from a number of separate surveys, it includes Hudson's explorations of the Hudson River in 1609, and good representations of the Kennebec and Penobscot rivers. Some of the inland detail "is done by the relation of Indians."*

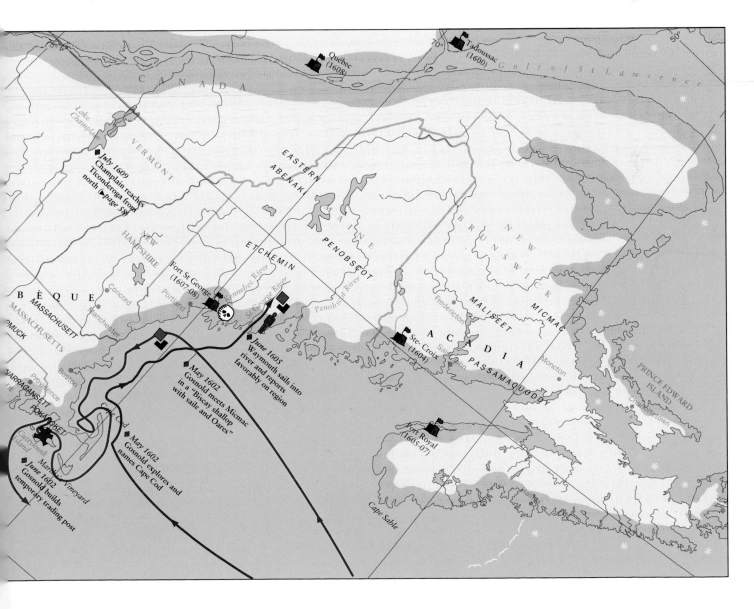

# The First English Colony

## CAPTAIN JOHN SMITH AND THE SETTLING OF VIRGINIA, 1607-12

*English settlers establish their first permanent colony in North America and explore the tidal rivers of Virginia.*

After Raleigh's settlers disappeared in the 1580s (▶ *page 48*), occasional, ill-documented voyages kept the memory of the lost colony alive and maintained a tenuous legal claim to the region. In 1606 the Virginia Company was founded to promote settlement and trade. It attempted to colonize "North Virginia" (later New England) but its settlement on the Sagadahoc River failed in 1607-08 (▶ *page 54*). Meanwhile better-capitalized shareholders were organizing another venture further south.

In April 1607 three ships carried 120 settlers into Chesapeake Bay. They settled 60 miles upriver at Jamestown, and the tiny colony survived dissension and hardship to become the first permanent English settlement in America. Captain John Smith soon emerged both as its political strong man and the most prominent of its early explorers. In May 1607 he traveled upriver from Jamestown with Christopher Newport, past Arrohattoc and as far as the falls of the James River. Newport, reported Smith, had secret instructions "not to returne without a lumpe of gold, a certainty of the south-sea or one of the lost colony of Sir Walter Rawley." But he

did bring back a map, drawn for him by an Indian, showing that far upriver were "certaine huge mountaines called Quirank." This was perhaps the first the Europeans heard of the Blue Ridge mountains.

In December 1607 Smith led a small party up the Chickahominy River, where he was captured by Indians and taken before the dominant chief, Powhatan. Smith's captivity, his dealings with Powhatan and his sub-chiefs, and the well-known part played in his release by Pocahontas, demonstrate the colony's early relations with the Indian inhabitants of the area: at times, help and co-operation, at others, ambushes and reprisals. In 1610 Powhatan delivered an ultimatum to the settlers to "depart his Country, or confine ourselves to James Towne only, without searching further up into his Land or Rivers."

Smith had already journeyed well beyond Powhatan's boundaries. In two expeditions in summer 1608 he explored Chesapeake Bay and the main rivers running into it, hoping to find a route to the Pacific. But after his second venture he became convinced that the stretches of salt water reported by the Indians lay to the north in Canada.

*Above: Powhatan's deerhide mantle, decorated with shells, was brought to England before 1656, when it was mentioned in the inventory of the Tradescants, who owned land in Virginia. The circles are believed to represent the many tribal groups under Powhatan's domination.*

T heir chiefe is called Powhatan... Some countries he hath which have been his ancestors, and came unto him by inheritance... All the rest of his Territories... have been his severall conquests... At Werewcomoco, he was seated on the river Pamauke, some 14 miles from James Towne, but he took so little pleasure in our nearer neighbourhood...that he retired himself to a place in the deserts at the top of the river Chickahamania

John Smith, A Map of Virginia, 1612

*Left: John Smith's* A Map of Virginia *(1612) outlined the main features of tidewater Virginia, with a mass of information about its Indian inhabitants. The crosses mark the limits of Smith's own explorations; everything beyond them he based on Indian information.*

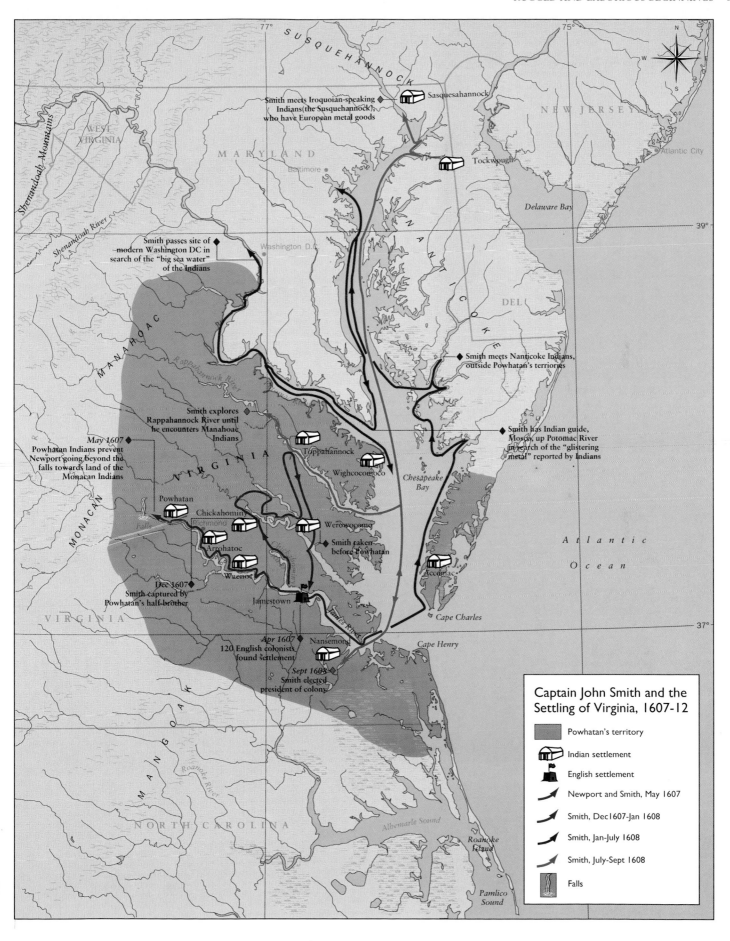

Smith meets Iroquoian-speaking
Indians (the Susquehannock),
who have European metal goods

Smith passes site of
modern Washington DC in
search of the "big sea water"
of the Indians

Smith explores
Rappahannock River until
he encounters Manahoac
Indians

May 1607
Powhatan Indians prevent
Newport going beyond the
falls towards land of the
Monacan Indians

Smith meets Nanticoke Indians,
outside Powhatan's territories

Smith has Indian guide,
Mosco, up Potomac River
in search of the "glistering
metal" reported by Indians

Smith taken
before Powhatan

Dec 1607
Smith captured by
Powhatan's half-brother

Apr 1607
120 English colonists
found settlement

Sept 1608
Smith elected
president of colony

Sasquesahannock
Tockwough
Toppahannock
Wighcocomoco
Werowocomo
Accomac
Powhatan
Chickahominy
Arrohatoc
Waenoc
Jamestown
Nansemond

SUSQUEHANNOCK
NEW JERSEY
WEST VIRGINIA
MARYLAND
Baltimore
Washington D.C.
Delaware Bay
Atlantic City
NANTICOKE
DEL
Shenandoah Mountains
Shenandoah River
MANAHOAC
Rappahannock River
VIRGINIA
MONACAN
Richmond
Falls
Chesapeake Bay
Atlantic Ocean
Cape Charles
Cape Henry
VIRGINIA
NORTH CAROLINA
MANGOAK
Roanoke River
Albemarle Sound
Roanoke Island
Pamlico Sound
James River

### Captain John Smith and the Settling of Virginia, 1607-12

- Powhatan's territory
- Indian settlement
- English settlement
- Newport and Smith, May 1607
- Smith, Dec 1607-Jan 1608
- Smith, Jan-July 1608
- Smith, July-Sept 1608
- Falls

# To the Great Lakes

## THE TRAVELS OF SAMUEL DE CHAMPLAIN, 1609-16

*Explorer, trader and empire-builder Samuel de Champlain secures Acadia and the St Lawrence for France. He pushes west, where Indians tell him of the Great Lakes.*

By 1603 Champlain had made short excursions along the Saguenay and Richelieu rivers and had sailed up the St Lawrence as far as the Lachine Rapids. His next six years were to be occupied with the foundling French settlement in Acadia and at Québec (▶ *page 52*).

In 1609 he returned to exploration. Entering the Richelieu River again, Champlain this time reached the lake soon to be named after him. Coming down from the north, Champlain and his two French companions set foot in what is now New York state a few months before Hudson arrived on its Atlantic coast (▶ *page 54*). This was the country of the Iroquois, that formidable group of tribes based on the Hudson and Mohawk rivers. At Ticonderoga, Champlain used his arquebus to help the Montagnais, Ottawa Algonquins and Hurons defeat the Iroquois.

In years to come Champlain used his relationships with the Ottawa and Huron

> I had much conversation with them [the Huron] regarding the source of the great river and regarding their country, about which they told me many things, both of the river, falls, lakes and of the tribes living there... They spoke to me of these things in great detail, showing me by drawings all the places they had visted.
>
> Champlain, *Voyages*, 1613

Indians, middlemen of the fur trade, to penetrate westward. It was no easy task, though, to persuade Indians to let Frenchmen through to the fur-trapping areas. In 1613 Champlain went by canoe along the Indian trade route of the Ottawa River as far as Allumette Lake, following the path of a young Frenchman, Nicolas de Vignau, whom he had left among the Indians two years earlier.

In 1615 Champlain made his most

A Montagnais woman and man. A contemporary engraving from Champlain's own drawing.

Below: Confrontation at Ticonderoga, 1609. Champlain, alongside his Montagnais, Algonquin and Huron allies, faces the Iroquois. From Champlain's Voyages.

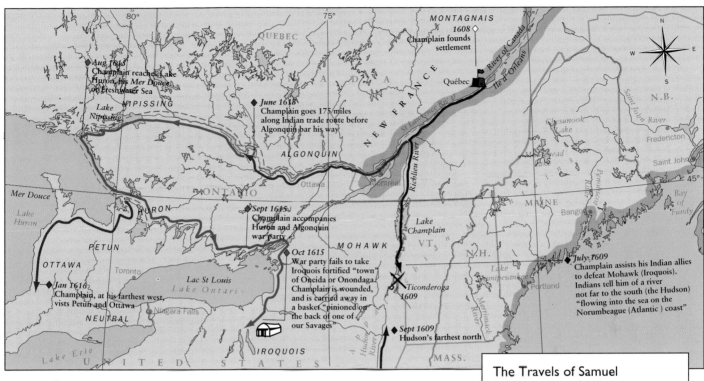

**The Travels of Samuel de Champlain, 1609-16**

Known to Europeans, 1609

French settlement

Indian settlement

Indian trade route

Hudson, 1609

Champlain

1609    1615

1613    1616

Battle

*Map annotations:*

MONTAGNAIS

1608 ◇ Champlain founds settlement

Québec

River of Canada

Aug 1615 ◆ Champlain reaches Lake Huron, his Mer Douce or Freshwater Sea

NIPISSING

Lake Nipissing

June 1618 ◆ Champlain goes 175 miles along Indian trade route before Algonquin bar his way

NEW FRANCE

N.B.

Chesuncook Lake

Saint John River

Fredericton

Saint John

Mer Douce

Lake Huron

HURON

MONTARIO

Ottawa

Montreal

Richlieu River

St Lawrence River

Sept 1615 ◆ Champlain accompanies Huron and Algonquin war party

Lake Champlain

VT.

N.H.

MAINE

Bangor

45°

Penobscot River

Bay of Fundy

PETUN

OTTAWA

Toronto

Lac St Louis
Lake Ontario

Jan 1616 ◆ Champlain, at his farthest west, visits Petun and Ottawa

NEUTRAL

Niagara Falls

Oct 1615 ◆ War party fails to take Iroquois fortified "town" of Oneida or Onondaga. Champlain is wounded, and is carried away in a basket "pinioned on the back of one of our Savages"

MOHAWK

✗ Ticonderoga 1609

Lake Winnipesaukee

Portland

Merrimack River

July 1609 ◆ Champlain assists his Indian allies to defeat Mohawk (Iroquois). Indians tell him of a river not far to the south (the Hudson) "flowing into the sea on the Norumbeague (Atlantic) coast"

IROQUOIS

Sept 1609 ◆ Hudson's farthest north

Hudson River

UNITED STATES

Lake Erie

MASS.

celebrated journey, 700 miles west from the Lachine Rapids to the land of the Huron. He traveled along the Ottawa River again, which was to become the main French route to the interior, and arrived at Lake Huron. After noting the fertility of the land under its Huron cultivators, Champlain accompanied a Huron band across the eastern tip of Lake Ontario on an unsuccessful campaign against the Iroquois. Before returning to Québec, Champlain explored in 1616 the eastern shores of Lake Huron to the land of the Petun or Tobacco Indians.

This was Champlain's last major expedition. His great concern was to persuade the home government to give more attention and more resources to Canada. He saw the trading and agricultural potential of "a country nearly 1800 leagues in length, watered by the fairest rivers in the world and by the greatest and most numerous lakes," from which might be found "the South Sea passage to China and the East Indies."

In 1610, Champlain sent a young Frenchman, Etienne Brulé, to live with an Indian chief and learn the Iroquois language. Brulé became the first of a new kind of explorer: the *coureurs de bois*. These fur traders lived among the Indians, learned Indian survival skills and traveled by Indian means, canoeing the rivers and portaging the falls. They became the outriders of French exploration in North America in the 17th and 18th centuries.

Brulé himself reached lakes Huron and Ontario before his mentor Champlain, and was probably the first white man to see lakes Erie and Superior. But he kept no written records. Champlain, by contrast, was a keen publicist. He described his travels in his *Voyages*, illustrated with drawings and maps, and published in successively larger editions in 1613, 1619 and 1632. These reveal greatly improved knowledge of northeast America, for much of which Champlain should be given credit. Champlain found no route to the western ocean but he established, through alliances with the Indian nations, a fur-trade network stretching from the Gulf of St Lawrence to Lake Huron and beyond.

**New France**

REDRAWN FROM SAMUEL DE CHAMPLAIN'S CARTE DE LA NOUVELLE FRANCE, 1632

This was the last of several maps made by Champlain of eastern Canada. It draws on his explorations in the St Lawrence valley and along the shores of lakes Huron (*Mer douce*) and Ontario (*Lac St Louis*). Champlain was able to use information given to him by Indians, and by his associates such as Etienne Brulé, about lakes Erie and Superior (*Grand Lac*). Only Lake Michigan is missing.

# The Great Lakes and Beyond

## THE JESUIT MISSIONARIES, 1630-1670

*Black-robed Jesuit missionaries probe the series of mighty lakes west of the St Lawrence. By the end of the 1640s all five Great Lakes begin to take shape on the maps.*

Champlain's successors around the Great Lakes were mainly Jesuits. Each year they sent reports back to France from their mission stations among the Indians. They gave a vivid picture of the various tribes at the moment they first met the material culture, aggressive religion and deadly diseases of Europe. They also reported the activities of the *coureurs de bois*. These French traders and adventurers, often the true European pathfinders, rarely left any written record of their travels.

In 1634 Champlain sent Jean Nicollet, an

*Indians wearing snow shoes visit the mission at Sault Saint-Louis. This pen and wash drawing was made by Father Claude Chauchetier.*

experienced trader with Indians, to the west. With help from Huron guides, Nicollet became the first European to see Lake Michigan, meet the Siouan-speaking Winnibago Indians, and hear of the mighty Sioux nation still farther west. Nicollet journeyed from Green Bay to the Fox River, only three days from the Wisconsin River, a tributary of the Mississippi – as yet unknown to the French but taking misty shape in Jesuit reports as a great river that might lead to China.

French traders and missionaries persistently speculated about a way to the western ocean but their immediate aim was to explore and exploit the area of the Great Lakes. The Jesuits followed Indian trails out of Huronia. They reached the strategic and

commercial "hinge" of Sault Sainte-Marie, an area between lakes Huron and Superior where Indian tribes came from all sides to trade. In another direction they reached the northern shores of Lake Erie. In 1642, they founded Montréal at a site on the St Lawrence where the Ottawa River led west, providing a safe route some distance from the Iroquois.

The expansion of French knowledge and influence was interrupted in the late 1640s and 1650s by the long-threatened Iroquois war over Huronia. Warriors from the Iroquois Confederacy wiped out most Huron villages, sent several Jesuits to a fiery death and wrecked the fur trade. The old Huron-dominated organization was broken and the French were forced west for furs. As the Iroquois raids died down in the mid-1650s dozens of *coureurs de bois* ventured westward to keep the faltering supply of furs on the move. During a lull in the fighting Jesuit fathers visited the Iroquois homeland and brought back first-hand accounts of a large area from Lake Ontario to the center of modern New York state. In the late 1650s the Iroquois returned to the attack. Regular French troops were brought in to defeat them finally in 1667.

Settlement and trade revived. Lake

Superior, still only known by Indian report, was a particular focus for the French. Father Jérôme Lalemant saw it as a nodal point providing waterways to the Hudson Bay, the Gulf of Mexico and the Gulf of California. The Jesuits, joined now by other missionaries, the Sulpicians and the Recollets, would soon determine the outline of the Great Lakes.

From Lake Michigan Father Allouez followed Nicollet's old route to Green Bay to establish a mission among the Siouan-

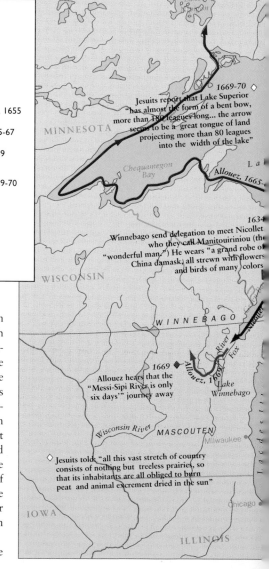

speaking Indians of Wisconsin. Pointing to the next phase of French expansion he described the land of the Mascouten Indians on the upper Fox River as "a very attractive place, where beautiful Plains and Fields meet the eye as far as one can see" – and only six days from the great river named "Messi-Sipi."

## Mapping the Lakes
REDRAWN FROM A JESUIT MAP OF THE GREAT LAKES, 1672

The Jesuit Fathers Dablon and Allouez produced this map to show the French missions in relation to "the tribes of these regions." It was the most accurate representation of Lake Superior until the 19th century, and the connection between Lake Illinois and Green Bay (*Baye des Puans*) is clearly marked.

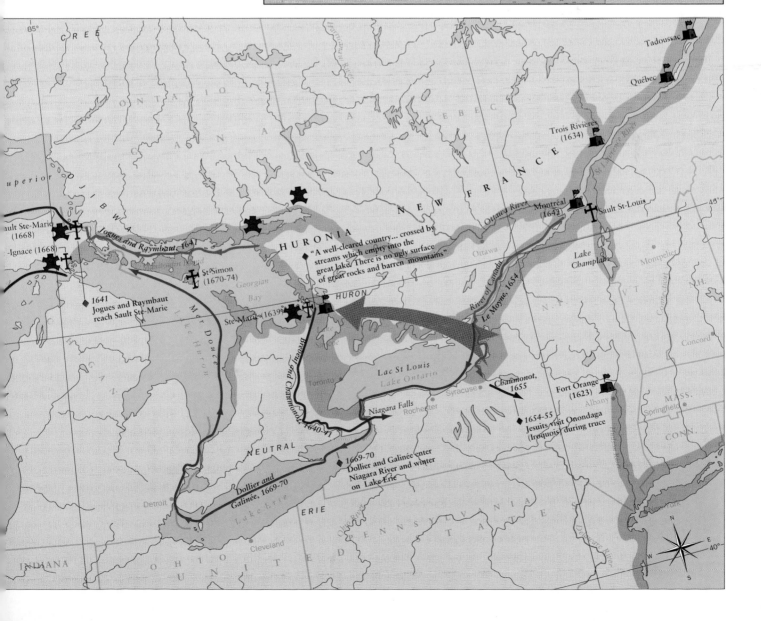

# Down the Mississippi
## THE JOURNEY OF JOLLIET AND MARQUETTE, 1673

*The French reach the great river of the interior and follow it towards the sea – not the western ocean as they had hoped, but the Gulf of Mexico.*

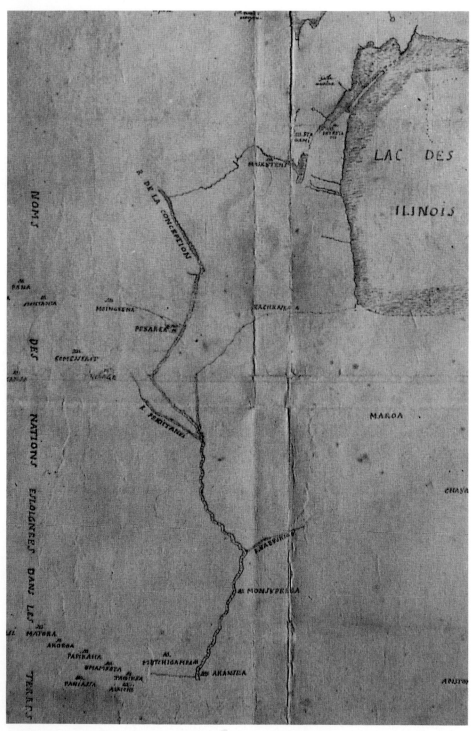

*This map was probably drawn by Father Marquette himself during the winter following his Mississippi expedition with Jolliet. Although the latitudes are one degree too far south, it is surprisingly accurate, and shows for the first time the mouths of the Missouri (Pekittan8i) and Ohio (Ouabougkigou).*

After the end of the Iroquois wars, at a ceremony at Sault Sainte-Marie in 1671, French officials told delegates from 17 Indian nations that the king of France was taking possession "of the territories from Montréal as far as the South Sea, covering the utmost extent and range possible." In May 1673 fur trader Louis Jolliet, with Father Jacques Marquette and five *voyageurs*, left to follow the great river to the south and find its outlet. Called the "Michissipi" by the Indians, the French believed it flowed into "the Sea of California."

Jolliet and Marquette canoed to the Fox River, crossed the Fox-Wisconsin portage and went on to the Mississippi. Paddling downstream, they saw fertile land on both banks, strange birds and plants and large herds of bison. It was 200 miles before they saw any Indians, poor though friendly Illinois displaced by the Iroquois wars. Further down, the placid waters of the Mississippi were disturbed by a large river thundering in from the west, the Missouri in full flood. Past the ox-bow bend of the Mississippi, they came to another great river, the "Ouabouskigan" or "Ohio." Jolliet and Marquette followed the Mississippi another 450 miles, but then, about 700 miles from the sea, fear of the Spaniards turned them back. Returning, they discovered an important short-cut to the Chicago Portage and Lake Michigan.

The explorers had found no precious metals, no furs, no wealthy Indian nations. Nor had they discovered a route to the Pacific, for clearly the Mississippi flowed into the Gulf of Mexico. But Indians reported that the Missouri led to the Western Ocean, and on the east bank the Ohio and Illinois rivers offered good commercial and strategic prospects. The Ohio provided a route into the backcountry behind the English seaboard settlements. Marquette wrote of the fertility of the Illinois valley, and their return route, modified, might take European boats all the way from the Great Lakes to the Gulf of Mexico. Lastly, they had made the link with the Great River – Espiritu Santo to the Spaniards – crossed by de Soto in 1541 (▶ *pages 34-35*). According to Father Dablon, Jesuit superior at Sault Ste-Marie: "It is certainly most probable that the river which geographers trace and call Saint Esprit is the Mississippi."

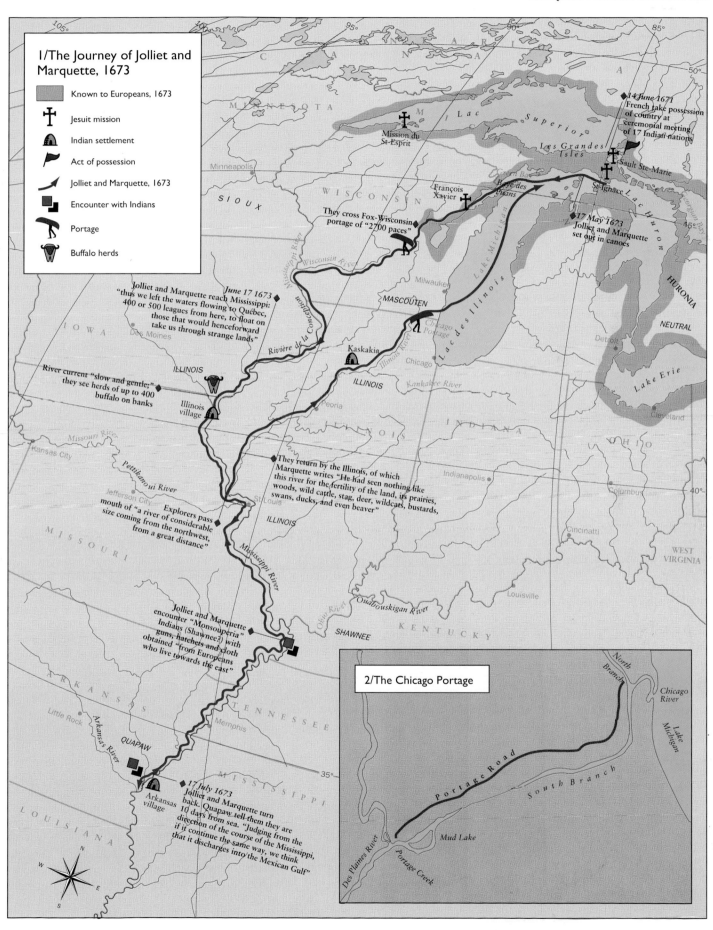

## 1/The Journey of Jolliet and Marquette, 1673

- Known to Europeans, 1673
- Jesuit mission
- Indian settlement
- Act of possession
- Jolliet and Marquette, 1673
- Encounter with Indians
- Portage
- Buffalo herds

14 June 1671
French take possession of country at ceremonial meeting of 17 Indian nations

Mission du St-Esprit

Les Grandes Isles

Sault Ste-Marie

St-Ignace

François Xavier

Baye des Puans

17 May 1673 Jolliet and Marquette set out in canoes

HURONIA

NEUTRAL

They cross Fox-Wisconsin portage of "2700 paces"

MASCOUTEN

Milwaukee

Chicago Portage

Lac des Illinois

Detroit

Lake Erie

Cleveland

Jolliet and Marquette reach Mississippi: "thus we left the waters flowing to Québec, 400 or 500 leagues from here, to float on those that would henceforward take us through strange lands"

June 17 1673

Kaskakia

Illinois River

Chicago

ILLINOIS

Kankakee River

River current "slow and gentle;" they see herds of up to 400 buffalo on banks

Rivière de la Conception

Illinois village

Peoria

INDIANA

Indianapolis

Columbus

OHIO

They return by the Illinois, of which Marquette writes "He had seen nothing like this river for the fertility of the land, its prairies, woods, wild cattle, stag, deer, wildcats, bustards, swans, ducks, and even beaver"

Missouri River

Kansas City

Pettikanoui River

Jefferson City

St Louis

ILLINOIS

Cincinatti

WEST VIRGINIA

Explorers pass mouth of "a river of considerable size coming from the northwest, from a great distance"

Mississippi River

Ohio River

Ouabouskigan River

Louisville

MISSOURI

KENTUCKY

Jolliet and Marquette encounter "Monsouperia" Indians (Shawnee?) with guns, hatchets and cloth obtained "from Europeans who live towards the east"

SHAWNEE

TENNESSEE

Memphis

ARKANSAS

Little Rock

QUAPAW

Arkansas River

Arkansas village

MISSISSIPPI

17 July 1673 Jolliet and Marquette turn back. Quapaw tell them they are 10 days from sea. "Judging from the direction of the course of the Mississippi, if it continue the same way, we think that it discharges into the Mexican Gulf"

LOUISIANA

MINNESOTA

Minneapolis

SIOUX

WISCONSIN

IOWA

Des Moines

ILLINOIS

## 2/The Chicago Portage

North Branch

Chicago River

Portage Road

Lake Michigan

South Branch

Des Plaines River

Mud Lake

Portage Creek

# The French Reach the Sea

## THE JOURNEY OF LA SALLE, 1682

*La Salle's canoe journey down the Mississippi to the sea opens the way to a French empire stretching from the St Lawrence to the Gulf of Mexico.*

When Jolliet and Marquette discovered the Mississippi River it seemed to hold out glittering prospects (▶ *page 62*), but the area was not explored any further for nine years. Although French fur traders were keen to expand their activities, the French government wanted to pursue a more cautious policy, preferring to develop a close-knit colony on the St Lawrence rather than far-flung trade with Indians.

The explorer who closed the gap between the sea and the farthest south point reached by Jolliet was the controversial French explorer, René-Robert, Cavalier de La Salle. La Salle spent much of the 1670s in arduous travels between Québec, the Great Lakes, and the country around the Illinois River. He was joined by his lieutenant, Henri de Tonty, and the Recollet order missionary, Louis Hennepin. In 1680, Hennepin and two companions went ahead to prepare the way for La Salle's Mississippi expedition. Traveling west, they were captured by the Sioux and carried off into captivity, before being rescued by the French explorer Dulhut (▶ *page 68*). Hennepin's account of his adventures, first published in France in 1697 and in an English translation the following year, became one of the most widely-read narratives of French exploration in North America. Yet it was scarcely a reliable source: Hennepin had much to say about his own exploits and his extravagant claims were part of the fabrications, intrigues and visionary plans which surrounded La Salle's career.

La Salle's Mississippi expedition of 1681-82 was part of the French attempt to dominate the western fur trade. It was also part of a grandiose project for a huge French commercial empire stretching from the St Lawrence to the ice-free ports of the Gulf of Mexico. The French commanded both the middle stretches of the continent and its strategic waterways. The way was open for the next great thrust westward.

Like most of La Salle's ventures, the expedition was much more modest than originally envisaged. He abandoned plans to sail downriver to the Gulf of Mexico in an armed sailing vessel. La Salle's party of about 40 French and Indians made the journey in less imposing fashion, by canoe. For much of the time they followed the route of Jolliet and Marquette, paddling past the mouths of the Missouri and Ohio rivers, and like them impressed by the fertility of the region and its abundant wildlife. As La Salle passed the furthest point of the earlier expedition they began to encounter Indians as yet unfamiliar to Europeans, people of the Taensa, Natchez and Choctaw tribes. Although La Salle assumed that he was the first European on these waters in fact he was following the track of the survivors of de Soto's expedition 140 years earlier, as they made their last bid to escape to the sea after de Soto's death (▶ *page 34*).

In April 1682 La Salle's expedition sighted the sea. Despite straightened circumstances he arranged as ambitious a ceremony as he could muster. He raised a cross and the arms of France and against a background of hymns and a fusillade of musket-fire declared that he "took possession of that river, of all rivers that enter it and of all the country watered by them." His exploration represented an expansionism in which commercial, spiritual and military motives were all present.

*Left: Louis Hennepin's 1697 engraving of a "vast and prodigious Cadence of Water" was the first printed illustration of the Niagara Falls. Hennepin, a relentless self-publicist, claimed that the falls were 600 feet high; they are actually only 193 feet.*

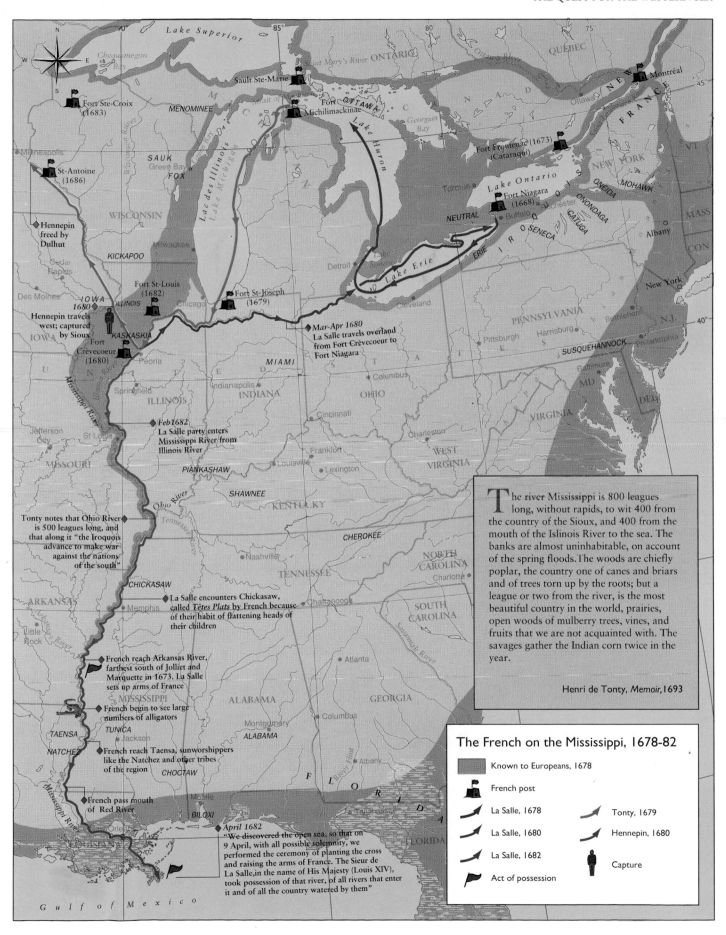

Fort Ste-Croix (1683)

Fort Michilimackinac

Sault Ste-Marie

Fort Frontenac (1673) (Cataraqui)

Montréal

St-Antoine (1686)

Fort Niagara (1668)

Hennepin freed by Dulhut

Fort St-Louis (1682)

Fort St-Joseph (1679)

Mar-Apr 1680
La Salle travels overland from Fort Crèvecoeur to Fort Niagara

Hennepin travels west; captured by Sioux

Fort Crèvecoeur (1680)

Feb 1682
La Salle party enters Mississippi River from Illinois River

Tonty notes that Ohio River is 500 leagues long, and that along it "the Iroquois advance to make war against the nations of the south"

La Salle encounters Chickasaw, called *Têtes Plats* by French because of their habit of flattening heads of their children

French reach Arkansas River, farthest south of Jolliet and Marquette in 1673. La Salle sets up arms of France

French begin to see large numbers of alligators

French reach Taensa, sunworshippers like the Natchez and other tribes of the region

French pass mouth of Red River

April 1682
"We discovered the open sea, so that on 9 April, with all possible solemnity, we performed the ceremony of planting the cross and raising the arms of France. The Sieur de La Salle, in the name of His Majesty (Louis XIV), took possession of that river, of all rivers that enter it and of all the country watered by them"

The river Mississippi is 800 leagues long, without rapids, to wit 400 from the country of the Sioux, and 400 from the mouth of the Islinois River to the sea. The banks are almost uninhabitable, on account of the spring floods. The woods are chiefly poplar, the country one of canes and briars and of trees torn up by the roots; but a league or two from the river, is the most beautiful country in the world, prairies, open woods of mulberry trees, vines, and fruits that we are not acquainted with. The savages gather the Indian corn twice in the year.

Henri de Tonty, *Memoir*, 1693

## The French on the Mississippi, 1678-82

- Known to Europeans, 1678
- French post
- La Salle, 1678
- La Salle, 1680
- La Salle, 1682
- Act of possession
- Tonty, 1679
- Hennepin, 1680
- Capture

# The Northern Approach

## TRADE AND EXPLORATION IN HUDSON BAY, 1659-90

*Rivalry between French and English fur traders fuels the exploration of the far north, and leads to armed conflict.*

In 1631-32 Foxe and James had failed to find a Northwest Passage through Hudson Bay (▶ *page 30*) and no European vessel entered the bay for almost 40 years. The French in Canada, after discovering that the Indians beyond the St Lawrence acquired beaver furs from the Cree Indians or "Christinos," revived interest in the far north. A Frenchman described these Algonquian-speaking Indians as "the best huntsmen of all America" at a time when they were

*Below: The beaver was the staple of the Canadian fur trade. This pen and ink drawing is believed to be the work of the Jesuit Louis Nicolas, c.1700.*

expanding along the southwest shores of Hudson Bay and past onto the plains.

Groseilliers and Radisson, two of the most enterprising *coureurs de bois*, reached the Lake Superior area in 1659-60, almost certainly not the coast of Hudson Bay as they claimed. They realized that the centre of Indian trade lay beyond Lake Superior and were convinced that the best way to bring back the furs of the Cree was not by the tortuous canoe route to the St Lawrence, but by the shorter carrydown to the shores of Hudson Bay, and then out by ship.

Officials in Québec were not impressed, but in England Groseilliers and Radisson gained the support of a consortium of businessmen and courtiers. In 1668 Groseilliers reached Hudson Bay in the 40-ton *Nonsuch*, wintered at Rupert River and returned with a cargo of furs. This was a decisive moment in the history of the Canadian fur trade. In 1670 some original subscribers, with other investors, were granted a royal charter incorporating the

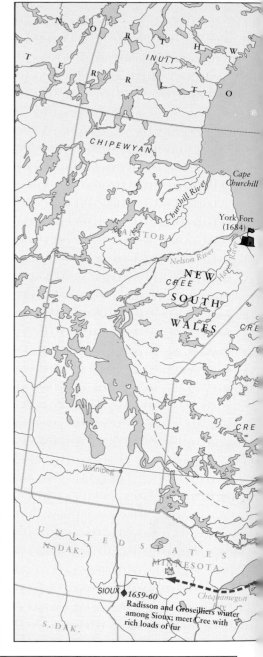

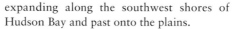

## Rival Claims

REDRAWN FROM SAMUEL THORNTON'S MAP, 1709

Thornton's map, prepared for the Hudson's Bay Company, shows the two rival routes to the fur-trading country of the Canadian interior: the English approach through Hudson Strait and Hudson Bay; and the French along the St Lawrence. The boundary between English and French territory in Labrador represents the English claim at the time.

Hudson's Bay Company. "Factories" or "forts" were soon established at Moose and Albany rivers. In 1684 the Company moved out of the James Bay ar ___ ___lt York Fort at Port Nelson, near ___ ___s of the Nelson and Hayes rivers, ___ ___ wnere it could tap the rich fur trade of the far interior.

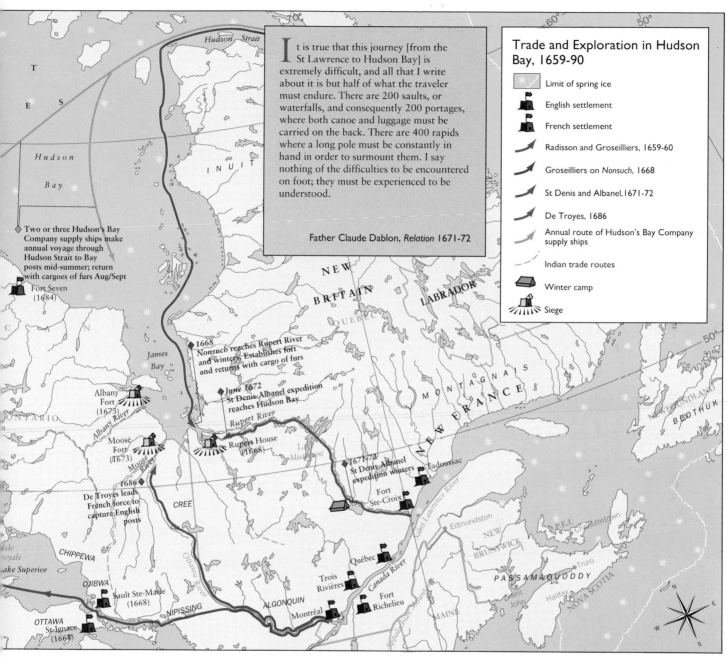

Two or three Hudson's Bay Company supply ships make annual voyage through Hudson Strait to Bay posts mid-summer; return with cargoes of furs Aug/Sept

Fort Seven (1684)

1668
*Nonsuch* reaches Rupert River and winters. Establishes fort and returns with cargo of furs

June 1672
St Denis-Albanel expedition reaches Hudson Bay

Albany Fort (1673)

Rupert River

Rupert House (1668)

James Bay

Moose Fort (1673)

1686
De Troyes leads French force to capture English posts

1671-72
St Denis-Albanel expedition winters

Fort Ste-Croix

Tadoussac

Québec

Trois Rivières

Montréal

Fort Richelieu

Sault Ste-Marie (1668)

St-Ignace (1668)

**Trade and Exploration in Hudson Bay, 1659-90**

- Limit of spring ice
- English settlement
- French settlement
- Radisson and Groseilliers, 1659-60
- Groseilliers on *Nonsuch*, 1668
- St Denis and Albanel, 1671-72
- De Troyes, 1686
- Annual route of Hudson's Bay Company supply ships
- Indian trade routes
- Winter camp
- Siege

It is true that this journey [from the St Lawrence to Hudson Bay] is extremely difficult, and all that I write about it is but half of what the traveler must endure. There are 200 saults, or waterfalls, and consequently 200 portages, where both canoe and luggage must be carried on the back. There are 400 rapids where a long pole must be constantly in hand in order to surmount them. I say nothing of the difficulties to be encountered on foot; they must be experienced to be understood.

Father Claude Dablon, *Relation* 1671-72

In Canada the French were concerned. Their earlier attempts to reach Hudson Bay overland from the St Lawrence had failed because of rough terrain. The Jesuits reached Lake Necouba in 1661 but this was only half way between Tadoussac and James Bay. In 1671-72, prompted by the news of the English arrival, another French group, including Jesuit Father Albanel, made the journey overland. Over two seasons they crossed 200 portages and 400 rapids. In 1674 and 1679 two more reconnaissance probes followed, prompted by a growing fear that the Bay posts w[...]ning the French hold on the north[...]de.

In the 1680s, as the French and English governments drifted into war in Europe,

hostilities broke out in Hudson Bay. In 1686 Pierre de Troyes led an armed force overland from Montréal, capturing all the Hudson's Bay Company posts except York. Open hostilities continued in a sporadic way for almost 30 years, with raids, counter-raids and seizures of posts and furs.

The rivalry between the traders of the St Lawrence and those of Hudson Bay was to last 150 years, and before it ended the fur trade had reached across the continent to the Pacific.

*Right: In 1670, two years after the* Nonsuch *arrived at Rupert River, a group of its original shareholders joined with other investors to form the Hudson's Bay Company. The Company's charter was granted by Charles II, whose portrait appears in the document's illuminated initial.*

# Towards the Prairies

## THE JOURNEYS OF DULHUT, NOYON AND KELSEY, 1678-92

*As the French push west towards the Winnipeg basin, they are outdistanced by a young English fur-trader from Hudson Bay.*

Despite the well-publicized exploits of La Salle in the Mississippi valley (▶ *page 64*), most of the furs traded by the French came from the upper country. Here, in the *pays en haut* beyond Lakes Michigan and Superior the *coureurs de bois* had traveled ever farther west since the mid-17th century, their search for furs often co-existing rather awkwardly with the missionaries' concern with souls.

Daniel Greysolon Dulhut (Duluth in modern usage) was one of the most important French agents in this region. He left Sault Sainte-Marie in 1679 on a peace-making mission among the Sioux and their neighbors the Cree, Assiniboin and Chippewa. These Indians lived west and north of Lake Superior, where river access to the English posts on Hudson Bay was a possibility which alarmed the French. Dulhut's farthest west point was Lake Mille Lacs in modern Minnesota, but during his winter stay at the western end of Lake Superior (on the site of modern Duluth) he sent three men to explore even farther west. Where they traveled is not clear, but they picked up reports from the Sioux of a "great lake" 20 days' journey away "whose water is not good to drink." The European preoccupation with finding a way through the continent to the Pacific was as strong as ever, and Dulhut took this as a reference to the Western Ocean.

By the mid-1680s the French presence in the area had been strengthened by the setting up of two posts, at Kaministiquia on the northwest shore of Lake Superior and at Lake Nipigon. In the late 1680s Jacques de Noyon canoed up the Kaministiquia River, perhaps as far as Lake of the Woods. Indians told him that from the lake a river flowed into the western ocean, presumably refering to the Winnipeg River and Lake Winnipeg. Noyon also thought he heard reports of bearded white men on horseback and stone cities. The French would not have an immediate opportunity to investigate these intriguing reports, for the tide of French westward expansion was interrupted by the Anglo-French wars of 1689-1713.

During these wars the Hudson's Bay Company maintained its cautious policy of waiting at its bayside posts for the Indians to come down to trade. Against this background in 1690-92, Henry Kelsey, "a very active Lad, delighting much in Indian Company," left York with a party of Cree. He was given instructions "to call, encourage, and invite,

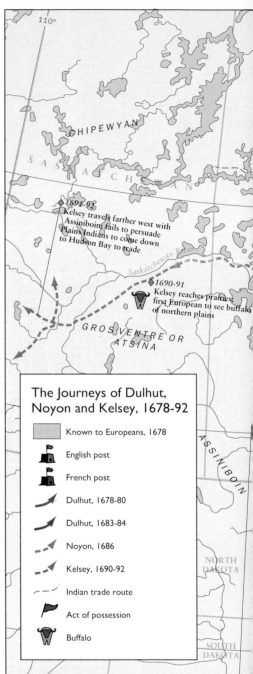

## The Journeys of Dulhut, Noyon and Kelsey, 1678-92

| | |
|---|---|
| | Known to Europeans, 1678 |
| | English post |
| | French post |
| | Dulhut, 1678-80 |
| | Dulhut, 1683-84 |
| | Noyon, 1686 |
| | Kelsey, 1690-92 |
| | Indian trade route |
| | Act of possession |
| | Buffalo |

*1691-92 Kelsey travels farther west with Assiniboin; fails to persuade Plains Indians to come down to Hudson Bay to trade*

*1690-91 Kelsey reaches prairies; first European to see buffalo of northern plains*

*Left: A buffalo, from the first English edition of Father Hennepin's A New Discovery of a Vast Country in America (1698). "Those Bulls ," Hennepin wrote, "have a very fine coat, more like wool than hair... Their Head is of a prodigious bigness... and they have between their two Horns an ugly Bush of Hair, which falls upon their Eyes, and makes them look horrid."*

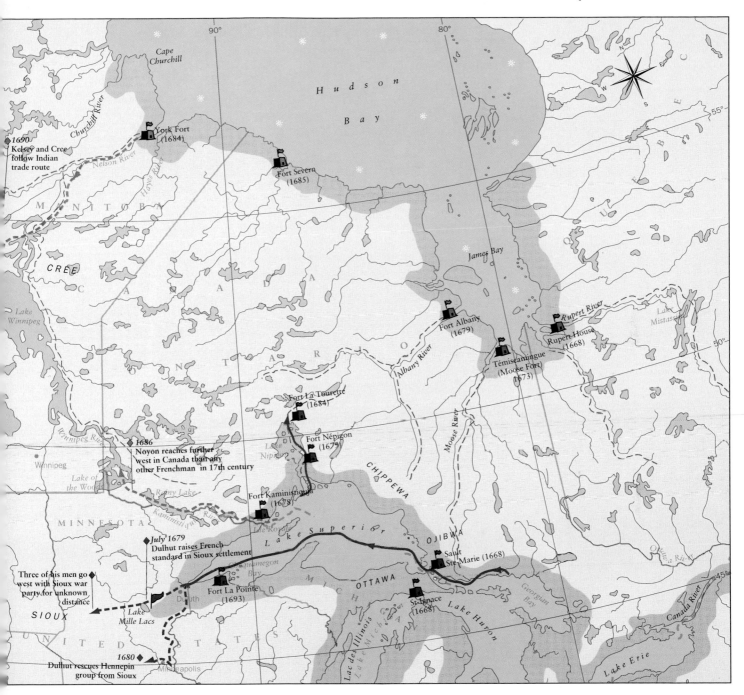

the remoter Indians to a trade with us." Traveling always with Indians, Kelsey seems first to have paddled along the Hayes or Nelson rivers to the Lake Winnipeg region, and then on to the Saskatchewan River, that great highway of the Indian trade. The next summer he followed the Cree on the track of the Assiniboin Indians southwest across the Saskatchewan River, and onto the great plains of western Canada. Here Kelsey saw buffalo herds, encountered grizzly bears and visited the Indians of the prairies, not just Assiniboin but also the mysterious "Naywatamee Poets" (probably Blackfoot Atsina).

The culture of the Plains Indians was based on the buffalo hunt and they declared themselves too fearful of the Cree and too unfamiliar with canoes to accept Kelsey's invitation to open trade with the distant Hudson's Bay posts. What the Company made of Kelsey's wanderings is not known. It neither used nor published his journal, the main part of which, with its curious rhyming prologue, was only discovered in the 20th century (*right*). No evidence of Kelsey's journey appeared on contemporary maps and in an era when Company servants were reluctant to leave the security of their bayside posts, his was undoubtedly a lone and adventurous undertaking.

I n sixteen hundred & ninety'th year
I set forth as plainly may appear
Through Gods assistance for to understand
The natives language & to see their land
And for my masters interest I did soon
Sett from ye house ye twealth of June
Then up ye River I with heavy heart
Did take my way & from all English part
To live amongst ye Natives of this place
If God permits me for one two years space
The Inland Country of Good report hath been
By Indians but by English not yet seen.

*From* Henry Kelsey his Book, *1690-91*

# Part III : Expanding Frontiers

As the English settlements on the east coast became more numerous and more secure, their traders pushed deeper into the interior, where they came into conflict with the French.

The rivalry which ensued was to dominate North American exploration in the first half of the 18th century, exploding into war in the 1750s. The British emerged the victors, but the new breed of colonists who had sprung up on the frontier would soon seize control of their own destiny. By the time traders and trappers had crossed the Mississippi to the foothills of the Rockies, the United States had declared independence, and was ready to explore its western lands.

During the 17th century English settlers established colonies along the Atlantic seaboard from New England to the Carolinas. There was some inland expansion along Indian trails with the help of Indian guides, but until the middle of the century, the tracks of the trader-explorers stopped short as they approached the Appalachian Mountains.

The deepest thrusts inland came in the south, where the mountain barrier fell away, allowing easier access to the interior. Deer skins rather than beaver furs were the main attraction here, but in many other ways the English traders of the region were the counterparts of the Canadian *coureurs du bois*. Much of their exploration was poorly recorded, but they reached far into the southern interior, towards the Mississippi. By the end of the century the English were challenging the long-established but weak Spanish grasp on Florida and the new French sphere of influence in Louisiana.

The first half of the 18th century saw exploration taking place in the context of fierce international rivalry as France, Spain and Britain struggled for control of the North American interior. A premature French attempt under La Salle to settle the Gulf coast of present-day Texas failed, but from their posts in the Mississippi valley the French edged westwards along the rivers towards New Spain. By the 1730s and 1740s the French seemed about to take control of the entire interior of the continent.

West of the Mississippi the Mallet brothers prospected the route to Santa Fé, while La Vérendrye reached the Upper Missouri from Canada. East of the great waterway the French pushed up the Ohio to confront the British traders who had filtered across the Appalachians. Despite the spider's web of their routes on the maps, French dominance was fleeting and illusory, and disappeared in the cannon-blasts of the Seven Years' War. The peace of 1763 gave the British sovereignty over Canada and all lands east of the Mississippi.

The remaining decades of the century saw the expansion of British settlement across the Appalachians. The American Revolutionary War checked this movement for a few years, but after the fighting ended American settlers flooded across the mountains into the fertile lowlands of Kentucky. A new type of American folk-hero emerged in the person of Daniel Boone – hunter, trailblazer and Indian fighter. Farther west, across the Mississippi, traders and explorers of several nations were active in the Missouri country. By the end of the century they were poised to cross the Rockies and fulfil the age-old dream of opening a trans-continental route to the Pacific.

# Inland from the Northeast Seaboard

## THE EXPANSION OF THE NORTHERN COLONIES, 1630-1700

*As European settlements spring up along the northeast coast, fur traders push inland along the river valleys.*

The settlement of New England, which began with the arrival of the Pilgrim Fathers at Plymouth in 1620, reached impressive proportions with the "Great Migration" to Massachusetts in the 1630s. But it was not accompanied by any immediate exploration of the interior. Although fur-traders soon pushed inland along the river valleys, their journeys were limited by the Indians. Only after disease and war had weakened the Pequot, Wampanoag and Narragansett was deep penetration of the interior possible. Even then the way was barred by the parallel ridges of the Appalachians.

In 1633 John Oldham opened up the overland trail from Boston to Connecticut,

*Right: Knives were among the goods most commonly exchanged with the Indians for furs. This mid-17th century Flemish knife has a brass handle in the shape of a hunter with gun and dog. It was found on the site of a Susquehannock village in Pennsylvania.*

and found fertile soil and plentiful supplies of beaver. He was followed by Edward Winslow, and William Pynchon, who traded and explored along the Connecticut River. Simon Willard in the 1640s pushed up the Merrimack River, and in 1652 John Sherman and Jonathan Ince reached its source at Lake Winnipesaukee. Further north Darby Field followed the Saco River to the White Mountains, and looked across to the Gulf of St Lawrence and into the region of French dominance. Boundary disputes between the separate colonies, wars with the Indians, and the traders' continuing search for furs, opened up more of the interior, but exploration remained mainly local.

To the south, Hudson's voyage of 1609

*Left: A 17th-century chevron bead, one and a half inches long, found at an Iroquois village site, probably Oneida.*

(▶ *page 54*) was followed by the arrival of Dutch traders and settlers. From Fort Orange, more than a hundred miles up the Hudson, the Dutch traded with the dominant Iroquois or Five Nations. The Iroquois were the middlemen in the fur trade; to preserve this position they discouraged exploration through their territory. In the winter of 1634-35, however, they allowed three Dutchmen to visit the chief fortified settlement or "castle" of the Oneida Indians. The Dutch saw French goods there, and were told how favorable the French trade terms were compared to their own.

Rivalry between the Hudson and Great Lakes trading areas became fiercer after the English annexed the Dutch settlements in 1664. Traders and interpreters from what was now the English colony of New York (formerly New Amsterdam) thrust deep into Indian country. In 1685 an Albany trader, James Roseboom, was guided by French deserters into the heart of the French trading empire at Michilimackinac, where he traded furs with the Ottawa. Even more enterprising was the journey of Arnout Viele, a Dutch trader and Indian interpreter working for the English. In 1692-94 he traveled from Albany at least as far southwest as the almost unknown Ohio valley to open trade with the Shawnees. Far-ranging though these journeys were, they were isolated forays rather than precursors of any systematic program of exploration and exploitation.

*Above: A Dutch flint-lock trade gun made around 1660. Such guns were often sold in the North American beaver trade.*

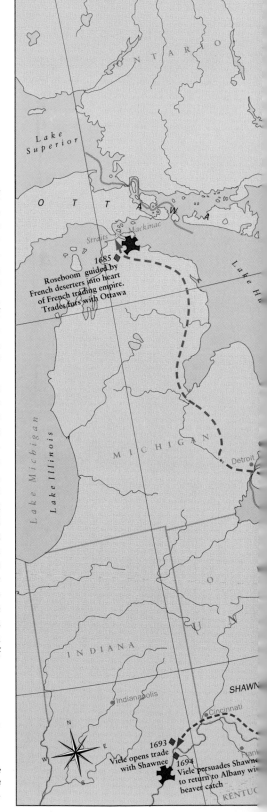

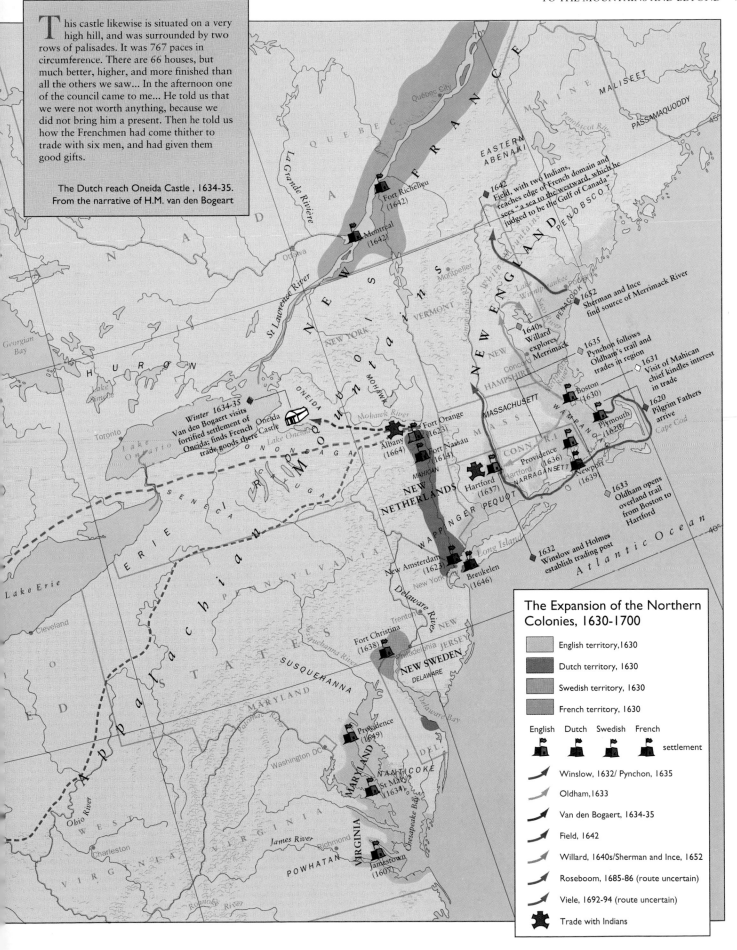

This castle likewise is situated on a very high hill, and was surrounded by two rows of palisades. It was 767 paces in circumference. There are 66 houses, but much better, higher, and more finished than all the others we saw... In the afternoon one of the council came to me... He told us that we were not worth anything, because we did not bring him a present. Then he told us how the Frenchmen had come thither to trade with six men, and had given them good gifts.

The Dutch reach Oneida Castle, 1634-35. From the narrative of H.M. van den Bogeart

1642 Field, with two Indians, reaches edge of French domain and sees "a sea to the westward, which he judged to be the Gulf of Canada."

1652 Sherman and Ince find source of Merrimack River

1640s Willard explores Merrimack

1635 Pynchon follows Oldham's trail and trades in region

1631 Visit of Mahican chief kindles interest in trade

1620 Pilgrim Fathers arrive

1633 Oldham opens overland trail from Boston to Hartford

1632 Winslow and Holmes establish trading post

Fort Richelieu (1642)
Montreal (1642)
Québec City
Boston (1630)
Plymouth (1620)
Providence (1636)
Newport (1639)
Hartford (1637)
Albany (1664)
Fort Orange (1623)
Fort Nassau (1614)
New Amsterdam (1623)
Breukelen (1646)
Fort Christina (1638)
Providence (1649)
St Mary's (1634)
Jamestown (1607)

Winter 1634-35 Van den Bogaert visits fortified settlement of Oneida; finds French trade goods there

## The Expansion of the Northern Colonies, 1630-1700

English territory, 1630
Dutch territory, 1630
Swedish territory, 1630
French territory, 1630

English  Dutch  Swedish  French   settlement

Winslow, 1632/ Pynchon, 1635
Oldham, 1633
Van den Bogaert, 1634-35
Field, 1642
Willard, 1640s/Sherman and Ince, 1652
Roseboom, 1685-86 (route uncertain)
Viele, 1692-94 (route uncertain)
Trade with Indians

# From Tidewater to Mountains

## EXPLORERS FROM VIRGINIA, 1670-1750

*Explorers and traders move inland from Virginia. They investigate the Appalachians and the fringes of the Mississippi river system.*

In the early years the settlers in Virginia, like those in New England, concentrated on survival and explored little inland. Settler knowledge stopped at the line of falls, and not until the 1640s were forts established upstream on the main rivers.

In 1650 Edward Bland and Abraham Wood led an expedition to the Roanoke River from the most important of these forts, Fort Henry on the Appomattox. William Berkeley, the Governor of Virginia during 1642-52 and 1660-77, believed that the Pacific Ocean lay in the near west (as shown in John Farrer's map of 1651) and encouraged the venture.

### Rich Adjacent Vallyes
REDRAWN FROM JOHN FARRER'S
*MAPP OF VIRGINIA,* 1651

Farrer was an official of the Virginia Company. His map, made in London, embodies the still-popular belief that the Pacific lay just beyond the Appalachians, not far from the English plantations. The reference to Francis Drake's Californian landing (▶ *page 40*) reinforces the English claim to the Pacific coast, "whose happy shores, (in ten dayes march... from the head of James River, over those hills and through the rich adjacent Vallyes...) may be discovered to the exceeding benefit of Great Brittain, and joye of all true English."

Berkeley's second term of office was marked by more serious exploration. In 1670 John Lederer, a young German doctor, made three journeys inland. His precise routes are far from certain, but he did climb the eastern slopes of the Blue Ridge mountains. Across the Shenandoah valley he saw in the distance, not the South Sea as some had hoped, but the looming peaks of the Appalachians. Lederer was thus able to correct the "great errour" of imagining the North American continent as being only 8 or 10 days' journey across. Lederer made his own errors however. Meeting strange Indians on his second journey, probably fugitive Erie from the northwest, Lederer suspected they had traveled from California "from whence we may imagine some great arm of the Indian Ocean or Bay streches into the Continent towards the *Apalataen* Mountains into the nature of a mid-land Sea."

After Lederer there began a more purposeful phase of exploration, much of it organized by Abraham Wood at Fort Henry. In 1671 Wood sent Thomas Batts and Robert Fallam inland with Indians who took them into the Appalachians, to a tributary of the Kanawha River. Predisposed to find oceans or seas to the west, they checked to see if the stream was tidal. But since the Kanawha

> I would not advise above half a dozen, or ten at the most, to travel together; and of these, the major part Indians: for the Nations in your way are prone to jealousies and mischief towards Christians in a considerable Body.
>
> John Lederer, *Discoveries,* 1672

flowed into the Ohio they were in fact on the eastern edge of the Mississippi system, two years before Jolliet and Marquette (▶ *page 62*) reached the great river from the north.

In 1673 Wood sent out James Needham and a youth, Gabriel Arthur. They were led along the well-worn Indian trade route of the Occaneechee Path, across Cherokee territory and probably as far as the Little Tennessee River. Needham was killed by an Occaneechee, but Arthur spent a terrified year with a band of Tomahitan Indians, "in a strange land, where never English man before had set foote, in all likelihood either slaine, or att least never likely to return to see the face of an English man." The Tomahitan took Arthur on their raids towards the Ohio and then south towards the Gulf coast, before he escaped.

By 1699 the Virginians knew enough about the land beyond the Appalachian mountains to realize how close they were to the French. The planter and explorer, Cadwallader Jones, proclaimed to the Governor of Virginia, Francis Nicholson, that it "cannot rationally be above one hundred miles into Louisiana Country." This was the year of the first French settlements in Louisiana, and Nicholson warned that if the French "settle that River [the Mississippi] that and the River of Canada will encompass all the English Dominions her." It was not from Virginia but from further south that the main English response would come.

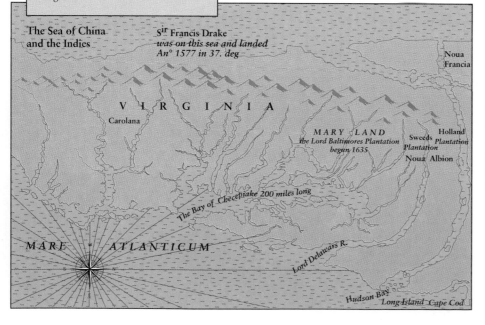

The Sea of China and the Indies

Sir Francis Drake *was on this sea and landed An° 1577 in 37. deg*

Noua Francia

V I R G I N I A

Carolana

MARY LAND
*the Lord Baltimores Plantation begun 1635*

Sweeds Plantation

Holland Plantation

Noua Albion

*The Bay of Checepiake 200 miles long*

MARE ATLANTICUM

*Lord Delawars R.*

Hudson Bay
Long Island Cape Cod

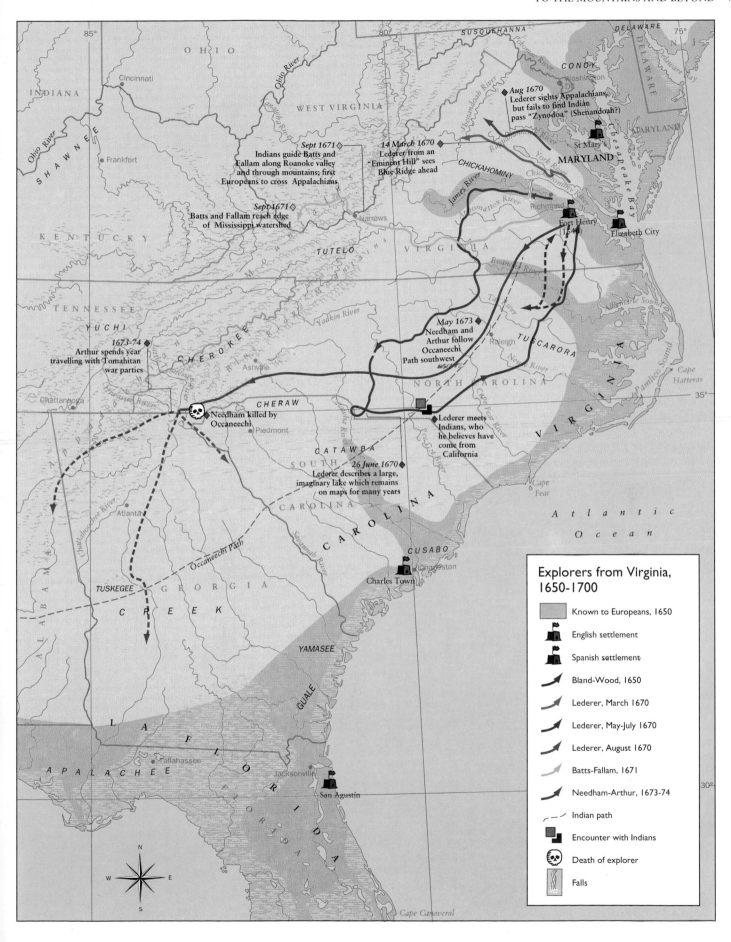

Aug 1670
Lederer sights Appalachians,
but fails to find Indian
pass "Zynodoa" (Shenandoah?)

Sept 1671
Indians guide Batts and
Fallam along Roanoke valley
and through mountains; first
Europeans to cross Appalachians

14 March 1670
Lederer from an
"Eminent Hill" sees
Blue Ridge ahead

Sept 1671
Batts and Fallam reach edge
of Mississippi watershed

1673-74
Arthur spends year
travelling with Tomahitan
war parties

May 1673
Needham and
Arthur follow
Occaneechi
Path southwest

Needham killed by
Occaneechi

Lederer meets
Indians, who
he believes have
come from
California

26 June 1670
Lederer describes a large,
imaginary lake which remains
on maps for many years

### Explorers from Virginia, 1650-1700

- Known to Europeans, 1650
- English settlement
- Spanish settlement
- Bland-Wood, 1650
- Lederer, March 1670
- Lederer, May-July 1670
- Lederer, August 1670
- Batts-Fallam, 1671
- Needham-Arthur, 1673-74
- Indian path
- Encounter with Indians
- Death of explorer
- Falls

# A Prospect into Unlimited Empires

## EXPLORATION AND TRADE FROM SOUTH CAROLINA, 1670-1715

*Traders from the new English colony of South Carolina follow Indian paths towards Florida and the Mississippi, challenging both the Spanish and the French.*

The founding of the colony of South Carolina in 1670 extended the southern frontier of English settlement and trade to within striking distance of the Spanish missions and garrisons in Florida. Inland, the southern ranges of the Appalachians were lower than those which hemmed in the Virginia settlements, and a network of Indian trails promised easier routes across them. Lederer (▶ *page 74*) dedicated his *Discoveries* (1672) to Lord Ashley, the proprietor of South Carolina. The preface pointed out that though the Appalachians "deny Virginia passage into the West Continent" they "stoop to your Lordships Dominions, and lay open a Prospect into unlimited Empires."

Among the first settlers at Charles Town (later Charleston) was Dr Henry Woodward. He made a series of probes deep into the back country: northwest to Catawba territory; west to open up trade with the warlike Westo on the Savannah River; and southwest to the lands of the powerful Creek confederacy. Woodward was followed by numerous Indian traders operating out of Charles Town, and later from Savannah, trading for deer skins, exploring and slave-raiding. Much of what they accomplished and where they went is unrecorded.

By the end of the century individual exploits emerge more clearly. In 1698 Thomas Welch followed the Indian paths all the way to the Mississippi to open trade contacts with the Chickasaw and Quapaw. The next year a Charles Town ship sailed a hundred miles up the Mississippi before being turned away by the French; but the main threat to France's planned empire in Louisiana came overland. In 1699 a renegade Canadian, Jean Couture, who had been with La Salle and Tonty (▶ *page 64*), led a trading party from Charles Town to the Mississippi. By February 1700 Couture, who was reputed to know eight or nine Indian languages, and to be "the Greatest Trader and Traveller amongst the Indians for more than Twenty years," had reached the mouth of the Arkansas, where he had commanded a French post in the 1680s.

Usually on foot, with a trail of pack-horses, the traders from Charles Town were spreading across the Southeast. By 1707 the Governor of South Carolina could claim that

"Charles Town trades near 1000 miles into the Continent." This expansion had a devastating impact on the Spaniards in Florida, where their missions among the Guale collapsed in the face of the English advance. The first Englishman to reach the Everglades was the trader Thomas Nairne. He accompanied a party of Yamasee Indians on a slave-raid in the region in 1702, and in 1705 boasted that "we have these past two years been intirely kniving all the Indian towns in Florida." In 1708 Nairne led a trading expedition into the Mississippi valley, and on his return drew up maps and proposals pleading for British government support for an aggressive trading policy based on alliances with the southern Indians.

Rather different in attitude and interest was John Lawson. A surveyor-explorer rather than a trader-explorer, he followed 600 miles of Indian paths to survey the interior of the Carolinas in 1700-01. But while their callings were different, the risks were the same: both Lawson and Nairne were killed by Indians, Lawson by Tuscarora in 1711, and Nairne at the outset of the Yamasee-Creek war of 1715.

*Above: Surveying with the Swiss colonist Baron von Graffenried in 1711, Lawson was captured by Tuscarora Indians. This pen and wash drawing by Graffenried's colleague Franz Louis Michel shows them, with their black servant, seated before the Indian tribunal which sentenced them to death. Graffenried secured his release, but Lawson was burned soon afterwards. The servant's fate is not known.*

### Map labels

The North Bounds of Carol

Green River

Wasatee
600 men

Arkansas River

the line of the present French Possessions seperates

Red River

1698 Trading po
established by W

Chicasa
600 men

Feb 1700
French post on Arkansas
reached by English expedition
from Charles Town led
by renegade Canadian
Jean Couture

Caphna 200 men

the line of divition

F R E N C H

Yassas 300

Tichee R

Nock
800 r

S E T T L E M E N

Mississippi River

May 1708
Nairne expedition
trades with Yazoo Indians

1700 English ship,
Carolina Galley, ent
Mississippi

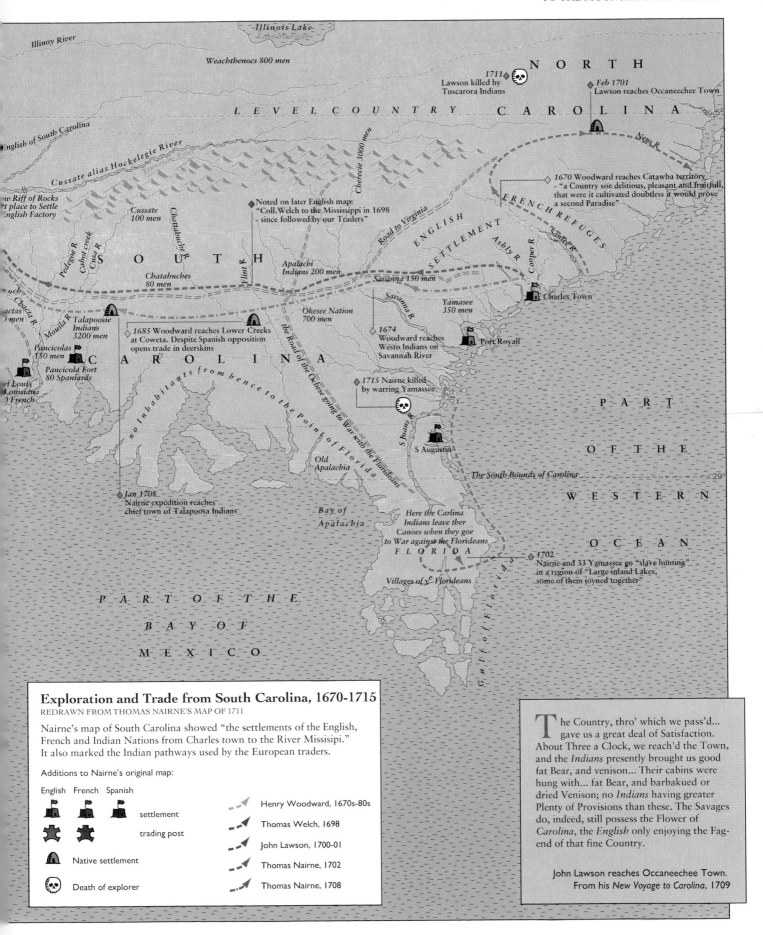

Illinois Lake
Lake Michigan

Illinoy River

Weachthenocs 800 men

1711 ☠ Lawson killed by Tuscarora Indians

N O R T H

Feb 1701 ◆ Lawson reaches Occaneechee Town

L E V E L   C O U N T R Y    C A R O L I N A

English of South Carolina

Cussate alias Hockelegie River

Tennessee River

w Riff of Rocks t place to Settle English Factory

Cherecie 3000 men

Noted on later English map: "Coll. Welch to the Mississipi in 1698 since followed by our Traders"

1670 Woodward reaches Catawba territory - "a Country soe delitious, pleasant and fruitfull, that were it cultivated doubtless it would prove a second Paradise"

F R E N C H   R E F U G E S

Neus R.

365°

Cussate 100 men

Pedegoe R. Cabot creek Cusa R.

Chattahuche

S O U T H

Flint R.

Apalachi Indians 200 men

Road to Virginia

E N G L I S H   S E T T L E M E N T

Ashly R. Cooper R. Santee R.

Chatahuches 80 men

Savanna 150 men

Savanna R.

Charles Town

nch Chacta men

Moulia R.

Talapoosie Indians 3200 men

1685 Woodward reaches Lower Creeks at Coweta. Despite Spanish opposition opens trade in deerskins

Okesee Nation 700 men

1674 Woodward reaches Westo Indians on Savannah River

Yamasee 350 men

Port Royall

ctas men

Pancicolas 130 men

C A R O L I N A

the Road of the Okesee going to War with the Florideans

1715 Nairne killed by warring Yamassee ☠

P A R T

Pancicola Fort 80 Spaniards

l Louis ouisiana ) French

no Inhabitants from hence to the Point of Florida

S Augustin

O F   T H E

Jan 1708 Nairne expedition reaches chief town of Talapoosa Indians

Old Apalachia

Bay of Apatachia

Here the Carlina Indians leave ther Canoes when they goe to War against the Florideans

The South Bounds of Carolina

W E S T E R N

29°

O C E A N

F L O R I D A

1702 ◆ Nairne and 33 Yamassee go "slave hunting" in a region of "Large inland Lakes, some of them joyned together"

Villages of ye Florideans

Gulf of Florida

P A R T   O F   T H E

B A Y   O F

M E X I C O

## Exploration and Trade from South Carolina, 1670-1715
REDRAWN FROM THOMAS NAIRNE'S MAP OF 1711

Nairne's map of South Carolina showed "the settlements of the English, French and Indian Nations from Charles town to the River Missisipi." It also marked the Indian pathways used by the European traders.

Additions to Nairne's original map:

English  French  Spanish

settlement

trading post

Native settlement

Death of explorer

Henry Woodward, 1670s-80s

Thomas Welch, 1698

John Lawson, 1700-01

Thomas Nairne, 1702

Thomas Nairne, 1708

The Country, thro' which we pass'd... gave us a great deal of Satisfaction. About Three a Clock, we reach'd the Town, and the *Indians* presently brought us good fat Bear, and venison... Their cabins were hung with... fat Bear, and barbakued or dried Venison; no *Indians* having greater Plenty of Provisions than these. The Savages do, indeed, still possess the Flower of *Carolina*, the *English* only enjoying the Fag-end of that fine Country.

John Lawson reaches Occaneechee Town.
From his *New Voyage to Carolina*, 1709

# Naturalists, Artists and Surveyors

## THE EXTENSION OF KNOWLEDGE IN THE SOUTHERN COLONIES, 1712-30

*In the wake of the explorers a new type of
visitor arrived at the frontier: the naturalists
and surveyors who set about recording the
area and its wildlife.*

As fear of French expansion from Louisiana
came to dominate official thinking in England's southern colonies in the early 18th
century, the attitude of the Cherokee, Creek
and Choctaw along the southern flanks of the
Appalachians became crucial. "While they are
our friends," a British official pointed out,
"they are the cheapest and strongest barrier
for the protection of our settlements." In the
struggle for the allegiance of the southern
Indian nations an unexpected part was played
by an eccentric Scottish baronet, Sir

Alexander Cuming. His scientific interests
had brought him membership of the Royal
Society. In 1730, during a specimen-collecting
journey from Charles Town westward into
the mountains, Cuming persuaded the
Cherokee to accept an alliance with the
British. He confirmed the treaty arrangements
by taking a delegation of Cherokee chiefs
back with him to London, where they
received a ceremonial welcome from the
British government.

Cuming's interest in natural history, if not
his political activities, indicated a new type of
visitor to the frontier. He had been preceded
some years earlier by Mark Catesby, "the
founder of American ornithology" as one
authority has described him. Between 1712
and 1725 Catesby traveled across the
southern colonies observing the natural
history of the region, collecting specimens,
and later painting them. Observers such as
Catesby, Lawson and Cuming were a

> However small this distance may
> seem to such as are us'd to travel at
> their Ease, yet our Poor Men, who were
> oblig'd to work with an unwieldy Load at
> their Backs, had reason to think it a long
> way; Especially in a Bogg where they had
> no firm footing, but every step made a deep
> Impression which was instantly fill'd with
> Water. At the same time they were
> labouring with their Hands to cut down the
> Reeds, which were Ten-feet high, Their
> Legs were hampered with the Bryars.
>
> **William Byrd's surveyors advance half a mile
> through the Great Dismal Swamp, from
> *History of the Dividing Line betwixt Virginia and
> North Carolina*, 1841**

*Below: This map by William Byrd shows the 1728
Dividing Line between Virginia and North
Carolina. To survey the line, Byrd and his fellow
commissioners would have used equipment like the
theodolite (above right) and level (opposite),
illustrated in William Gardiner's 1737 book
Practical Surveying.*

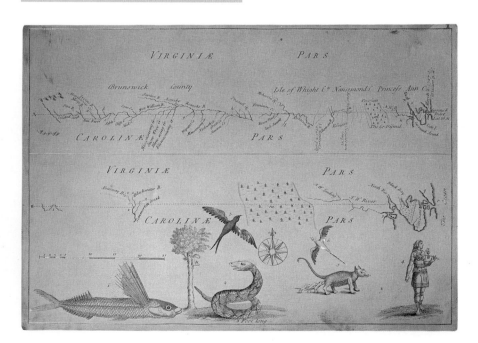

different sort of explorer from those who had
gone before them, but they were representative of many who were to follow. John
and William Bartram, the Swede Peter Kalm,
the Frenchman André Michaux, found a new
world of nature in North America which
caught both the imagination and scientific
curiosity of their contemporaries. Their
interests were wide and varied: a careful
listing and drawing of a plant or bird one
moment, a description of Indian customs or
some spectacular landscape scene the next.
The title of Mark Catesby's two-volume work
indicated the range both of area and subject
which might be covered by these polymaths:
*The Natural History of Carolina, Florida, and
the Bahama Islands; Containing the Figures
of Birds, Beasts, Fishes, Serpents, Insects, and
Plants: Particularly the Forest-Trees, Shrubs,
and Other Plants... To Which are added
Observations on the Air, Soil and Waters;
with Remarks upon Agriculture, Grain, Pulse,*

*Pfittacus Carolinensis Linnæi*
The Parrot of Carolina.

*Roots, Etc. To the Whole is prefixed a New and Correct Map of the Countries Treated of.*

While the naturalists roamed at will along the frontier, those who labored behind them had a narrower but no less dedicated intent; for as settlement moved into the interior, so the land had to be surveyed, and boundaries established. One of the best-known examples of this activity was the survey of 1728 which laid down the boundary between Virginia and North Carolina. This drove a line 240 miles west from the coast through forests, across rivers and swamps, to the Blue Ridge Mountains. One of the Virginia commissioners was William Byrd, whose account of the survey, *History of the Dividing Line*, was a graphic description of the back country in this period, its terrain, wild life, and human inhabitants, both European and Indian. The survey, like others of its kind, formed an intermediate stage between primary exploration and settlement. It marked the beginning of a process of recording the main features of a region after the first wave of European intruders had passed across it.

*Above: The Parrot of Carolina and the Cypress of America, from Mark Catesby's* The Natural History of Carolina, Florida and the Bahama Islands *(1731).*
*"This Bird," Catesby wrote, "is of the bigness, or rather less than a Black-bird weighing three ounces and a half: The fore-part of the Head Orange-Colour, the hind-part of the Head and Neck yellow. All the rest of the Bird appears green; but upon nearer scrutiny the interior vanes of most of the wing-feathers are dark-brown... The Legs and Feet are white: the small Feathers covering the Thighs, are green, ending at the Knees with a verge of Orange-colour. They feed on Seeds and Kernels of Fruit, particularly those of Cypress and Apples. The Orchards in Autumn are visited by numerous flights of them; where they make great destruction... Their Guts is certain and speedy*

*poison to Cats. This is the only one of the Parrot kind in Carolina; some of them breed in the Country; but most of them retire more South..."*
*"The Cypress (except the Tulip-tree) is the tallest and largest in these parts of the world. Near the Ground some of 'em measure 30 foot in circumference... the tree increases only by seed- which in form are like the common Cypress, and contain a balsamic consistance of a fragrant smell. The Timber this Tree Affords, is excellent, particularly for covering Houses with, it being light, of a free Grain, and resisting the injuries of the weather better than any other here. It is Aquatic, and usually grows from one, five or six foot deep in water; which secure situation seems to invite a great number of different Birds to breed in its lofty branches; amongst which these Parrots delight to make their Nests..."*

*Mathematical Instruments Contrived & Made in Metal, Ivory, or Wood, according to the latest Observations of Philosophers and Practitioners of Mathematical Arts, by Thoˢ Heath at the Hercules next the Fountain in yᵉ Strand, London. With Books of their Use: Thos Platt sculp*

# The Race for the Ohio

## TRADE AND DIPLOMACY IN THE OHIO COUNTRY, 1729-54

*Traders from the English colonies follow migrating Indians into the Ohio valley, bringing them into direct conflict with the French.*

Since La Salle's time, the French trade routes from the Great Lakes to the Upper Mississippi had hinged on the Wisconsin and Illinois portages, well to the northwest of the Ohio; and apart from Arnout Viele's journey of 1692-94 (▶ page 72), the English had made little attempt to exploit the little-known country west of the Pennsylvanian settlements. But a war with the Fox Indians during the early 1700s forced the French to re-route their trade along the Wabash and Maumee rivers. In 1729 Chaussegros de Léry, Chief Engineer of Canada, made the first proper survey of the Allegheny and Upper Ohio rivers; and by the 1730s the French were building posts at Fort Vincennes, Fort Oniatenon and Fort Miami.

But as the Delaware and Shawnee Indians migrated west from the Pennsylvania backcountry across the Alleghenies towards the Forks of the Ohio, English traders worked their way along the Susquehanna, West Branch and Juanita rivers in an effort to keep in touch with the retreating Indian groups.

These sporadic ventures turned into more purposeful expansion in the mid-1740s, as war in Europe prevented goods reaching the French merchants in North America. The Pennsylvania trader George Croghan took advantage of the lessening of French activity to build advanced posts at Logstown on the Monongahela, where there was an important Indian trading village, and at other locations on the Upper Ohio. In 1748 he set up a post at Pickawillany, deep in the French trading area among the Miami Indians. Helped by the German, Conrad Weiser, who had traveled widely among the Indians, Croghan negotiated in 1751 and 1752 treaties with the Six Nations and with the Miami, Shawnee and Delaware tribes. With perhaps as many as 300 English traders on or near the Ohio, the whole region seemed about to fall British.

The French response, as war clouds gathered again in Europe, was a military one, a devastating attack on Croghan's post at Pickawillany in 1752, followed the next year by an ambitious fort-building program farther east along a line stretching from Lake Erie to the Forks of the Ohio. It was at the last of these establishments, Fort Duquesne, that fighting broke out in 1754 between French troops and Virginian militia under George

> **B**rethren: it is a great while since we, your Brothers the English, first came over the Great Water; as soon as our ships struck the Land you the Six Nations took hold of her and tyed her to the Bushes, and for fear the Bushes would not be strong enough to hold her you removed the Rope and tyed it about a great Tree; then fearing the winds would blow the Tree down, you removed the Rope, and tyed it about a great Mountain in the Country (meaning the Onondaga), and since that time we have lived in true brotherly Love and Friendship together.
>
> **George Croghan's speech to the Six Nations, 28 May 1751**

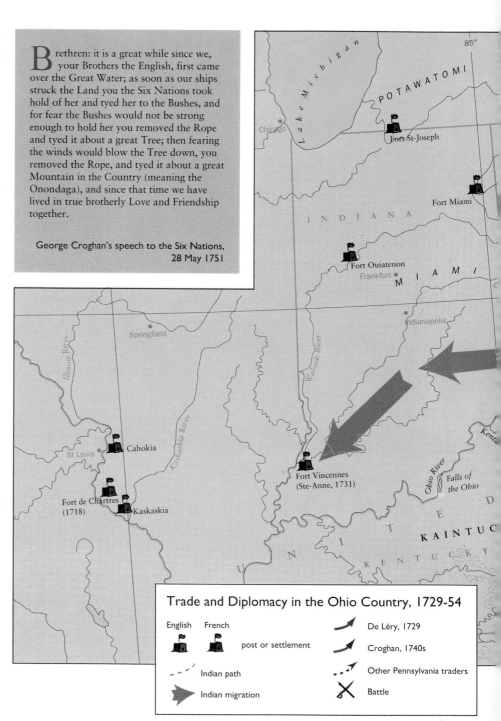

### Trade and Diplomacy in the Ohio Country, 1729-54

English — post or settlement

French — post or settlement

- - - Indian path

▶ Indian migration

↗ De Léry, 1729

↗ Croghan, 1740s

↗ Other Pennsylvania traders

✕ Battle

Washington. The clash marked the beginning of large-scale hostilities between Britain and France in America which continued until the final French defeat in 1760. Three years later the Treaty of Paris confirmed that North America east of the Mississippi was to be British, and the way seemed open for the next phase of frontier expansion.

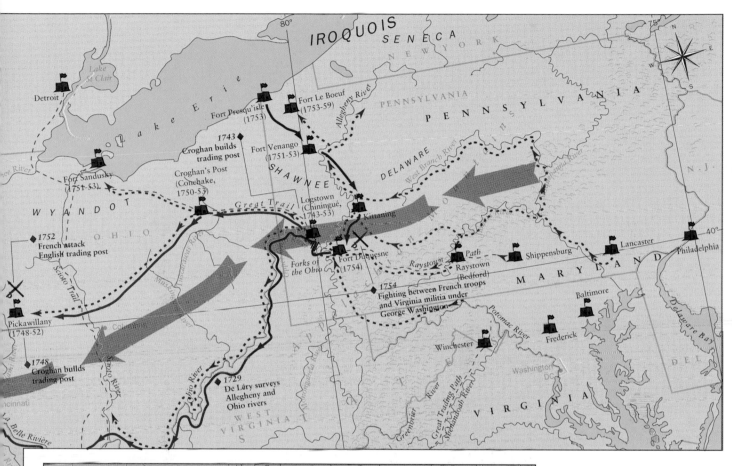

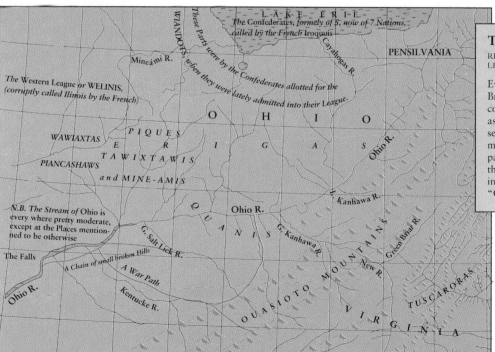

## The Colonial Frontier

REDRAWN FROM A MAP BY
LEWIS EVANS, 1755

Evans's "general map of the Middle
British Colonies, in America" was
commissioned by the Pennsylvania
assembly to encourage permanant
settlement in the frontier areas. The
mapping of the Ohio region is
particularly accurate, and draws upon
the knowledge George Croghan gained
in the course of his journeys. Evans's
"Quani" Indians are Shawnee.

# From the Blue Ridge to Cumberland Gap

## THE EXPLORATIONS OF SALLEY, WALKER AND GIST, 1742-52

*The English settlements expand westwards. Along the frontiers routes are found through the Appalachians into the bluegrass country of the Kentucky valley.*

By the 1740s the Indian traders pushing west across the Appalachians from the English middle colonies were being joined by frontiersmen with different objectives. They were looking for land suitable for settlement. In Virginia, particularly, land speculators and land companies found a favorable environment, for the colony's founding charter gave it claims stretching far to the west from the Atlantic seaboard. Some indication of Virginian ambitions was given as early as 1716. The governor, Alexander Spottswood, led his gentlemen companions, the Knights of the Golden Horseshoe, through the James River gap in the Blue Ridge, and on to the Shenandoah valley. One aim of this ceremonial procession, he explained, was "to satisfy myself whether it was practicable to come at the [Great] Lakes."

As passes through the Blue Ridge were discovered and negotiated, so land grants were assigned west of the mountains. In 1737 the Virginia Council allocated 10,000 acres of land to John Howard on the understanding that he carried out exploration west to the Mississippi. In 1742, joined by the experienced traveler John Peter Salley, Howard led a small group out of the Valley of Virginia at the James River, down the New and Kanawha rivers, onto the Ohio, and so down the Mississippi. There the venture came to an abrupt end as the group were "suddenly surprised by a Company of Men, Viz. to the Number of Ninety, consisting of French men Negroes, & Indians, who took us prisoners and carried us to the Town of New Orleans."

In 1749 the Loyal Land Company received a huge grant of 800,000 acres west of the Alleghenies, and the next year sent Dr Thomas Walker from Virginia to investigate settlement sites and routes. Walker crossed the Blue Ridge and the Holston valley, and reached Cumberland Gap – the gateway through which thousands of settlers were later to flood into the bluegrass country of Kentucky. Walker never reached the fertile lowlands himself, for he worked along the Indian trail, the Warriors' Path (used by the Cherokee in their incursions into Shawnee territory), to the north, before turning east along the Big Sandy River, across the Cumberland Mountains, and back to the Staunton River.

> W e killed in the Journey [of four months] 13 Buffaloes, 8 Elks, 53 Bears, 20 Deer, 4 Wild Geese, about 150 Turkeys, besides small Game. We might have killed three times as much meat, if we had wanted it.
>
> Thomas Walker's *Journal*, 1750

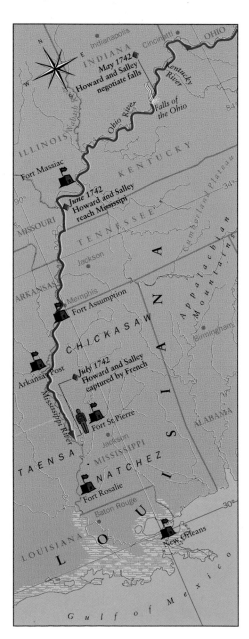

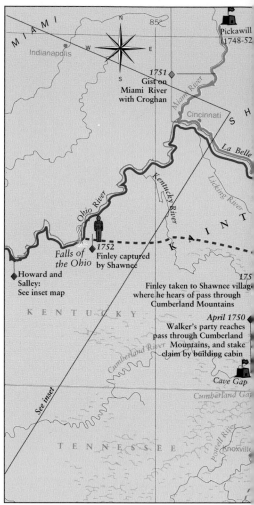

The next year Christopher Gist of Maryland reached the bluegrass country from the north. An associate of George Croghan (▶ *page 80*), and recently appointed agent of the Ohio Company, Gist crossed the Ohio, and in a huge sweep struck into Kentucky, crossing the upper reaches of the Kentucky River before bearing away east. It was left to a Pennsylvania trader, John Finley, to discover the connection between Cumberland Gap and the fertile Kentucky lowlands. Finley was captured on the Ohio by the Shawnee in 1752, and taken to their village near the Upper Kentucky River. There he learned of a pass through the mountains, clearly the one found by Walker, and soon to be known as the Cumberland Gap. Finley returned to Pennsylvania with the news, and although the looming hostilities with the French prevented any immediate response, his knowledge was to play an important part in the opening up of the region after the war.

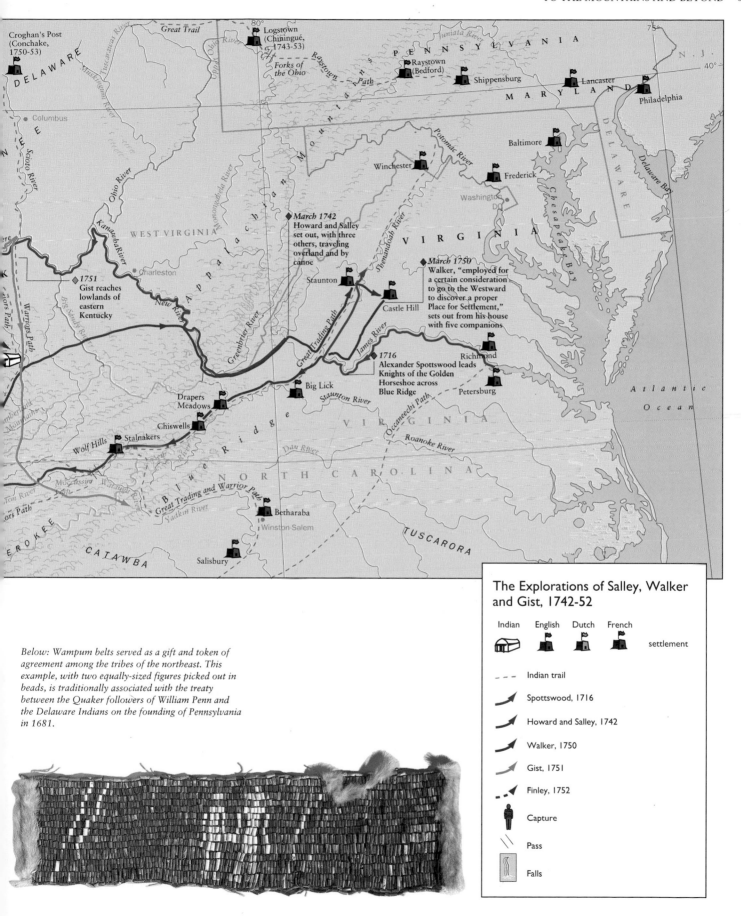

Croghan's Post (Conchake, 1750-53)

DELAWARE

Great Trail

Logstown (Chiningué, c. 1743-53)

Forks of the Ohio

PENNSYLVANIA

Raystown (Bedford)

Raystown Path

Shippensburg

Lancaster

N.J.

Philadelphia

MARYLAND

DELAWARE

Columbus

Scioto River

Muskingum River

Tuscarawas River

Upper Ohio River

Monongahela River

Ohio River

Juniata River

Appalachian Mountains

Winchester

Potomac River

Baltimore

Frederick

Washington DC

Chesapeake Bay

Delaware Bay

WEST VIRGINIA

Kanawha River

Charleston

New River

Greenbrier River

**March 1742**
Howard and Salley set out, with three others, traveling overland and by canoe

Staunton

Shenandoah River

V I R G I N I A

**March 1750**
Walker, "employed for a certain consideration to go to the Westward to discover a proper Place for Settlement," sets out from his house with five companions

**1751**
Gist reaches lowlands of eastern Kentucky

Warriors Path

Big Sandy River

Castle Hill

Great Trading Path

James River

**1716**
Alexander Spottswood leads Knights of the Golden Horseshoe across Blue Ridge

Richmond

Petersburg

Atlantic Ocean

Drapers Meadows

Big Lick

Staunton River

V I R G I N I A

Oceaneechi Path

Chiswells

Cumberland Mountains

Wolf Hills

Stalnakers

Blue Ridge

Dan River

Roanoke River

N O R T H   C A R O L I N A

Moccasin Gap

Watauga River

Great Trading and Warrior Path

Yadkin River

Betharaba

Winston-Salem

TUSCARORA

Salisbury

CHEROKEE

CATAWBA

*Below: Wampum belts served as a gift and token of agreement among the tribes of the northeast. This example, with two equally-sized figures picked out in beads, is traditionally associated with the treaty between the Quaker followers of William Penn and the Delaware Indians on the founding of Pennsylvania in 1681.*

## The Explorations of Salley, Walker and Gist, 1742-52

| Indian | English | Dutch | French | |
|---|---|---|---|---|
| | | | | settlement |

– – –  Indian trail

Spottswood, 1716

Howard and Salley, 1742

Walker, 1750

Gist, 1751

Finley, 1752

Capture

Pass

Falls

# Lands Further Off

## DANIEL BOONE AND THE OPENING OF THE TRANS-APPALACHIAN WEST, 1763-76

*As the French and Indian War dies away, Daniel Boone and others on the frontier scout paths across the Appalachians for settlers to follow.*

The influx of traders and land scouts did little to reassure the Indian nations, already nervous after the ponderous exercise of British military power that had crushed the French. In 1763 Indian resentments and fears exploded: an Ottawa chief, Pontiac, led an uprising of Shawnee, Delaware, Ojibwa and other western tribes. It was only suppressed at a fearful cost in lives to both sides.

The British government tried to stabilize the situation with the Proclamation of 1763,

*Daniel Boone's, adventures in the fertile valleys west of the Appalachians made him a legendary figure. A colonel in the 1763 war against France, Boone went west when victory gave Britain a claim to the Mississippi. The defeat of the Shawnee in 1774 made a major expansion west feasible, and Boone helped drive a road across to the new frontier settlements.*

which virtually banned settlement west of the Appalachians. But this was only, in George Washington's words, "a temporary expedient to quiet the minds of the Indians," and successive revisions changed both the boundary lines and the conditions under which settlement and trade were allowed. Land-hungry colonists in Pennsylvania, Virginia and North Carolina pressed on the central Appalachian frontier, where military

roads cut by the British during the war afforded settlers easy access. One official noted that the eager groups which pressed against the frontier always thought that "the lands further off, are still better than those upon which they are already settled."

The Forks of the Ohio, the Kanawha valley and the Tennessee River all attracted settlers, but most alluring were the hills and blue-grass meadows of "Kaintuck" or Kentucky. Gist and Finley (▶ *page 82*) had brought back reports of a lush and bountiful land, with fertile soil and plentiful game. It was here that the most spectacular expansion was to occur, but first routes suitable for settlers had to be found. While military surveyors mapped the former French territory along the Ohio, Illinois and Mississippi rivers, hunters and landscouts fanned out across the intervening country. In 1766 separate parties led by James Smith and Isaac Lindsey passed through Cumberland Gap, and news of their travels attracted the attention of the man who was to become the most celebrated "frontiersman" of the period, Daniel Boone.

While serving with the British army during the war, Boone had met Gist and Finley, and heard details from them about the bluegrass country. Working for a North Carolina land speculator, Judge Richard Henderson, and also trapping on his own account, Boone made his first attempt to reach Kentucky in 1767-68, but fell short of the Cumberland Gap as he hunted in the hill country around the Big Sandy River. In 1769, with Finley as guide, Boone's party reached Cumberland Gap, and followed the Warrior's Path into eastern Kentucky. Two years of wandering, exploring and fighting gave Boone a unique knowledge of the country between the Cumberland and Ohio rivers, where his

> S ometimes I feel like a leaf carried on a stream. It may whirl about and turn and twist, but it is always carried forward.
>
> Daniel Boone, after the death of his son at the hands of Indians in 1773

adventurous exploits made him the embodiment of the American "frontiersman."

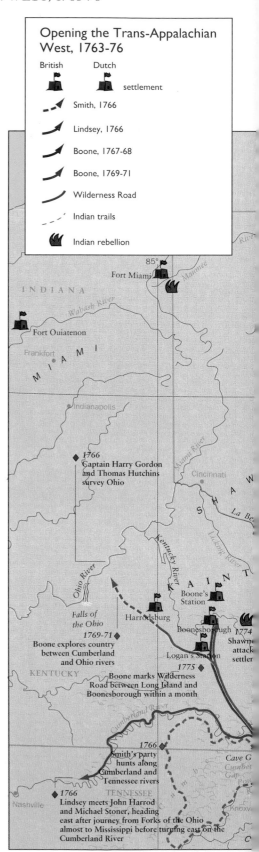

By 1774 there was settlement as far west as Harrodsburg, though in that year Indian war broke out as the Shawnees tried desperately to retain their hunting grounds in the face of settler encroachment. Their defeat cleared the way for the settlement of Kentucky. Boone helped to mark and clear the Wilderness Road between the Holston River and the new settlements. By the outbreak of the Revolution in 1776, the western frontier had moved forward massively, and by 1790 Kentucky had a population of 70,000 settlers.

*Right: One of Daniel Boone's beaver traps. Boone, who spent over thirty years trapping and hunting buffalo and game in the trans-Appalachian West, used this trap on his journey along the Kanawha River with Paddy Huddleston in 1789*

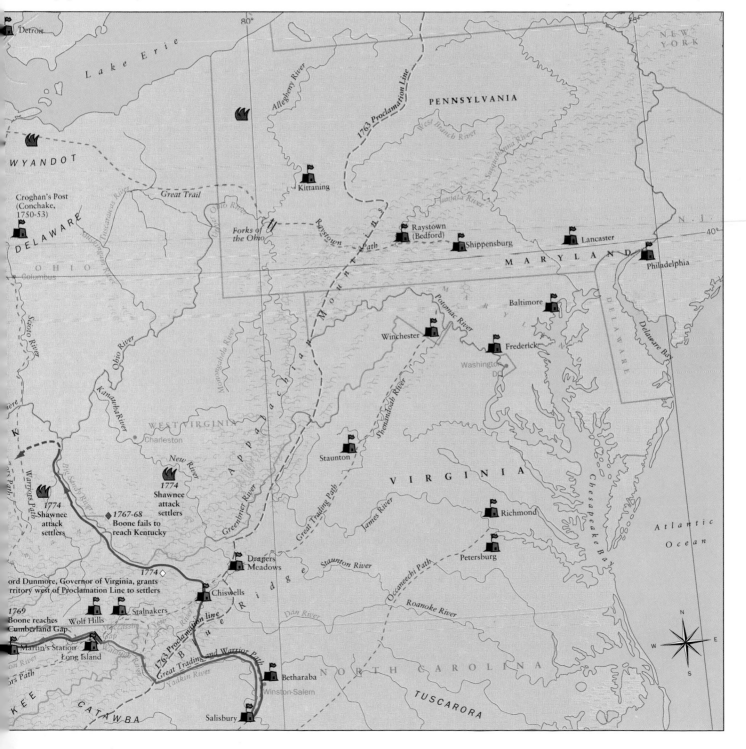

# To Explore the Most Unknown Parts

## THE TRAVELS AND WRITINGS OF JONATHAN CARVER, 1766-78

*The war with France finally over, gradually the British explore their new territory. Jonathan Carver winters with Plains Sioux and keeps a record of his experiences.*

The French had been defeated in North America by 1760, but it was three years before Britain and France reached a negotiated settlement. This, plus the disruption of Pontiac's Rebellion (▶ *page 84*), delayed British activity beyond the Great Lakes for a few years.

> N ear this nation [Cheyenne] I learned is a river rising from mountains in their neighbourhood and running north of the west till it falls into salt water, enlarging much in its course. On enquiring after a passage from the Indians they wou'd speak and make signs of great waters to the north west but whether salt or fresh, straits, rivers, seas, or inland lakes is hardly to be gathered from people whose way of life leads them into no such researches.
>
> From Jonathan Carver's manuscript journal

In October 1765 Ranger leader, Major Robert Rogers, was put in command of the strategic post at Michilimackinac. He made plans for moving westward on the upper Mississippi, hoping to find goods to trade and new areas to explore. Although the French had lost their territorial rights there were still French traders on the Mississippi. And although part of the treaty meant that New Orleans was now under Spanish control it still continued as a French trading entrepôt. In 1766 Rogers sent out some small-scale expeditions, not just to divert trade towards the Great Lakes, but also to undertake some exploration.

In 1764 Rogers had informed the British government that beyond "the Head of the Mississippi" lay a river "called by the Indians

*Below: This engraving, from the 1778 edition of Carver's* Travels, *shows the portage around the Falls of St Anthony. Situated on the Mississippi at modern Minneapolis, they were named by Louis Hennepin (▶ page 64) in 1680-81. "This amazing*

Ouragan" which flowed to the Pacific. This reincarnation of the French "River of the West" caught the imagination of at least one of the men sent out by Rogers, Jonathan Carver. Carver had been a captain in the colonial forces during the recent war with France. After leaving the army he taught himself map-making and surveying in Boston since, as he put it, he was determined "to explore the most unknown parts" of the "vast acquisition of territory" that Britain had gained as a result of the war.

Rogers employed Carver to explore west of Michilimackinac. Accompanied by traders and Indians, Carver left Michilimackinac in September 1766, taking the old French route first prospected by Jolliet and Marquette (▶ *page 62*). He journeyed through Lake

*body of waters," wrote Carver, "which are above 250 yards over, form a most pleasing cataract; they fall perpendicularly about 30 feet, and the rapids below... render the descent considerably greater."*

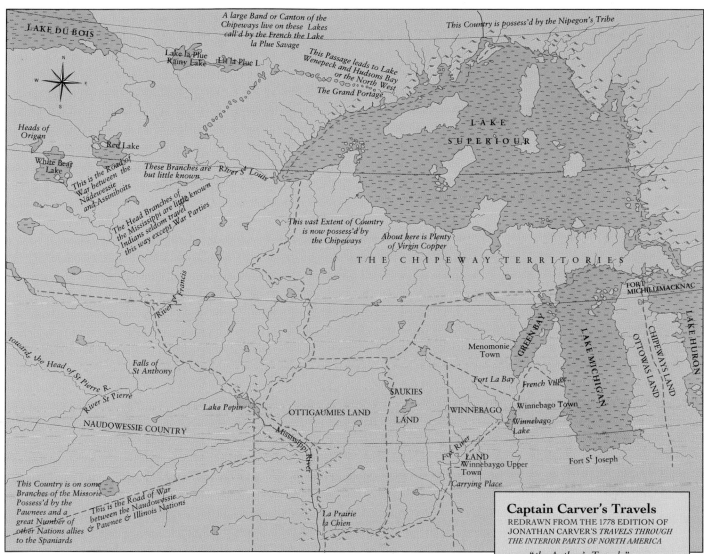

LAKE DU BOIS

A large Band or Canton of the Chipeways live on these Lakes call'd by the French the Lake la Plue Savage

This Country is possess'd by the Nipegon's Tribe

Lake la Plue Rainy Lake

Lit la Plue L.

This Passage leads to Lake Wenepeck and Hudsons Bay or the North West

The Grand Portage

Heads of Origan

Red Lake

LAKE SUPERIOUR

White Bear Lake

This is the Road of War between the Nadewessie and Assiniboits

These Branches are but little known

River St Louis

The Head Branches of the Mississippi are little known Indians seldom travel this way except War Parties

This vast Extent of Country is now possess'd by the Chipeways

About here is Plenty of Virgin Copper

THE CHIPEWAY TERRITORIES

FORT MICHILLIMACKNAC

River Francis

LAKE HURON

GREEN BAY

CHIPEWAYS LAND

Menomonie Town

LAKE MICHIGAN

OTTOWAS LAND

towards the Head of St Pierre R.

Falls of St Anthony

Fort La Bay

French Ville

River St Pierre

SAUKIES LAND

Winnebago Town

Lake Pepin

OTTIGAUMIES LAND

WINNEBAGO

Winnebago Lake

NAUDOWESSIE COUNTRY

Mississippi River

Fo. River

Fort St Joseph

LAND

Winnebago Upper Town

This Country is on some Branches of the Missorie Possess'd by the Pawnees and a great Number of other Nations allies to the Spaniards

This is the Road of War between the Naudowessie Pawnee & Illinois Nations

Carrying Place

La Prairie la Chien

**Captain Carver's Travels**
REDRAWN FROM THE 1778 EDITION OF JONATHAN CARVER'S *TRAVELS THROUGH THE INTERIOR PARTS OF NORTH AMERICA*

----- "*the Author's Travels*"

Michigan, Green Bay, and Fox River to the upper Mississippi. Once on the Mississippi, Carver followed a route taken by Hennepin while he was a prisoner of the Sioux, the Falls of St Anthony and Lake Pepin (▶ *page 64*). He described a cave 30 miles below the Falls. "The Indians term it Wakon-teebe, that is the Dwelling of the Great Spirit... I found in this cave many Indian hieroglyphicks, which appeared very ancient."

In November Carver encountered Sioux for the first time. They were Dakota or Plains Sioux, Naudouwessie, as Carver called them. He then followed the Minnesota River about 200 miles to the main Sioux encampment, where he spent the winter. The Sioux told him of further Indian nations to the west: the Mandan and, beyond them, the Cheyenne. In April 1767 he left for Michilimackinac following a more northerly return route.

Carver's journey was longer than any other made between 1763 and 1775, but he was handicapped by the lack of trade goods that

had been promised by Rogers. In practical terms Carver achieved little and as the threat of revolution in America grew, both Rogers and Carver were unable to persuade the British government to mount further western expeditions. Both men fell on hard times.

Carver's account of his exploits, heavily re-written, was republished in 1778 as *Travels through the Interior Parts of North America*. A bestseller, it was translated into several European languages. But it was too late to be of help and in 1780 Carver died in a state of abject poverty. Despite an element of plagiarism and tall stories, Carver's account remains more than an engaging travel narrative. It is one of the first detailed accounts of the Plains Sioux and makes some perceptive comments on North American geography.

Carver's map shows his routes between the Great Lakes and the Upper Mississippi, and is extensively annotated. In print, though not on this map, he was one of the first to sense the existence of a great range of mountains running from north to south down the centre of the continent, forming a barrier to explorers trying to reach the Pacific from the east.

The Shining Mountains, as he called them, formed a true continental divide, with rivers flowing to all points of the compass – and that to the west was the River "Oregon." Although Carver sited the range too far east, in all except location his remarks conjured up the mighty spectacle of the Rockies:

"This extraordinary range of mountains is calculated to be more than three thousand miles in length, without any very considerable intervals, which I believe surpasses anything of the kind in other quarters of the globe."

# The Country of His Discovery

## LA SALLE IN THE GULF OF MEXICO, 1684-86

*La Salle tries to return to the Mississippi to found a French colony, but the attempt ends in confusion and tragedy.*

In 1682 La Salle's journey down the Mississippi (▶ *page 64*) opened vistas of a French empire commanding the heartland of the North American continent from Louisiana to the Great Lakes. After failing to win support in Québec for his plan to establish a chain of forts stretching from his new post (Fort St-Louis) on the Illinois River to the mouth of the Mississippi, La Salle returned to France at the end of 1683. There, Diego Dionisio de Peñalosa, the exiled former Spanish governor of New Mexico, had approached French ministers with plans for seizing the allegedly silver-rich territories of Gran Quivira and Teguayo which he said lay on New Mexico's eastern frontier. It was supported by La Salle's first-hand knowledge of the Mississippi valley. With France and Spain at war his proposal was approved and although the two countries signed a truce in August 1684, by then La Salle's expedition of four ships and 300 settlers was already at sea.

The expedition has been surrounded by controversy. La Salle missed the Mississippi delta completely, landing some 400 miles to the west at present-day Matagorda Bay. Here he founded his settlement, naming it Fort St-Louis.

Some historians have accused La Salle of deliberate deception, claiming that he knew where he was all along but placed the mouth of the Mississippi far to the west in order to increase French territorial claims at the expense of the Spanish. As a result, some cartographers even showed it as a branch of the Rio Grande. But it now seems that La Salle was genuinely mistaken. When he had journeyed down the Mississippi in 1682, he had tried to determine the longitude of the delta, but a broken compass and an "unsuitable" astrolabe led him to calculate it inaccurately. He appears not to have realized his error and was baffled to find that the dry coastal plains around his little outpost bore no resemblance to the silt-filled channels of the Mississippi he had negotiated three years earlier.

La Salle's forays from Matagorda Bay are as obscure as much else in these years. In the winter of 1685-86, if Indian reports are accurate, he seems to have reached as far west as the Rio Grande, possibly in search of Gran Quivira and its silver. In the summer of 1686, with the settlement marooned after the shipwreck or departure of its vessels, La Salle made an unsuccessful attempt to find the Mississippi, and follow it to the other Fort St-Louis on the Illinois River, where his trusted lieutenant, Tonty, was in command. Deaths, desertions and disputes weakened the little colony and led to a final desperate attempt by La Salle in 1687. Somewhere near the Brazos River violent quarrels resulted in the deaths of La Salle and six other members of the party.

The survivors, under Henri Joutel, eventually reached Fort St-Louis (Illinois) in September 1687, but Tonty had already launched a relief expedition in which he reached the mouth of the Mississippi and founded a French post on the Arkansas River. In 1689 he tried again by way of the Red River, but fell short of Matagorda Bay. It was left to Spanish search parties to piece together the story of the settlement's final days (▶ *page 90*). At the end of 1688, most of the few remaining colonists had been wiped out by the Karankawa Indians and the fort pillaged. They were still incensed, a young survivor later reported, by La Salle's behavior when he, "on coming, arbitrarily took their canoes for ascending the river to establish a settlement."

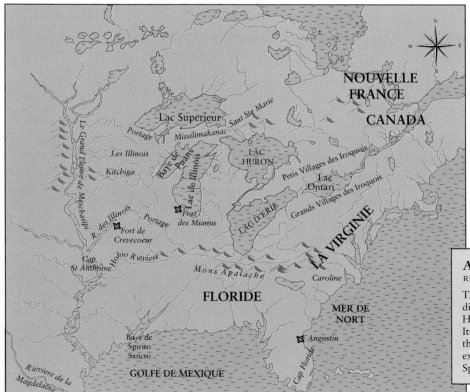

### A Very Great Country
REDRAWN FROM LOUIS HENNEPIN'S MAP, 1697

This influential map of "a very great country discovered in America" draws on both La Salle's and Hennepin's own explorations down the Mississippi. Its one major error reflects the territorial rivalries of the period: the great river has been pushed westward, extending the French claim at the expense of the Spanish.

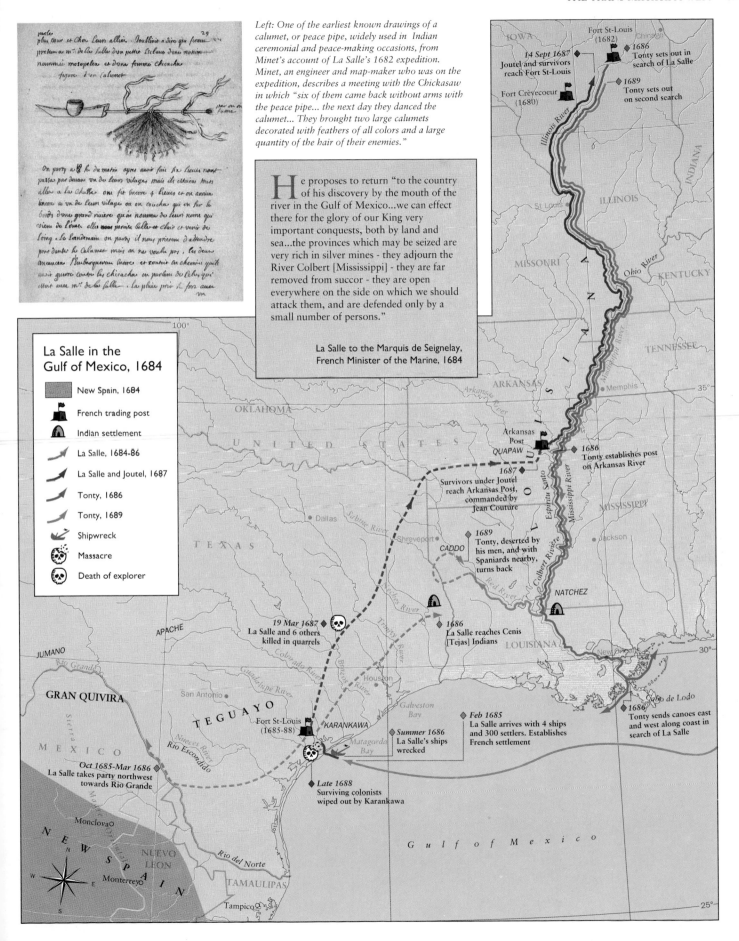

*Left: One of the earliest known drawings of a calumet, or peace pipe, widely used in Indian ceremonial and peace-making occasions, from Minet's account of La Salle's 1682 expedition. Minet, an engineer and map-maker who was on the expedition, describes a meeting with the Chickasaw in which "six of them came back without arms with the peace pipe... the next day they danced the calumet... They brought two large calumets decorated with feathers of all colors and a large quantity of the hair of their enemies."*

He proposes to return "to the country of his discovery by the mouth of the river in the Gulf of Mexico...we can effect there for the glory of our King very important conquests, both by land and sea...the provinces which may be seized are very rich in silver mines - they adjourn the River Colbert [Mississippi] - they are far removed from succor - they are open everywhere on the side on which we should attack them, and are defended only by a small number of persons."

La Salle to the Marquis de Seignelay,
French Minister of the Marine, 1684

## La Salle in the Gulf of Mexico, 1684

- New Spain, 1684
- French trading post
- Indian settlement
- La Salle, 1684-86
- La Salle and Joutel, 1687
- Tonty, 1686
- Tonty, 1689
- Shipwreck
- Massacre
- Death of explorer

Fort St-Louis (1682)

1686 Tonty sets out in search of La Salle

14 Sept 1687 Joutel and survivors reach Fort St-Louis

1689 Tonty sets out on second search

Fort Crèvecoeur (1680)

1686 Tonty establishes post on Arkansas River

Arkansas Post
QUAPAW

1687 Survivors under Joutel reach Arkansas Post, commanded by Jean Couture

1689 Tonty, deserted by his men, and with Spaniards nearby, turns back

CADDO

NATCHEZ

19 Mar 1687 La Salle and 6 others killed in quarrels

1686 La Salle reaches Cenis [Tejas] Indians

APACHE

JUMANO

GRAN QUIVIRA

TEGUAYO

Fort St-Louis (1685-88)

KARANKAWA

Summer 1686 La Salle's ships wrecked

Feb 1685 La Salle arrives with 4 ships and 300 settlers. Establishes French settlement

1686 Tonty sends canoes east and west along coast in search of La Salle

Oct 1685-Mar 1686 La Salle takes party northwest towards Rio Grande

Late 1688 Surviving colonists wiped out by Karankawa

MEXICO

NEW SPAIN

NUEVO LEON

Monclova

Monterrey

Rio del Norte

TAMAULIPAS

Tampico

Gulf of Mexico

# A Thorn in the Heart of America

## LAND AND SEA SEARCHES FOR LA SALLE, 1686-90

*The Spanish hear of La Salle's colony and send out expeditions to "pluck out the thorn which has been thrust into the heart of America."*

Since the collapse of Oñate's high-flown schemes (▶ *page 40*) the frontier province of New Mexico had settled into a humdrum existence. Less than 3,000 Spanish settlers were scattered along the upper valley of the Rio Grande from Socorro to Santa Fé, and only occasional missionaries, traders or punitive parties pushed east into the country of the Jumano Indians. The Pueblo Uprising of 1680, which drove Spanish settlers from Santa Fé and back to El Paso, stifled thoughts of expansion in the upper valley.

To the south, Bosque and Larios crossed the lower Rio Grande in 1675. And Mendoza responded in 1684 to Jumano appeals for help against the Apache. In 1685 a more immediate threat than the Apache emerged. A French deserter from La Salle's expedition (▶ *page 88*) reported that the French had arrived on the Gulf coast.

During the next five years, five sea and six land expeditions were sent out to find the French intruders, who threatened to push a wedge between the Spanish settlements in Mexico and Florida. As the Council of the Indies put it in 1686, "prompt action is necessary to pluck out the thorn which has been thrust into the heart of America."

The settlement proved difficult to find. The knowledge that 16th century Spanish explorers had gained of the Gulf area had been mostly forgotten. Spanish expeditions deciphered the complex maze of the Mississippi delta. In 1687 and 1688 they entered San Bernardo (now Matagorda) Bay and saw the wrecks of La Salle's ships, but they missed the settlement on the bay's northwest arm. Land searches fared no better. A lone Frenchman was found living among the Indians. There were doubts that this French colony existed.

Then, in April 1689, Indians handed papers obtained from Tejas (Texas) Indians to the

### San Bernardo Bay

REDRAWN FROM CARDENAS'S MAP OF SAN BERNARDO BAY, 1691

De Cárdenas's map, the first detailed survey of "San Bernardo" (now Matagorda) Bay, showing the route explored in 1690 by Francisco de Llanos in a Spanish frigate. La Salle's Fort St-Louis is shown here as "Pueblo de los Franceses" and the wreck of one of his ships, *Aimable*, is shown by the letter "H."

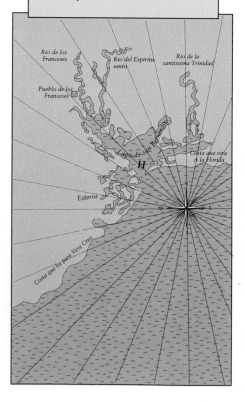

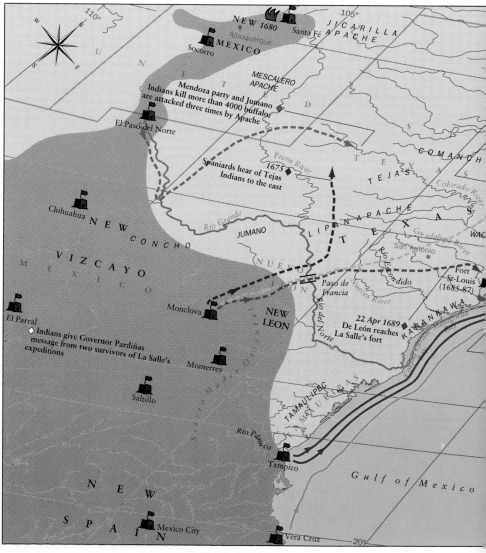

east, to officials in New Mexico. Among them was a parchment painting of a frigate, with a handwritten plea for help from two Frenchmen living among the Tejas. In the same month, the most persistent Spanish searcher, Alfonso de León, found the ruins of Fort St-Louis. De León rescued the two Frenchmen and the following year a few more survivors were found living among the Tejas, mostly children. Father Damián Massenet founded two missions and in 1691 Domingo de Terán, governor of the new province of Texas, led an expedition as far as the Red River. But the dispersal of the La Salle colony, problems with the Tejas and other calls on resources led the Spanish to abandon the new missions in 1693 and withdraw to the Rio Grande.

*Right: Two of La Salle's men, Jean l'Archevêque and Jacques Grollet, scrawled a desperate rescue plea on this parchment painting of a frigate. The Tejas Indians passed it to Jumano and Cíbolo Indians, who passed it to the Spanish governor of New Vizcaya at El Parral in 1689. The message reads: "We are sorely grieved to be among beasts like these who believe neither in God nor in anything. Gentlemen, if you are willing to take us away, you have only to send a message."*

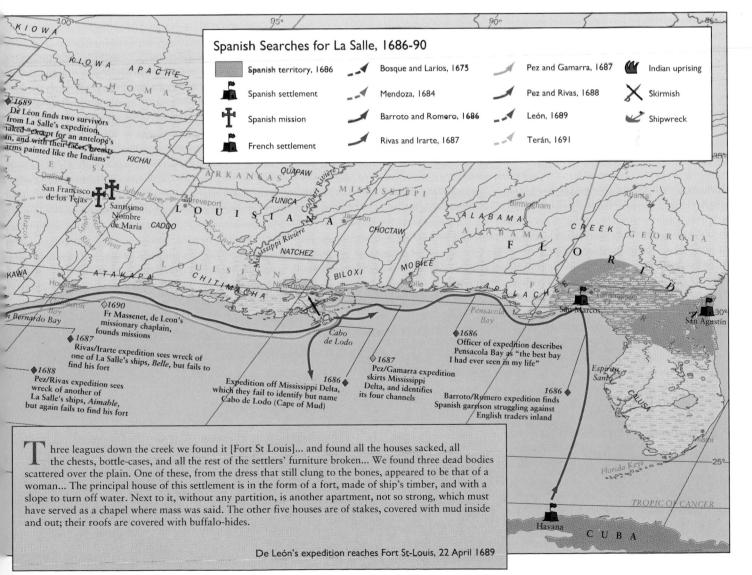

## Spanish Searches for La Salle, 1686-90

De León's expedition reaches Fort St-Louis, 22 April 1689

Three leagues down the creek we found it [Fort St Louis]... and found all the houses sacked, all the chests, bottle-cases, and all the rest of the settlers' furniture broken... We found three dead bodies scattered over the plain. One of these, from the dress that still clung to the bones, appeared to be that of a woman... The principal house of this settlement is in the form of a fort, made of ship's timber, and with a slope to turn off water. Next to it, without any partition, is another apartment, not so strong, which must have served as a chapel where mass was said. The other five houses are of stakes, covered with mud inside and out; their roofs are covered with buffalo-hides.

# New Frontiers

## EUROPEAN BEGINNINGS IN LOUISIANA AND TEXAS, 1698-1722

*Amid tense rivalry, the Spaniards and French explore inland from the coast of the Gulf of Mexico. The French found a settlement at present-day New Orleans.*

There had been a flurry of activity along the Gulf coast, prompted by La Salle's arrival at present-day Matagorda Bay, which lasted only until Spanish search parties revealed the expedition's fate. There was then a short-lived lull. But by the late 1690s rumors and counter-rumors of French, Spanish and English activities heightened the tension around these early European ventures into Louisiana and Texas.

In 1698 the Spaniards established a fort at Pensacola Bay. The following year a French expedition, commanded by Sieur d'Iberville, arrived on the coast but after the Spaniards turned them away from Pensacola, Iberville sailed on to the Mississippi delta. As La Salle had foreseen, a French base at the mouth of the Mississippi would be safely distant from the Spanish bases in Florida. Meanwhile English overseas expansion towards the Mississippi valley from the Carolinas posed a commercial rather than a military challenge.

Under Iberville and his brother Sieur de Bienville the French built forts at Biloxi and Mobile and on the Mississippi. They also negotiated alliances with the Natchez, Choctaw and other Indian tribes, and sent out exploring expeditions. Iberville himself investigated the maze of the delta and Bienville reached the Red River. The new settlements were a magnet for explorers. In

1700 Tonty came down the Mississippi from Illinois and the mining prospector Pierre Le Sueur made them his base for a remarkable upriver journey to the Sioux country of Minnesota, returning with samples of lead and copper in 1702.

The French traveled in heavy dugout boats, for the bark canoes of the north were unsuited to the sluggish, snag-ridden waterways of Louisiana. La Salle's plan of shipping out the furs of the north from a warm-water port on the Gulf still had appeal, but they were equally beguiled by prospects to the west – the trade and silver of New Spain. In 1714 Louis de St Denis journeyed from his new post at Natchitoches to the presidio of San Juan Bautista on the lower Rio Grande. When St Denis surprised the Spaniards by arriving on the Rio Grande this led to some uneasy collaboration between the Spaniards and French.

This was brought to an end as war broke out between the two nations in Europe and as Spanish expeditions drove deep into Texas. The French from the Mississippi and the Spanish from New Mexico approached each other, in places crossing and touching, in the vast new frontier area of eastern Texas.

For the French, Bénard de La Harpe broke new ground in 1719 when he reached the plains between the Red and Arkansas rivers

looking for Indian trade and for a route to New Mexico. Yet it was the Spanish thrusts which were the more purposeful, showing the distinctive characteristics of Spanish expansion elsewhere in the Americas. Expeditions of Ramón and St Denis in 1716, of Alarcón in 1718, and Aguayo in 1721-22, the last two including settlers and stock, left in their wake a chain of Franciscan missions and fortified presidios. The farthest east, at Los Adaes, was only a dozen miles from the French fortified post at Natchitoches.

For their part the French tightened their grip on the lower Mississippi. In 1718 they founded a settlement at New Orleans as well as other settlements among the Natchez, on the east bank of the Mississippi, above its confluence with the Red River. Since the new Spanish establishments in eastern Texas blocked any southerly route westward, the French began to look farther north for a way through. In that direction would lie "a great river, which comes from the west, on which there are numerous nations." The words were Tonty's; the river was the Missouri.

*Right: The French frontier post at New Biloxi, Louisiana, was sited across the bay from Fort Maurepas (Old Biloxi). This drawing, by Jean Baptiste Le Buteaux, shows the post in December 1720. Buildings are still going up, and already the camp is bustling with boat-construction and other activity. A flat-bottomed boat typical of the Mississippi region, lies near its moorings. Within two years, however, the settlement was transfered to New Orleans.*

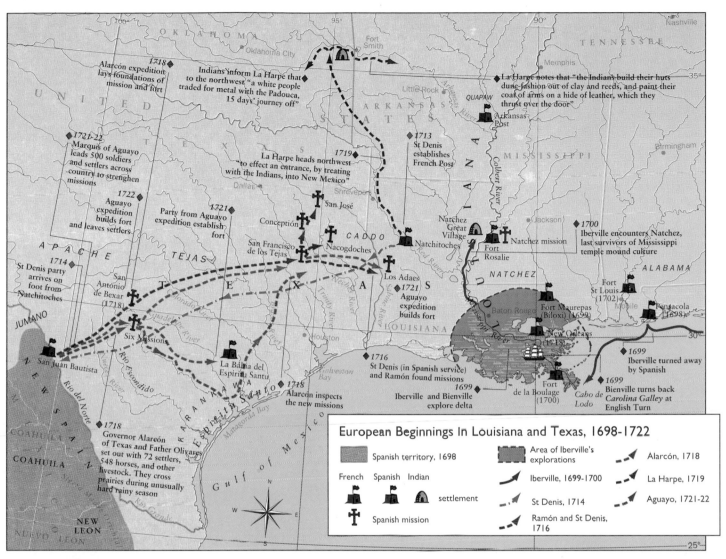

Indians inform La Harpe that to the northwest "a white people traded for metal with the Padouca, 15 days' journey off"

1718
Alarcón expedition lays foundations of mission and fort

1721-22
Marquis of Aguayo leads 500 soldiers and settlers across country to strenghen missions

1722
Aguayo expedition builds fort and leaves settlers

1721
Party from Aguayo expedition establish fort

1719
La Harpe heads northwest "to effect an entrance, by treating with the Indians, into New Mexico"

1713
St Denis establishes French Post

La Harpe notes that "the Indians build their huts dune-fashion out of clay and reeds, and paint their coat of arms on a hide of leather, which they thrust over the door"

QUAPAW
Arkansas Post

1700
Iberville encounters Natchez, last survivors of Mississippi temple mound culture

1714
St Denis party arrives on foot from Natchitoches

1721
Aguayo expedition builds fort

1716
St Denis (in Spanish service) and Ramón found missions

1699
Iberville and Bienville explore delta

1699
Iberville turned away by Spanish

1699
Bienville turns back Carolina Galley at English Turn

1718
Governor Alarcón of Texas and Father Olivares set out with 72 settlers, 548 horses, and other livestock. They cross prairies during unusually hard rainy season

San José
Conception
Nacogdoches
San Francisco de los Tejas
Natchez Great Village
Natchitoches
Natchez mission
Los Adaes
Fort Rosalie
San Antonio de Bexar (1718)
San Juan Bautista
Six Missions
La Bahía del Espíritu Santu
Alarcón inspects the new missions
Fort St Louis (1702)
Pensacola (1698)
Fort Maurepas (Biloxi) (1699)
New Orleans (1718)
Fort de la Boulage (1700)
Cabo de Lodo

OKLAHOMA
Oklahoma City
Fort Smith
TENNESSEE
Nashville
Memphis
ARKANSAS
Little Rock
Arkansas River
MISSISSIPPI
Jackson
Birmingham
Colbert River
LOUISIANA
ALABAMA
Mobile
UNITED STATES
TEXAS
TEJAS
CADDO
NATCHEZ
APACHE
JUMANO
KARANKAWA
NEW SPAIN
COAHUILA
NUEVO LEON
NEW LEON
Dallas
Shreveport
Houston
Red River
Neches River
Trinity River
Sabine River
Rio del Norte
Rio Escondido
Galveston Bay
Matagorda Bay
Espíritu Santo
Gulf of Mexico
Baton Rouge
Mississippi River

### European Beginnings In Louisiana and Texas, 1698-1722

Spanish territory, 1698

Area of Iberville's explorations

French  Spanish  Indian   settlement

Spanish mission

Iberville, 1699-1700

St Denis, 1714

Ramón and St Denis, 1716

Alarcón, 1718

La Harpe, 1719

Aguayo, 1721-22

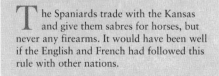

The Spaniards trade with the Kansas and give them sabres for horses, but never any firearms. It would have been well if the English and French had followed this rule with other nations.

Bénard de La Harpe, 1719

## The Mouth of the Mississippi

REDRAWN FROM GUILLAUME DE L'ISLE'S 1718 MAP OF LOUISIANA

Drawing from d'Iberville, St Denis and others, de L'Isle's map was the major authority on the Mississippi valley and delta for travelers and cartographers for over 50 years to come. This inset map of the "Embouchure du Mississippi" shows the delta in detail, including Lakes Maurepas and Ponchartrain, and the newly-established French settlements. New Orleans, founded in 1718, was not on de L'Isle's original map, although it was added to later editions.

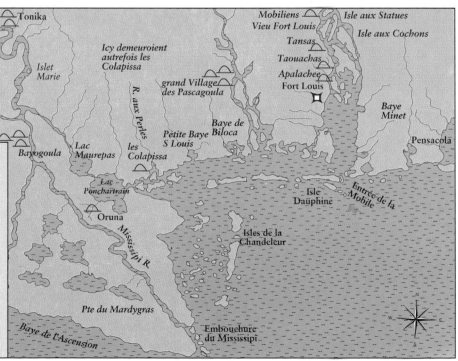

Tonika
Islet Marie
Bayogoula
Islet demeuroient autrefois les Colapissa
R. aux Perles
grand Village des Pascagoula
Lac Maurepas
Petite Baye S Louis
les Colapissa
Lac Ponchartrain
Oruna
Mississipi R.
Pte du Mardygras
Baye de l'Ascension
Embouchure du Mississipi
Mobiliens
Vieu Fort Louis
Tansas
Taouachas
Apalachee
Fort Louis
Baye de Biloca
Isle aux Statues
Isle aux Cochons
Baye Minet
Pensacola
Isle Dauphine
Isles de la Chandeleur
Entrée de la Mobile

# The Muddy River

## BOURGMONT'S EXPLORATIONS ALONG THE MISSOURI, 1712-24

*The French attempt to expand their trading
empire along the Missouri in a search for
silver and a river route to the Pacific.*

After Jolliet and Marquette sighted the mouth of the Missouri in 1673 (▶ *page 62*) there began a new phase of speculation and exploration. That the "Pekitanoui" or Muddy River was a major waterway was not in doubt, but its length, direction and source were all unknown. First reports placed the upper Missouri far south of its true location, and consequently much nearer Spanish settlements than was actually the case. Indian reports of other waterways to the west – the Osage, Kansas and Platte rivers – added to the confusion.

At the turn of the century the French had begun to establish posts on the Mississippi near its juncture with the Missouri. But it was some ten to twenty years before reliable first-hand reports of the Missouri country became available. The most important of these came from the French soldier and trader, Etienne Veniard de Bourgmont. In 1712 Bourgmont, who had been commander at Fort Detroit, returned with the Missouri Indians to their homeland after they had fought as allies of the French against the Fox Indians. He lived among them for the next five or six years, had

a child by a Missouri woman, and traveled widely. In 1714 he journeyed about 600 miles up the Missouri to the mouth of the Platte, persuading successive Indian tribes, jealous of their privileges as trading middlemen, to let him pass through their territory. From the Missouri Indians he reached the Osage, and from there he moved on to the Pawnee. The Pawnee, however, refused to let him through to the territory of the "Padouca," the fearsome Comanche of the plains.

A more official French initiative was made in 1719, when du Tisné, one of Bienville's

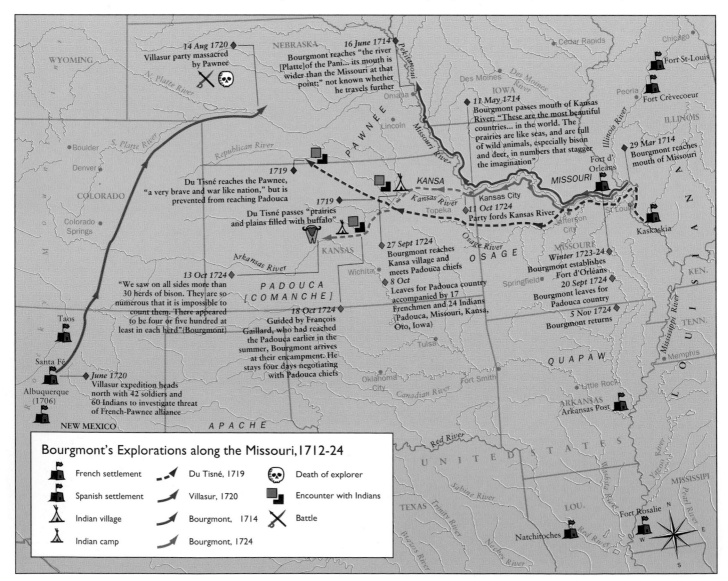

**Bourgmont's Explorations along the Missouri, 1712-24**

| | | |
|---|---|---|
| French settlement | Du Tisné, 1719 | Death of explorer |
| Spanish settlement | Villasur, 1720 | Encounter with Indians |
| Indian village | Bourgmont, 1714 | Battle |
| Indian camp | Bourgmont, 1724 | |

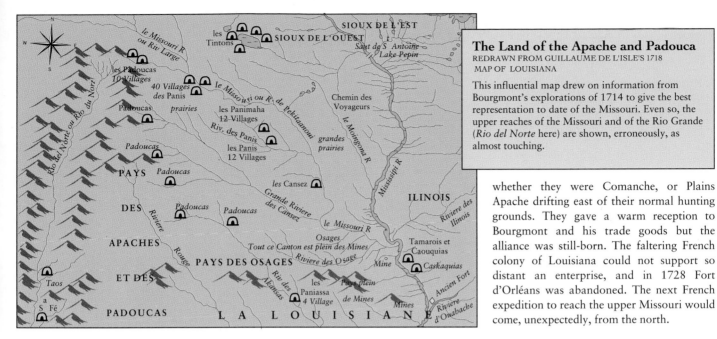

**The Land of the Apache and Padouca**
REDRAWN FROM GUILLAUME DE L'ISLE'S 1718
MAP OF LOUISIANA

This influential map drew on information from Bourgmont's explorations of 1714 to give the best representation to date of the Missouri. Even so, the upper reaches of the Missouri and of the Rio Grande (*Rio del Norte* here) are shown, erroneously, as almost touching.

whether they were Comanche, or Plains Apache drifting east of their normal hunting grounds. They gave a warm reception to Bourgmont and his trade goods but the alliance was still-born. The faltering French colony of Louisiana could not support so distant an enterprise, and in 1728 Fort d'Orléans was abandoned. The next French expedition to reach the upper Missouri would come, unexpectedly, from the north.

officers, tried to follow Bourgmont's steps with a treaty-making expedition. From the French post at Kaskaskia he entered Osage territory and, with difficulty, Pawnee country, but he, also, was prevented from reaching the Padouca. Exaggerated reports of du Tisné's exploits reached the Spanish authorities, who were already worried that Plains Indians on New Mexico's eastern borders would obtain guns. By this time most southern Plains Indians had acquired horses, originally traded or stolen from Spanish ranches in New Mexico. This had already increased their mobility and the range of their buffalo hunts and war parties. If they were to acquire guns this would give them a formidable increase in firepower.

The Spaniards were further alarmed by the prospect of a French-Pawnee alliance. In 1720 they sent Don Pedro de Villasur north to investigate, with nearly a hundred soldiers and Indians. The expedition reached the Platte River, where it was attacked by Pawnee. Most of the party was massacred.

Since both the French and Spanish persistently underestimated the distance between

them, Indian reports of strange white men in the interior kept nerves on edge in both Louisiana and Mexico. In response to the Villasur expedition the French entrusted Bourgmont with a mission to find the mysterious Padouca. In doing so Bourgmont might open up a way to the silver mines, and beyond them, the *Mer de l'Ouest*.

Bearing the grand title of "Commandant of the Missouri River," Bourgmont established Fort d'Orléans on the north bank of the Missouri. In 1724 he left on his best-known exploring venture. With a few Frenchmen, his young mixed-blood son and large numbers of Indians, he journeyed westward. In October he finally reached the Padouca, in an encampment on the prairies east of the Big Bend of the Arkansas. Scholars are divided as to

*Below: Kansa on the move. Bourgmont wrote that women and dogs carried skins for shelters and other utensils in bundles weighing 300 lbs. This engraving is from* Histoire de la Louisiane *by Le Page du Pratz, who described how Bourgmont traveled through the territory of these "naturels du nord" on his 1724 mission to make peace with the Padouca. Settled in Natchez, du Pratz later lived amongst Natchez Indians and described the tragic deportation by the French of a tribe he saw as most civilized.*

> I t is true that we go to the home of the Spaniards, but they trade to us only some horses, a few knives, and some inferior axes; they do not trade in fusils, or lead, or gunpowder, or kettles, or blankets, or any of the goods that the great French chief has given us. Thus, the French are our true friends.
>
> Speech of the Padouca chief to Bourgmont, October 1724

# The Land of the Mandan

## THE EXPLORATIONS OF THE VÉRENDRYES, 1738-43

*La Vérendrye was the last great French explorer of North America. He and his sons reveal the geography of an immense area stretching from the Saskatchewan to the Missouri.*

"After sailing up the Missouri as far as it is navigable," the Jesuit geographer and traveler Father Charlevoix had written, "you come to a great river which runs westward and discharges into the sea." There were also numerous Indian reports which told of a light-skinned, bearded people of advanced civilization, called "Mantannes," who lived on the banks of "a great river which flowed west."

These reports prompted Sieur de La

> On the morning of the 28th we arrived at the place indicated as a rendezvous for the Mandan, who arrived in the evening, one chief with thirty men and four Assiniboin... I confess I was greatly surprised, as I expected to see people quite different from the other savages according to the stories that had been told us. They did not differ from the Assiniboin, being naked except for a garment of buffalo skin carelessly worn without any breechcloth. I knew then that there was a large discount to be taken off all that had been told me.
>
> La Vérendrye reaches the Mandan, November 1738

### Fact and Fantasy
REDRAWN FROM PHILIPPE BUACHE'S 1754 MAP

Buache's map intended to show the "discoveries of French officers to the west of Lake Superior." La Vérendrye's explorations are set in the context of the theoretical geography of the period: the 1738 route to the Mandan or the "Ouachipouanes," for example, is shown ending on a River of the West, which flows into a gigantic Sea of the West (▶ page 42).

Vérendrye's expedition of 1738. A French fur trader from Canada, he had outflanked the troublesome Sioux with a chain of posts from Lake Superior to Fort La Reine on the Assiniboine River (▶ page 104); now he was in a position to expand his trading empire south westward.

In October they left the woods, waters and their bark canoes, striking across the prairies on foot. They followed Indian trails and were accompanied by Assiniboin, plains Indians who hunted buffalo for the expedition as it marched southwest. Early in December they reached the first Mandan village, 150 cabins surrounded by fortifications. The inhabitants were neat, industrious, well-provided, and if lighter-skinned than most, unmistakably Indian. Other Mandan villages lay further along the banks of a wide, muddy river flowing southwest – a local, reverse twist of the Missouri. Here La Vérendrye left two of his men. The following summer they would meet Indians from further west who not only had horses but also oddments of Spanish manufacture. In 1741 La Vérendrye's eldest son, Pierre, brought back two horses from the Mandan villages to Fort La Reine.

In 1742 La Vérendrye sent two of his sons, Louis-Joseph (the

*Above: La Vérendrye's sons buried this lead plate at an Indian village on the Missouri River, nearby present-day Pierre, South Dakota. It was not discovered until 1913. Stamped on the front is a formal act of possession on behalf of the French crown. On the back, the Vérendryes scratched their own message: "Deposited by the Chevalier and de La Vérendrye witnesses – St. Louy de Londette A. Miotte, the 30th March 1743."*

Chevalier) and François, on a renewed search for the western sea. They reached the Mandan villages again, crossed the Missouri and traveled with "Bow" Indians across the Badlands of North Dakota. Their precise journey is unknown but early in 1743 their apprehensive Indian companions forced them to turn back from the mountains – probably the Black Hills of Dakota – from whose summit they hoped to see the sea. In reality they were not only more than a thousand miles from the Pacific, but in between lay the massive barrier of the Rocky Mountains.

Some of the information the Vérendryes received from Indians was either fanciful to begin with, or seriously misinterpreted by the explorers, but it provided glimpses of Spaniards in distant New Mexico or Frenchmen in Illinois. They now knew about the Mandan, although the plains Indians remained mysterious. Contemporary French maps hint that La Vérendrye had come close to both the western sea and the River of the West, but in reality he found neither. His sons revealed that the river of the Mandan flowed southeast, and that it must be the Missouri. But the link between the northern and southern approaches to the upper Missouri had still not been made.

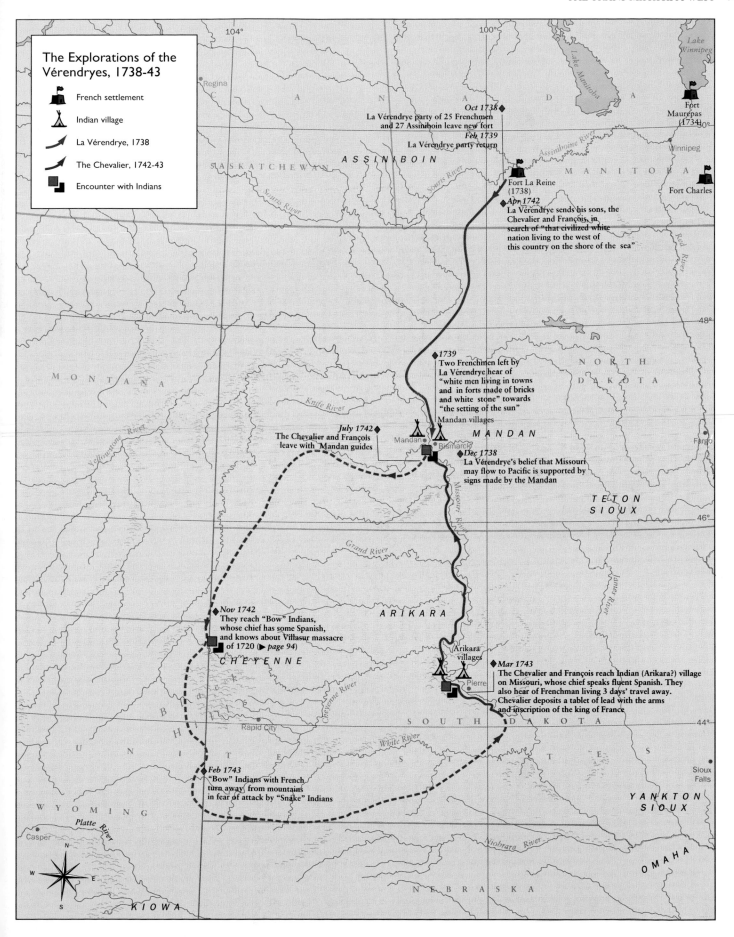

## The Explorations of the Vérendryes, 1738-43

- French settlement
- Indian village
- La Vérendrye, 1738
- The Chevalier, 1742-43
- Encounter with Indians

Fort Maurepas (1734)

Lake Winnipeg

Winnipeg

*Oct 1738*
La Vérendrye party of 25 Frenchmen and 27 Assiniboin leave new fort
*Feb 1739*
La Vérendrye party return

Fort La Reine (1738)

Fort Charles

*Apr 1742*
La Vérendrye sends his sons, the Chevalier and François, in search of "that civilized white nation living to the west of this country on the shore of the sea"

*1739*
Two Frenchmen left by La Vérendrye hear of "white men living in towns and in forts made of bricks and white stone" towards "the setting of the sun"
Mandan villages

NORTH DAKOTA

Fargo

*July 1742*
The Chevalier and François leave with Mandan guides

Mandan   Bismarck

*Dec 1738*
La Vérendrye's belief that Missouri may flow to Pacific is supported by signs made by the Mandan

MANDAN

TETON SIOUX

*Nov 1742*
They reach "Bow" Indians, whose chief has some Spanish, and knows about Villasur massacre of 1720 (▶ page 94)

ARIKARA

CHEYENNE

Rapid City

*Mar 1743*
The Chevalier and François reach Indian (Arikara?) village on Missouri, whose chief speaks fluent Spanish. They also hear of Frenchman living 3 days' travel away. Chevalier deposits a tablet of lead with the arms and inscription of the king of France

Arikara villages   Pierre

*Feb 1743*
"Bow" Indians with French turn away from mountains in fear of attack by "Snake" Indians

SOUTH DAKOTA

Sioux Falls

WYOMING

Platte River

Casper

YANKTON SIOUX

Niobrara River

NEBRASKA

OMAHA

KIOWA

MONTANA

SASKATCHEWAN

ASSINIBOIN

CANADA

MANITOBA

Regina

Souris River

Knife River

Yellowstone River

Grand River

Cheyenne River

White River

Missouri River

Assiniboine River

Souris River

Red River

James River

Lake Manitoba

# To Santa Fé from the East

## THE EXPLORATIONS OF PIERRE AND PAUL MALLET, 1739-40

*In their quest for trade with the silver-rich provinces of New Spain, the Mallet brothers are the first French traders to reach the frontier town of Santa Fé from the east.*

Throughout the 18th century the French hoped to find a practicable route between the Mississippi valley and New Mexico which would lead them to Spain's rich sources of silver. Initially it was French traders from Illinois and Louisiana who were most active in their attempts to reach New Spain for trade and possibly conquest.

The French were mistaken, however, for the silver provinces of northern Mexico – New Galicia, New Vizcaya and New León – did not stretch up the Rio Grande as far as New Mexico and Santa Fé. It was a triumph of illusion over reality that a sleepy little town of adobe huts should take on the semblance of an El Dorado.

In 1739 the first French trading party, nine Canadians led by Pierre and Paul Mallet, arrived in Santa Fé from New Orleans. They had successfully crossed what was thought to be unpassable wilderness inhabited by hostile Jumano, Apache and Comanche. Their circuitous route had been based on another common misconception of the French, that the best way to New Mexico lay along the Missouri River. When the Mallet brothers were at their furthest point north on the Missouri, Pawnee Indians advised them to cut back southwest. They therefore crossed the Platte and Arkansas Rivers to reach Taos and Santa Fé. For their return, the expedition was able to take a more direct route. They crossed the head of the Pecos Valley to a river, from now on to be called the Canadian, which brought them to the more familiar reaches of the Arkansas.

> Santa Fé is a town built of wood and without any fortification. There are about 800 Spanish and mulatto families there, and in the surrounding area are a number of villages of settled Indians, each with a Padre running the mission. There are only eighty soldiers in the garrison, poorly trained and badly armed. And there are other soldiers in this province, in the pay of the king of Spain, who transport silver every year to Old Mexico by caravan.
>
> The Mallet brothers' report on Santa Fé, 1739

The French traders had received a friendly reception at Santa Fé. Although trade with foreigners was officially prohibited, Santa Fé's frontier position meant that few goods ever reached there and those that did were expensive after the long trail from Mexico. Unfortunately, the Mallets' expedition had lost its trade goods as they crossed the Saline River.

In the years after the Mallets' journey the Jumano and Comanche made peace and the route became slightly less dangerous. A trickle of Frenchmen managed to make their way through to Santa Fé. In 1741 Pierre and Paul Mallet were part of a more official but less successful expedition from New Orleans, led by Fabry de la Bruyère. They had set out to open trade links between Louisiana and Santa Fé and followed the more direct route used by the Mallets on their return in 1740. However the expedition failed to reach Santa Fé because of Bruyère's bumbling leadership and low water on the Canadian River.

In the following years various Frenchmen, including Pierre Mallet, made successful journeys to Santa Fé. But most were individual, haphazard ventures which achieved little except to put the Spanish authorities on the alert. Even these ceased as to the east French forces became involved in the great war with Britain which had begun in 1754. The peace between France and Britain, in 1763, was to change the whole power balance in the North American continent. France lost Canada to Britain, and also gave up to Spain its Louisiana territory west of the Mississippi.

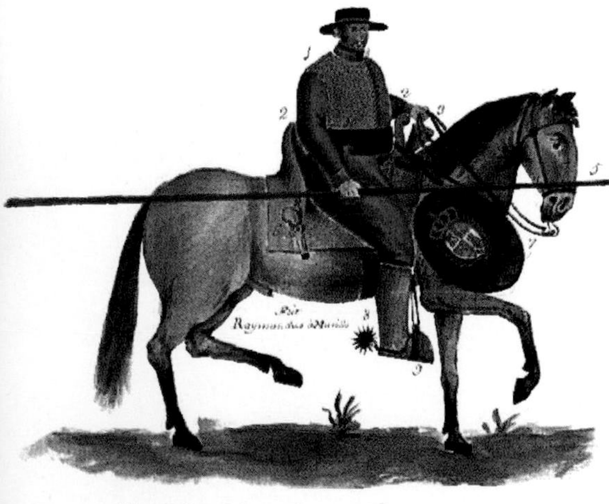

*Above: Spanish cavalry men fighting Indians and intruders on the northern frontier were known as "leatherjackets." Though lances were still prefered to pistols for horse combat, this one carries both. He was painted by a fellow leatherjacket, Ramón de Murillo, to show his commanders how different frontier soldiers were.*

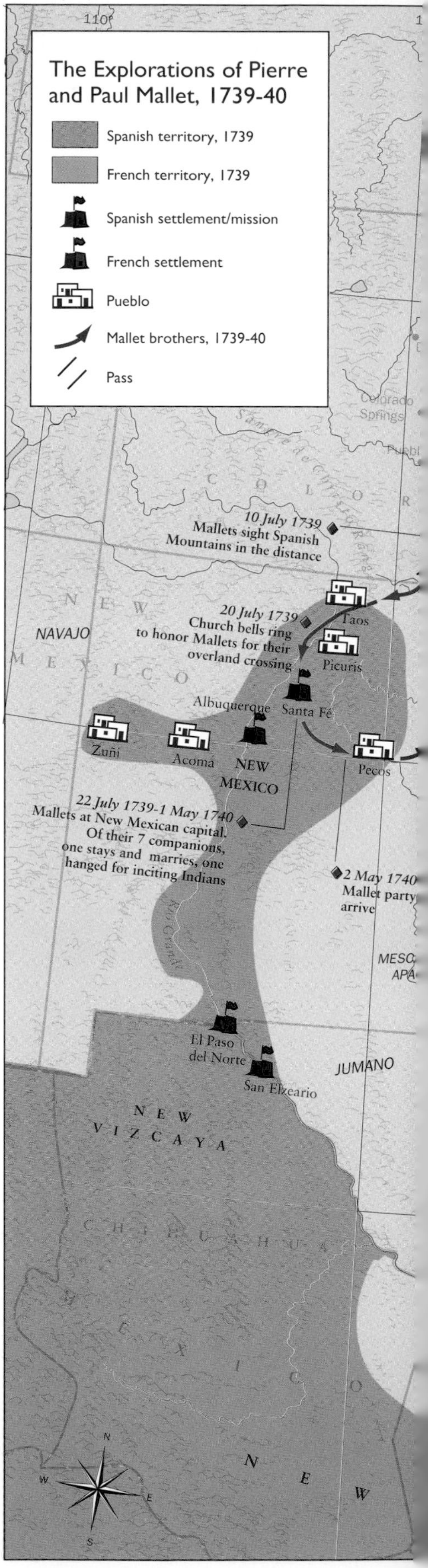
The Explorations of Pierre and Paul Mallet, 1739-40
Spanish territory, 1739
French territory, 1739
Spanish settlement/mission
French settlement
Pueblo
Mallet brothers, 1739-40
Pass
110°
Colorado Springs
C O L O R
10 July 1739 Mallets sight Spanish Mountains in the distance
N E W M E X I C O
NAVAJO
20 July 1739 Church bells ring to honor Mallets for their overland crossing
Taos
Picuris
Albuquerque
Santa Fé
Zuñi
Acoma
NEW MEXICO
Pecos
22 July 1739-1 May 1740 Mallets at New Mexican capital. Of their 7 companions, one stays and marries, one hanged for inciting Indians
2 May 1740 Mallet party arrive
Rio Grande
El Paso del Norte
San Elzeario
JUMANO
N E W V I Z C A Y A
C H I H U A H U A
N E W

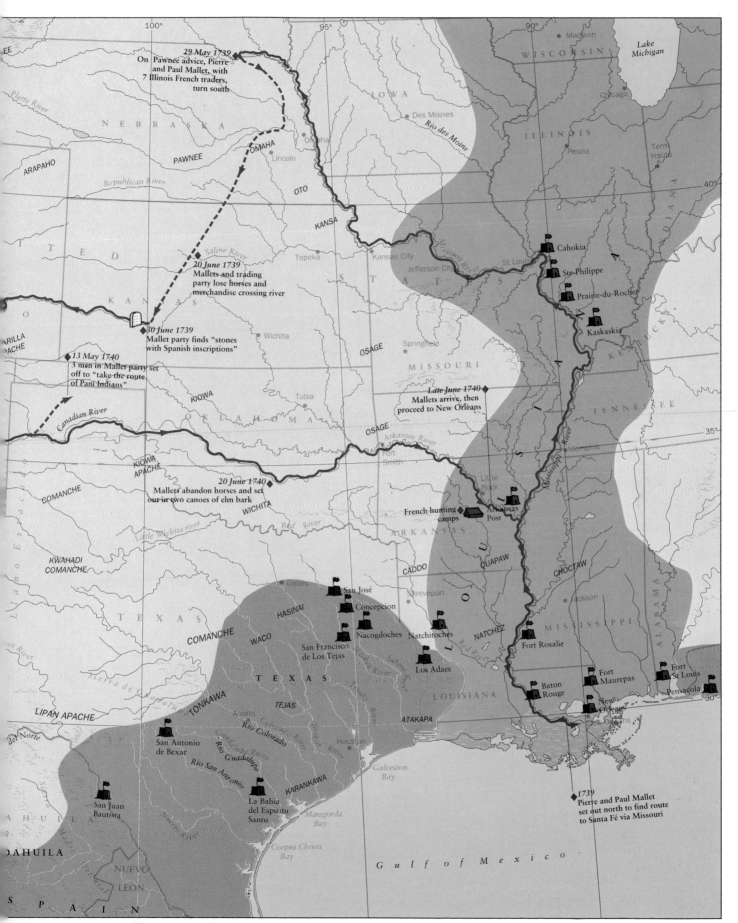

**29 May 1739**
On Pawnee advice, Pierre and Paul Mallet, with 7 Illinois French traders, turn south

**20 June 1739**
Mallets and trading party lose horses and merchandise crossing river

**30 June 1739**
Mallet party finds "stones with Spanish inscriptions"

**13 May 1740**
3 men in Mallet party set off to "take the route of Pani Indians"

**20 June 1740**
Mallets abandon horses and set out in two canoes of elm bark

French hunting camps

**Late June 1740**
Mallets arrive, then proceed to New Orleans

**1739**
Pierre and Paul Mallet set out north to find route to Santa Fé via Missouri

# Part IV : Ocean to Ocean

Between the northernmost point reached by Spanish ships coasting up from Mexico, and the easternmost fringe of the Russian empire, lay the longest unexplored coast in the world. During the eighteenth century, Spanish, Russian, and British ships edged their way along this broken and convoluted 5000-mile coastline, while Canadian fur traders struck out boldly across the middle of a continent that proved vaster than they had ever imagined.

By 1800, the outlines of North America had at last been established. It fell to a new century, and a new republic, to explore the interior. United States soldiers and scientists, trappers and traders, emigrants and entrepreneurs, as well as a host of map-makers, artists and photographers, pushed west across the Rockies to the Pacific, unveiling the mysteries of the Western interior.

In the eastern and southern parts of North America, exploration was steady rather than dramatic throughout the 18th century. But far away to the north and west explorers were making journeys of continental proportions. Their travels were closely associated with the demands of the fur trade, and with the continuing hope that a way might be found to the western ocean. In quest of such a route, British ships probed the ice-bound shores of Hudson Bay for an entrance to a Northwest Passage, and French canoes pushed along the river routes west of their trading empire on the St Lawrence and the Great Lakes. Indian reports of great waters just over the western horizon lured the explorers on, but they found instead the vastness of the northern plains. By the 1770s Hearne had reached the northern edge of the continent as he crossed overland from Hudson Bay to the Arctic Ocean. It was the western – or Pacific – ocean, not Hearne's polar sea, that was the objective of most explorers, but unknown to them the way was blocked by the barrier of the Rocky Mountains.

For all their flamboyant enterprise, the explorers of the north were as blind about the location of the Pacific as Cartier had been more than two centuries earlier. At the beginning of the 16th century, no European knew which direction the west coast followed, north of California. Many believed that California was an island until Kino established its connection with the mainland at the turn of the 18th century.

The Spanish made no further movement to the north until the 1760s. When they did, it was in reaction to the activities of the Russian explorers and traders who followed the tracks of Bering to the Alaskan coast. Slowly the Spaniards and Russians groped their way towards each other along the labyrinthine inlets of the northwest coast. But in the end it was an Englishman, James Cook, who closed the gap between them. In the last decades of the century, seaborne expeditions traced the outline of the mainland coast from Oregon to Alaska, penetrating beyond the screen of outlying islands.

It was in these same years that the first overland explorer arrived on the northwest coast. The outriders of the Canadian fur trade had reached Lake Athabasca in the 1770s, and Great Slave Lake in the 1780s. Then, after a false start which took him first to the Arctic Ocean, Mackenzie crossed the Rockies in 1793 to reach the Pacific "from Canada, by land."

To the south, the newly-independent United States saw its future in the vast territories that lay to the west. In the spring of 1803, President Thomas Jefferson bought Louisiana – a great tract of largely unexplored territory west of the Mississippi – from the French for 15 million dollars.

To Jefferson's opponents, the Louisiana Purchase was the "wildest chimera of a moonstruck brain." Published maps of the day displayed an almost total ignorance of the West. Leading mapmakers seemed scarcely aware of the existence of the Rockies. Americans circulated incredible tales about what these lands might hold. The President himself believed that mastodons might wander the western plains. Others told stories of gem-like "shining mountains," unicorns, giant water serpents, beavers seven feet tall, a mountain of salt, cliffs of flawless gems, silver nuggets the size of bricks.

Yet this was probably the most inspired coup of Jefferson's presidency. The following year, Lewis and Clark set off up the Missouri, over the Rockies and down the Columbia to the Pacific. It was to be the first of many military scientific expeditions that opened the West to settlement during the 19th century. Trappers and traders also played their part: John Jacob Astor's Pacific Fur Company found the South Pass through the Rockies, and trappers streamed into the Green River valley.

To the southwest, American expansion led to conflict with Spain's ailing empire and then to war with its successor, the Mexican republic. While mountain men Jedediah Smith, Tom Fitzpatrick and Joseph R. Walker, as well as Captain John C. Frémont, pioneered emigrant routes, the US Army's Corps of Topographical Engineers painstakingly recorded the dramatic terrain. As railroads took the place of wagon trains, survey teams scoured the Rockies for passes. They described, drew and photographed the landscape in meticulous detail. A new era of scientific exploration had begun.

# "Yellow Mettle" and the Strait of Anian

## THE TRAGIC VOYAGE OF JAMES KNIGHT, 1719

*The prospect of gold and a passage to the
West leads the veteran fur trader James
Knight and his expedition to an icy death in
Hudson Bay.*

The long bout of Anglo-French hostilities, which had begun in 1689, came to an end in 1713 with the Treaty of Utrecht. Hudson Bay and its fur-trading posts were thus restored to the English Hudson's Bay Company. In 1714 James Knight, a veteran trader who had been made the first post-war governor in the Bay arrived at Fort York. According to Knight's journals, kept over four years, he hoped not only to expand trade but also to discover a land of treasure somewhere to the northwest. The "Northern" or Chipewyan Indians, lived in that direction, fearful of the Bay area Cree and their firearms, but a potential source of information and furs.

In 1715, to make peace between the Indians and to explore the country, Knight sent William Stuart inland with a band of Cree and with a Chipewyan woman slave as their guide. Stuart was away almost a year, dependent on the Indians for survival and equipped only with a compass. He brought back ten more Chipewyan to York and a confused report which claimed he had traveled 1000 miles to latitude 67°N. This claim was exaggerated, but Stuart was the first white man to travel onto the Barrens and he probably reached the area between Lake Athabasca and Great Slave Lake.

Back at York, Knight eagerly questioned the Chipewyan who told him about "Ships in the Western Seas," rivers and straits, deposits of copper and "a Yellow Mettle" which Knight believed to be gold. He persuaded the Indians "to lay down there Rivers along Shore to the Norward they chalked 17 Rivers some of them very Large." With this information he drew up a map and convinced himself that the 17th river was the Northwest Passage.

In 1717 Knight established a new post

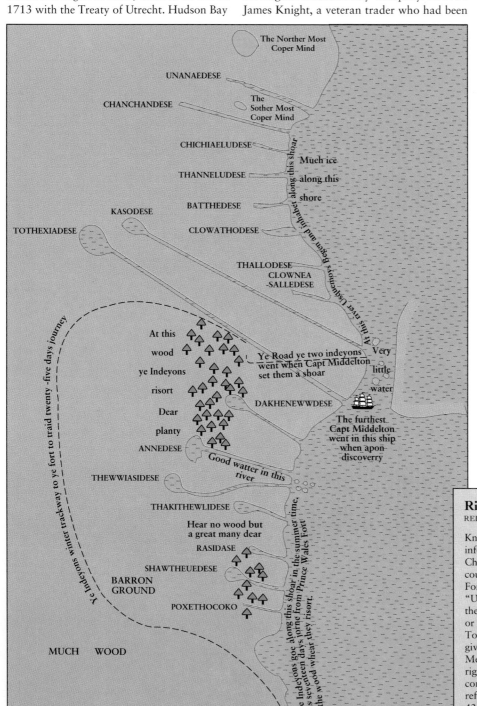

### Rivers of the North
REDRAWN FROM A MAP BY JAMES KNIGHT, *c.*1716

Knight based this map on sketches and information brought to him at Fort York by Chipewyan Indians. The map shows the country north of Churchill (Prince of Wales Fort); the division between Indians and "Usquemay" (Eskimo or Inuit) territory; and the rivers as far as the Coppermine (the 16th or "Chanchandese") River.
To modern eyes its main deficiencies are that it gives no indication of the great bulges of the Melville and Boothia peninsulas, nor of the right-angled westward turn the coast makes to come round to the Coppermine River. The references to Middleton's expedition of 1741-42 (▶ *page 106*) are later additions.

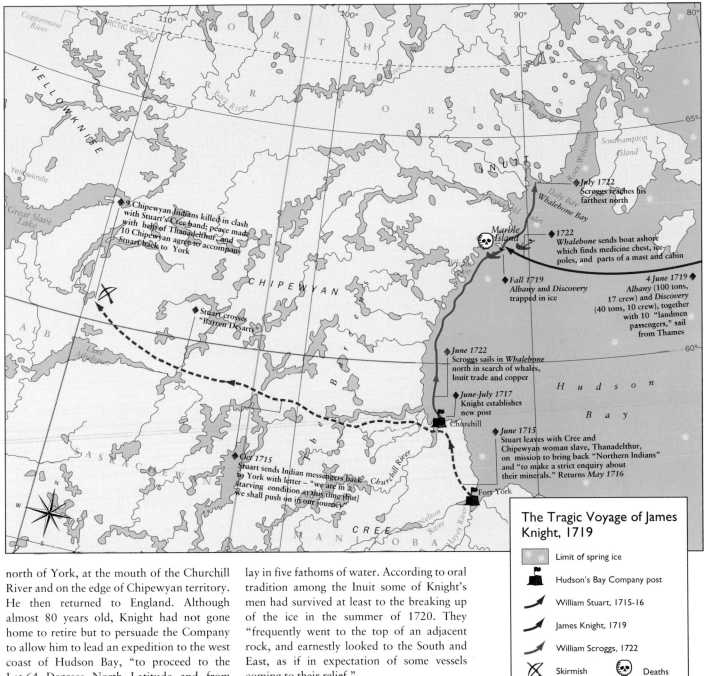

## The Tragic Voyage of James Knight, 1719

Stuart crosses "Barren Desarts"

9 Chipewyan Indians killed in clash with Stuart's Cree band; peace made with help of Thanadelthur, and 10 Chipewyan agree to accompany Stuart back to York

*July 1722* Scroggs reaches his farthest north

*1722 Whalebone* sends boat ashore which finds medicine chest, ice-poles, and parts of a mast and cabin

*Fall 1719 Albany* and *Discovery* trapped in ice

*4 June 1719 Albany* (100 tons, 17 crew) and *Discovery* (40 tons, 10 crew), together with 10 "landmen passengers," sail from Thames

*June 1722* Scroggs sails in *Whalebone* north in search of whales, Inuit trade and copper

*June–July 1717* Knight establishes new post

*June 1715* Stuart leaves with Cree and Chipewyan woman slave, Thanadelthur, on mission to bring back "Northern Indians" and "to make a strict enquiry about their minerals." Returns *May 1716*

*Oct 1715* Stuart sends Indian messengers back to York with letter – "we are in a starving condition at this time [but] we shall push on in our journey."

| | |
|---|---|
| ❄ | Limit of spring ice |
| 🏭 | Hudson's Bay Company post |
| ➤ | William Stuart, 1715–16 |
| ➤ | James Knight, 1719 |
| ➤ | William Scroggs, 1722 |
| ✕ | Skirmish |
| ☠ | Deaths |

north of York, at the mouth of the Churchill River and on the edge of Chipewyan territory. He then returned to England. Although almost 80 years old, Knight had not gone home to retire but to persuade the Company to allow him to lead an expedition to the west coast of Hudson Bay, "to proceed to the Lat.64 Degrees North Latitude and from thence Northward to find out the Streights of Anian." This expedition became one of the tragedies of Arctic exploration. Knight's two ships, *Albany* and *Discovery*, sailed in 1719 but were trapped during the fall in a small harbor at Marble Island. In that desolate spot where, a later explorer wrote, "the winds of almost perpetual winter blow in pitiless and withering blasts," every member of the expedition died.

Three years later a Company sloop off Marble Island found local Inuit with debris from the ships. Almost half a century later Company whalers came across ruins and graves near where the hulks of Knight's ships

lay in five fathoms of water. According to oral tradition among the Inuit some of Knight's men had survived at least to the breaking up of the ice in the summer of 1720. They "frequently went to the top of an adjacent rock, and earnestly looked to the South and East, as if in expectation of some vessels coming to their relief."

### The Strait of Anian
REDRAWN FROM A SECTION OF J.B. NOLIN'S
*GLOBE TERRESTRE*, 1708

The mythical Strait of Anian, leading from Hudson Bay to the Pacific, obsessed European explorers and cartographers in the 18th century. Reports Knight received from Chipewyans at Fort York in 1716 led him to believe "there may be a Passage or Straits that parts America from Asia..."

He also heard of Indians to the west who had "a Yellow Mettle," and "every Summer see Sevl Ships in the Western Seas wch I cannot think to be Spaniards... I rather take them to be Tartars or Jappannees Vessels."

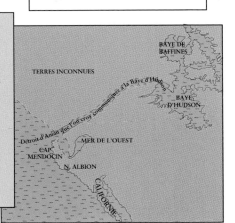

# The Search for the River of the West

## FRENCH EXPLORATIONS FROM LAKE SUPERIOR TO THE SASKATCHEWAN, 1731-53

*La Vérendrye presses far into the west and builds up the rich French fur trade of the Lower Saskatchewan River. The myth of a great inland sea is slowly demolished.*

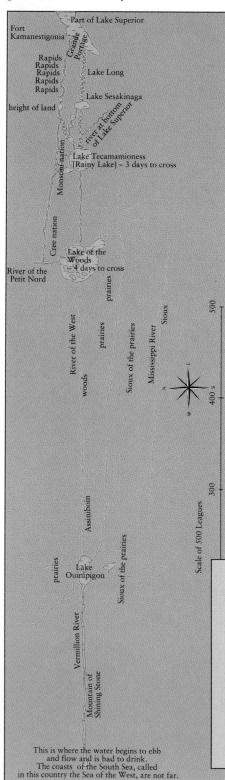

After the Treaty of Utrecht of 1713, French fur traders were denied access to the sea-route of Hudson Bay. They once more turned to westward expansion along the canoe-trails beyond Lake Superior, establishing new posts and reviving old ones. In 1717 these included Kaministiquia, linking the fur trade of the west with the 1000-mile route back to Montréal. Pierre Gaultier de Varennes, de La Vérendrye, took command of these *postes du nords* in 1728. Like his predecessors, La Vérendrye was as much trader as explorer. Beyond expansion of the fur trade the French government would do no more than finance his search for a sea and river of the west.

During his first stay at the *postes du nord* the Cree brought La Vérendrye familiar reports: "they had been beyond the height of land and reached a great river which flows straight towards the setting sun, and which widens continually as it descends." La Vérendrye turned to the west. In 1731 he opened a new route to Rainy Lake by way of Grand Portage and Pigeon River. In 1732 he built Fort St Charles, a palisaded depot, at Lake of the Woods. In 1734 his sons established Fort Maurepas where the Red River of the North divided the eastern woodlands of the beaver and marten hunts from the buffalo plains of the west. Finally, in

1738 Fort La Reine was built on the Assiniboine River. It looked out to the plains and, in another direction, across "the road to the English posts" on Hudson Bay.

As the French reached the Winnipeg basin it became clear that many earlier reports about great stretches of water to the west were merely references to the Winnipeg River and Lake Winnipeg. In search of the western sea La Vérendrye then moved southwest towards the Missouri (▶ *page 96*). But he turned back north in 1738-39, disappointed by a journey to the Mandan who told him that the Blanche, or Poskioac, River (later the Saskatchewan) flowed into the western end of Lake Winnipeg.

In 1739-40 La Vérendrye's youngest son, Louis-Joseph the Chevalier, circled Lake Winnipeg and reached the Forks of the Saskatchewan, "a great crossroads of the northern fur trade, the rendezvous every spring of the Crees of the Mountains, Prairies and Rivers to deliberate as to what they shall do, go and trade with the French or with the English." The Cree told him that farther up-river there were mountains, and beyond them water which was undrinkable. But geographers were reluctant to accept that a great mountain range, rather than an inland sea, lay between the French fur traders and the ocean.

*Right: Beaver were the staple of the fur trade. This 1703 illustration shows a variety of methods used by Canadian Indians to hunt beaver with firearms, bow and arrow, nets and traps.*

### Auchagach's Map

REDRAWN FROM AN INDIAN MAP MADE FOR LA VÉRENDRYE, 1728-29

La Vérendrye's map was drawn from sketches made by the Cree Indian Auchagach and others. It shows the two main canoe routes west from Lake Superior, and a River of the West flowing across the prairies, past the mountain of shining stone, and on towards the western ocean. Modern scholars have suggested that if Lake Winnipeg (at this time still unknown to Europeans) is swiveled approximately 90° to its correct north-south orientation, the River of the West will flow from its northern end, and follow roughly the course of the Nelson River towards Hudson Bay.

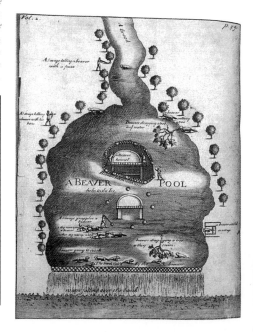

It was along the Saskatchewan River that La Vérendrye intended to make his final journey, but in 1749 he died. De Niverville attempted the journey two years later and claimed to have traveled 1000 miles upriver from Le Pas to the "Montagnes des Roches"(Rocky Mountains), where he established Fort La Jonquière. There is no hard evidence for such a claim.

Under La Vérendrye the French worked out the relationship between the Great Lakes Winnipeg, Manitoba and Winnipegosis. It was under La Vérendrye, too, that they controlled the rich fur trade of the Lower Saskatchewan. After they built Fort La Corne near the Forks, in 1753, French dominance of the interior routes seemed complete.

It was the Chevalier de La Vérendrye who first discovered it [the Saskatchewan] and who ascended it as far as the fork... It was there that he was in the spring [1740] at the meeting of all the Cree, and where he enquired minutely, according to his father's orders, where the source of this great river was. They all replied with one voice that it came from very far, from a height of land where there were very high mountains; that they knew of a great lake on the other side of the mountains, the water of which was not good to drink.

The Chevalier's account of his discoveries of 1739-40

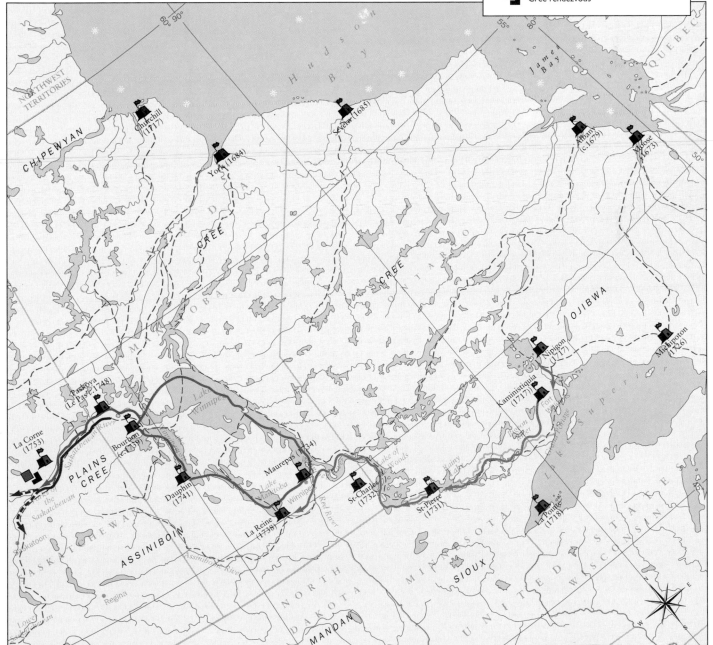

### French Explorations from Lake Superior to the Saskatchewan, 1731-53

- English trading post
- French trading post
- Indian trade route
- Pierre de La Vérendrye and his sons, 1731-38
- Louis-Joseph de La Vérendrye (the Chevalier)1739-40
- Boucher de Niverville, 1751
- Cree rendezvous

# Asleep at the Edge of a Frozen Sea

## THE VOYAGES OF MIDDLETON, MOOR AND COATS, 1741-49

*A renewed search for the Northwest Passage leads to the exploration of the remaining uncharted coasts of Hudson Bay.*

The Hudson's Bay Company had been granted vast territories when it acquired its charter in 1670 (▶ *page 66*). But for the first 70 years of its incorporation, the Company kept to its bayside posts, waiting for Indians to come down from the interior to trade. It made little effort to send out expeditions for either trade or exploration. Nor had the Bay itself been explored to any great extent; as yet no map showed its outline accurately. In the words of Joseph Robson, a former employee, the Hudson's Bay Company had "slept at the edge of a frozen sea."

The awakening was marked by a flurry of activity in the 1740s in which exploration was pursued along the west and east coasts of Hudson Bay. It was also marked by a challenge to the Company's trade monopoly.

The expeditions to the west coast were prompted by a resurgence of hope that that elusive dream, a Northwest Passage, might yet be found. Arthur Dobbs, an Irish Member of Parliament, was fearful that the westward expansion of the French would lead them to reach the Pacific coast before the English, and that they were cutting across the hinterland of some of the Company's most profitable posts at York and Churchill. In 1741 Dobbs persuaded the Admiralty to send a naval expedition out to Hudson Bay, to search for a navigable passage to the Pacific which would outflank the French and open up new trade areas.

Commanded by Christopher Middleton, a former Company captain, this first naval Arctic expedition wintered in the Bay before exploring its west coast in the summer of 1742. Middleton was to sail farther north along the coast than any previous explorer.

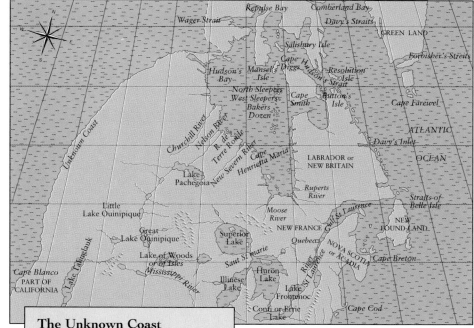

### The Unknown Coast

REDRAWN FROM *A NEW MAP OF PART OF NORTH AMERICA* BY ARTHUR DOBBS, 1741

The map illustrates Dobbs's interpretation of Middleton's voyage, suggesting that three openings in the northwest corner of Hudson Bay led to an "unknown coast" which swung southwest to California. The central area is based on the travels of Joseph de La France, a "French Canadese Indian" trader. A friend of Dobbs described how La France "gave thise Description in my Dineing Room at the Golden fleece in New Bondstreet, when onto the floor we chalkt out this map."

*Below: An engraving of Inuit from* A Voyage to Hudson's Bay *(1748), by Henry Ellis, agent on William Moor's expedition. "These people," Ellis wrote, "are of a middle Size, robust, and inclinable to be fat,... The Mens clothes are of Seal Skins, Deer Skins, and... the skins of Land and Sea Fowl; each of their Coats has a Hood like that of Capuchin... The Women have a Train to their Jackets, that reaches down to their Heels... when they want to lay their Child out of their Arms they slip it into one of their Boots."*

He discovered Wager Bay and sailed up Roes Welcome to Repulse Bay. Although his map included the main features of the west coast, Middleton omitted Chesterfield Inlet, having mistaken it for a deep bay.

Dobbs refused to accept Middleton's findings and in 1746 he organized a private expedition commanded by William Moor. Moor had been first mate with Middleton, both in the Company's service and on the expedition of 1741-42. After wintering near the Company's post at York, in 1747 Moor followed Middleton's track. But apart from entering Chesterfield Inlet he added little to Middleton's surveys. In 1762 the Hudson's Bay Company itself brought this phase of exploration to an end when one of its sloops traced the whole of Chesterfield Inlet.

The Company also carried out less-publicized explorations along the east coast of the Bay, the East Main. Since Hudson's voyage of 1610, later explorers as well as the Company's annual supply ships sailing for James Bay or points farther west kept well clear of the uncharted islands which lay off the East Main coast. What little was known of the coast and interior did not entice them to investigate. But in 1739 Indians told the mas-

ter of Eastmain House that to the north there were three large lakes with plenty of wood, fish and deer visited by Indians and Inuit.

Attracted by the possibility of opening a new trade area, and anxious to determine the truth or otherwise of rumors in England that the difficult route through Hudson Strait could be by-passed by a more southerly route through the middle of the Labrador peninsula, the Company sent two sloops to survey the East Main coast in 1744. The expedition's only discovery of note was Richmond Gulf, possibly the most westerly of the "lakes" described by the Indians. In 1749 the initial survey was followed by a more elaborate expedition. Commanded by one of the Company's senior captains, William Coats, from Cape Digges, it explored south to Little Whale River.

Coats produced detailed but unpublished surveys, of 500 miles of the East Main coast from Cape Digges southward. He also recommended that a trading post should be set up in Richmond Gulf. Richmond House was built in 1750, only to be abandoned in 1759 after its officials failed in their attempts to open trade with the Naskapi Indians and to establish a white whale fishery.

> No ship was ever pester'd with such a set of rogues, most of them having deserved hanging before they entered with me, and not three seamen among the whole number of private men, so that had it not been for the officers, who, every one of them, worked like common men, I should have found no little difficulty to get the ships to England.
>
> Captain Christopher Middleton on the crew of the *Furnace*, August 1742

## Discovery Voyages to Hudson Bay, 1741-49

- Limit of spring ice
- Known to Europeans, 1741
- Hudson's Bay Company post
- Middleton, 1742
- Moor, 1747
- Longland/Mitchell, 1744
- Coats, 1749
- Death of explorer

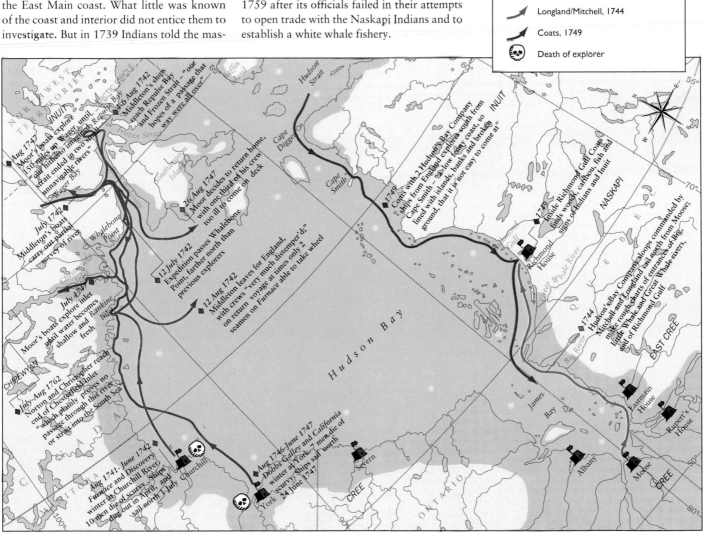

# To the Arctic Ocean

## THE JOURNEY OF SAMUEL HEARNE, 1771-72

*In one of the great journeys of North American exploration, Hearne is guided by Indians to the northernmost edge of the continent.*

In 1762 when Moses Norton became factor at Prince of Wales's Fort, Churchill, he again took up the quest for a river of copper and furs. Since Knight's day (▶ *page 102*) this dream had dominated thinking about the area of country northwest of Hudson Bay. Norton, investigating Chesterfield Inlet by sloop in the summer of 1762, saw that it did not harbor the hoped-for route deep into the interior.

In the same year Norton sent two Northern or Chipewyan Indians, Mattonabbee and Idotliaze, to investigate the far country. In 1767 they returned to Churchill with exciting news. They had found a river which ran between three copper mines and a wooded country rich in furs. They illustrated these dramatic and impressive findings in a map (*opposite*).

Armed with the map, Norton sent Samuel Hearne, mate of one of the sloops at Churchill, on an overland journey in search of "the Far Off Metal River," new fur areas and the Northwest Passage. After two false starts, Hearne, with a band of Chipewyan Indians led by Mattonabbee, pursued his task in 1771-72. They traveled on foot across the Barrens of the northern tundra, "scarcely any thing but one solid mass of rock and stones," Hearne wrote, "in general a total want of soil." The Indians lived on fish and caribou, the streams were usually too shallow for canoes, and the best time for traveling was in winter when the frozen land gave a reasonable surface for snowshoes and sledges.

In July 1771 Hearne reached the Coppermine River. He followed it downstream until he sighted the Arctic Ocean, becoming the first European to see the northern coastline of the American continent. He viewed it "with the assistance of a good pocket telescope. The ice was not then broke up, but was melted away for about three quarters of a mile from the main shore."

The Coppermine River itself was a sad disappointment, shallow and unnavigable, and offering up only a few scattered lumps of copper. Hearne placed its mouth in latitude 71°54'N, almost four degrees too far north. This was a colossal error and a reminder of the lack of training and instruments of many of the Company explorers: Kelsey, Stuart, Henday and now Hearne. Hearne's return track opened up new areas to European gaze, for Mattonabbee's band turned southwest to Great Slave Lake in search of beaver and moose. They finally returned to Churchill after a journey of almost 19 months. Hearne, traveling with his Chipewyan guides, had displayed qualities of perseverance and endurance as he crossed one of the harshest landscapes in North America.

Samuel Hearne's journal, published in 1795, showed him to be an exceptional observer of the Indians and of the wildlife of the Canadian north. His journal also significantly observed that "the Continent of America is much wider than many people imagine... When I was at my greatest Western distance, upward of five hundred miles from Prince of Wales's Fort, the natives, my guides, well knew that many tribes of Indians lay to the West of us, and they knew no end to the land in that direction; nor have I ever met with any Indian, either Northern or Southern, that ever had seen the sea to the Westward."

Hearne's journey shattered any remaining hopes that a passage for shipping might be found through the continent. He had reached its northern shoreline without crossing a strait or even a river of note. If a passage existed, it must lie still farther north, in the polar sea which Hearne had glimpsed from the mouth of the Coppermine River. This was where James Cook (▶ *page 130*) would be sent to renew the search for a passage a few years after Hearne's return.

## Hearne's Route to the Arctic Ocean

REDRAWN FROM SAMUEL HEARNE'S MANUSCRIPT MAP OF 1771

The map shows the country traveled by Hearne and his Chipewyan guides in 1771-72. A dotted line traces Hearne's outward route to the Arctic Ocean; a solid one his track back to Churchill. Hearne's "Arathapescow Lake" was to be the source of much confusion; it is Great Slave Lake which here appears for the first time on a European map, but was thought for some years to be Lake Athabasca, 200 miles to the southeast. The line of trees represents the "wood's edge" – between it and Hudson Bay were the treeless Barrens.

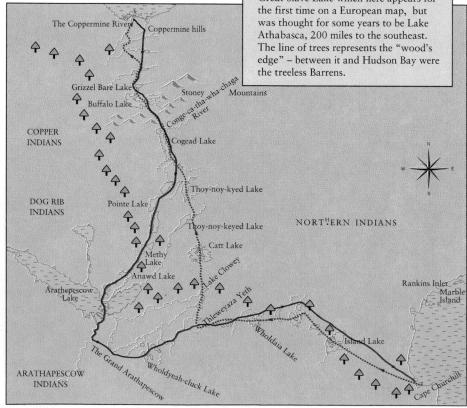

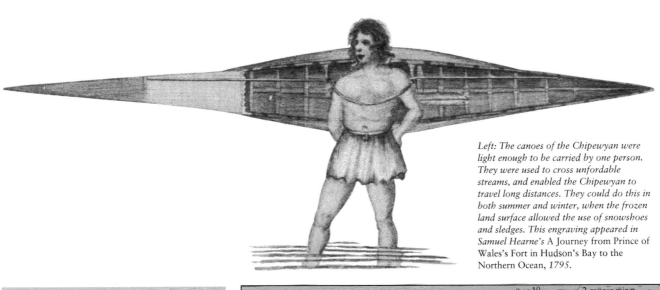

*Left: The canoes of the Chipewyan were light enough to be carried by one person. They were used to cross unfordable streams, and enabled the Chipewyan to travel long distances. They could do this in both summer and winter, when the frozen land surface allowed the use of snowshoes and sledges. This engraving appeared in Samuel Hearne's* A Journey from Prince of Wales's Fort in Hudson's Bay to the Northern Ocean, *1795.*

The Continent of America is much wider than many people imagine...when I was at my greatest Western distance, upward of five hundred miles from Prince of Wales's Fort, the natives, my guides, well knew that many tribes of Indians lay to the West of us, and they knew no end to the land in that direction; nor have I ever met with any Indian, either Northern or Southern, that ever had seen the sea to the Westward.

Samuel Hearne, A Journey from Prince of Wales's Fort, 1795

## Chipewyan Knowledge
REDRAWN FROM A MAP MADE IN 1767 BY MATTONABBEE AND IDOTLIAZE

The original map seems to be a copy made and annotated by Norton in 1767-68 from "A Draught of ye Coast" drawn by Mattonabee and Idotliaze. The version here is based on a redrawing by Professor Richard Ruggles. It shows an immense area of the Canadian Northwest that was totally unknown to Europeans at the time. Its focal point is Great Slave Lake, drawn for the first time in recognizable shape, and its drainage systems.

As with Knight's Chipewyan map (▶ *page 102*), allowances must be made for proportion and direction. The coast was not a feature of great interest to inland Indians and is shown running straight north-south. It lacks the great right-angle turn above Hudson Bay which gives the Arctic coastline its east-west orientation.

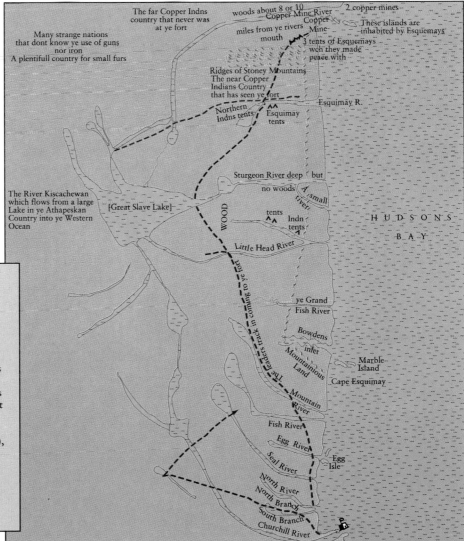

# Inland from Hudson Bay

## FUR TRADERS ON THE CANADIAN PRAIRIES, 1754-74

*Under pressure from Canadian rivals, the explorer-traders of the Hudson's Bay Company journey far into the western interior.*

By 1750 French expansion into the Winnipeg basin and beyond was making a serious dent in the Hudson Bay trade. James Isham, factor at York Fort, the most important bayside post, began a series of efforts to attract the distant "Archithinues" (Blackfoot) of the prairies, who reportedly had "great plenty of the best and finest of furs."

In June 1754 a "bold, enterprizing" laborer and netmaker at York, Anthony Henday, left the post on the first major inland journey since Kelsey's in 1690-92 (▶ *page 68*). He lived and traveled with the Indians, accom-panying the returning Cree along their canoe route from York to the lower Saskatchewan, past "a Hogstye" of a French post at Le Pas. By the end of July Henday was encountering Assiniboin, and in September saw the great buffalo herds of the plains. They were so numerous that Henday's Indians had to "make them sheer out of our way" and when they hunted the buffalo they took only the tongue and other delicacies. In October Henday's Cree band reached the horsed Blackfoot, somewhere south of Red Deer River. The "king" or "great leader" of their impressive camp told Henday that he would not send men to trade at the Bay because his people rode horses rather than paddled canoes, and they lived off the buffalo. Henday and his few remaining Cree companions now drifted farther west and should have been within sight of the Rocky Mountains. But there is no mention of the mountains in the different versions of his journal and the map he made of his journey has disappeared.

Henday revealed that the new French posts were intercepting furs going down to Hudson Bay. But the Seven Years' War brought

*Left: A plan drawing of the Hudson's Bay Company post at Fort York, by its factor James Isham (c.1750). The numbered key to Isham's plan, has unfortunately, been lost. To the top is the Hayes River, on which Indian canoes carry furs to the fort. Andrew Graham, who succeeded Isham, described York as a "handsome, well-built Fort... consisting of four bastions with sheds between them, and a breast work on which are mounted twelve small carriage guns... and on the bank's edge abreast the fort are two fascine batteries...on which are mounted thirteen heavy cannon."*

<blockquote>
We mett the Earchitinue [Blackfoot] men on horse back 40 in number they were out on a Scout from the main body... upon the top of a Hill I seed 200 tents, where they were pitched in 2 Rows, and an opening Right through the middle, and att ye farther End of the Street, their was a Large tent pitcht in front, where all the old Men were seated and their King in the middle, and in the middle of the tent was full of fatt Buffaloes flesh, and after that we had all smoakt round.

From Henday's journal, 14 October 1754
</blockquote>

dramatic changes in North America, and Canada was ceded to Britain in 1763. The French formally relinquished their trading posts, seeming to give the Hudson's Bay Company total control of the northern fur trade.

By the mid-1760s the river routes westward from Montréal were busy again, with French canoemen and interpreters now financed by British businessmen in Canada and also the American colonies. By 1770 the "English pedlars" had reoccupied the former French posts at Le Pas and elsewhere, and the Company's trade declined sharply. Reconnaissance trips from York which covered a great arc from Churchill River to Lake Manitoba, taking Matthew Cocking well beyond the Forks of the Saskatchewan to the Eagle Hills, revealed the extent of the threat. In 1773 the Hudson's Bay Company decided on a far-reaching change of policy, ordering Samuel Hearne to establish an inland post at or near Le Pas. The next year Hearne built Cumberland House at Pine Island Lake, 60 miles beyond Le Pas, and about 700 miles by canoe from York. Though strategically situated at a crossroads of the Indian trade, Cumberland House in isolation could only offer feeble competition to the Canadians, but it was important as a symbol of the Company's new policy. Its establishment marked the beginning of 50 years of strenuous competition which was to take the rival fur traders of Hudson Bay and the St Lawrence to Athabasca, across the Rockies, and finally to the Pacific slopes.

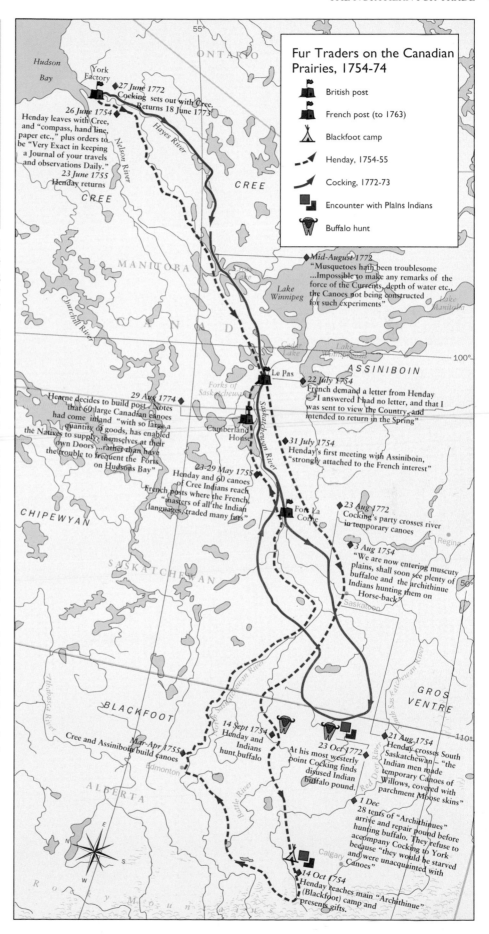

**Fur Traders on the Canadian Prairies, 1754-74**

- British post
- French post (to 1763)
- Blackfoot camp
- Henday, 1754-55
- Cocking, 1772-73
- Encounter with Plains Indians
- Buffalo hunt

*27 June 1772* Cocking sets out with Cree. Returns 18 June 1773.

*26 June 1754* Henday leaves with Cree, and "compass, hand line, paper etc.," plus orders to be "Very Exact in keeping a Journal of your travels and observations Daily."

*23 June 1755* Henday returns

*Mid-August 1772* "Musquetoes hath been troublesome ...Impossible to make any remarks of the force of the Currents, depth of water etc., the Canoes not being constructed for such experiments"

*22 July 1754* French demand a letter from Henday "I answered I had no letter, and that I was sent to view the Country, and intended to return in the Spring"

*29 Aug 1774* Hearne decides to build post. Notes that 60 large Canadian canoes had come inland "with so large a quantity of goods, has enabled the Natives to supply themselves at their own Doors...rather than have the trouble to frequent the Forks on Hudsons Bay"

*31 July 1754* Henday's first meeting with Assiniboin, "strongly attached to the French interest"

*23-29 May 1755* Henday and 60 canoes of Cree Indians reach French posts where the French, "masters of all the Indian languages, traded many furs"

*23 Aug 1772* Cocking's party crosses river in temporary canoes

*3 Aug 1754* "We are now entering muscuty plains, shall soon see plenty of buffaloe and the archithinue Indians hunting them on Horse-back"

*14 Sept 1754* Henday and Indians hunt buffalo

*23 Oct 1772* At his most westerly point Cocking finds disused Indian buffalo pound.

*Mar-Apr 1755* Cree and Assiniboin build canoes

*21 Aug 1754* Henday crosses South Saskatchewan – "the Indian men made temporary Canoes of Willows, covered with parchment Moose skins"

*1 Dec* 28 tents of "Archithinues" arrive and repair pound before hunting buffalo. They refuse to accompany Cocking to York because "they would be starved and were unacquainted with Canoes."

*14 Oct 1754* Henday reaches main "Archithinue" (Blackfoot) camp and presents gifts.

York Factory
Hudson Bay
ONTARIO
Hayes River
Nelson River
Churchill River
CREE
MANITOBA
CANADA
Lake Winnipeg
Lake Manitoba
Cedar Lake
Le Pas
Forks of Saskatchewan
Cumberland House
Saskatchewan River
ASSINIBOIN
Fort La Corne
Regina
Saskatoon
CHIPEWYAN
SASKATCHEWAN
Athabasca River
GROS VENTRE
North Saskatchewan River
South Saskatchewan River
BLACKFOOT
Edmonton
Red Deer River
Battle River
Calgary
ALBERTA
ROCKY MOUNTAINS

# Pond and the Northwesters

## THE EXPANSION OF THE FUR TRADE INTO ATHABASCA, 1778-1787

*Ruthless fur trader and eccentric visionary
Peter Pond reaches and explores the Great
Slave Lake, and revives hopes of finding a
waterway to the Pacific.*

By the time the Hudson's Bay Company had established its first inland post at Cumberland House in 1774 (▶ *page 110*), its Montréal rivals were sweeping past. Led by Thomas and Joseph Frobisher and the American Alexander Henry, they pushed further up the Saskatchewan and moved northwest onto English River. The further these "Pedlars" went, the harder it became for them to bring up supplies by river from Montréal, or even from the halfway station at Michilimackinac. So, to shorten their supply lines, they set up a new base at Grand Portage, at the western end of Lake Superior.

In 1778 one of the most enterprising and combative of them, the New Englander Peter Pond, did not even come down to Grand Portage from the interior. Using supplies still left in the trading areas, he followed the Indian trails to cross the height of land at the 13-mile Methy Portage and reached the Athabasca basin. His journey was a notable, if ill-defined, feat of exploration into what a contemporary described as "a country hitherto unknown but from an Indian report."

It was also a lucrative one: when Pond came out of Athabasca in 1779 he had traded twice as many fine beaver skins as his canoes

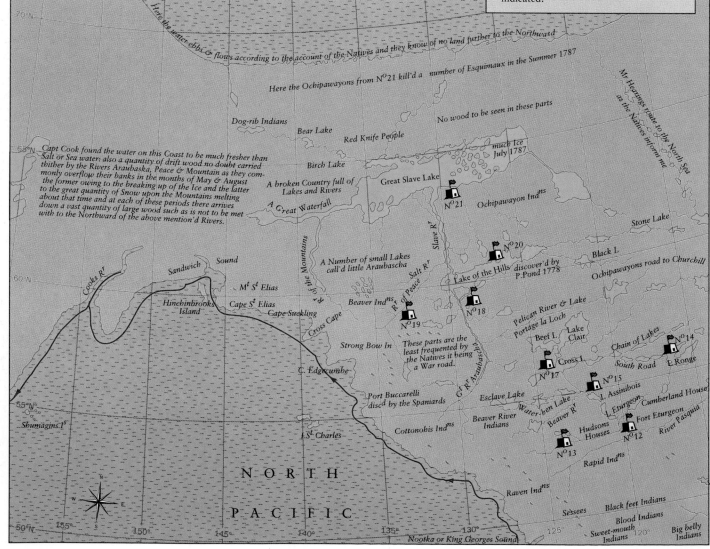

could carry. His revelation of the rich fur country of Athabasca helped the formation in 1779 of a new partnership of Montréal merchants. In 1783 it adopted the name by which it became famous: the North West Company.

Meanwhile, at his post near Lake Athabasca, Pond was collecting information from the Indians about the country to the north and west, of another great lake or sea (the Great Slave Lake), of rivers and mountains. He returned to Montréal in 1784 with a grandiose scheme for a chain of posts stretching to the Pacific coast, recently explored by Cook (▶ *page 130*). He drew up a series of maps and proposals aimed at enlisting support for his plan, but they attracted little interest.

Undeterred, Pond went back to Athabasca in 1785 and organized the establishment of new posts at Great Slave Lake and on the Peace River. The evidence of his maps indicates that he also explored Great Slave Lake. This second spell in Athabasca gave Pond more evidence of possible routes to the Pacific coast which would save the exhausting two-year canoe trip back to the St Lawrence. He claimed that at Great Slave Lake he met Indians who had seen Cook's ships on the coast, and possessed articles which seemed to be of English manufacture. On the strength of these reports, he estimated that he had been "within six days travel of the Grand Pacific Ocean."

In 1787, Pond left the Canadian northwest for good. He devoted the rest of that year to drawing a series of maps intended to illustrate and promote his visionary ideas, sending them off to influential figures such as the governor of Québec and the empress of Russia. The maps show a gigantic Great Slave Lake, with a massive river flowing from its western end towards "Cook's River." The inference is clear: the two rivers were one and the same. Pond had revived the old fantasy of a navigable inlet stretching from the Pacific far into the North American interior (▶ *page 52*). Along this channel, supplies could be brought to the fur traders in Athabasca.

Pond was one of the last of the old explorers, tough in body and mind, but technically unskilled in representing where they had been or what they had seen. A ruthless, obsessive character suspected of killing two rival fur traders, Pond knew the northwest better than any other white man. But as one perceptive observer in Québec put it, Pond's longitudes seemed "to be guesswork and not in any respect accurate enough to be depended upon." Pond's theories were soon put to the test, not by himself as he once hoped, but by his young second-in-command in Athabasca, Alexander Mackenzie.

*This engraving of* A Winter View in the Athapuscow Lake *was based on a drawing by Samuel Hearne (*▶page 108*), and appeared in his* Journey... to the Northern Ocean *(1795). "The point where we crossed" Hearne wrote, "is said to be the narrowest. It is full of islands; most of which are clothed with tall poplars, birch and pines, and are well stocked with Indian deer. On some of the large islands we also found several beaver..."*

That the great Slave Lake is the most northerly large piece of water before you arrive at the Northern Ocean, and that the River which rises from that Lake empties into the Northern Pacific Ocean, and is the River that Cook discovered... another man by the name of McKanzie was left by Pond at Slave Lake with orders to go down the River, and from thence to Unalaska, and so to Kamchtaka, and then to England through Russia.

Report from Quebec on Pond's proposals, November 1789

# From Canada, by Land
## THE JOURNEYS OF ALEXANDER MACKENZIE, 1789 AND 1793

*Traveling in harsh conditions overland*
*Alexander Mackenzie reaches both the Arctic*
*and Pacific oceans.*

In June 1789 Alexander Mackenzie, a young Scot in the service of the North West Company, set out from Fort Chipewyan on Lake Athabasca in an attempt to reach the Pacific coast.

Mackenzie took with him three canoes and was accompanied by five *voyageurs* and five Indians, including Mattonabbee's successor as Chipewyan leader, "the English Chief." By the end of June the expedition reached the river at the western end of Great Slave Lake and found that it flowed west, as Peter Pond had predicted (▶ *page 112*). Disappointment came on 2 July, when they faced high mountains, looming "as far as we could see."

> The immense ridge, or succession of ridges of stony mountains, whose Northern extremity dips in the North [Arctic] Sea, in latitude 70 North, and longitude 135 West, running nearly South-East... to divide the waters of the Atlantic from those which run into the Pacific. In those snow-clad mountains rises the Mississippi, if we admit the Missouri to be its source, which flows into the Gulph of Mexico; the River Nelson, which is lost in Hudson's Bay; Mackenzie's River, that discharges itself into the North Sea; and the Columbia emptying itself into the Pacific Ocean.
>
> Mackenzie's description of the Rocky Mountains, from his *Voyages*, 1801

and found that the river started to bend north, along the barrier of the Rockies. By 12 July Mackenzie had reached the tidal waters of the Arctic Ocean at America's northern coastline and produced a more accurate reading of his location, latitude 67°47'N, than Samuel Hearne had made (▶ *page 108*) 18 years before.

In September Mackenzie was back at Fort Chipewyan after canoeing almost three thousand miles in three months. "My expedition," he noted, "was hardly spoken of but that is what I expected." As with many of his predecessors, Mackenzie's journey was made possible only with the help of Indian guides, interpreters and canoemen. If the comment of a recent scholar that Mackenzie was taken on "a conducted tour" of the river soon to be named after him makes scant acknowledgement of the Scotsman's qualities of willpower and determination, it illustrates an essential truth of these expeditions.

Mackenzie had lacked adequate surveying instruments and skills on his first expedition. He acquired these in England and by the fall of 1792 returned to Fort Chipewyan to investigate a second river the Hare Indians had told him about, which flowed into the sea on the far side of the mountains.

After wintering west of Great Slave Lake, Mackenzie headed up Peace River crammed into a 25ft canoe with six *voyageurs*, two Indians and 3000lbs of goods and provisions. They soon became the first Europeans to reach

the northern Rockies from the east, where men and boat received a terrible battering from the seething waters and jagged rocks of Peace River Canyon. After they crossed the continental divide, a confusing tangle of rivers, mountains and forests almost brought the expedition to a halt. On 4 July 1793 they abandoned their canoe and, with 90lb packs on their backs, struggled towards the ocean on foot. They were on the moist western slopes, where the Indian inhabitants lived mainly on salmon and in large, decoratively-carved wooden dwellings. Passing from one Indian guide to another they reached the Pacific at Dean Channel, less than seven weeks after the arrival of Vancouver's survey boats (▶ *page 132*).

Mackenzie had not found a trade route to the Pacific, but he was the first white man to cross the American continent north of Mexico. He therefore established the true distance between Athabasca and the Pacific. He also confronted the harsh reality of the northern Rockies and while not following it far, he had found a "big river," called by Indians the Tacoutche Tesse (▶ *page 118*), which they said flowed into the sea far to the south. As Mackenzie simply inscribed on a rock on 22 July 1793, he had come "from Canada, by land."

*Below: Cedar-plank houses similar to those seen by Mackenzie on the western slopes of the Rockies. This Nootka village, at Friendly Cove, was painted by John Webber, who accompanied Captain Cook on his 1778 expedition (▶ page 130).*

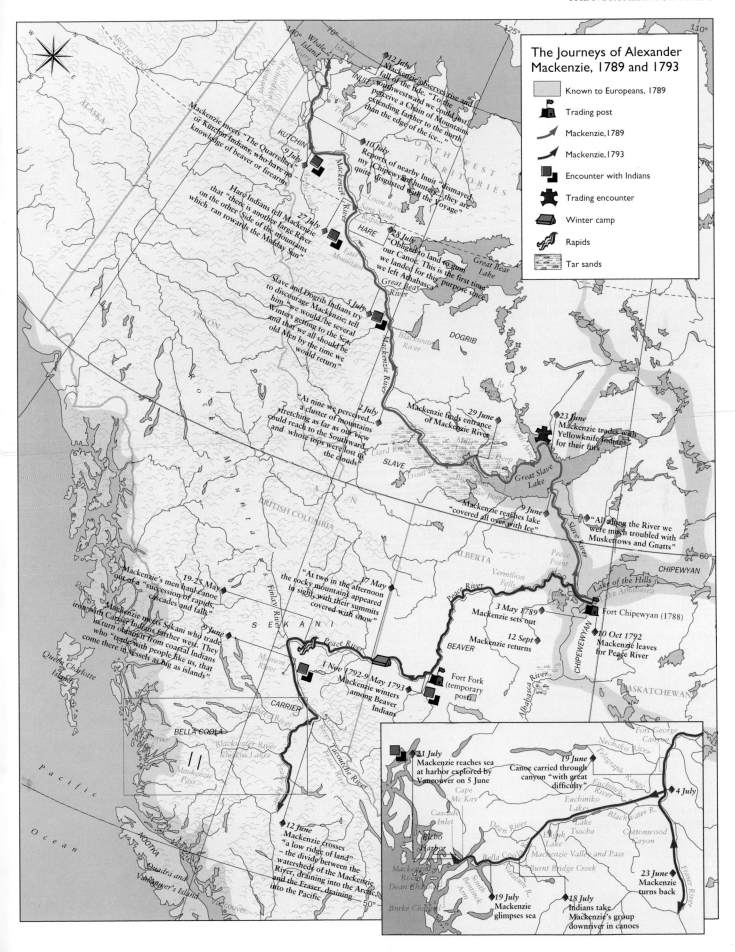

## The Journeys of Alexander Mackenzie, 1789 and 1793

| | |
|---|---|
| | Known to Europeans, 1789 |
| | Trading post |
| | Mackenzie, 1789 |
| | Mackenzie, 1793 |
| | Encounter with Indians |
| | Trading encounter |
| | Winter camp |
| | Rapids |
| | Tar sands |

**12 July**
Mackenzie observes rise and fall of the tide. "To the southwestward we could just perceive a Chain of Mountains extending farther to the north than the edge of the ice..."

**9 July**
Mackenzie meets "The Quarrellers" or Kutchin Indians, who have no knowledge of beaver or firearms

**10 July**
Reports of nearby Inuit "dismayed my Chipewyan hunters; they are quite disgusted with the voyage"

**27 July**
Hare Indians tell Mackenzie that "there is another large River on the other Side of the mountains which ran towards the Midday Sun"

**28 July**
"Obliged to land to gum our Canoe. This is the first time we landed for this purpose since we left Athabasca"

**5 July**
Slave and Dogrib Indians try to discourage Mackenzie; tell him "we would be several Winters getting to the Sea, and that we all should be old Men by the time we would return"

**2 July**
"At nine we perceived... a cluster of mountains stretching as far as our view could reach to the Southward and whose tops were lost in the clouds"

**29 June**
Mackenzie finds entrance of Mackenzie River

**23 June**
Mackenzie trades with Yellowknife Indians for their furs

**9 June**
Mackenzie reaches lake "covered all over with Ice"

"All along the River we were much troubled with Musketows and Gnatts"

**19-25 May**
Mackenzie's men haul canoe out of a "succession of rapids, cascades and falls"

**17 May**
"At two in the afternoon the rocky mountains appeared in sight, with their summits covered with snow"

**9 June**
Mackenzie meets Sekani who trade iron with Carrier Indians farther west. They in turn obtained it from coastal Indians who "trade with people like us, that come there in vessels as big as islands"

**3 May 1789**
Mackenzie sets out

**12 Sept**
Mackenzie returns

**10 Oct 1792**
Mackenzie leaves for Peace River

**Fort Chipewyan (1788)**

**1 Nov 1792–9 May 1793**
Mackenzie winters among Beaver Indians

**Fort Fork (temporary post)**

**12 June**
Mackenzie crosses "a low ridge of land" – the divide between the watersheds of the Mackenzie River, draining into the Arctic, and the Fraser, draining into the Pacific

**21 July**
Mackenzie reaches sea at harbor explored by Vancouver on 5 June

**19 June**
Canoe carried through canyon "with great difficulty"

**4 July**

**23 June**
Mackenzie turns back

**19 July**
Mackenzie glimpses sea

**18 July**
Indians take Mackenzie's group downriver in canoes

# From Hudson Bay to the Rockies

## THE INLAND SURVEYS OF THE HUDSON'S BAY COMPANY, 1778-1812

*In the late 18th century trained surveyors, Philip Turnor, Peter Fidler and David Thompson, map the trade routes of the Canadian West.*

In 1774 the Hudson's Bay Company began to move inland. From Cumberland House, traders slowly moved their operations up the Saskatchewan River until in 1786 the Company appointed William Tomison, chief at Fort York, to reside inland. These activities signaled the beginning of a war of attrition with the North West Company which lasted until they amalgamated in 1821. For the first time the Bay posts were relegated to a subordinate status, and the extension of Company posts deep into the interior can be followed through Tomison's movements as he shifted headquarters steadily upstream on the North Saskatchewan. By 1795 he was at Edmonton House, and four years later Acton House was built on the fringes of the Rocky Mountains.

In expansion of posts, development of more flexible transport systems, and opening up of trade with the Indians of the plains and mountains, the Hudson's Bay Company had advanced far in the generation following its first tentative move inland; but it still lagged behind its rivals. Flamboyant and ruthless, the Northwesters had reached Great Slave Lake, the Peace and Mackenzie rivers and even, momentarily, the Pacific, by the time the Hudson's Bay men established their first post in Athabasca in 1802. But slowness and steadiness had compensations, and the surveyors of the Hudson's Bay Company mapped the inland routes with a thoroughness never approached by the Northwesters.

A new era in the exploration of the north began in 1778 when the Hudson's Bay Company hired Philip Turnor as "their Surveyor for settling the Latitudes, Longitudes, Courses and distances of the different Settlements Inland." For the distant London directors, it was the logical and essential consequence of the Company's shift into the unmapped interior. In the next 15 years Turnor produced detailed surveys of the trade routes, many near Hudson Bay but others as far distant as the Northwesters' run from the Methy Portage into Athabasca. The surveys of Turnor and his colleagues in 1791-92 established the position of Lake Athabasca and Great Slave Lake, and corrected the huge inaccuracies of Pond's longitudes. It was a chance meeting with Turnor in 1790 which

prompted Mackenzie to return to England to acquire the necessary skills (▶ *page 114*). Not the least of Turnor's contributions was the training of younger men, Peter Fidler and David Thompson in particular. In 1794, after his retirement, Turnor incorporated his surveys into a superb general map which formed the basis for Aaron Arrowsmith's *Map Exhibiting all the New Discoveries in the Interior Parts of North America* (1795). In Arrowsmith's words, Turnor and his associates "had laid the permanent foundation of that part of the globe." From Kelsey to Pond, the explorers of the interior until this time had been more notable for their qualities of endurance and courage than for any skill in surveying.

After David Thompson switched allegiance to the North West Company in 1797, Peter Fidler became Turnor's acknowledged successor and outdid his mentor both in years of service and in surveys accomplished. In a career of more than 30 years he traveled 48,000 miles, by canoe, on horseback and on foot, and completed 7,300 miles of surveys. He ranged across vast areas of western Canada, and became more familiar with the prairies and its Indians than any other white man. He was more than a surveyor in a narrow, technical sense, for his journals are a treasure-house of information about the regions he traversed. They include some of the earliest descriptions of the Athabasca tar sands, "great quantities of bitumen a kind of liquid tar oozing out of the banks;" as well as the eastern Rockies, described as "awfully grand... similar to dark rain like clouds rising above the Horizon in a fine summer's evening;" the destruction of the Piegan buffalo hunts, and much else. Fidler's most active period of field work ended in 1812, but by then he had made a massive contribution to the revolutionary new maps by Arrowsmith and others of the Canadian interior.

> The Buffalo are very numerous on the NE side the Red Deers River...the ground is entirely covered by them & appears quite black. I never saw such amazing numbers together before. I am sure there was some millions in sight as no ground could be seen for them in that compleat semicircle & extending at least 10 miles.
>
> Peter Fidler's journal, February 1793

### The Canadian West and the Fur Trade, c.1812

- Limit of spring ice
- Known to people of European descent, c.1812

Hudson's Bay Company

North West Company

Post

Trade route

Portage

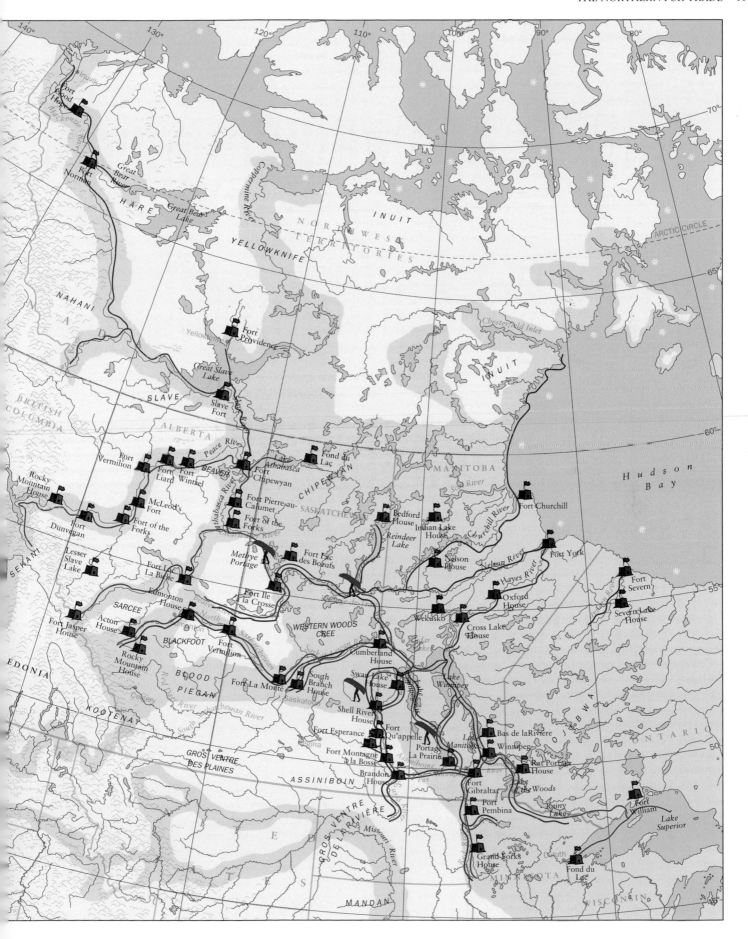

# Traders to the Pacific

## THE EXPLORATIONS OF FRASER AND THOMPSON, 1805-11

*Soon after Lewis and Clark reach the Pacific overland, Canadian fur traders renew their search for a northerly route to the mouth of the Columbia River.*

Early in the 19th century the North West Company was near the eastern slopes of the Rockies. Simon Fraser headed explorations to the north, planning to follow the southward-flowing "big river" down to the coast that had been found, and then left, by Alexander Mackenzie in 1793 (▶ *page 114*). Like Mackenzie, Fraser assumed this was the Columbia River.

Between 1805 and 1807 Fraser and his associates explored along and beyond Mackenzie's track. Traveling up the Peace River and among Indians who had never seen a white man, Fraser built the first trading posts on the Pacific slope. One of these, later Fort George, was the starting point for his journey to the sea in 1808. By canoe and on foot Fraser followed Mackenzie's "Tacoutche Tesse" for more than 500 miles. It could not be the Columbia, as Fraser would establish, for it ran into the sea at the Strait of Georgia. Moreover a dangerous and hair-raising sequence of rapids, cascades and whirlpools made it impossible as a trade route. It was later reported that in nine attempts out of ten the passage downriver would lead to certain death. In 1813 David Thompson, master surveyor of the North West Company, named it the Fraser River.

David Thompson, "the Astronomer," would succeed where Fraser had failed. Working first for the Hudson's Bay Company, then the better-resourced North West Company, Thompson covered in all a prodigious 56,000 miles, surveying 13,000 of them. Thompson's story of his surveys, recounted late in life, has become a classic of its kind. He mapped the country on both sides of the Canadian-American border of 1783, from Sault Sainte-Marie and Grand Portage to Lake Winnipeg, the Red River, the Upper Missouri and the headwaters of the Mississippi. He worked his way along both banks of the Saskatchewan, the Churchill River and into Athabasca. In 1801 he failed in an attempt to cross the Rockies from the Northwesters' new post at Rocky Mountain House. Thompson then turned to the south.

From 1807 to 1810 Thompson traded and explored a great arc from the Upper Columbia across the border to the Clark Fork region of Idaho. During this time, his trading activities and the hostility of the Piegan Indians stopped

> July 14th [1811] brought us to a full view of the Pacific Ocean; which to me was a great pleasure, but my men seemed disappointed; they had been accustomed to the boundless horizons of the great Lakes of Canada, and their high rolling waves; from the Ocean they expected a more boundless view... and my informing them, that directly opposite to us at the distance of five thousand miles was the Empire of Japan added nothing to their Ideas.
>
> **From Thompson's *Narrative***

*Above: Fort William, on the northwest shore of Lake Superior (▶ page 116), was the effective headquarters of the North West Company. When Thompson retired from the fur trade, he produced a map of the Northwest, which hung for many years in the Great Hall of Fort William. This watercolor view of the fort was painted by Robert Irvine in 1812.*

his efforts to reach the ocean to the west.

In 1810 Thompson was at Rainy Lake, on his return east, when news arrived that John Jacob Astor had formed the American Fur Company and was sending a ship from Boston to the Columbia River. "I was now obliged" wrote Thompson "to take 4 canoes and to proceed to the mouth of the Columbia to oppose them."

To avoid the Piegan, Thompson followed his Iroquois guide north to make a winter crossing through the unmapped Athabasca Pass. The mountains were "far north in a rugged country" a companion noted. After three months in a miserable winter camp, deserted by most of his men, Thompson resumed his journey in April 1811. Then, threading his way through the tangled skein of rivers on the Pacific slope in June he reached the Columbia River at Kettle Falls, and became the first white man to follow the river downstream to its fork with the Snake River. From here he followed the track taken by Lewis and Clark six years earlier, past the fearsome Dalles and the Cascades, down to the sea.

There the American flag flew over Astoria, built by Astor's men three months earlier.

# The Explorations of Fraser and Thompson, 1805-11

Known to people of European descent, 1805

North West Company post

US post

Fraser, 1808

Thompson, 1810-11

Winter camp

Act of possession

Rapids

Falls

Portage

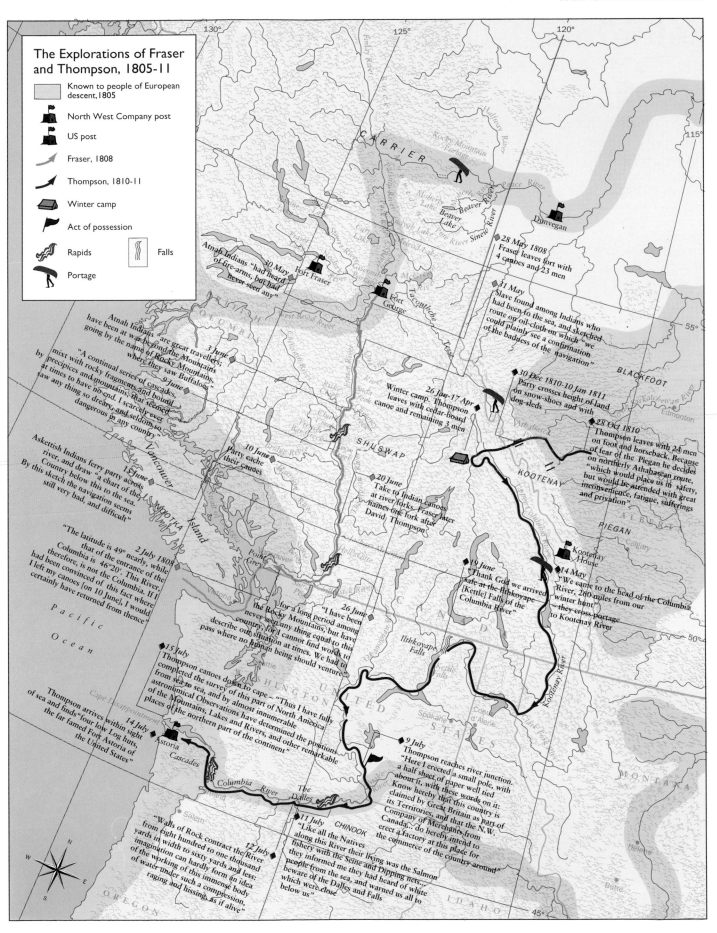

Atnah Indians "had heard of fire-arms, but had never seen any"
30 May

Atnah Indians "are great travellers: have been at war beyond the Mountains, going by the name of Rocky Mountains, where they saw Buffaloes."

"A continual series of cascades; mixt with rocky fragments, and bound by precipices and mountains, that seemed at times to have no end. I scarcely ever saw any thing so dreary, and seldom so dangerous in any country"
9 June

3 June

Askettish Indians ferry party across the river, and draw "a chart of the Country below this to the sea. By this sketch the navigation seems still very bad, and difficult"
15 June

Party cache their canoes
10 June

"The latitude is 49° nearly, while that of the entrance of the Columbia is 46°20'. This River, therefore, is not the Columbia. If I had been convinced of this fact where I left my canoes [on 10 June], I would certainly have returned from thence"
2 July 1808

Winter camp. Thompson leaves with cedar-board canoe and remaining 3 men
26 Jan-17 Apr

20 June
Take to Indian canoes at river forks. Fraser later names one fork after David Thompson

19 June
"Thank God we arrived safe at the Ilthkoyape [Kettle] Falls of the Columbia River"

"for a long period among the Rocky Mountains, but have never seen any thing equal to this country, for I cannot find words to describe our situation at times. We had to pass where no human being should venture"
26 June

Ilthkoyape Falls

15 July
Thompson canoes down to cape – "Thus I have fully completed the survey of this part of North America from sea to sea, and by almost innumerable astronomical Observations have determined the positions of the Mountains, Lakes and Rivers, and other remarkable places of the northern part of the continent"

14 July
Thompson arrives within sight of sea and finds "four low Log huts, the far famed Fort Astoria of the United States"

Astoria
Cascades

"Walls of Rock contract the River from eight hundred to one thousand yards in width to sixty yards and less: imagination can hardly form an idea of the working of this immense body of water under such a compression, raging and hissing, as if alive"

Columbia River
The Dalles

11 July
"Like all the Natives along this River their living was the Salmon fishery with the Seine and Dipping nets... they informed me they had heard of white people from the sea, and warned us all to beware of the Dalles and Falls which were close below us"
CHINOOK

12 July

9 July
Thompson reaches river junction. "Here I erected a small pole, with a half sheet of paper well tied about it, with these words on it: Know hereby that this country is claimed by Great Britain as part of its Territories, and that the N.W. Company of Merchants, from Canada... do hereby intend to erect a factory at this place for the commerce of the country around"

Spokane
Coeur d'Alene

28 May 1808
Fraser leaves fort with 4 canoes and 23 men

31 May
Slave found among Indians who had been to the sea, and sketched route on oil-cloth on which "we could plainly see a confirmation of the badness of the navigation"

Dunvegan

BLACKFOOT

30 Dec 1810-10 Jan 1811
Party crosses height of land on snow-shoes and with dog-sleds

28 Oct 1810
Thompson leaves with 24 men on foot and horseback. Because of fear of the Piegan he decides on northerly Athabascan route, "which would place us in safety, but would be attended with great inconvenience, fatigue, sufferings and privation"

PIEGAN

Kootenay House

14 May
"We came to the head of the Columbia River, 260 miles from our winter hunt" – they cross portage to Kootenay River

KOOTENAY

ALBERTA

Edmonton

Calgary

Fort Fraser

Fort George

CARRIER

SHUSWAP

Vancouver Island

NOOTKA ISLAND

Pacific Ocean

Point Grey

Cape Disappointment

Victoria

WASHINGTON

UNITED STATES

CANADA

OREGON

IDAHO

MONTANA

Salem

Helena

Butte

Kettle Falls

Kootenay River

Clark Fork

# California: Island or Peninsula?

## THE JOURNEYS OF FATHER KINO, 1687-1702

*The Jesuit Father Eusebio Kino tirelessly journeys around the fringes of New Spain, and dispels the myth that California is an island.*

Throughout the 17th century, Lower or *Baja* California lay on the very edge of the northwest frontier of New Spain. What was known of it from earlier coasting voyages was not reassuring: mountains, deserts and a forbidding coastline with few harbors, and no sign of precious metals or of populous Indian nations.

Even its basic geography was the subject of contention. Although Francisco de Ulloa's 1539 voyage to the head of the Gulf of California (▶ *page 38*) had shown that California was a peninsula, this knowledge had been obscured by later misunderstandings. Father Ascensión, who had sailed with Vizcaíno in 1602 (▶ *page 40*), claimed that beyond Cape Mendocino the coast turned northeast into the Strait of Anian, "having joined the Oceanic Sea which surrounds Cape Mendocino and the Mediterranean Sea of California." An account written in 1626 of Oñate's 1604-05 journey to the Colorado River made much the same point: "the Gulf of California is not closed, but is an arm of the sea."

During the 17th century the Spanish frontier advanced slowly along the mainland coast of the Gulf. Missions and presidios were established in Sinaloa and Sonora, and ranching activity spread north. Even so, not until the next century was it accepted that California was a peninsula. This was the individual achievement of another in the long line of Jesuit missionary explorers, Father Eusebio Francisco Kino. In the mid-1680s, he made a series of explorations across the gusty waters of the Gulf of California, and in 1685 reached the Pacific coast. Kino then moved north into the Sonoran frontier area. From the mission post at Dolores, which he founded in 1687, he pushed north to the Colorado and Gila Rivers. Accompanied by Indian guides and carriers, Father Kino made more than 50 journeys on horseback and on foot through Pimeria Alta (northern Sonora and southern Arizona) – the first exploration of the region.

By the late 1690s Kino was absorbed in the quest for a land route to California, and in 1698 described how he saw land across the head of the Gulf of California. It took another four years for Kino to be convinced of the reality of his discovery, and he himself never made the journey across the head of the Gulf

and on to the Pacific coast. But the issue of the insularity – or otherwise – of California remained unresolved. For casual callers to the coast, such as the English privateer George Shelvocke in 1721, this was proof that "the Spaniards are now grown indolent and incurious." It was not until 1747, after the voyage of Father Fernando Consag right round the Gulf of California, that the Spanish authorities publicly declared that California was a part of the North American mainland.

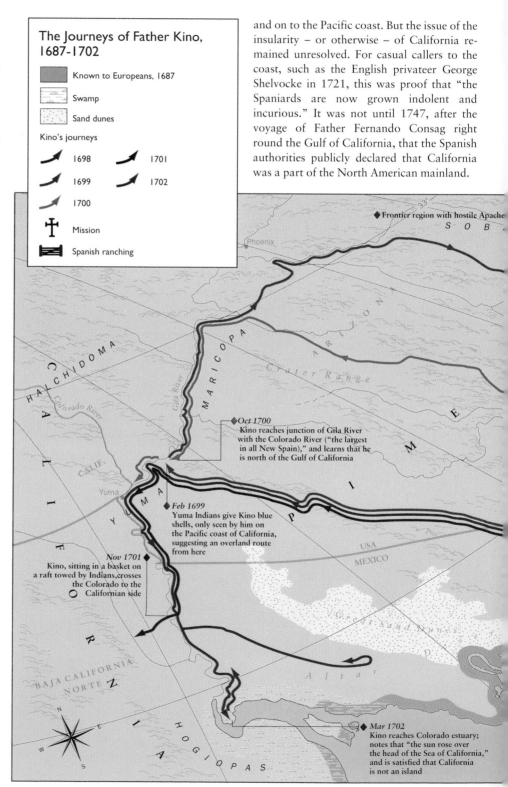

The Journeys of Father Kino, 1687-1702

Known to Europeans, 1687

Swamp

Sand dunes

Kino's journeys

1698     1701

1699     1702

1700

✝ Mission

Spanish ranching

◆ Frontier region with hostile Apache

**Oct 1700**
Kino reaches junction of Gila River with the Colorado River ("the largest in all New Spain)," and learns that he is north of the Gulf of California

**Feb 1699**
Yuma Indians give Kino blue shells, only seen by him on the Pacific coast of California, suggesting an overland route from here

**Nov 1701**
Kino, sitting in a basket on a raft towed by Indians, crosses the Colorado to the Californian side

**Mar 1702**
Kino reaches Colorado estuary; notes that "the sun rose over the head of the Sea of California," and is satisfied that California is not an island

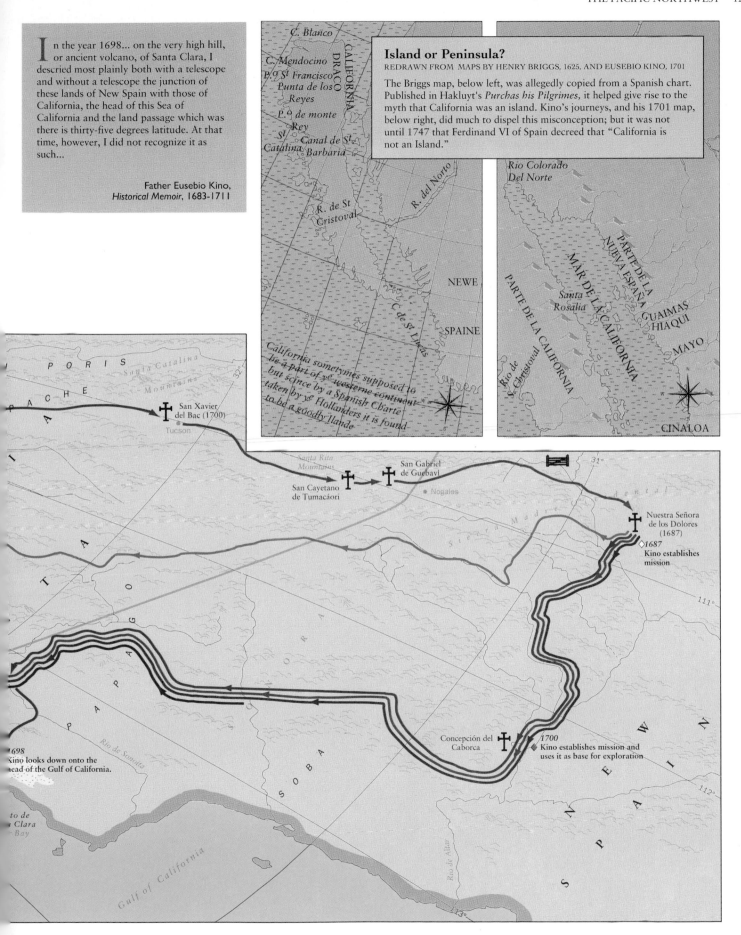

In the year 1698... on the very high hill, or ancient volcano, of Santa Clara, I descried most plainly both with a telescope and without a telescope the junction of these lands of New Spain with those of California, the head of this Sea of California and the land passage which was there is thirty-five degrees latitude. At that time, however, I did not recognize it as such...

Father Eusebio Kino,
*Historical Memoir*, 1683-1711

## Island or Peninsula?
REDRAWN FROM MAPS BY HENRY BRIGGS, 1625, AND EUSEBIO KINO, 1701

The Briggs map, below left, was allegedly copied from a Spanish chart. Published in Hakluyt's *Purchas his Pilgrimes*, it helped give rise to the myth that California was an island. Kino's journeys, and his 1701 map, below right, did much to dispel this misconception; but it was not until 1747 that Ferdinand VI of Spain decreed that "California is not an Island."

California sometymes supposed to be a part of ye westerne continent but since by a Spanish Charte taken by ye Hollanders it is found to be a goodly Ilande

1698
Kino looks down onto the head of the Gulf of California.

San Xavier del Bac (1700)
Tucson

San Cayetano de Tumacáori
San Gabriel de Guebavi
Nogales

Nuestra Señora de los Dolores (1687)
1687 Kino establishes mission

Concepción del Caborca
1700 Kino establishes mission and uses it as base for exploration

Gulf of California

# From Asia to America

## THE VOYAGES OF BERING AND THE RUSSIANS, 1728-68

*The Russians, having expanded to the Pacific, investigate the* bolshaya zemlya *(great land) rumored to lie across the sea to the east.*

As early as 1648, a Cossack, Semen Dezhnev, had claimed that he had rounded the eastern cape of Asia (now Mys Dezhneva), but his report had been lost and his discovery forgotten. So in 1724 Tsar Peter I ordered the Danish seaman Vitus Bering to sail from Kamchatka and "determine where it joins with America." Four years later, in the *St Gabriel* (a vessel built in Kamchatka), Bering reached the strait now known by his name, but fog hid the opposite shore. In 1732 Mikhail Gwosdev reached a shoreline across the strait, although no report of this was published.

In 1731 Bering took charge of a second, more ambitious expedition. After years of struggle on the long overland route from St Petersburg and Kamchatka, he sailed from Petropavlovsk in the spring of 1741. On the voyage Bering's two ships became separated, with dire results. His second-in-command, Chirikov, sighted the American coast in latitude 55°21'N., but there lost both his ship's boats with their crews, and was unable to land. Bering, meanwhile, had swung north towards the Alaskan coast, and landed at Kayak Island. He stayed there only long enough to take on water, to the irritation of his German naturalist, Georg Steller. Bering's ship, with its crew suffering from scurvy, threaded its way homeward, only to be wrecked on an island near Kamchatka where Bering and many of his crew died.

The survivors reported that the area was rich in fur seals, foxes, and above all sea otters, and at least 30 trading ventures sailed from Kamchatka in the next 20 years. In crazy vessels often held together by leather thongs, the *promysheniki* visited the stark volcanic islands of the Aleutian chain. They had no interest in exploration, and killed not only sea otters but almost exterminated the native Aleuts, turning the intimidated survivors into hunters. But the naval escort expeditions of Lieutenant Synd (1764-68), and Captain Krenitsyn and Lieutenant Levashev (1764-71), did some useful survey work. Unfortunately, their maps languished in the archives, and the only published map issued from St Petersburg, Jacob von Stählin's, was to mislead rather than guide future explorers (▶ *page 130*).

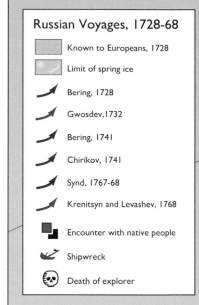

### Russian Voyages, 1728-68

| | |
|---|---|
| ▢ | Known to Europeans, 1728 |
| ✳ | Limit of spring ice |
| ⬆ | Bering, 1728 |
| ⬆ | Gwosdev, 1732 |
| ⬆ | Bering, 1741 |
| ⬆ | Chirikov, 1741 |
| ⬆ | Synd, 1767-68 |
| ⬆ | Krenitsyn and Levashev, 1768 |
| ◼ | Encounter with native people |
| ⚓ | Shipwreck |
| ☠ | Death of explorer |

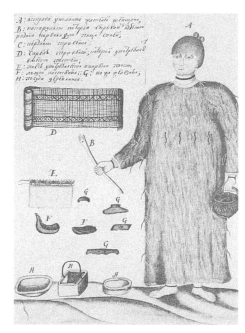

*Above: Russian expeditions to Alaska were keen to record both the people and the wildlife they encountered. Levashev sketched this Aleut woman (above), surrounded by her belongings, on Unalaska Island in 1767.*

### The Russian Discoveries

REDRAWN FROM GERHARDT MÜLLER'S *NOUVELLE CARTE*, 1754-58

Published by the Academy of Sciences in St Petersburg, Müller's map reflects the official Russian view that all Bering's sightings were of the American mainland. This led him to conjecture that a vast peninsula stretched along the line of the Aleutian Islands towards Kamchatka. Dreams of a passage through the continent had lingered in the "River of the West" and in the "discoveries" of Juan de Fuca and Bartholomew de Fonte(▶ *page 42*). Otherwise, this was the most accurate map of the northwest coast yet produced.

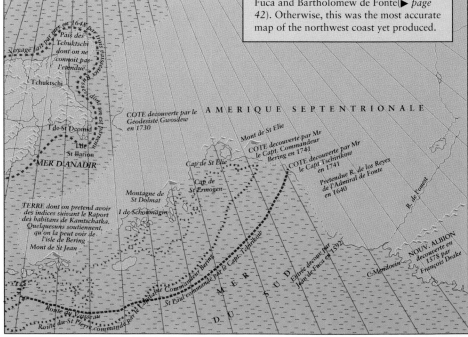

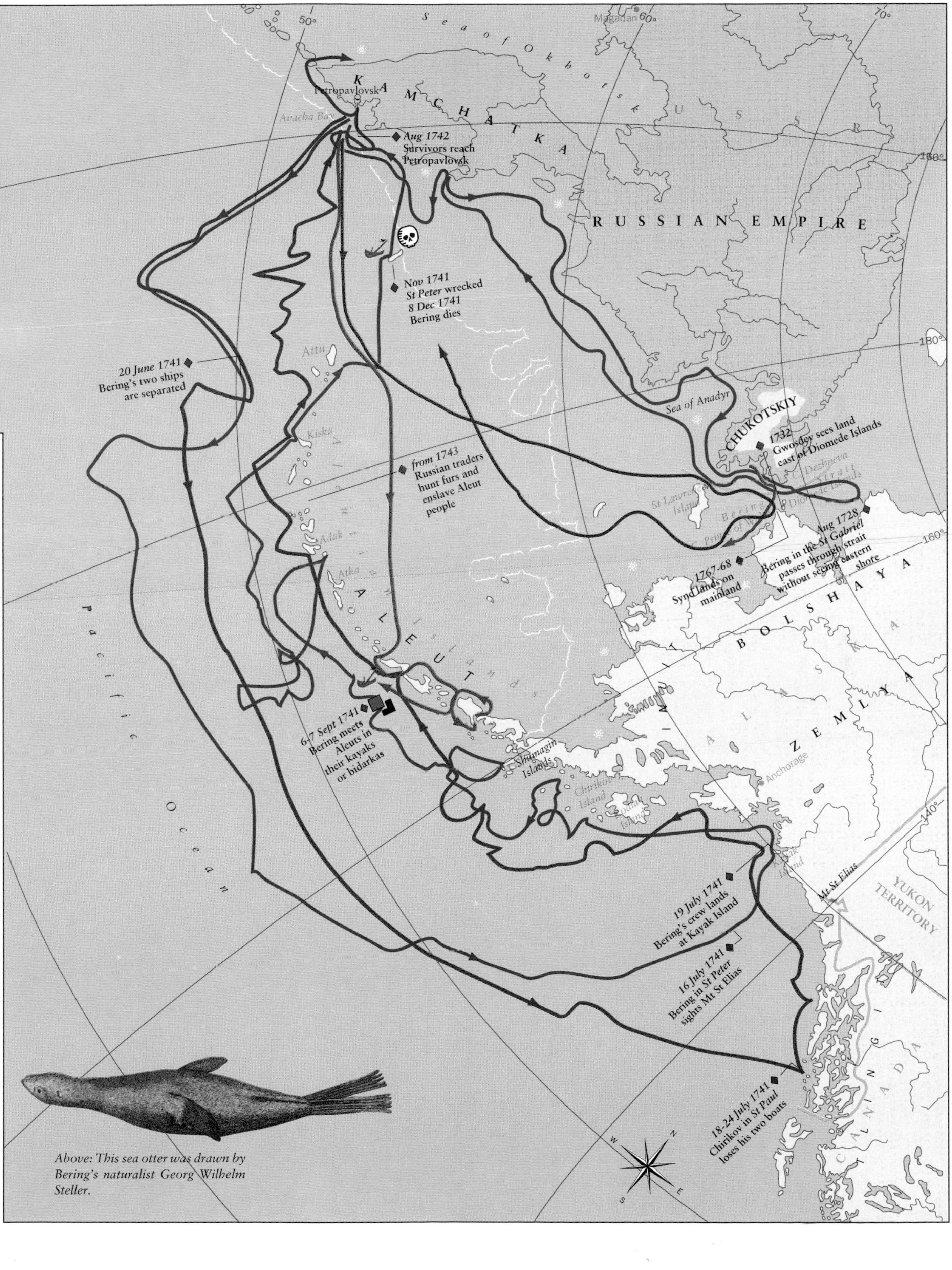
Sea of Okhotsk
Magadan
KAMCHATKA
Petropavlovsk
Avacha Bay
USSR
RUSSIAN EMPIRE
Aug 1742
Survivors reach
Petropavlovsk
Nov 1741
St Peter wrecked
8 Dec 1741
Bering dies
20 June 1741
Bering's two ships
are separated
Attu
Kiska
Adak
Atka
ALEUTIAN ISLANDS
from 1743
Russian traders
hunt furs and
enslave Aleut
people
Sea of Anadyr
CHUKOTSKIY
1732
Gwosdev sees land
east of Diomede Islands
Diomede Islands
Bering Strait
St Lawrence Island
Aug 1728
Bering in the St Gabriel
passes through strait
without seeing eastern
shore
1767-68
Synd lands on
mainland
BOLSHAYA ZEMLYA
ALASKA
Anchorage
Shumagin Islands
Chirikov Island
Kodiak Island
Kayak Island
Mt St Elias
YUKON TERRITORY
CANADA
6-7 Sept 1741
Bering meets
Aleuts in
their kayaks
or bidarkas
19 July 1741
Bering's crew lands
at Kayak Island
16 July 1741
Bering in St Peter
sights Mt St Elias
18-24 July 1741
Chirikov in St Paul
loses his two boats
Pacific Ocean
50°
60°
70°
160°
180°
160°
140°
N
E
S
W

*Above: This sea otter was drawn by Bering's naturalist Georg Wilhelm Steller.*

# The Golden Gate

## SPANISH EXPANSION INTO UPPER CALIFORNIA, 1769-1776

*In a burst of military and missionary activity, the Spanish move into Alta California, where they establish missions and discover the incomparable harbor of the Golden Gate.*

For a century and a half, New Spain had made no sustained attempt to advance its northern frontiers, but by the 1760s alarmist reports of Russian activity along the Alaskan coast, rumors of British expeditions to the North Pacific, and Indian uprisings in northern Sonora, prompted a change of policy.

José de Galvéz, the energetic *visitador-general* of New Spain, and Junípero Serra, Father-President of the Franciscan missions, set about extending their military and missionary activity into Alta California. The first objective was Monterey, discovered by Vizcaíno in 1603 (▶ *page 40*). In 1769, land and sea expeditions left La Paz for the north. San Diego was reached by sea in April, and by land in May. Then in a journey along hundreds of miles of shoreline never before trodden by Europeans, a party of soldiers, Indian muleteers and carriers led by the governor of Alta California, Gaspar de Portolá, headed north. Suffering from heat by

day and cold by night, the expedition plodded for 11 weeks across the hilly terrain between the mountains and the shore to reach Monterey. Its open bay proved so unlike Vizcaino's flattering description – "the best port that could be desired, sheltered from all the winds" – that scouts were sent further on to see if Monterey lay to the north. Instead, they stumbled on the great bay of San Francisco. On this journey the Spaniards saw for the first time at close quarters the giant redwood trees, so vast that eight men with arms outstretched could not encircle one.

At first, the Spaniards thought that the vast expanse of sheltered water they had discovered was a great estuary, barring the coastal route to the north. In the next few years, further land approaches from Monterey to the southern and eastern shores of the bay added some piecemeal information, but the reality of the incomparable harbor was not grasped until 1775. In August of that

year Juan de Ayala made the first recorded sailing through the Golden Gate, difficult to discern against the hills even in clear weather. The expedition's sailing master, Cañizares, surveyed the waters of the bay, marking numerous soundings, and on his return Ayala reported that the harbor was the best he had seen "in these seas from Cape Horn northwards." So extensive were its various bays and passages that many squadrons could anchor there without sight or knowledge of each other. The next year, a group of settlers led by an army officer, Juan Bautista de Anza, and accompanied by Father Pedro Font, arrived from Sonora to establish a presidio and a mission. Anza and Pedro Font surveyed the bay from the land side, and their maps and descriptions left no doubt about its potential.

Although San Diego, Monterey and San Francisco had been secured, and in 1771 another mission established at San Gabriel (modern Los Angeles), the Spanish position in

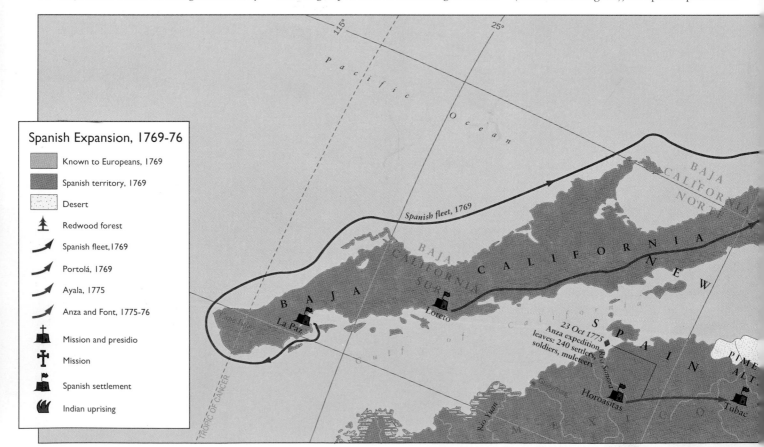

Spanish Expansion, 1769-76

- Known to Europeans, 1769
- Spanish territory, 1769
- Desert
- Redwood forest
- Spanish fleet, 1769
- Portolá, 1769
- Ayala, 1775
- Anza and Font, 1775-76
- Mission and presidio
- Mission
- Spanish settlement
- Indian uprising

Alta California was still precarious. Penin-sular or *Baja* California had few resources, and supplies for the new establishments had to be brought by sea from Mexican ports. The northward voyage could take three or four months against headwinds, and the alternative of crossing the stormy waters of the Gulf of California was not an appealing one. The next stage of Spanish exploration was to find a land trail from Sonora to the Californian posts.

*Right: Father Pedro Font, who accompanied Anza on his 1776 voyage, made this map of the Golden Gate the following year. "The port of San Francisco," he wrote, "is a marvel of nature, and might well be called the harbor of harbors, because of its great capacity..." Below: Along the Californian coast, the Spanish planted a string of missions. This one, the Mission del Carmelo, was painted by José Cardero in 1791 (▶ page 132).*

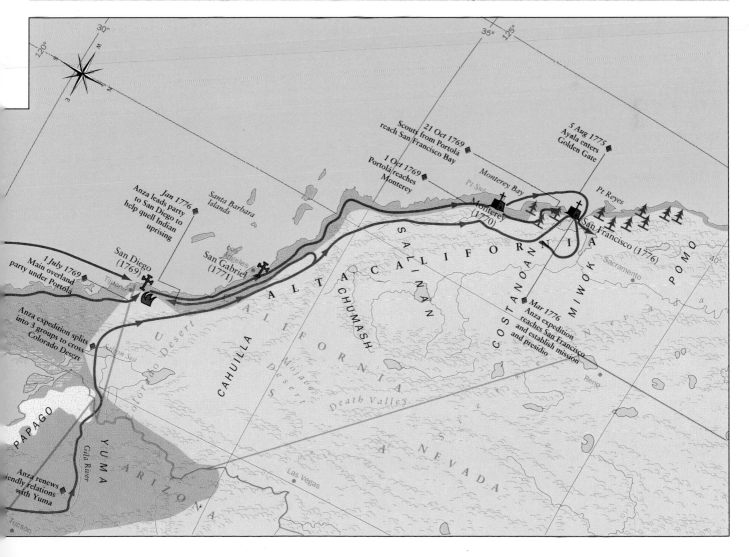

# Deserts, Mountains and Canyons

## SPANISH INTERIOR EXPLORATIONS, 1774-76

*Spanish missionaries and soldiers reach further into the interior than any explorers since the 16th century, and discover the Great Basin.*

In 1774 Juan Bautista de Anza (▶ *page 124*) and the Franciscan missionary Father Garcés led a party from Tubac to the coast. The Colorado Desert almost defeated them, but at a second attempt they skirted the waterless, trackless wastes and climbed the Sierra Nevada. From here they descended the San Jacinto Valley through the fertile Californian coastal plain, "full of flowers, fertile pastures, and other vegetation, useful for the raising of cattle," to the mission at San Gabriel.

The next year Anza proved that the route was practicable by leading 240 soldiers, settlers and muleteers, with more than 1000 animals, along it. Meanwhile Garcés searched for a more northern route which would avoid the Colorado desert. Traveling alone among the Indians, he spent much of 1775 and 1776 on or near the Colorado and Mohave rivers. He ranged as far as the Hopi pueblos, saw the Grand Canyon (the first European to do so since 1540), and reached the coast at San Gabriel. But the hardships he suffered were proof that the route was not suitable for supply expeditions. He was also the first European to enter the Great Basin that stretches from the Sierra Nevadas to central Utah, dispelling the myth of the great inland sea, the *Mer de l'Ouest*, that cartographers had placed here (▶ *page 42*).

In 1776 the Franciscan Fathers Escalante and Domínguez left Santa Fé in search of a route to Monterey. If a route could be found to the north, avoiding hostile Hopi and Apache Indians, it would strengthen the Spanish frontier which now stretched from Upper California to Texas. They failed in their main task, but the 1500-mile circle they cut through country never seen by Europeans was one of the most important interior journeys of the century. Escalante's diary tells of months of struggling with their Indian guides, horses and mules across a stark landscape of high plateaus, awesome canyons, of featureless deserts, splintered hillsides and salt lakes. Only in the quiet beauty of the Utah valley did they see any potential for future settlement. But their journey was one of the last feats of Spanish exploration, and when settlers reached the Great Basin in the next century they came from the east, and they were American.

*Below: The Escalante expedition was recorded in magnificent unpublished maps drawn by its soldier-cartographer Miera y Pacheco. This manuscript shows bearded Ute Indians. A note on the map explains the growing pressures on the Spanish frontier as horsed Comanche displaced the Apache to dominate the buffalo plains.*

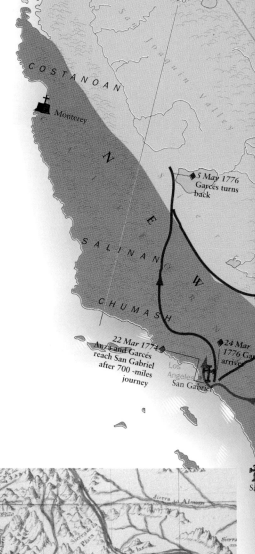

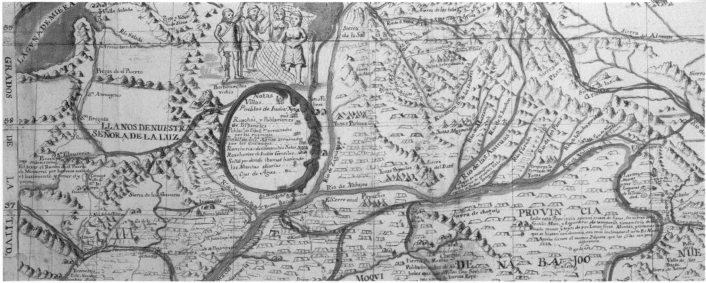

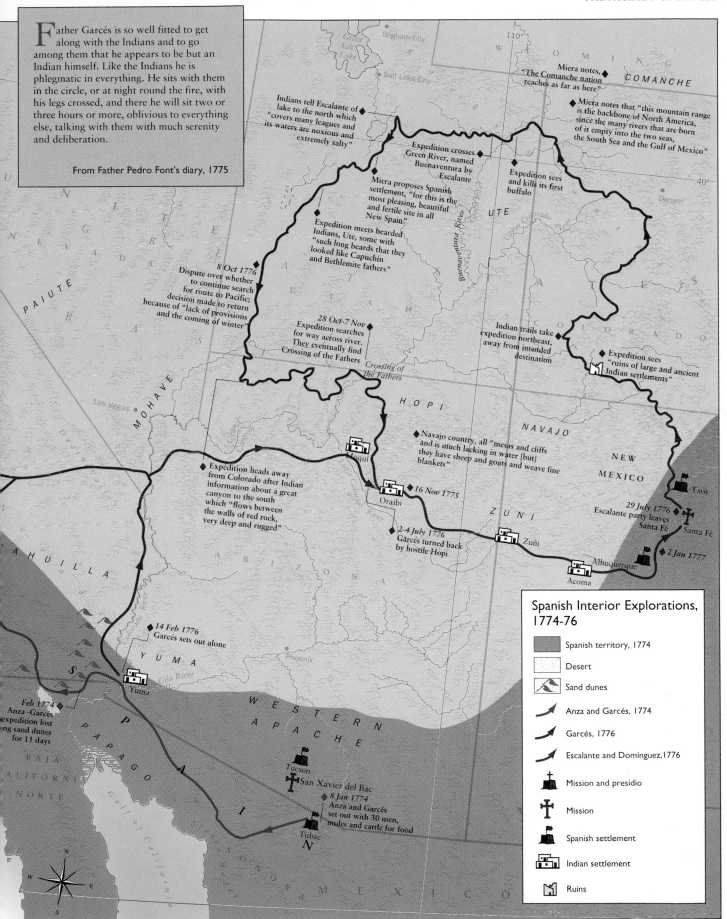

Father Garcés is so well fitted to get along with the Indians and to go among them that he appears to be but an Indian himself. Like the Indians he is phlegmatic in everything. He sits with them in the circle, or at night round the fire, with his legs crossed, and there he will sit two or three hours or more, oblivious to everything else, talking with them with much serenity and deliberation.

From Father Pedro Font's diary, 1775

Miera notes, "The Comanche nation reaches as far as here"

Miera notes that "this mountain range is the backbone of North America, since the many rivers that are born of it empty into the two seas, the South Sea and the Gulf of Mexico"

Indians tell Escalante of lake to the north which "covers many leagues and its waters are noxious and extremely salty"

Expedition crosses Green River, named Buenaventura by Escalante

Expedition sees and kills its first buffalo

Miera proposes Spanish settlement, "for this is the most pleasing, beautiful and fertile site in all New Spain"

Expedition meets bearded Indians, Ute, some with "such long beards that they looked like Capuchin and Bethlemite fathers"

8 Oct 1776 Dispute over whether to continue search for route to Pacific; decision made to return because of "lack of provisions and the coming of winter"

28 Oct-7 Nov Expedition searches for way across river. They eventually find Crossing of the Fathers

Indian trails take expedition northeast, away from intended destination

Expedition sees "ruins of large and ancient Indian settlements"

Navajo country, all "mesas and cliffs and is much lacking in water [but] they have sheep and goats and weave fine blankets"

Expedition heads away from Colorado after Indian information about a great canyon to the south which "flows between the walls of red rock, very deep and rugged"

16 Nov 1775

2-4 July 1776 Garcés turned back by hostile Hopi

29 July 1776 Escalante party leaves Santa Fé

2 Jan 1777

14 Feb 1776 Garcés sets out alone

Feb 1774 Anza-Garcés expedition lost ng sand dunes for 11 days

8 Jan 1774 Anza and Garcés set out with 30 men, mules and cattle for food

### Spanish Interior Explorations, 1774-76

- Spanish territory, 1774
- Desert
- Sand dunes
- Anza and Garcés, 1774
- Garcés, 1776
- Escalante and Domínguez, 1776
- Mission and presidio
- Mission
- Spanish settlement
- Indian settlement
- Ruins

# North to Alaska

## SPANISH COASTAL VOYAGES, 1774-79

*To protect their settlements in Upper California from their European rivals, the Spanish sail up the northwest coast and claim new possessions.*

Although the Spanish had settled far into Upper California, Antonio María Bucareli y Ursúa, the Viceroy of New Spain, was aware that Spain was vulnerable to the north. He knew the Russians were active in Alaska but was unsure how far south they had reached.

Other nations were also drawn to the northwest coast when published maps suggested a network of straits linking it with Hudson Bay and Baffin Bay. The maps showed the strait supposedly found by Juan de Fuca in 1592 as well as the one associated with Bartholomew de Fonte's imaginary voyage (▶ *page 42*). Bucareli was rightly sceptical, but sent precautionary expeditions far north along the unknown coast.

In 1774 Juan Pérez, an experienced pilot, sailed in the *Santiago* with secret instructions to take possession of all places suitable for European settlement up to 60°N. At the northern end of the Queen Charlotte Islands the Spaniards traded with Haida Indians who came out to their vessel in large, decorated canoes, beating drums and offering furs and fine wool blankets. Contrary winds and currents then forced Pérez to turn back. On the return voyage they sighted the great mass of Vancouver Island at Nootka Sound. Here the Spaniards again traded without leaving their ship; it was dark and cold, and they feared a shortage of water and the unknown coast. This was the first contact between Europeans and the Indians of the northwest coast, whose culture was very different from that of the Californian tribes.

The following year Bucareli sent two vessels north, Bruno de Hezeta in command of the *Santiago* and Peruvian-born Juan Francisco de la Bodega y Quadra in the tiny *Sonora*. As the *Santiago* coasted back south because of sickness on board, the crew sighted a large bay through which "the sea penetrates far into the land, making a horizon to the east." Lack of experience prevented them from going any closer. Hezeta thought this might be the entrance of Fuca's strait. But what he had seen was the entrance of one of North America's major rivers, the Columbia, 17 years before the American Robert Gray sighted and claimed to have discovered it.

Meanwhile, Quadra had sailed far north, becoming the first Spaniard to reach Alaska. He was also the first Spaniard to land on the northwest coast (though not the mainland) as he searched near Bucareli Bay for signs of Fonte's supposed strait.

In 1779, hearing of Cook's arrival on the coast the previous year, the Spanish sent a further expedition to Alaska. Ignacio de Arteaga in the flagship *Princesa* and Quadra in command of the *Favorita* spent a month exploring the intricate waterways near Bucareli Bay. On their way north they took ceremonial possession of several points along the coast, including Hinchinbrook Island, the farthest north of all Spanish acts of possession in America. When Arteaga and Quadra turned back near Kodiak, they had seen neither English nor Russians, nor found any strait which might be the entrance to a Northwest Passage. Arteaga's report gave the Spanish authorities a sense of security. It would be short-lived.

*Below: An Indian burial place, sketched by José Cardero, artist on Malaspina's expedition (▶ page 132). The massive wooden sculpture and architecture is typical of the northwest coast.*

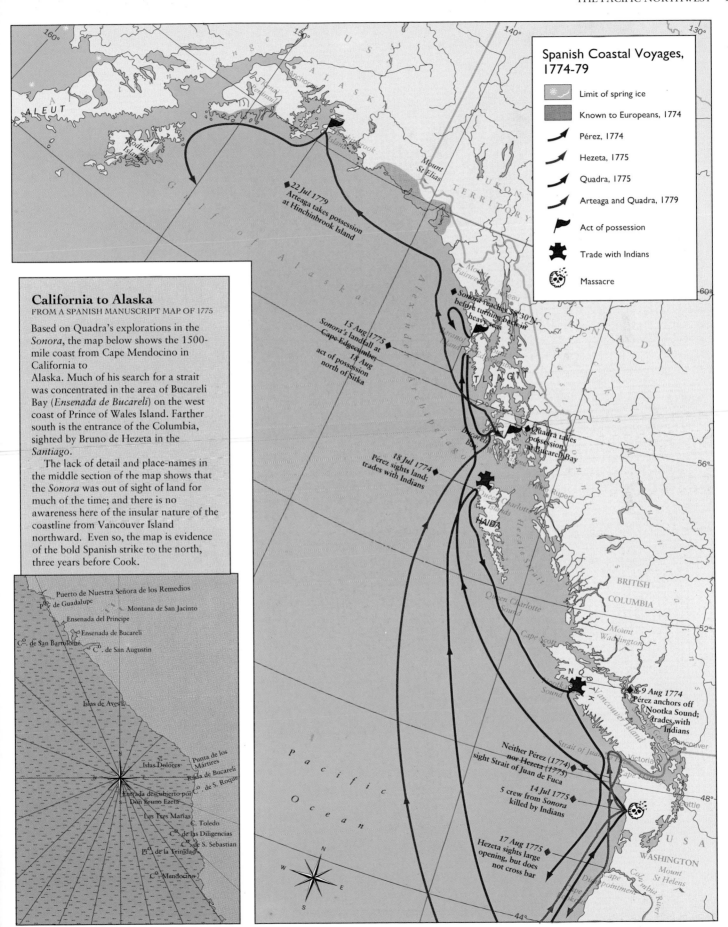

## Spanish Coastal Voyages, 1774-79

- ☀ Limit of spring ice
- Known to Europeans, 1774
- Pérez, 1774
- Hezeta, 1775
- Quadra, 1775
- Arteaga and Quadra, 1779
- Act of possession
- Trade with Indians
- Massacre

22 Jul 1779
Arteaga takes possession
at Hinchinbrook Island

15 Aug 1775
Sonora's landfall at
Cape Edgecumbe

18 Aug
act of possession
north of Sitka

Sonora reaches 58°30'N
before turning back in
heavy seas

Quadra takes
possession
at Bucareli Bay

18 Jul 1774
Pérez sights land;
trades with Indians

9 Aug 1774
Pérez anchors off
Nootka Sound;
trades with
Indians

Neither Pérez (1774)
nor Hezeta (1775)
sight Strait of Juan de Fuca

14 Jul 1775
5 crew from Sonora
killed by Indians

17 Aug 1775
Hezeta sights large
opening, but does
not cross bar

### California to Alaska
FROM A SPANISH MANUSCRIPT MAP OF 1775

Based on Quadra's explorations in the
*Sonora*, the map below shows the 1500-
mile coast from Cape Mendocino in
California to
Alaska. Much of his search for a strait
was concentrated in the area of Bucareli
Bay (*Ensenada de Bucareli*) on the west
coast of Prince of Wales Island. Farther
south is the entrance of the Columbia,
sighted by Bruno de Hezeta in the
*Santiago*.

The lack of detail and place-names in
the middle section of the map shows that
the *Sonora* was out of sight of land for
much of the time; and there is no
awareness here of the insular nature of the
coastline from Vancouver Island
northward. Even so, the map is evidence
of the bold Spanish strike to the north,
three years before Cook.

Puerto de Nuestra Señora de los Remedios
Pta. de Guadalupe
Montaña de San Jacinto
Ensenada del Principe
Ensenada de Bucareli
Cº. de San Bartolomé
Cº. de San Augustin
Islas de Aves
Islas Dolores
Punta de los
Martires
Rada de Bucareli
Cº. de S. Roque
Entrada descubierto por
Don Bruno Ezeta
Las Tres Marias
C. Toledo
Cº. de las Diligencias
Cº. de S. Sebastian
Pta. de la Trinidad
Cº. Mendocino

# The Northwest Coast Revealed

## THE VOYAGE OF JAMES COOK, 1778

*As the Russians and Spaniards edge towards
each other along the northwest coast, James
Cook bridges the gap between them.*

Russian and Spanish activity in the North
Pacific was interrupted by the arrival on the
northwest coast in 1778 of a British naval
expedition commanded by James Cook. The
motivation for this third Pacific voyage by
Europe's most celebrated explorer owed
much to Hearne's sighting in 1771 of the
polar sea (▶ *page 108*). This raised hopes that
a Northwest Passage might be found along
the Arctic coastline of the American
continent. Such hopes were buoyed by
fashionable theories that the polar seas were
ice-free and by publication of a map by Jacob
von Stählin. Stählin showed a wide strait
between the island of "Alaschka" and the
American continent. The optimistic plan
assumed that Cook would head north along
the northwest coast until he found the strait,
sail through it into an ice-free polar sea, and
so back into the Atlantic.

The *Resolution* and *Discovery* arrived on

the northwest coast in March 1778, from
Cook's new discovery of the Sandwich or
Hawaiian Islands. The ships anchored in
Nootka Sound on the oceanic coast of Vancouver Island, where the local Indians proved
keen traders, displayed spectacular skills in
handling their canoes, and built wooden
buildings with intricate totemic carvings. In
late April the ships sailed north, keeping well
offshore because of bad weather. On 1 May
they sighted the coast of Alaska, and the
shoreline, all dark-green forest near Nootka,
became bleaker. The scenery was dramatic,
with towering, snow-capped volcanic peaks,
including Bering's Mt St Elias a hundred miles
inland. Expectation ran high of the imminent
discovery of a strait leading north, but the
coast turned inexorably to the west. The ships
followed Prince William Sound until its shores
closed in, and traced Cook Inlet far inland.
The crews saw Alaskans in their sealskin
craft, and old Greenland hands had no doubt
that these were "Esquimaux."

Once out to sea again, the vessels were
forced away to the southwest, edging along
the tongue of the Alaskan peninsula until at
last they were able to head north through the
channel east of Unalaska Island. Aleut of Inuit
stock appeared in their kayaks, begging
tobacco and repeating the word "Russ." On 9
August the expedition finally reached a strait -

too far west to be Stählin's yet, with shores
almost in sight of each other, too narrow to be
Bering's if the Russian maps were correct.

Once through the strait the reality of polar
navigation was brought home to the crews. A
massive wall of ice threatened to crush the un-
strengthened ships. As the expedition retreated it was clear that this was indeed the

*Above: The* Resolution *and* Discovery *in Nootka
Sound, by the Cook expedition's artist John
Webber. The ships are surrounded by the canoes of
Nootka Indians coming to trade.*

strait reached by Bering 50 years earlier (▶
*page 122*). Of Stählin's strait there was no
sign, nor did the Russian fur-traders
encountered during Cook's stay at Unalaska
before he headed back to Hawaii (and his
death) have any knowledge of it.

In his final sustained feat of exploration
Cook had achieved much. In a single season
he had traced hundreds of miles of difficult
coastline, defined the Alaskan peninsula, and
confirmed the existence of Bering's strait.
While neither Cook, nor his Russian and
Spanish predecessors, had determined whether the long stretches of coastline north of
Nootka were islands or mainland, in outline
at least the shape and position of the
northwest coast of America were now known.

## A Confusion of Islands

REDRAWN FROM JACOB VON STÄHLIN'S
MAP, 1774

One of Cook's officers recalled that
Stählin's map, which drew on Russian
discoveries in the northwest, was
"constantly in our hands." But its errors
– it showed Alaska as a large island and
misplaced several of the Aleutians –
proved exasperating. "Many of these
islands," Cook furiously noted in his log,
"are jumbled in regular confusion..." The
explorer dismissed Stählin's work as "a
Map that the most illiterate of his
illiterate Sea-faring men would have been
ashamed to put his name to."

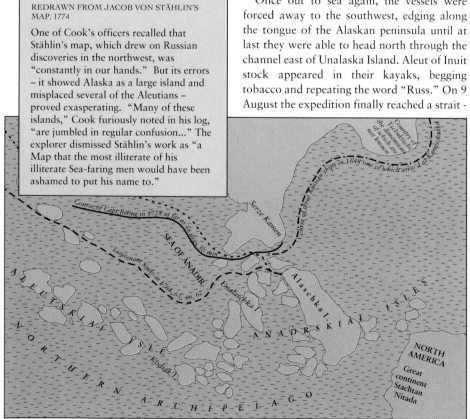

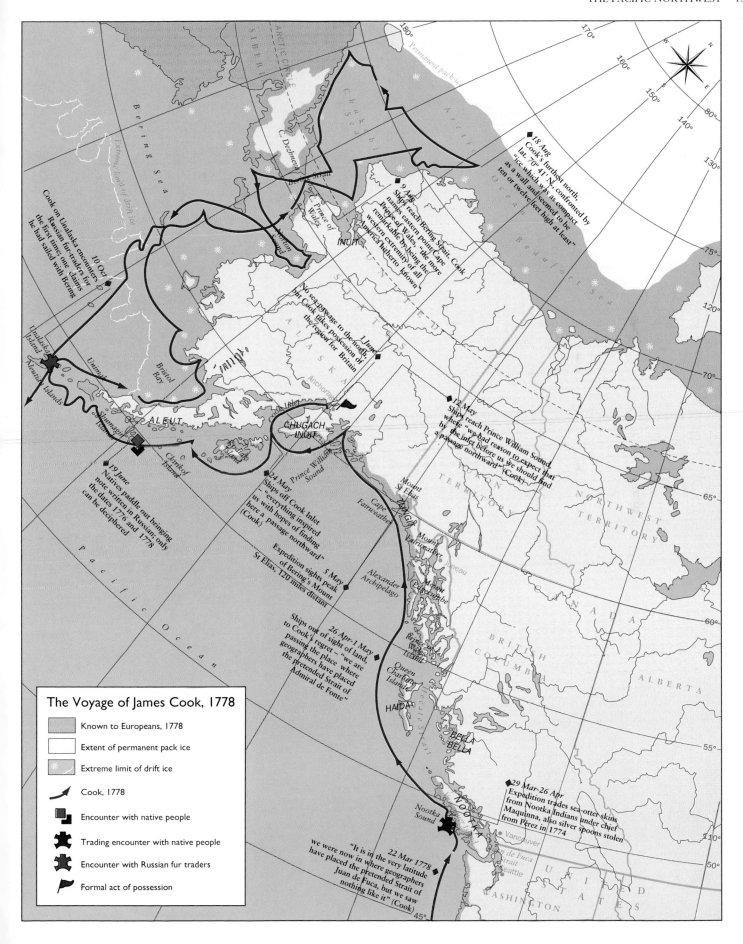

18 Aug
Cook's furthest north,
lat. 70° 41' N, confronted by
"ice which was as compact
as a wall, and seemed to be
ten or twelve feet high at least"

9 Aug
Ships reach Bering Strait. Cook
names eastern point Cape
Prince of Wales, "the more
remarkable by being the
western extremity of all
America hitherto known"

1 June
No sea-passage to the north,
but Cook takes possession of
the region for Britain

12 May
Ships reach Prince William Sound
where "we had reason to expect that
by the inlet before us we should find
a passage northward" (Cook)

10 Oct
Cook on Unalaska encounters
Russian fur-traders for
the first time; one claims
he had sailed with Bering

19 June
Natives paddle out bringing
note written in Russian; only
the dates 1776 and 1778
can be deciphered

24 May
Ships off Cook Inlet
– everything inspired
us with hopes of finding
here a passage northward"
(Cook)

5 May
Expedition sights peak
of Bering's Mount
St Elias, 120 miles distant

26 Apr–1 May
Ships out of sight of land,
to Cook's regret – we are
passing the place where
geographers have placed
the pretended Strait of
Admiral de Fonte"

29 Mar–26 Apr
Expedition trades sea-otter skins
from Nootka Indians under chief
Maquinna, also silver spoons stolen
from Perez in 1774

22 Mar 1778
"It is in the very latitude
we were now in where geographers
have placed the pretended Strait of
Juan de Fuca, but we saw
nothing like it" (Cook)

## The Voyage of James Cook, 1778

Known to Europeans, 1778

Extent of permanent pack ice

Extreme limit of drift ice

Cook, 1778

Encounter with native people

Trading encounter with native people

Encounter with Russian fur traders

Formal act of possession

# Tracing the Mainland Coast

## TRADERS AND EXPLORERS, 1785-94

*Following Cook's voyage, the northwest coast becomes the scene of intense trading, exploring and diplomacy.*

Cook's crew reported good prices at Canton for sea-otter skins and this led to a scramble in both Europe and the new United States to fit out expeditions to the northwest coast. Their commanders soon realized that what Cook, sailing largely offshore in 1778, had assumed to be the mainland coast, was a screen of islands. Where the straits supposedly found by Juan de Fuca and Bartholomew de Fonte (▶ *page 42*) lay was still unknown.

In 1786 La Pérouse, the French explorer, had searched around Lituya Bay for signs of a strait or river leading eastward. In 1787,

George Dixon thought Hecate Strait was Fonte's strait and William Barkley, sighting an opening south of Nootka, thought he had found "the long lost strait of Juan de Fuca."

In 1792 the American Robert Gray entered the river which Hezeta had sighted from outside its bar in 1775 (▶ *page 128*). Named after Gray's ship, the Columbia River was the most important waterway of the Pacific northwest. In the next century Gray's exploit would buttress the American claim to Oregon.

By 1790 Spain and Britain had clashed over the possession of Nootka Sound and both

powers were determined to settle the rumors of a navigable Northwest Passage. During the three summers of 1790-92, Spanish vessels explored the intricate waterways inside the opening sighted by Barkley (now the Strait of Juan de Fuca). They established that far from leading inland, the passage turned back to the sea through the Strait of Georgia and Queen Charlotte Sound. Farther north, Martínez in 1788 and Fidalgo in 1790 had reached Russian trading posts along the Alaskan peninsula. In 1791 Malaspina searched the Alaskan coast for a strait supposedly discovered by Maldonado in 1588; and in 1792 Caamaño made yet another search for evidence of Fonte's strait.

By the time George Vancouver's British

> I trust the precision with which the survey of the coast of North West America has been carried into effect, will... set aside every opinion of a north-west passage... no small portion of facetious mirth passed among the seamen, in consequence of our sailing from old England on the *first of April,* for the purpose of discovering a north-west passage, by following up the discoveries of De Fuca, De Fonte, and a numerous train of hypothetical navigators.
>
> George Vancouver, *A Voyage of Discovery to the North Pacific Ocean,* 16 April 1794

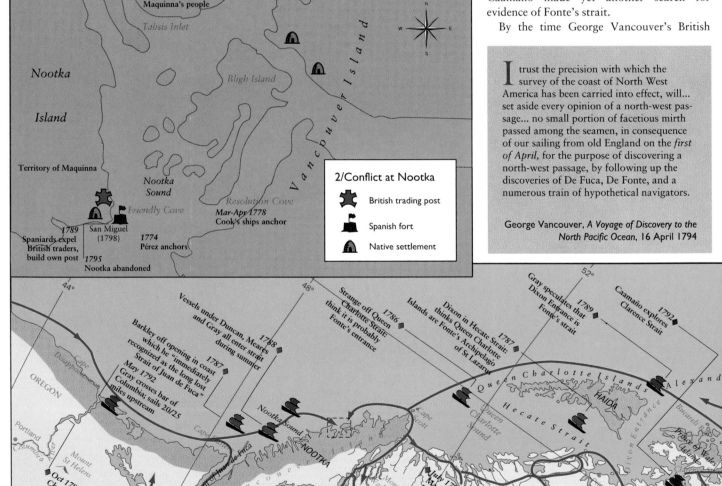

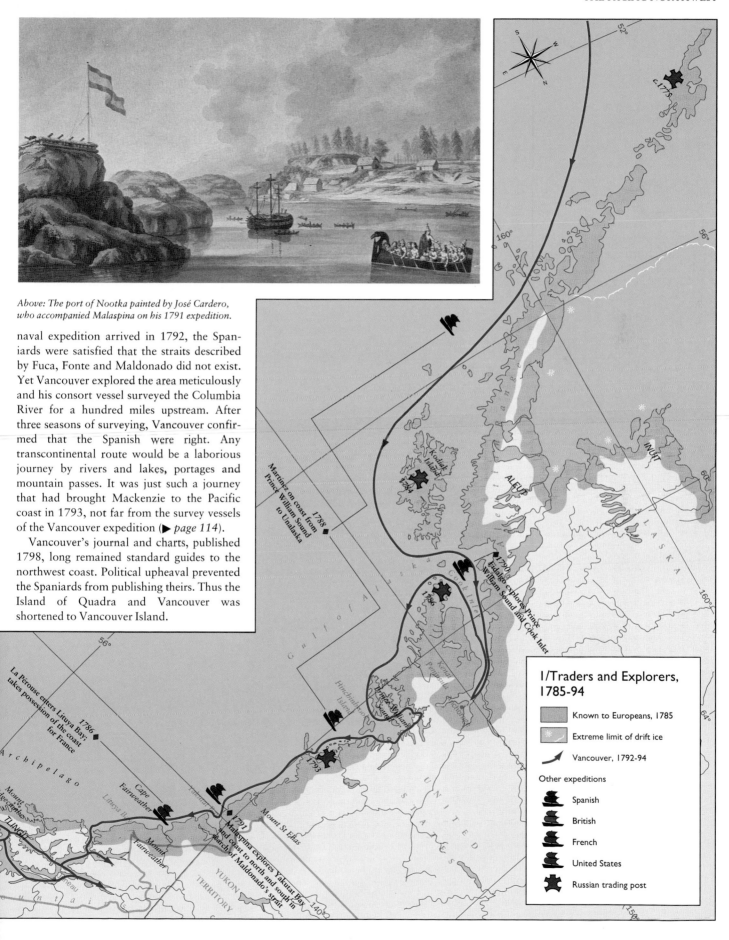

*Above: The port of Nootka painted by José Cardero, who accompanied Malaspina on his 1791 expedition.*

naval expedition arrived in 1792, the Spaniards were satisfied that the straits described by Fuca, Fonte and Maldonado did not exist. Yet Vancouver explored the area meticulously and his consort vessel surveyed the Columbia River for a hundred miles upstream. After three seasons of surveying, Vancouver confirmed that the Spanish were right. Any transcontinental route would be a laborious journey by rivers and lakes, portages and mountain passes. It was just such a journey that had brought Mackenzie to the Pacific coast in 1793, not far from the survey vessels of the Vancouver expedition (▶ *page 114*).

Vancouver's journal and charts, published 1798, long remained standard guides to the northwest coast. Political upheaval prevented the Spaniards from publishing theirs. Thus the Island of Quadra and Vancouver was shortened to Vancouver Island.

Martinez on coast from Prince William Sound to Unalaska

Fidalgo explores Prince William Sound and Cook Inlet

La Pérouse enters Lituya Bay; takes possession of the coast for France

Malaspina explores Yakutat Bay and coast to north and south in search of Maldonado's strait

**I/Traders and Explorers, 1785-94**

| | Known to Europeans, 1785 |
| --- | --- |
| | Extreme limit of drift ice |
| | Vancouver, 1792-94 |

Other expeditions

| | Spanish |
| --- | --- |
| | British |
| | French |
| | United States |
| | Russian trading post |

# Forerunners of Lewis and Clark

MISSOURI EXPLORATIONS, 1792-97

*The Spanish authorities send British and
French traders far up the Missouri to explore
the remote fringes of their dying empire.*

By the late 1780s Spanish officials had long been concerned about the frontiers of their enlarged North American empire in California, New Mexico and Louisiana. Now, rumors that British traders from Canada had followed La Vérendrye's old route to the Mandan (▶ *page 96*) meant that foreigners could infiltrate or even invade the Upper Missouri. The British threat from the north, "which seemed a dream to us on account of the distance, is today at our doors."

Spanish resources were being spent on holding the Mississippi against the Americans, so their expeditions were private rather than official. They were led by French and British traders, "since no native of the country has been found with sufficient intelligence."

In 1792 the Frenchman, Jacques d'Eglise, left St Louis for the Mandan villages, "to which no one had ever gone in this direction and by this river." In 1793 St Louis merchants formed the Company of Explorers of the Upper Missouri (the Missouri Company) and sent another Frenchman, Jean Baptiste Truteau, to the Mandan villages in 1794.

With only a single pirogue of trade goods, Truteau could not get through the upper valley, past the Ponca, Omaha and Sioux. Painfully poling and paddling upriver, slipping past hostile villages at night, Truteau may have reached no farther than the Arikara villages near Grand River. But there were echoes of La Vérendrye when he asked the Indians about a river "the waters of which might possibly flow towards the setting sun."

A Scot, James Mackay, followed Truteau in the service of Spain. Mackay, an experienced trader with the North West Company in Canada, had already visited the Mandan in 1787. He was accompanied by John Evans, a remarkable young Welshman who had come to America in quest of Welsh Indians, descendants of Madoc. He hoped to find them among the light-skinned Mandan or the "White Padoucas" (Comanche).

In 1795 Mackay left St Louis with four pirogues, the largest Spanish venture on the Upper Missouri, with instructions "to open commerce with those distant and unknown nations in the upper parts of the Missouri and to discover all the unknown parts... through

## West of the Mandan
REDRAWN FROM A MANUSCRIPT MAP
BY JOHN EVANS, 1797

Relying on Indian information, Evans showed the Missouri west of the Mandan villages, the Yellowstone River ("River yellow rock"), the Falls of the Missouri, several ranges of mountains, and a westward-flowing river with what appears to be a European trading post. The map was taken by Lewis and Clark on their expedition in 1804.

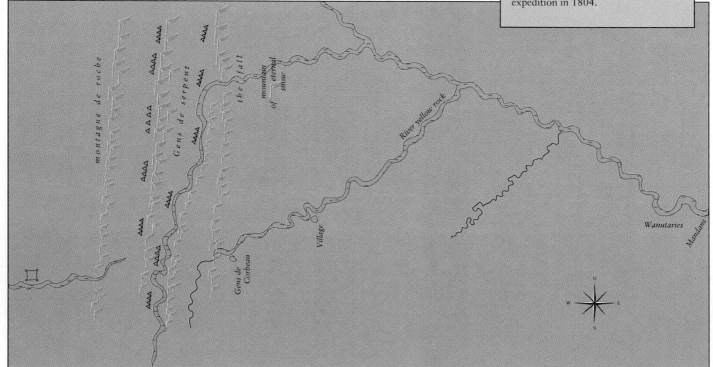

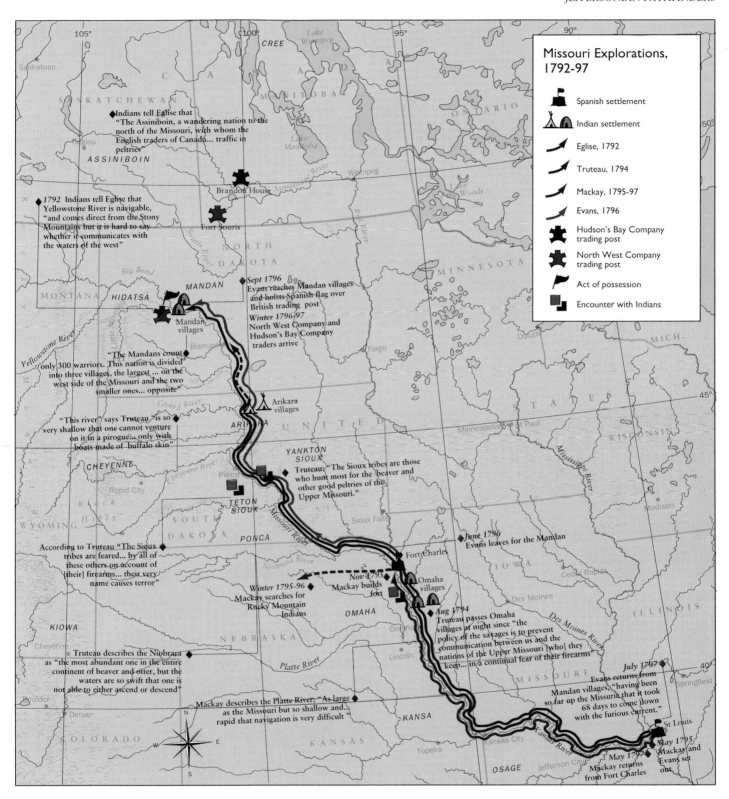

**Missouri Explorations, 1792-97**

Spanish settlement

Indian settlement

Eglise, 1792

Truteau, 1794

Mackay, 1795-97

Evans, 1796

Hudson's Bay Company trading post

North West Company trading post

Act of possession

Encounter with Indians

Indians tell Eglise that "The Assiniboin, a wandering nation to the north of the Missouri, with whom the English traders of Canada... traffic in peltries"

1792 Indians tell Eglise that Yellowstone River is navigable, "and comes direct from the Stony Mountains but it is hard to say whether it communicates with the waters of the west"

Brandon House

Fort Souris

Sept 1796 Evans reaches Mandan villages and hoists Spanish flag over British trading post

Winter 1796-97 North West Company and Hudson's Bay Company traders arrive

Mandan villages

"The Mandans count only 300 warriors. This nation is divided into three villages, the largest ... on the west side of the Missouri and the two smaller ones... opposite"

Arikara villages

"This river" says Truteau "is so very shallow that one cannot venture on it in a pirogue... only with boats made of buffalo skin"

Truteau "The Sioux tribes are those who hunt most for the beaver and other good peltries of the Upper Missouri."

According to Truteau "The Sioux tribes are feared... by all of these others on account of [their] firearms... their very name causes terror"

June 1796 Evans leaves for the Mandan

Fort Charles

Nov 1795 Mackay builds fort

Omaha villages

Winter 1795-96 Mackay searches for Rocky Mountain Indians

Aug 1794 Truteau passes Omaha villages at night since "the policy of the savages is to prevent communication between us and the nations of the Upper Missouri [who] they keep... in a continual fear of their firearms"

Truteau describes the Niobrara as "the most abundant one in the entire continent of beaver and otter, but the waters are so swift that one is not able to either ascend or descend"

Mackay describes the Platte River: "As large as the Missouri but so shallow and... rapid that navigation is very difficult"

July 1797 Evans returns from Mandan villages, "having been so far up the Missurie that it took 68 days to come down with the furious current."

St Louis

May 1795 Mackay and Evans set out

May 1797 Mackay returns from Fort Charles

that continent as far as the Pacific Ocean." Mackay built a post, Fort Charles, in Nebraska, and then sent Evans on to the Mandan country in search of trade, alliances, and a route to the Pacific. But by the time Evans reached the Mandan there was a Canadian trading post among the earth-lodges of the Indians, he was unable to travel farther west along the Missouri and he found no sign of any Welsh Indians.

Nevertheless Mackay and Evans had gathered detailed knowledge of the course of the Missouri from St Louis to the Mandan, later to be used by Lewis and Clark (▶ page 136). They also gleaned information from the Indians about the country to the west. As a result the Yellowstone River and the Great Falls of the Missouri appeared on the map for the first time, while Mackay and Evans began to see the Rockies as a complex series of ranges rather than a single ridge.

# Across the Continent

## THE JOURNEY OF LEWIS AND CLARK, 1805-06

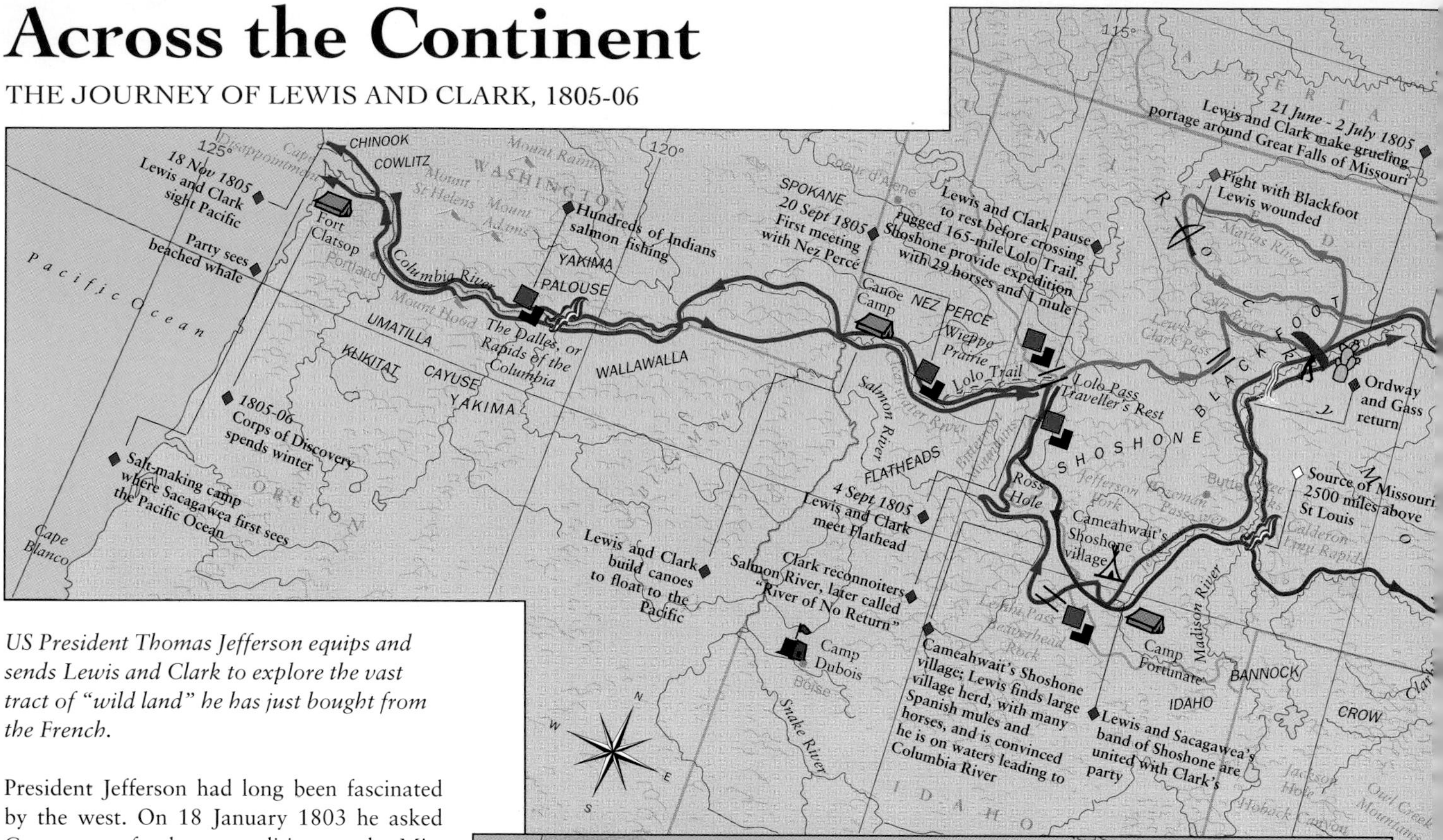

**Map labels (region 1):**

CHINOOK
COWLITZ
WASHINGTON
Mount Rainier
Mount St Helens
Mount Adams
18 Nov 1805 Lewis and Clark sight Pacific
Cape Disappointment
Party sees beached whale
Fort Clatsop
Portland
Columbia River
Mount Hood
YAKIMA
PALOUSE
The Dalles, or Rapids of the Columbia
Hundreds of Indians salmon fishing
SPOKANE 20 Sept 1805 First meeting with Nez Percé
Coeur d'Alene
Lewis and Clark pause to rest before crossing rugged 165-mile Lolo Trail. Shoshone provide expedition with 29 horses and 1 mule
Canoe Camp NEZ PERCE
Weippe Prairie
Lolo Trail
Lolo Pass Traveller's Rest
21 June - 2 July 1805 Lewis and Clark make grueling portage around Great Falls of Missouri
Fight with Blackfoot Lewis wounded
Marias River
BLACKFOOT
Lewis & Clark Pass
Ordway and Gass return
Pacific Ocean
Cape Blanco
1805-06 Corps of Discovery spends winter
OREGON
Salt-making camp where Sacagawea first sees the Pacific Ocean
UMATILLA
KLIKITAT
CAYUSE
YAKIMA
WALLAWALLA
Salmon River
FLATHEADS
4 Sept 1805 Lewis and Clark meet Flathead
Lewis and Clark build canoes to float to the Pacific
Salmon River, later called "River of No Return"
Clark reconnoiters
SHOSHONE
Ross' Hole
Jefferson River
Bitterroot
Cameahwait's Shoshone village
Butte
Source of Missouri 2500 miles above St Louis
Calderon
Lemhi Pass
Beaverhead Rock
Camp Dubois
Boise
Snake River
Cameahwait's Shoshone village; Lewis finds large village herd, with many Spanish mules and horses, and is convinced he is on waters leading to Columbia River
Camp Fortunate
Madison River
BANNOCK
IDAHO
Lewis and Sacagawea's band of Shoshone are united with Clark's party
CROW
IDAHO
Jackson Hole
Owl Creek Mountains
Hoback Canyon

*US President Thomas Jefferson equips and sends Lewis and Clark to explore the vast tract of "wild land" he has just bought from the French.*

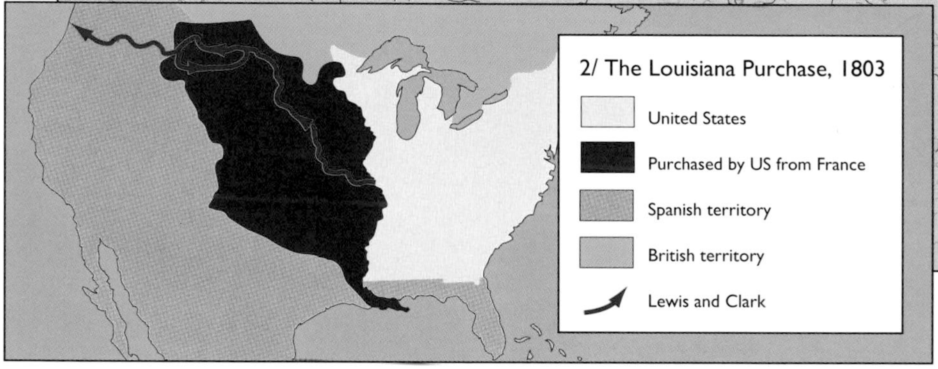

President Jefferson had long been fascinated by the west. On 18 January 1803 he asked Congress to fund an expedition up the Missouri, stressing that the journey over Spanish soil would bring great commercial gain.

Congress agreed. Jefferson's private secretary, the young army captain Meriwether Lewis, was sent to Philadelphia to learn natural history. In the spring, Jefferson bought Louisiana from Napoleon, lending impetus to the project. Lewis asked Jefferson to appoint William Clark, his friend and former commanding officer, co-captain of the expedition. By fall, they had recruited 36 "stout, single woodsmen," a half-Indian interpreter, and Clark's black slave, York.

On 14 May 1804 Clark and the Corps of Discovery put their 55-foot, 22-oared keelboat and two pirogues (flat-bottomed dugouts) into the Mississippi at Wood River, and rowed downstream to the Missouri. Lewis joined them at Saint-Charles, a French settlement. The shallow, serpentine Missouri was filled with the green, rotting carcasses of buffalo killed by Indians. Caved-in banks and shifting sandbars lined its course. Stiff breezes and a strong current meant that the men sometimes had to get out and pull their boats through with ropes.

Occasionally they met white traders on the river. Several times they stopped to pay tribute to local Indians. Beyond the mouth of the Platte they found large numbers of buffalo, which they hunted for meat, and they regularly sighted deer, elk and antelope.

**Legend box:**

### 2/ The Louisiana Purchase, 1803

- United States
- Purchased by US from France
- Spanish territory
- British territory
- Lewis and Clark

In November, after high winds and the first snow, they built a winter fort, watched by curious Mandan. Toussaint Charbonneau, a French Canadian trapper who had lived for five years among the Hidatsa, arrived and Lewis and Clark hired him as an interpreter. A week later his pregnant wife, a Shoshone named Sacagawea, joined them.

Winter temperatures at Fort Mandan dipped almost 50° below zero. The hunting was poor, but the Corps built canoes and made clothes and moccasins. Lewis and Clark traded with the Indians, who told them of great waterfalls and mountains ahead.

Early in April, the keelboat, under Corporal Richard Warfington, headed back down the Missouri with specimens for Jefferson and a letter. The rest of the expedition paddled upstream. Late in May, Lewis glimpsed the distant Rockies for the first time. The explorers were in "high broken rockey" country populated by grizzly bears and bighorn sheep. On 13 June Lewis found the 80-foot waterfalls the Mandan had told him marked the Missouri, and dispatched one of his men with a letter to Clark.

For two hot weeks, the men pulled their boats up steep slopes, through rocky gullies and around great stands of prickly pear until they were back on the Missouri. They then hiked over the Continental Divide. Through rain, hail and snow they crossed the Bitterroot Range of the Rockies and along an old Nez Percé trail, the Lolo Pass, to the coastal plain.

At the Clearwater River, they left their mounts with the Nez Percé, burned out five canoes from logs, and took to the water again. Riding the rapids they followed the Clearwater, the Snake and then the Columbia River, reaching the Pacific early in November.

11

11

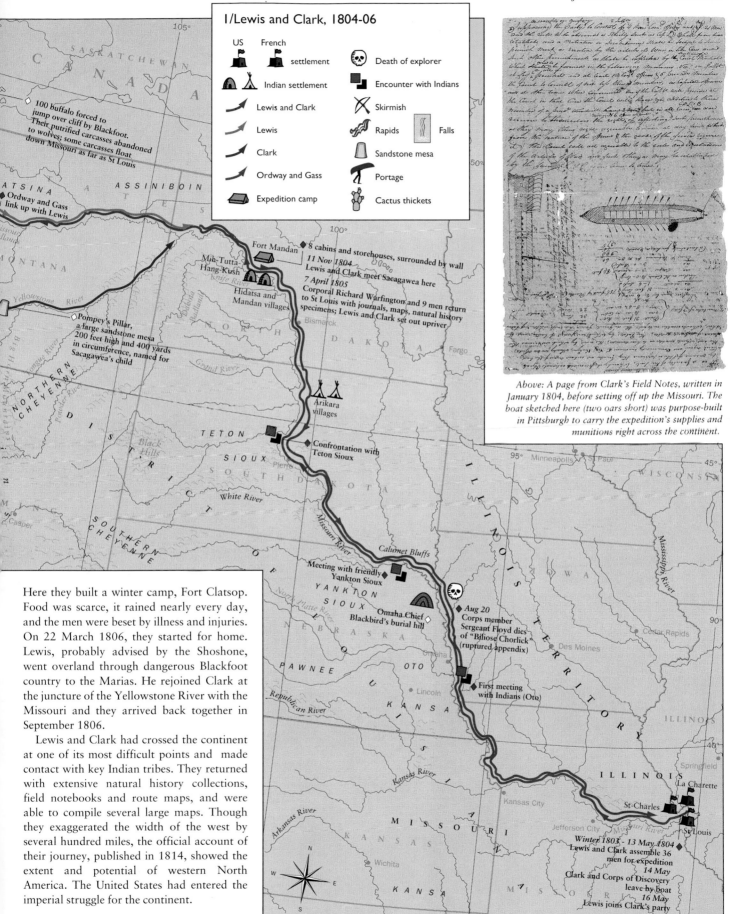

**I/Lewis and Clark, 1804-06**

US | French
- settlement
- Indian settlement
- Lewis and Clark
- Lewis
- Clark
- Ordway and Gass
- Expedition camp
- Death of explorer
- Encounter with Indians
- Skirmish
- Rapids | Falls
- Sandstone mesa
- Portage
- Cactus thickets

100 buffalo forced to jump over cliff by Blackfoot. Their putrified carcasses abandoned to wolves; some carcasses float down Missouri as far as St Louis

Ordway and Gass link up with Lewis

Fort Mandan

Mih-Tutta-Hang-Kush

Hidatsa and Mandan villages

8 cabins and storehouses, surrounded by wall
11 Nov 1804 Lewis and Clark meet Sacagawea here
7 April 1805 Corporal Richard Warfington and 9 men return to St Louis with journals, maps, natural history specimens; Lewis and Clark set out upriver

Pompey's Pillar, a large sandstone mesa 200 feet high and 400 yards in circumference, named for Sacagawea's child

Knife River
NORTHERN CHEYENNE
Yellowstone River
Big Horn River
MONTANA
Powder River
Dakota Badlands
NORTH DAKOTA
Grand River
Bismarck
Fargo

Arikara villages

TETON SIOUX
Black Hills
SOUTH DAKOTA
Pierre
White River

Confrontation with Teton Sioux

SOUTHERN CHEYENNE

Calumet Bluffs
Meeting with friendly Yankton Sioux
YANKTON SIOUX
North Platte River
Omaha Chief Blackbird's burial hill
NEBRASKA
Omaha
Lincoln
PAWNEE
OTO
Republican River
KANSAS
First meeting with Indians (Oto)

Aug 20 Corps member Sergeant Floyd dies of "Biliose Chorlick" (ruptured appendix)

IOWA
Cedar Rapids
Des Moines
ILLINOIS TERRITORY
Minneapolis St Paul
WISCONSIN

Kansas River
Kansas City
MISSOURI
Jefferson City
Arkansas River
Wichita
KANSAS

Springfield
ILLINOIS
La Charette
St-Charles
St Louis
Winter 1803 - 13 May 1804 Lewis and Clark assemble 36 men for expedition
14 May Clark and Corps of Discovery leave by boat
16 May Lewis joins Clark's party

Casper
WYOMING

CANADA
SASKATCHEWAN
ASSINIBOIN
ATSINA

Missouri River

Above: A page from Clark's Field Notes, written in January 1804, before setting off up the Missouri. The boat sketched here (two oars short) was purpose-built in Pittsburgh to carry the expedition's supplies and munitions right across the continent.

Here they built a winter camp, Fort Clatsop. Food was scarce, it rained nearly every day, and the men were beset by illness and injuries. On 22 March 1806, they started for home. Lewis, probably advised by the Shoshone, went overland through dangerous Blackfoot country to the Marias. He rejoined Clark at the juncture of the Yellowstone River with the Missouri and they arrived back together in September 1806.

Lewis and Clark had crossed the continent at one of its most difficult points and made contact with key Indian tribes. They returned with extensive natural history collections, field notebooks and route maps, and were able to compile several large maps. Though they exaggerated the width of the west by several hundred miles, the official account of their journey, published in 1814, showed the extent and potential of western North America. The United States had entered the imperial struggle for the continent.

# The Scouts of New Spain

## SPANISH TRAILBLAZERS IN THE OLD SOUTHWEST, 1786-1808

*Spanish explorers forge paths between
frontier posts in Texas and Louisiana. But
the area they open is hotly contested by both
the United States and the Plains Indians.*

In 1763 the French ceded their Louisiana possessions to Spain to spite the English and suddenly the Spanish frontier advanced to Mississippi country. The Spanish bureaucracy eventually realized the value of establishing links between their remote frontier outposts. In 1786 they hired a mysterious Frenchman and former *contrabandista* or illegal trader, Don Pedro (Pierre) Vial, to blaze a trail from San Antonio to Santa Fé. Vial was a former gunsmith who had spent years living with Indians and repairing their French weapons. He crossed the plains wilderness from east to west but his diary entries were meager and much of his winding route is now conjectural.

New Mexico's governor then sent a retired corporal, José Mares, to find a more direct route. Mares was the first known explorer on the featureless plains of the Llano Estacado since the Martin-Castillo expedition of 1650. Shortly after Mares' return to San Antonio, New Mexico's governor dispatched Vial, with diarists Fragoso and Fernandez, and four com-

panions, to find a direct route from Santa Fé to Natchitoches in Louisiana. On their return they found even shorter routes to San Antonio and from there to Santa Fé. Then in 1792 Vial was ordered to blaze a trail from Santa Fé to "St Louis of Illinois, province of Louisiana."

Although Spanish officials had laid out a planned interstate network of trails linking New Mexico, Texas and Louisiana, the expected trading caravans simply never materialized. When France reacquired Louisiana and sold it to the Americans, the Spanish became concerned with Anglo penetration. In 1806 Spain's frontier officials dispatched Don Facundo Malgares to intercept Zebulon Pike (▶ *page 144*). They missed him. In 1808 Lieutenant Francisco Amangual left San Antonio to make a show of force in finding a northern route to Santa Fé.

The 18th and early 19th century trailblazers of the Spanish northeast frontier covered vast distances, left significant accounts of their travels and operated with a minimum of violence. Some, like Vial, were also important intermediaries in the establishment of peaceful relations between native tribes and the Spanish.

### The Spanish Southwest

REDRAWN FROM A MAP BY PEDRO VIAL, 1787

Vial's hand-drawn map shows the main Spanish settlements in New Mexico and Texas. Drawing on his own travels in the region, it represents the best Spanish knowledge of the region at the time. He shows the Canadian River, but depicts its flowing into the Red River (Rio Colorado) instead of the Arkansas (Rio de la arga).

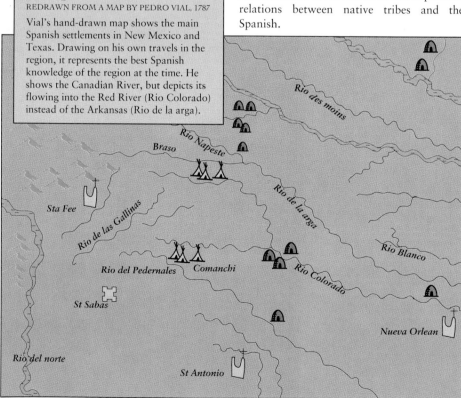

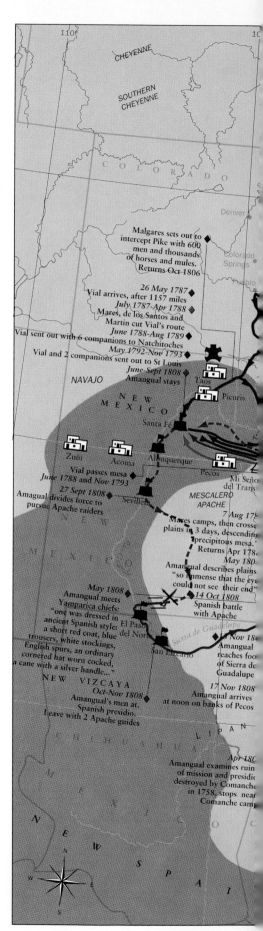

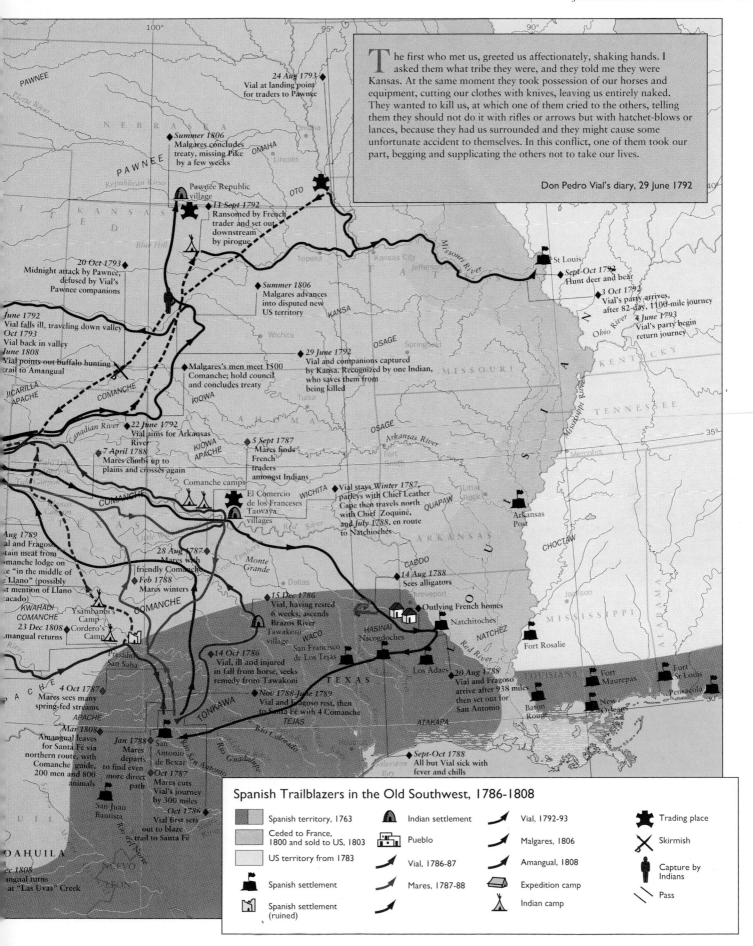

The first who met us, greeted us affectionately, shaking hands. I asked them what tribe they were, and they told me they were Kansas. At the same moment they took possession of our horses and equipment, cutting our clothes with knives, leaving us entirely naked. They wanted to kill us, at which one of them cried to the others, telling them they should not do it with rifles or arrows but with hatchet-blows or lances, because they had us surrounded and they might cause some unfortunate accident to themselves. In this conflict, one of them took our part, begging and supplicating the others not to take our lives.

Don Pedro Vial's diary, 29 June 1792

**24 Aug 1793**
Vial at landing point for traders to Pawnee

**Summer 1806**
Malgares concludes treaty, missing Pike by a few weeks

Pawnee Republic village

**11 Sept 1792**
Ransomed by French trader and set out downstream by pirogue

**20 Oct 1793**
Midnight attack by Pawnee, defused by Vial's Pawnee companions

**Sept-Oct 1792**
Hunt deer and bear

**3 Oct 1792**
Vial's party arrives, after 82-day, 1100-mile journey

**4 June 1793**
Vial's party begin return journey

**Summer 1806**
Malgares advances into disputed new US territory

**June 1792**
Vial falls ill, traveling down valley
**Oct 1793**
Vial back in valley
**June 1808**
Vial points out buffalo hunting trail to Amangual

**29 June 1792**
Vial and companions captured by Kansa. Recognized by one Indian, who saves them from being killed

Malgares's men meet 1500 Comanche; hold council and concludes treaty

**22 June 1792**
Vial aims for Arkansas River

**7 April 1788**
Mares climbs up to plains and crosses again

**5 Sept 1787**
Mares finds French traders amongst Indians

**Vial stays Winter 1787,**
parleys with Chief Leather Cape then travels north with Chief Zoquiné, and *July 1788*, en route to Natchioches

El Comercio de los Franceses
Taovaya villages

Comanche camps

**Aug 1789**
al and Fragoso
tain meat from
manche lodge on
e "in the middle of
e Llano" (possibly
st mention of Llano
acado)

**28 Aug 1787**
Mares with friendly Comanche

**Feb 1788**
Mares winters

**14 Aug 1788**
Sees alligators

**15 Dec 1786**
Vial, having rested 6 weeks, ascends Brazos River

Tawakoni village

Outlying French homes

Natchitoches

*KWAHADI COMANCHE*
**23 Dec 1808**
mangual returns
Cordero's Camp
Ysambanbi's Camp

**14 Oct 1786**
Vial, ill and injured in fall from horse, seeks remedy from Tawakoni

San Francisco de Los Tejas

Hasinai
Nacogdoches

**20 Aug 1788**
Vial and Fragoso arrive after 938 miles then set out for San Antonio

Los Adaes

Presidio San Saba

**4 Oct 1787**
Mares sees many spring-fed streams
*APACHE*

**Nov 1788-June 1789**
Vial and Fragoso rest, then to Santa Fe with 4 Comanche

*TONKAWA*
*TEJAS*

**Mar 1808**
Amangual leaves for Santa Fe via northern route, with Comanche guide, 200 men and 800 animals

**Jan 1788**
Mares departs to find even more direct path
San Antonio de Bexar

**Oct 1787**
Mares cuts Vial's journey by 300 miles

**Oct 1786**
Vial first sets out to blaze trail to Santa Fe

**Sept-Oct 1788**
All but Vial sick with fever and chills

San Juan Bautista

*e 1808*
ngual turns
at "Las Uvas" Creek

Fort Maurepas
Fort St Louis
Pensacola

Baton Rouge
New Orleans

## Spanish Trailblazers in the Old Southwest, 1786-1808

| | | | |
|---|---|---|---|
| ■ Spanish territory, 1763 | Indian settlement | Vial, 1792-93 | Trading place |
| ■ Ceded to France, 1800 and sold to US, 1803 | Pueblo | Malgares, 1806 | ✕ Skirmish |
| ■ US territory from 1783 | Vial, 1786-87 | Amangual, 1808 | Capture by Indians |
| Spanish settlement | Mares, 1787-88 | Expedition camp | Pass |
| Spanish settlement (ruined) | | Indian camp | |

# Pathfinders of the Old Southwest

## TRAPPERS AND TRADERS IN LOUISIANA AND TEXAS, 1792-1827

*US government expeditions and freelance traders and horse hunters explore the fiercely contended no-man's land between the lower Red River and central Texas.*

Following the Louisiana Purchase, it became urgent for the United States to determine its uncertain boundary with New Spain. As early as 1791, Phillip Nolan, a friend of both Wilkinson and Jefferson, had penetrated Texas, trading horses with the Comanche. In 1794 he reached San Antonio. By 1800 he had led a party of filibusters who built a fort on Nolan Creek, near present-day Temple, Texas, where he was killed by the Spaniards.

Once he became president, Thomas Jefferson sent official expeditions to the region. In 1804 Scottish-born planter William Dunbar and Philadelphia naturalist George Hunter rowed up the Ouachita accumulating data on the region's geography, flora, fauna, fossils, Indian sign language and astronomical phenomena. Two years later Thomas Freeman led a party up the Red River to locate its source. Despite a 100-mile detour to avoid the log "rafts" which jammed the river, they arrived at its upper reaches before being turned back by a Spanish force under Francisco Viana.

Meanwhile a host of horse traders and gold seekers from Natchitoches contributed to knowledge of the Texas plains. Jacques Clamorgan had made his way to Santa Fé in 1807, undoubtedly invited by the Spaniards. Anthony Glass regularly led parties out onto the plains to trade with the Comanche and Pawnee for horses. So friendly was he with the Pawnee that they showed him their sacred stone, a meteorite 3 foot 4 inches long and 2 foot 4.5 inches wide. Believing that it was pure platinum, Glass stole it in 1809. In 1812 John Maley led a party up the Red River

seeking abandoned Spanish gold and silver mines. Far out on the prairie Maley and his partners were robbed by the Osage. Stripped and left with only their wallets and knives, Maley and his men wandered for nearly two grueling months before they finally staggered back into Natchitoches.

The stream of traders and trappers continued, despite frequent imprisonment by the Spanish authorities. Three civilian parties - under William Becknell, Thomas James and

*Below: This oil painting by George Catlin depicts "Comanches giving the arrows to the Medecine Rock." The Comanche believed that fallen meteorites, such as the one Glass stole in 1809, had medicinal properties, and made offerings to them.*

### The Internal Part of Louisiana
REDRAWN FROM AN 1807 MAP BY ANTOINE NAU

Nau, a French draftsman who had served on Wilkinson's staff, based his map on a chart by Pike (▶ *page 144*). It was one of the first to incorporate the discoveries of Freeman, Dunbar and Hunter. It also shows the neutral border zone agreed by Wilkinson and the Spanish Colonel Herrera, and an 1806 confrontation between them in which armed conflict was narrowly avoided.

Hugh Glenn - were all en route to Santa Fé when Glenn met some Mexican emissaries who told him "that the mackeson province Has de Clared Independance of the mother Cuntry and is desirous of a traid With the people of the united States." With this new willingness to trade, a regular Santa Fé Trail was established by the end of 1824.

A person is mounted on a fleet horse, round the neck of which a rope is tied; and the other end of the rope is formed into a noose... and singling out one of [the wild horses], rides at full speed after him, and when he has come within the required distance, throws the noose over his head... The rider then gets off his horse and immediately mounts the other animal, and continues to ride him at full speed till he is fairly overcome, and properly broken in...

Francis Bailey, an English scientist
with Philip Nolan

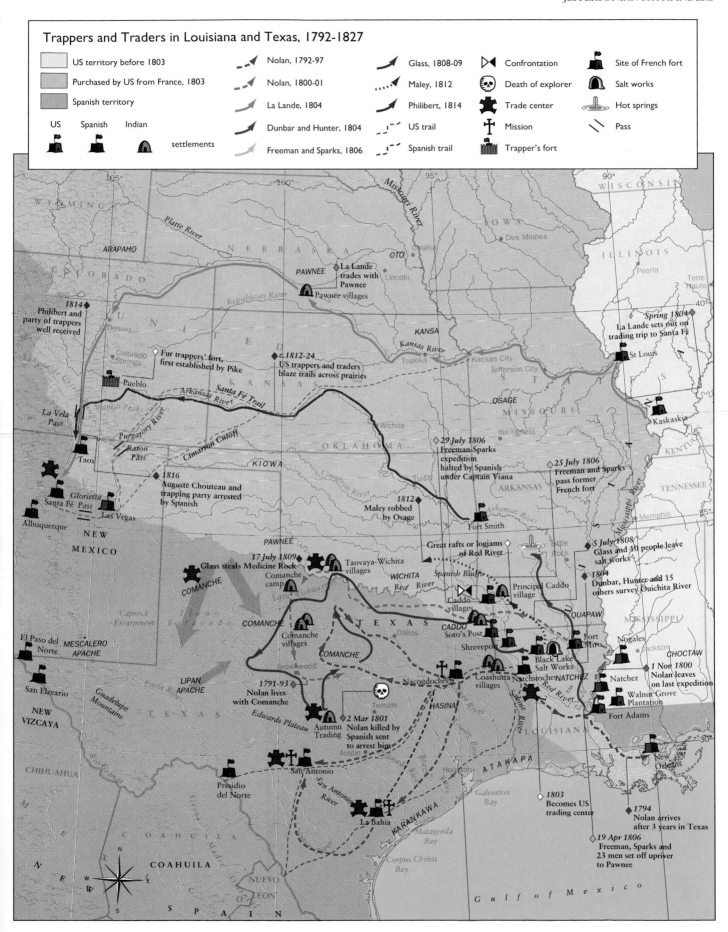

## Trappers and Traders in Louisiana and Texas, 1792-1827

- US territory before 1803
- Purchased by US from France, 1803
- Spanish territory

settlements: US  Spanish  Indian

- Nolan, 1792-97
- Nolan, 1800-01
- La Lande, 1804
- Dunbar and Hunter, 1804
- Freeman and Sparks, 1806
- Glass, 1808-09
- Maley, 1812
- Philibert, 1814
- US trail
- Spanish trail
- Confrontation
- Death of explorer
- Trade center
- Mission
- Trapper's fort
- Site of French fort
- Salt works
- Hot springs
- Pass

WISCONSIN

WYOMING

ARAPAHO

Platte River

Missouri River

IOWA

• Des Moines

Omaha

ILLINOIS

NEBRASKA

OTO

Peoria

Terre Haute

COLORADO

La Lande trades with Pawnee

PAWNEE

Republican River

Lincoln

40°

Spring 1804
La Lande sets out on trading trip to Santa Fé

St Louis

KANSA

Kansas River

Topeka

Kansas City

Jefferson City

MISSOURI

Kaskaskia

1814
Philibert and party of trappers well received

Denver

Colorado Springs

Fur trappers' fort, first established by Pike

c.1812-24
US trappers and traders blaze trails across prairies

Santa Fé Trail

KANSAS

Wichita

OSAGE

Springfield

KENTUCKY

La Vela Pass

Pueblo

Arkansas River

Spanish Peaks

OKLAHOMA

Cimarron Cutoff

ARKANSAS

TENNESSEE

Taos

Purgatory River

Raton Pass

Cimarron River

Tulsa

29 July 1806
Freeman-Sparks expedition halted by Spanish under Captain Viana

25 July 1806
Freeman and Sparks pass former French fort

Memphis

85°

Glorietta Pass

Santa Fé

1816
Auguste Chouteau and trapping party arrested by Spanish

KIOWA

1812
Maley robbed by Osage

Fort Smith

Arkansas River

Little Rock

5 July 1808
Glass and 10 people leave salt works

Albuquerque

Las Vegas

NEW MEXICO

PAWNEE

Great rafts or logjams of Red River

Spanish Bluffs

Principal Caddo village

1804
Dunbar, Hunter and 15 others survey Ouichita River

17 July 1809
Glass steals Medicine Rock

Taovaya-Wichita villages

Comanche camp

COMANCHE

Little Wichita River

WICHITA

Red River

Caddo villages

QUAPAW

MISSISSIPPI

Nogales

Jackson

El Paso del Norte

MESCALERO APACHE

Llano Estacado

COMANCHE

Comanche villages

COMANCHE

TEXAS

Dallas

CADDO

Soto's Post

Shreveport

Fort Miro

CHOCTAW

Caprock Escarpment

Black Lake Salt Works

Natchez

1 Nov 1800
Nolan leaves on last expedition

San Elzeario

LIPAN APACHE

1791-93
Nolan lives with Comanche

Brownwood

COMANCHE

Nacogdoches

Coashutta villages

Natchitoches

Red River

Walnut Grove Plantation

NEW VIZCAYA

Guadelupe Mountains

Pecos River

Edwards Plateau

Autumn Trading

2 Mar 1801
Nolan killed by Spanish sent to arrest him

HASINAI

Sabine River

NATCHEZ

Fort Adams

CHIHUAHUA

Rio Grande

Temple

Austin

LOUISIANA

Houston

ATAKAPA

New Orleans

Presidio del Norte

San Antonio

San Antonio River

Galveston Bay

1803
Becomes US trading center

Sierra Madre

La Bahia

KARANKAWA

Matagorda Bay

1794
Nolan arrives after 3 years in Texas

COAHUILA

NUEVO LEON

SPAIN

Corpus Christi Bay

19 Apr 1806
Freeman, Sparks and 23 men set off upriver to Pawnee

Gulf of Mexico

# Vanguard of Empire

## THE ASTORIANS 1810-12

*John Jacob Astor's attempt to corner the north American fur trade leads to the discovery of the South Pass through the Rockies.*

On 8 September 1810 John Jacob Astor launched the ship *Tonquin* on a course around Cape Horn and via Hawaii to the mouth of the Columbia River. There, under the leadership of two of his Canadian associates, Duncan McDougall and Robert Stuart, the Pacific Fur Company established Fort Astoria on the south bank of the Columbia.

Captain Thorne then took the *Tonquin* north to Vancouver Island where Salish Indians overwhelmed his ship, killing all aboard save two. One Jack Ramsay survived by jumping overboard. Another wounded sailor touched off the powder magazine, blowing up the *Tonquin* and 200 Salish, whose "arms, legs, and heads," according to Ramsay, "were flying in all directions."

Shortly after the *Tonquin* sailed from New York, Wilson Price Hunt, a St Louis clerk without any exploring experience, together with Canadian fur trader, Donald Mackenzie and 60 men, left St Louis and headed up the Missouri for the mouth of the Columbia. Hunt took with him the English botanist John Bradbury and Thomas Nuttall, a Philadelphia naturalist.

Though furnished with a map by William Clark, Hunt decided to try a shortcut to the Columbia. After suffering great hardships in the stony badlands, they eventually confronted the towering Big Horn Mountains crossing them with great difficulty. Most of the party were French Canadian rivermen – indeed, Robinson, Hoback, and Reznor were the only experienced mountain men in the party – and Hunt hoped to build canoes and cruise down the Snake to the Columbia. They should have taken note of Clark's map. They got tangled up in the rocky cliffs of Hoback Canyon, and were near starving by the time, with the help of the Shoshone, they reached the ruins of Andrew Henry's fort.

Here, Hunt made his most critical mistake. He left his few horses behind and tried to sail down the Snake. By the time they reached the rolling rapids of Calderon Linn, in present-day Idaho, the party had broken up. One detachment, led by Ramsay Crook, walked along the south bank of the Snake. Another detachment, headed by Robert McClellan, joined Hoback and Reznor and abandoned the trek to live with the Shoshone.

Meanwhile Hunt followed the north bank of the mighty Snake. Indians warned him of the 5000-foot Hell's Canyon of the Snake. He heeded their advice and later met up with Cayuse and Nez Percé Indians, who supplied the exhausted explorers with horses and pointed them toward the Columbia. At last, Hunt consulted Clark's map and realized they were in familiar country. They made their way down the Columbia. On 15 February 1812, paddling six canoes through rain and fog, they reached Fort Astoria. Mackenzie had arrived there a month earlier. Ramsay Crook, John Day and two other members of the party were robbed by Indians near the Salmon River and remained stranded until late spring when they were rescued by a party from Astoria. Dogs, horses, beaver paws, animal skins and stomach-wrenching roots were providential fare for all the explorers. Out of the 60 men who started on the expedition only 45 were to reach Fort Astoria alive.

The Astoria venture was proving to be a disaster. Few furs were taken at the fort. In July 1811 David Thompson of the North West Company arrived (▶ *page 118*), after claiming all of the Columbia River country for Britain, although the Astorians from the United States had beaten him to the mouth of the Columbia. On 19 June 1812 war was declared between Britain and the United States. By March 1813, Astoria was besieged by the North West Company and then later by the British man-o-war HMS *Raccoon*. Macdougall and Mackenzie gave up without a fight.

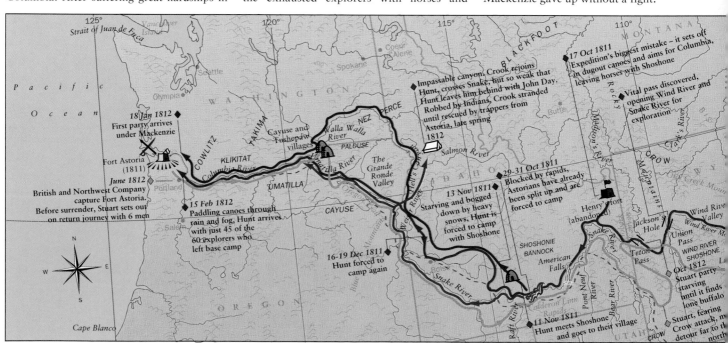

Mr Crook's indisposition increased so much this afternoon that I insisted on his taking a dose of castor oil, which fortunately had the desired effect, but he... is withal so weak as to preclude all idea of continuing our journey untill his recovery... The sensations excited on this occasion, and by the view of an unknown and untravelled wilderness, are not such as to arise in the artificial solitude of parks and gardens... the phantoms which haunt a desert are want, misery, and danger, the evils of which... rush upon the mind; man is made unwillingly acquainted with his own weakness and meditation shews him how little he can sustain and how little he can perform.

*Robert Stuart's journal, 1 October 1812*

One of the Canadians advanced towards me with his rifle in his hand saying that as there was no appearance of our being able to procure any provisions... that lots should be cast and one die to preserve the rest... I snatched up my rifle cocked and leveled it at him with firm resolution to fire if he persisted...

*Robert Stuart's journal, 12 October 1812*

It was a very real pleasure for travelers harassed by fatigue to rest in quiet and be surrounded by friends after so long a journey in the midst of savages of whom it is always prudent to be wary. We had covered 2073 miles since leaving the Aricara's village.

*Wilson Price Hunt's diary, on reaching Fort Astoria, 16 February 1812*

Before the surrender, on 29 June 1812, Robert Stuart and six men started the return march back across the continent. This would prove to be the most important of Astor's contributions to continental exploration. Part of their route was along what would become the Oregon Trail. The crossing was extremely difficult – even more so than that of Hunt's westbound party. John Day went insane and had to be returned to Astoria even before they crossed the Grand Ronde and the Blue Mountains of Oregon. Stuart's party avoided Hell's Canyon and followed the Snake River as it curved far south through desolate parts of present-day Idaho. Then, fearing Indians, they made a detour far to the north into Jackson's Hole. Only the shooting of a lone buffalo bull saved them from starvation.

From Jackson's Hole, they followed an Indian trail through Hoback Canyon, west of the Wind Rivers. Then they discovered the South Pass of the Rocky Mountains, soon to become the gateway to the West, as thousands of emigrants would pass through on their way to Oregon and California.

For over a decade, however, Robert Stuart's discovery remained private, known only to Astor. It was not until 1824, that the mountain men Jedediah Smith and Tom "Broken Hand" Fitzpatrick (▶ *page 152*) rediscovered it with the help of Crow Indians.

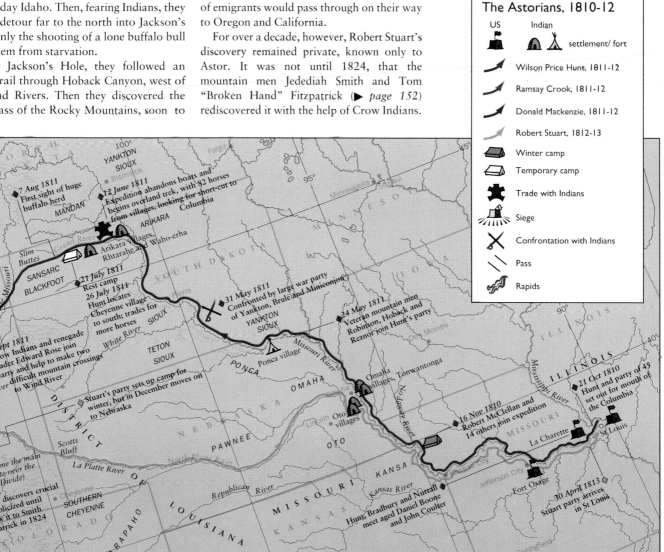

# The Great American Desert
## THE EXPEDITIONS OF PIKE AND LONG, 1806-20

*Two military expeditions cross the Great Plains to the Rockies and explore the area between Lewis and Clark's discoveries and the mysterious Spanish territory to the south.*

In July 1806 General James Wilkinson, US Governor of the Louisiana Territory, sent Lieutenant Zebulon Pike to visit Osage, Pawnee and Comanche villages and to determine the source of the Red River, regarded by the US as its southern boundary. The story of Pike's expedition is the stuff of romance and intrigue. Wilkinson harbored ambitions to capture Santa Fé from the Spaniards. He gave Pike secret orders to scout out the road there, reassuring him that, as far as the Spanish were concerned, he would be "as safe as in Philadelphia," he had only hostile plains Indians to fear. But then Wilkinson, the master intriguer, leaked word of Pike's mission to the Spanish authorities, who sent Malgares out to capture Pike (▶ *page 138*).

Pike's 23 men included Lieutenant James Wilkinson, the general's own son, and a mysterious Dr John Robinson. Pike followed Malgares' broad trail towards Santa Fé. Following orders, he sent Wilkinson and five men down the Arkansas River to safety. They carried Pike's maps and final dispatches. Then Pike turned toward the Rockies, which he sighted on 15 November, 1806, looking like "a small blue cloud." Pike and his men failed in several attempts to climb what is now Pike's Peak, but he did climb Cheyenne Peak which afforded him a panoramic view of the southern Rockies. On the Arkansas the severe winter forced Pike to leave some of his men

> I n regard to this extensive section of country,... it is almost wholly unfit for cultivation, and of course, uninhabitable by a people depending upon agriculture for their subsistence... The scarcity of wood and water, almost uniformly prevalent, will prove an insuperable obstacle in the way of settling the country...
>
> Major Stephen H. Long,
> *General Description of the Country Traversed by the Exploring Expedition*

behind. At the Rio Conejos, at the end of their endurance, Pike's men built a crude fort and awaited rescue.

Dr Robinson went on to Santa Fé, showing that Pike knew approximately where he was, but he claimed innocence when he and his men were arrested by Malgares and Spanish cavalry. At Chihuahua the Governor confiscated Pike's notes and sent him back across Texas to Louisiana. This gave Pike a matchless opportunity to spy out virtually all of New Spain and Texas. He secretly made new notes, hiding them in the barrels of his men's guns. In 1810, four years before Lewis and Clark's report, Pike made an extensive report on the Great American Desert, the road to Santa Fé, hitherto obscure northern New Spain and Texas. Wilkinson was later

tried for treason, but acquitted much to Jefferson's disgust.

In 1819, the US Secretary of War sent General Henry Rice Atkinson and 1000 men to control the Indians and drive out the British fur traders. After heading up the Missouri in five steamboats, the troops became ill and the Indians would not let them pass. Major Stephen H. Long had accompanied them, in a sixth steamboat, with scientists and army topographical engineers. After Atkinson's failure, Long was given permission to explore the Great Plains. They headed along the North and then the South Platte and, after climbing Pike's Peak, marched south. At the Arkansas River, Long sent Captain John Bell, the artist Samuel Seymour and the expedition's geologist Dr Thomas Say downriver with several riflemen. Returning, Bell's party passed through large numbers of threatening Cheyenne, Arapaho and Kiowa. Some soldiers deserted, taking most of the expedition's scientific collections and notebooks. Long continued south, at one point mistaking the Canadian River for the Red River, the boundary between United States and Spanish territory.

Originally criticized for this blunder, Long's foray is now seen to have had great merit. The US government published Long's map with "Great Desert" printed across the western prairies; a misleading description which was to deter thousands of potential emigrants. A report was privately published, with a small atlas, in 1823. It included Thomas Say's finding of marine fossils millions of years old, indicating that a great inundation had once covered the Great Plains.

The headwaters of the Red River were not discovered until 1852, by Captain Randolph Barnes Marcy, by which time they no longer had any political significance.

*Left: Unlike previous expeditions, Long's had two artists. One of them, Samuel Seymour painted this view of the Rockies from Fifty miles out.Titian Peale, who also traveled with Long, illustrated the abundant wildlife to be seen on the plains. Their work provided the American public with their first visual impressions of the West.*

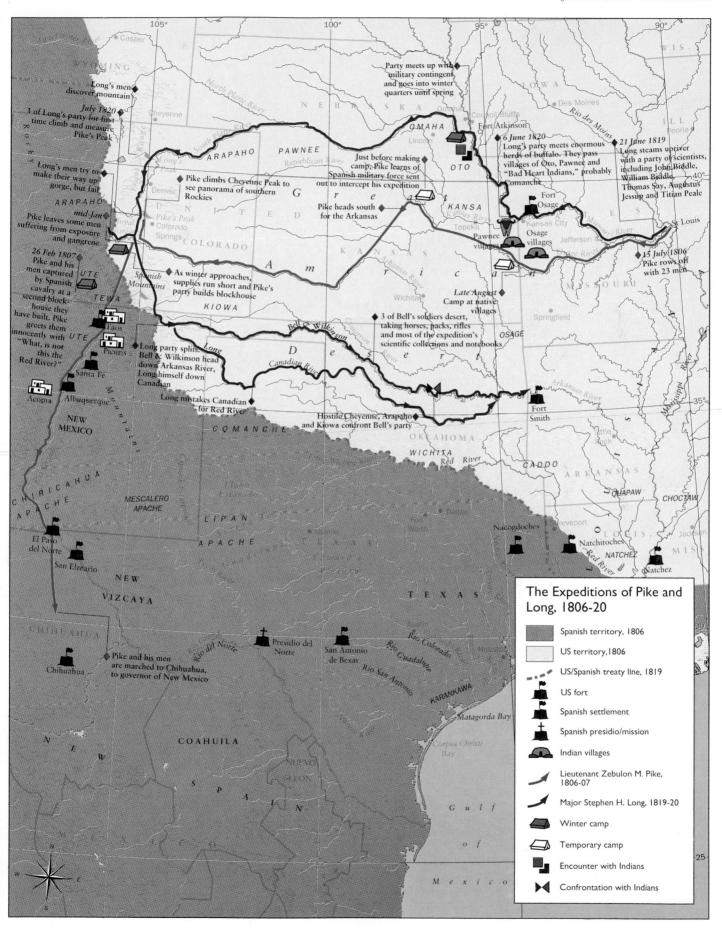

Long's men discover mountain

July 1820

3 of Long's party for first time climb and measure Pike's Peak

Long's men try to make their way up gorge, but fail

mid-Jan
Pike leaves some men suffering from exposure and gangrene

26 Feb 1807
Pike and his men captured by Spanish cavalry at a second block-house they have built. Pike greets them innocently with "What, is not this the Red River?"

Pike climbs Cheyenne Peak to see panorama of southern Rockies

Pike heads south for the Arkansas

As winter approaches, supplies run short and Pike's party builds blockhouse

Long party splits. Bell & Wilkinson head down Arkansas River, Long himself down Canadian

Long mistakes Canadian for Red River

Pike and his men are marched to Chihuahua, to governor of New Mexico

Party meets up with military contingent and goes into winter quarters until spring

Just before making camp, Pike learns of Spanish military force sent out to intercept his expedition

6 June 1820
Long's party meets enormous herds of buffalo. They pass villages of Oto, Pawnee and "Bad Heart Indians," probably Comanche

21 June 1819
Long steams upriver with a party of scientists, including John Biddle, William Biddle, Thomas Say, Augustus Jessup and Titian Peale

15 July 1806
Pike rows off with 23 men

Late August
Camp at native villages

3 of Bell's soldiers desert, taking horses, packs, rifles and most of the expedition's scientific collections and notebooks

Hostile Cheyenne, Arapaho and Kiowa confront Bell's party

## The Expeditions of Pike and Long, 1806-20

- ▨ Spanish territory, 1806
- ▫ US territory, 1806
- — · — US/Spanish treaty line, 1819
- ⚑ US fort
- ⚑ Spanish settlement
- ✝ Spanish presidio/mission
- ⌂ Indian villages
- ➤ Lieutenant Zebulon M. Pike, 1806-07
- ➤ Major Stephen H. Long, 1819-20
- ⛺ Winter camp
- ⛺ Temporary camp
- ◼ Encounter with Indians
- ◪ Confrontation with Indians

# Intrigue beyond the Rockies

## EXPEDITIONS FROM LISA'S FORT RAYMOND, 1807-12

*Drawn by the promise of riches and
adventure, fur traders explore the rugged
and uncharted Rocky Mountains.*

In 1806, as Lewis and Clark coursed back down the Missouri, they met American fur traders heading upriver. They had been sent by Spanish-born Manuel Lisa, a brilliant St Louis entrepreneur.

Lisa was quick to grasp the potential riches of the country crossed by Lewis and Clark and dreamed of trading with Santa Fé. Denied permission by the US military governor of Louisiana, James Wilkinson, Lisa turned his interests to the north, beyond effective United States jurisdiction. In 1807 he established a trade fort at the junction of the Yellowstone and the Big Horn. His partner, Andrew Henry, headed due west and in 1810 established a trading post among the Shoshone on a fork of the Snake River. It was the first American post west of the Continental Divide. Lisa sent a number of expeditions out from his fort, including those of John Colter, George Drouillard, and Jean Baptiste Champlain; for one of Lisa's objectives was to find a route that ran west of the Rockies to Santa Fé.

The most important expedition was undertaken by Colter, one of Lewis and Clark's men. Lisa's other men always ventured out in teams, but in winter 1807 Colter headed out of Lisa's fort alone, with orders to make trade alliances with the tribes of the Big Horn Basin, notably the Absaroka, or Crow.

Colter's exact route is conjectural. Armed with only a rifle and a pack of trade goods, he made his way through Crow country. He received nothing but friendship from the Crow, who led him to the sulfurous geysers on the Shoshone, or Stinking Water, River, which were dubbed "Colter's Hell" by his incredulous contemporaries.

From there he went back through Jackson Hole and north through present day Yellowstone Park. He was the first white man to see its geysers and other marvels. Then he crossed eastward out of the Park through a pass in the Snowy Range and then moved south through Sunlight Basin back into Crow country, eventually reaching Lisa's Fort Raymond.

The following year Colter made his way to the Three Forks, source of the Missouri. He had thus located the sources of two, and possibly four, of the West's greatest rivers, counting the Snake River as it flows from

Jackson's Hole and the Green as it flows from Green Lake at the head of the Wind River Mountains. He came close to proving the contention of Jonathan Carver and Zebulon Pike that in the central Rockies was "a grand reservoir" out of which all the major rivers of the west flowed. In 1809 Colter was stripped and chased by a band of Blackfoot, and forced to run miles for his life across the Three Forks of the Missouri. Colter retired early from furtrapping and exploration but he remains a legendary figure.

George Drouillard was less lucky. He was killed by the Blackfoot at the Three Forks in 1810. Earlier, in 1808, he too explored the Yellowstone and the Big Horn Basin, though his real mission seems to have been to reach the Spaniards to the south. He believed that Santa Fé was about ten days' march away or even less via the "Salt Fork" – where the Spaniards supposedly obtained their salt. Drouillard's opinions were noted on Governor William Clark's master map of the

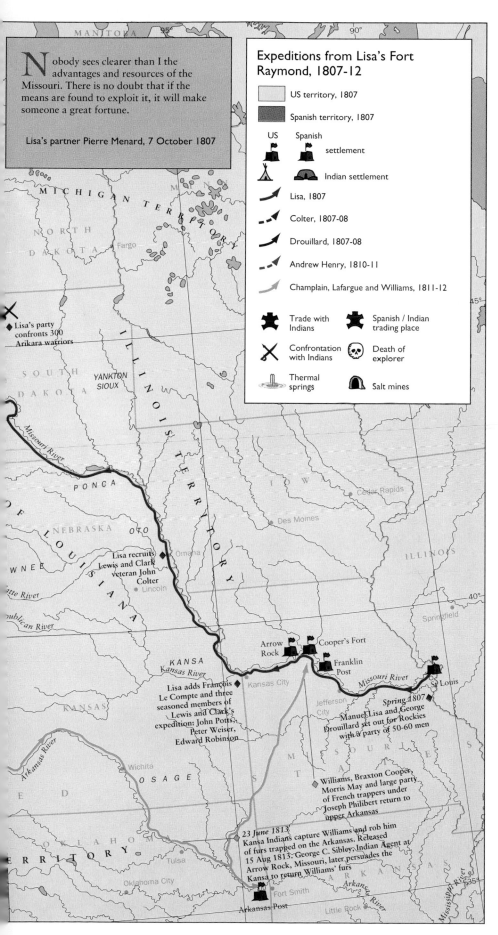

Nobody sees clearer than I the advantages and resources of the Missouri. There is no doubt that if the means are found to exploit it, it will make someone a great fortune.

Lisa's partner Pierre Menard, 7 October 1807

## Expeditions from Lisa's Fort Raymond, 1807-12

- US territory, 1807
- Spanish territory, 1807

| US | Spanish | |
|---|---|---|
| | | settlement |
| | | Indian settlement |

- Lisa, 1807
- Colter, 1807-08
- Drouillard, 1807-08
- Andrew Henry, 1810-11
- Champlain, Lafargue and Williams, 1811-12

| | |
|---|---|
| Trade with Indians | Spanish / Indian trading place |
| Confrontation with Indians | Death of explorer |
| Thermal springs | Salt mines |

MANITOBA

MICHIGAN TERRITORY

NORTH DAKOTA    Fargo

X Lisa's party confronts 300 Arikara warriors

SOUTH DAKOTA    YANKTON SIOUX

ILLINOIS TERRITORY

PONCA

OF LOUISIANA

NEBRASKA    OTO

Omaha

Lisa recruits Lewis and Clark veteran John Colter

PAWNEE

Lincoln

ttle River

Republican River

KANSA
Kansas River

Lisa adds François Le Compte and three seasoned members of Lewis and Clark's expedition: John Potts, Peter Weiser, Edward Robinson

Kansas City

Arrow Rock    Cooper's Fort

Franklin Post

Jefferson City

Spring 1807
Manuel Lisa and George Drouillard set out for Rockies with a party of 50-60 men

Missouri River    St Louis

KANSAS

Wichita

Arkansas River

OSAGE

Williams, Braxton Cooper, Morris May and large party of French trappers under Joseph Philibert return to upper Arkansas

23 June 1813
Kansa Indians capture Williams and rob him of furs trapped on the Arkansas. Released 15 Aug 1813. George C. Sibley, Indian Agent at Arrow Rock, Missouri, later persuades the Kansa to return Williams' furs

OKLAHOMA TERRITORY

Tulsa

Oklahoma City

Fort Smith
Arkansas Post

Little Rock

Cedar Rapids

IOWA

Des Moines

ILLINOIS

Springfield

MISSOURI

ARKANSAS

Arkansas River

Mississippi River

*Above: An early painting of a Blackfoot Indian, a warrior of the Piegan tribe. His elk hide robe illustrates his many war "coups," including wounded enemies and stolen horses and weapons. The Blackfoot menaced trappers of the Missouri Company from the time of their first skirmish with Lewis and Clark. The artist, Karl Bodmer, traveled with an ethnologist recording Indian culture.*

west, which he kept up-to-date in his St Louis office. Drouillard thus eliminated what is now Colorado and much of Wyoming from early knowledge of the west.

Champlain's expedition southward from Lisa's Fort Raymond in 1811 should have reinstated them. He headed for Arapaho country in present-day Colorado. But his company was shattered by dissension, fear and Blackfoot attacks. Seven men turned back to the Big Horn Valley. Champlain and one companion elected to stay with the Arapaho permanently and were never heard from again. Four other men from Champlain's band, led by Jean Baptiste Lafargue, actually reached Santa Fé. But only one man, Ezekiel Williams, returned. He made his way down the Arkansas River to Arrow Rock with a very large cargo of furs, only to meet the charge that he had murdered Champlain. No one knows the truth, but he was exonerated.

# The Snake Country Brigades

## CANADIANS IN THE AMERICAN WEST, 1818-30

*American, Canadian and British fur trappers
and traders range across the West, in search
of the lucrative beaver. They bring back
valuable information for map-makers.*

As the fur trade pushed westward across the Rockies, competition between Canadian and US trappers intensified. Thompson (▶*page 118*) had attempted to beat the Astorians (▶page *142*) to the Pacific in 1811, only to find them safely ensconced in their fort at the mouth of the Columbia River. But the network of trading posts he had set up, and the relations he had built with the Indians, paved the way for the North West Company to expand south.

Perhaps the most important of the company's explorers of the western interior was Donald Mackenzie, a huge, fat man who once stood off a party of hostile Shoshone by holding a match to a keg of powder and threatening to blow them all to pieces.

In 1818 Mackenzie organized the Snake country fur brigades for the North West Company. Sometimes numbering as many as 55 people, including Iroquois brought over from the east, Mackenzie's brigades followed the Snake River east, into the region next to the Green River. Mackenzie was one of the first white explorers to follow the Green River to its source in the magnificent Green Lake, high up in the Wind River Mountains, and he made camp in Jackson's Hole in the shadow of the Grand Tetons. In all, Mackenzie made three trips at the head of Snake country fur

brigades. On one of these, he shot the rapids of Hell's Canyon of the Snake in a crude boat, a feat no white man, and probably no Indian, had done before.

Mackenzie's concept of the Snake country fur brigade was a huge success, in exploration as well as fur-hunting. He was succeeded by William Kittson, Michel Bourdon, who reached Bear Lake in Utah, and by Finian McDonald. McDonald wrote that he got "as far as the Croe Indian Cuntre on the rail Spanish river" (Green River). He also "sa the Musosoury Last fall down as far as the falls", meaning that he passed safely through Blackfoot country to the Great Falls of the Missouri River.

Still other brigade leaders from Canada followed the trails laid out by Mackenzie. Alexander Ross brought American trappers back to Flathead Post, thereby driving a rival wedge into the domain now claimed by the Hudson's Bay Company. The latter rose to the challenge, however. At the behest of Governor George Simpson, brigade leader Peter Skene Ogden set out to turn the Snake country into a "fur desert." For six years he led parties into the interior until, in 1825, he reached the country east of the Great Salt Lake. There he clashed with American trappers, though since they were below the

42nd parallel they were in Mexican territory.

Ogden also discovered and mapped the entire length of the Humboldt River, which became the main emigrant route to California. In 1829-30 he made his way from Fort Clatsop on the Columbia River south and across what is now the whole American West to the Gulf of California. Near the site of present-day Needles, California, Mohave Indians attacked his party. A pitched battle ensued in which 26 Mohave were killed.

As an explorer Ogden was second to none. Much of the information he brought back, together with that of the Canadian Snake Country Brigades and the work of explorers of the North West Company and the Hudson's Bay Company, was added to maps made by A.H. Brué in Paris and the leading map-maker of the day, Aaron Arrowsmith in London.

> On seeing the number of their fellows who in a single moment were made to lick the dust, the rest ingloriously fled... Twenty-six remained dead on the field
>
> **Peter Skene Ogden describes his battle with the Mohave, 1829**

> There were times when we tasted no food and were unable to discover water for several days together... our horses were reduced to great weakness so that many of them died, on whose emaciated carcases we were constrained to satisfy the intolerable cravings of our hunger, and as a last resource, to quench our thirst with their blood.
>
> **Peter Skene Ogden in Nevada's Great Basin, winter 1829**

*Left: The Kootenay River was the main route of the North West Company trappers as they headed south into the United States. Here, a supply party makes the southernmost crossing of the river, in an 1860 watercolor by James Madison Alden.*

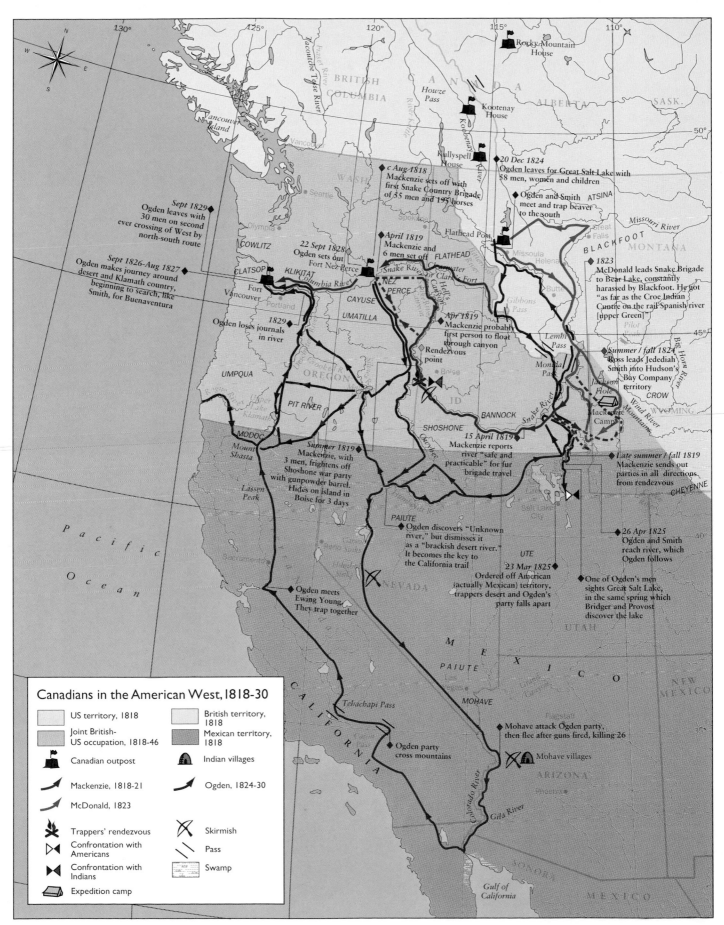

## Canadians in the American West, 1818-30

US territory, 1818

Joint British-
US occupation, 1818-46

British territory,
1818

Mexican territory,
1818

Canadian outpost

Indian villages

Mackenzie, 1818-21

Ogden, 1824-30

McDonald, 1823

Trappers' rendezvous

Skirmish

Confrontation with
Americans

Pass

Confrontation with
Indians

Swamp

Expedition camp

*Sept 1829*
Ogden leaves with
30 men on second
ever crossing of West by
north-south route

*Sept 1826-Aug 1827*
Ogden makes journey around
desert and Klamath country,
beginning to search, like
Smith, for Buenaventura

*22 Sept 1828*
Ogden sets out
Fort Nez Perce

*c Aug 1818*
Mackenzie sets off with
first Snake Country Brigade
of 55 men and 195 horses

*April 1819*
Mackenzie and
6 men set off

*20 Dec 1824*
Ogden leaves for Great Salt Lake with
58 men, women and children

*Ogden and Smith*
meet and trap beaver
to the south

*1823*
McDonald leads Snake Brigade
to Bear Lake, constantly
harassed by Blackfoot. He got
"as far as the Croe Indian
Cuntre on the rail Spanish river
[upper Green]"

*Apr 1819*
Mackenzie probably
first person to float
through canyon

*1829*
Ogden loses journals
in river

*Summer 1819*
Mackenzie, with
3 men, frightens off
Shoshone war party
with gunpowder barrel.
Hides on island in
Boise for 3 days

*15 April 1819*
Mackenzie reports
river "safe and
practicable" for fur
brigade travel

*Summer / fall 1824*
Ross leads Jedediah
Smith into Hudson's
Bay Company
territory

*Late summer / fall 1819*
Mackenzie sends out
parties in all directions
from rendezvous

Ogden discovers "Unknown
river," but dismisses it
as a "brackish desert river."
It becomes the key to
the California trail

*23 Mar 1825*
Ordered off American
(actually Mexican) territory,
trappers desert and Ogden's
party falls apart

*26 Apr 1825*
Ogden and Smith
reach river, which
Ogden follows

One of Ogden's men
sights Great Salt Lake,
in the same spring which
Bridger and Provost
discover the lake

Ogden meets
Ewing Young.
They trap together

Ogden party
cross mountains

Mohave attack Ogden party,
then flee after guns fired, killing 26

Mohave villages

# All for the Seeds-Kee-Dee

## TRAPPERS AND TRADERS IN THE CENTRAL ROCKIES, 1822-26

*The Green River – known to the Indians as the Seeds-Kee-Dee – becomes a magnet for fur trappers as they penetrate deeper into the Rockies and discover the Great Salt Lake.*

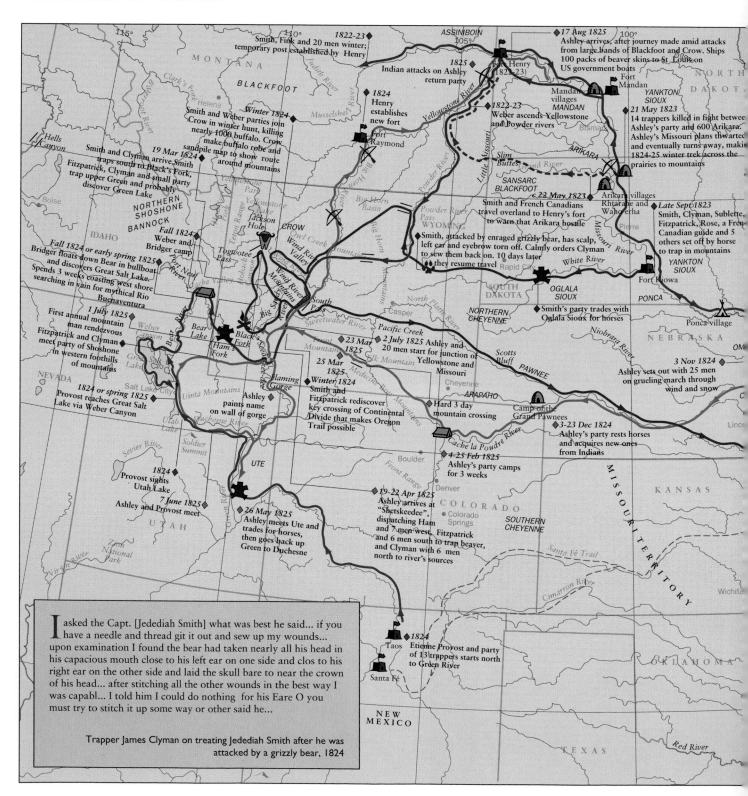

Smith, Fink and 20 men winter; temporary post established by Henry

1822-23

ASSINIBOIN

17 Aug 1825
Ashley arrives, after journey made amid attacks from large bands of Blackfoot and Crow. Ships 100 packs of beaver skins to St Louis on US government boats

1825
Indian attacks on Ashley return party

Fort Henry (1822-23)

Fort Mandan

Mandan villages
MANDAN

YANKTON SIOUX

NORTH DAKOTA

MONTANA

BLACKFOOT

Helena

Winter 1824
Smith and Weber parties join Crow in winter hunt, killing nearly 1000 buffalo. Crow make buffalo robe and sandpile map to show route around mountains

1824
Henry establishes new fort

Fort Raymond

1822-23
Weber ascends Yellowstone and Powder rivers

Bismark

21 May 1823
14 trappers killed in fight between Ashley's party and 600 Arikara. Ashley's Missouri plans thwarted and eventually turns away, making 1824-25 winter trek across the prairies to mountains

19 Mar 1824
Smith and Clyman arrive. Smith traps south to Black's Fork; Fitzpatrick, Clyman and small party trap upper Green and probably discover Green Lake

Slim Buttes

ARIKARA

SANSARC BLACKFOOT

22 May 1823
Smith and French Canadians travel overland to Henry's fort to warn that Arikara hostile

Arikara villages
Rhtarahe and Waho'erha

Late Sept 1823
Smith, Clyman, Sublette, Fitzpatrick, Rose, a French Canadian guide and 5 others set off by horse to trap in mountains

NORTHERN SHOSHONE
BANNOCK

Boise

IDAHO

Fall 1824
Weber and Bridger camp

Jackson Hole

CROW

WYOMING

Smith, attacked by enraged grizzly bear, has scalp, left ear and eyebrow torn off. Calmly orders Clyman to sew them back on. 10 days later they resume travel

Rapid City

YANKTON SIOUX

Fort Kiowa

Fall 1824 or early spring 1825
Bridger floats down Bear in bullboat and discovers Great Salt Lake. Spends 3 weeks coasting west shore searching in vain for mythical Rio Buenaventura

Togwotee Pass

Wind River Valley

Wind River Mountains

White River

OGLALA SIOUX

PONCA

1 July 1825
First annual mountain man rendezvous

Fitzpatrick and Clyman meet party of Shoshone in western foothills of mountains

Bear Lake

Black's Fork

Ham's Fork

South Pass

Sweetwater River

North Platte River

Casper

NORTHERN CHEYENNE

Smith's party trades with Oglala Sioux for horses

Ponca village

NEBRASKA

NEVADA

1824 or spring 1825
Provost reaches Great Salt Lake via Weber Canyon

Salt Lake City

Flaming Gorge

23 Mar 1825

2 July 1825 Ashley and 20 men start for junction of Yellowstone and Missouri

Scotts Bluff

PAWNEE

3 Nov 1824
Ashley sets out with 25 men on grueling march through wind and snow

Ashley paints name on wall of gorge

25 Mar 1825
Winter 1824
Smith and Fitzpatrick rediscover key crossing of Continental Divide that makes Oregon Trail possible

Cheyenne

ARAPAHO

Hard 3 day mountain crossing

Camp of the Grand Pawnees

Uinta Mountains

Duchesne River

Utah Lake

Soldier Summit

UTE

3-23 Dec 1824
Ashley's party rests horses and acquires new ones from Indians

Cache la Poudre River

Boulder

Front Range

4-25 Feb 1825
Ashley's party camps for 3 weeks

1824
Provost sights Utah Lake

Sevier River

7 June 1825
Ashley and Provost meet

26 May 1825
Ashley meets Ute and trades for horses, then goes back up Green to Duchesne

Denver

19-22 Apr 1825
Ashley arrives at "Shetskeedee", dispatching Ham and 7 men west, Fitzpatrick and 6 men south to trap beaver, and Clyman with 6 men north to river's sources

Colorado Springs

COLORADO

SOUTHERN CHEYENNE

Santa Fé Trail

MISSOURI TERRITORY

KANSAS

Wichita

Virgin River

Zion National Park

Green River

Cimarron River

Taos

1824
Etienne Provost and party of 13 trappers starts north to Green River

Santa Fé

OKLAHOMA

NEW MEXICO

TEXAS

Red River

I asked the Capt. [Jedediah Smith] what was best he said... if you have a needle and thread git it out and sew up my wounds... upon examination I found the bear had taken nearly all his head in his capacious mouth close to his left ear on one side and clos to his right ear on the other side and laid the skull bare to near the crown of his head... after stitching all the other wounds in the best way I was capabl... I told him I could do nothing for his Eare O you must try to stitch it up some way or other said he...

Trapper James Clyman on treating Jedediah Smith after he was attacked by a grizzly bear, 1824

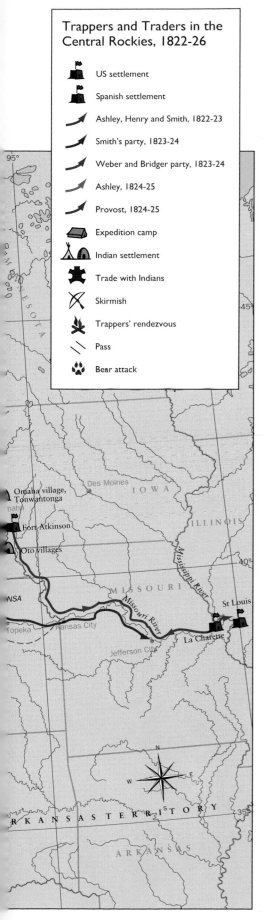

## Trappers and Traders in the Central Rockies, 1822-26

- US settlement
- Spanish settlement
- Ashley, Henry and Smith, 1822-23
- Smith's party, 1823-24
- Weber and Bridger party, 1823-24
- Ashley, 1824-25
- Provost, 1824-25
- Expedition camp
- Indian settlement
- Trade with Indians
- Skirmish
- Trappers' rendezvous
- Pass
- Bear attack

In February 1822, the politician and would-be entrepreneur William Ashley teamed up with Andrew Henry to form the Rocky Mountain Fur Company. He advertised for "Enterprising Young Men... to ascend the Missouri to its source" as fur trappers: their harrowing adventures did much to create the heroic image of the mountain man.

Ashley's first keelboat sank in the Missouri, costing $10,000 in trade goods and on his second venture Arikara Indians killed 14 of his party. Andrew Henry tried to set up a post on the Yellowstone. When he took a party of trappers across the plains two more were killed by Indians. Few Indians wanted to trap furs for the white man, so Henry sent John Weber with a party to trap with the friendly Crow in the valley of the Wind River.

In September 1823 Jedediah Smith, (▶ *page 152-3*), led a second party that included James Clyman, Tom "Broken Hand" Fitzpatrick, and William Sublette. They headed out along the White River guided by a French veteran of Pierre Chouteau's Missouri Fur Company. They traded with the Sioux, but, towards winter moved west to the Black Hills of the Rockies. When Jedediah Smith was attacked by a grizzly bear, Clyman sewed his scalp and ear back on without anaesthetic.

Eventually Smith and his men joined Weber's party in the freezing Wind River valley, where they helped the Crow kill over a thousand buffalo. The Crow made a deerskin and sandpile map showing a pass over the Continental Divide. This would become the Oregon Trail, the main route for American

*Alfred Jacob Miller, one of the greatest artists of the American West, painted this watercolor of trappers' annual rendezvous on Green River around 1839, just a few years before it faded into history.*

emigrants heading west.

Smith and a few men went on to trap successfully on the Green River. At Henry's Fork of the Snake they met Alexander Ross with a group of Canadians. Together they reconnoitred most of what had been the prime Hudson's Bay Snake River trapping preserve.

In July, Weber and his men followed Smith's trail and eventually holed up in Cache Valley for the winter. In the late fall of 1824 or the early spring of 1825, Jim Bridger, on a bet, floated down the Bear River in a bullboat into the Great Salt Lake. The water being salty, he took it to be an arm of the Pacific. Thus Bridger was probably the first white man to discover the Great Salt Lake, although Etienne Provost, a band of Taos trappers and Peter Skene Ogden also saw it in spring 1825.

In November 1825 Ashley led a further party across the plains. Clyman was their guide as they struggled, starving, across the wintery plains to the comparative safety of the Pawnee villages at the forks of the Platte River. They eventually reached the Green River, by then the "Main Street" of the Rocky Mountain fur trappers.

Ashley immediately sent trapping parties out in all directions, while he himself set out in bull boats down the Green River past the Uinta Mountains and the Ladore canyons. Ashley met up with Provost's party and they headed toward a designated rendezvous in July 1825. He thus created the annual rendezvous or fur trade fairs, attracting free trappers, Hudson's Bay men, Taos trappers and thousands of Indians. The second, in 1826, was a bacchanal that made Ashley so rich that he quit the mountains forever, to pursue an indifferent political career.

# Across Mountain and Desert

## THE EXPEDITIONS OF JEDEDIAH SMITH, 1826-31

*Mountain man Jedediah Smith makes a series of epic journeys from the Rockies into California, including a grueling crossing of the Great Basin.*

Jedediah Smith was the greatest explorer of the American West. One of William Ashley's men (▶ *page 150*), by 1824 he had led a small brigade up the Green River and over to the Snake River. There he met Alexander Ross of the Hudson's Bay Company who had come down from Flathead Post. Ross invited Smith to accompany him back to Flathead Post, and this afforded Smith the opportunity to spy out the far reaches of the Hudson's Bay Snake Country Brigades' beaver haunts. In June 1826, Smith set out from the Cache Valley rendezvous to explore the area south-west of the Great Salt Lake. He had heard from Ute Indians that the lake had an arm to the Pacific; he thought this could be the Rio Buenaventura, much fabled by the Spanish.

In July, William Ashley sold out his interest in the Rocky Mountain Fur Company to Smith, Bill Sublette and David Jackson. Sublette went north to the Snake and encountered a large freshwater lake "one hundred by forty miles in diameter and clear as crystal." This was Yellowstone Lake, discovered almost twenty years before by John Colter (▶ *page 146*) but then forgotten.

Meanwhile Smith set out south with 18 men. In barren, rocky Black Mountain country his party subsisted largely on insects and rodents. Then in November they crossed the Mohave Desert, following an ancient Indian trade route from spring to spring and helped by Mohave Indians. After going south to San Diego, Smith returned by sea to the San Gabriel Mission in California. Here they were suspected of being spies, but eventually traveled west to the San Joaquin Valley, where they found beaver in abundance. In May 1827, far north at the American River, Smith's party failed in its first attempt to cross the snowbound Sierras. Jedediah Smith, Silas Gobel and Robert Evans then set out on what would become a great feat of exploration history. It is recounted in Smith's journal which came to light 150 years later.

The three men struggled across the vast, barren wastes of the Great Basin. After 32 days, dehydrated and near starvation, they pushed on day and night, making sometimes 40 miles in 24 hours. In July 1827 they rode down into the trappers' rendezvous in Cache Valley. "My arrival," wrote Smith, "caused considerable bustle in camp, for myself and party had been given up for lost. A small cannon brought up from St Louis was loaded and fired for a salute."

Only ten days later Smith began to retrace his route to California. The Mohave, having recently been attacked by Taos trappers, ambushed Smith's party as they crossed the Colorado. On reaching California, Smith was detained by Governor Echeandia, accused of staking an American claim to Mexican lands. A Boston shipmaster posted a $30,000 bond for Smith, but he jumped bond and sailed for San Francisco aboard an American ship. Here he was jailed and delayed again but escaped with his men and 250 horses and mules. Heading north along the western slopes of the Sierras, Smith found the head of the Sacramento and then veered west to the Umpqua River. Here Smith and two others went hunting. After narrowly surviving an attack by their Indian guides, Smith returned to find that Indians had slaughtered all but one of those left behind. Smith and his companions took to the woods, arriving safely at Fort Vancouver in August 1828. From there his Hudson's Bay rivals accompanied him back to the scene of the massacre to recover horses, equipment and journals.

In March 1829 Smith began another great journey, going far north to the heart of fur country, then turning south through the Bitterroot Valley and along a fork of the Snake. Within a year, Jedediah Smith, lonely for family and old friends, left behind the life of the mountain man. In 1830, however, he could not resist a journey over the Santa Fé trail via the Cimarron cut-off and early in 1831 he was killed by the Comanche.

> I t is that I may be able to help those who stand in need, that I face every danger – it is for this that I traverse the Mountains covered with eternal snow... that I pass over Sandy Plains, in heat of Summer, thirsting for water... and most of all, it is for this that I deprive myself of the privilege of Society...
>
> **Jedediah Smith to his brother Ralph, 24 December 1829**

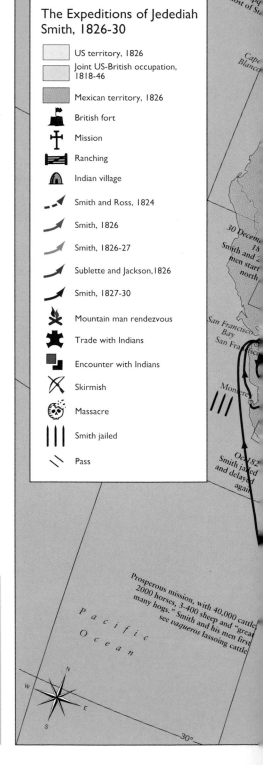

### The Expeditions of Jedediah Smith, 1826-30

- US territory, 1826
- Joint US-British occupation, 1818-46
- Mexican territory, 1826
- British fort
- Mission
- Ranching
- Indian village
- Smith and Ross, 1824
- Smith, 1826
- Smith, 1826-27
- Sublette and Jackson, 1826
- Smith, 1827-30
- Mountain man rendezvous
- Trade with Indians
- Encounter with Indians
- Skirmish
- Massacre
- Smith jailed
- Pass

Umpq most of S

Cape Blanco

30 Decembe 18 Smith and 2 men start north

San Francisco Bay San Fra

Monter

Oct 182 Smith jailed and delayed agai

Prosperous mission, with 40,000 cattle, 2000 horses, 3-400 sheep and "great many hogs." Smith and his men first see vaqueros lassoing cattle

Pacific Ocean

N
W E
S

30°

CANADA

WASHINGTON

ALBERTA

SASKATCHEWAN

Seattle

Olympia

Mt St Helens

CHINOOK

Cape Disappointment

Fort Okanagan

Fort Colville

10 August 1828 Smith given shelter by rivals from Hudson's Bay company

Fort Vancouver

COWLITZ

KLIKITAT

YAKIMA

Spokane

Flathead Post

Clark Fork

Flathead Lake

Teton

1829 Smith meets David Jackson

1830 Smith heads South for rendezvous then retires and returns to St. Louis and his fate on the Cimarron

ATSINA

Marias River

Missouri River

ASSINIBOIN

MONTANA

PALOUSE

FLATHEAD

Columbia River

Walla Walla R

Hell's Canyon

Blue Mountains

WALLA WALLA

NEZ PERCE

Snake River

Helena

BLACKFOOT

Butte

BLACKFOOT

Clark Fork

Bitterroot Mountains

Sublette discovers geysers, fountains and Firehole Basin "paint pots." On return narrowly escapes Blackfoot

Musselshell River

Yellowstone River

CHEYENNE

Tongue River

Powder River

OREGON COUNTRY

UMATILLA

CAYUSE

IDAHO

Party divides. Sublette goes north into Yellowstone, while Jackson probably goes north towards Missouri and Flathead Post

12 Mar 1829 Smith leaves to scout for British fur posts

Sublette finds sources of Snake in Jackson Hole

SHOSHONE

Sublette harassed by Blackfoot

Snake River Fall 1826

BLACKFOOT

Yellowstone Lake

Pierre's Hole

Jackson Hole

Wind River Mountains

Big Horn Mountains

Big Horn Basin

Owl Creek

CROW

UNITED STATES

CHEYENNE

Sublette party leaves rendezvous for Snake

Bear River

June 1826 Smith explores north and west shores of lake

Wind River Valley

South Togo-Agie River

Sweetwater River

South Pass

WYOMING

MODOC

PIT RIVER INDIANS

MAIDU

Attacked by Paiute

Deep snows prevent crossing of Sierras

River

WASHOE

Appelaman's R.

25 June 1827 Evans collapses, Smith and Gobel leave him behind. Find spring 3 miles on. They returned and revive Evans

3 July 1827 Smith arrives back for annual rendezvous

ARAPAHO

M.D.

Casper

North Platte River

S.D.

Cheyenne

NEVADA

Great Salt Lake

Salt Lake

Smith almost drowns

Ogden Pass

Soldier Summit

Uinta Mountains

UTE

Duchesne River

2 June 1827 Smith, Gobel and Evans probably first people to cross Great Basin

MIWOK

25-27 May 1827 Smith finally crosses Sierras

1 June 1827 Smith, Gobel and Evans first Americans to see vast lake

Wheeler Peak

Smith meets Ute. Tries to persuade Ute to make peace with Shoshone

Denver

Colorado Springs

Sukuevutnine

Wowol Yokut village

Chin-ta-che

Zion National Park

PAIUTE

UTAH

SANPITS

Smith party meets Sanpits and Paiute. First non-Indians to notice smoke signals

40°

Colorado River

Front Range

SOUTHERN PAIUTE

Nov 1826 Smith follows native trade route

Las Vegas

Sangre de Cristo Mountains

COLORADO

Arkansas River

San Gabriel Mission

San Pedro Harbor

Santa Catalina

San Juan Capistrano

San Bernardino Mountains

San Diego

Mohave River

MOHAVE

Smith trades with Mohave

Mohave villages

MEXICO

Late 1827 Smith and party attacked by Mohave. 10 explorers, 2 Mohave killed

ARIZONA

Colorado River

NAVAJO

JICARILLA APACHE

Flagstaff

Rio San Jose

Santa Fé

Albuquerque

5 Jan 1827 Smith sails aboard brig Courier

American smugglers tan contraband hides and keep small ranches with cattle and hogs

Sept 1827 Smith sails north for San Francisco aboard US ship Franklin

Gila River

MEXICO

NEW MEXICO

TEX.

35°

125°    120°    115°    110°    105°
50°    45°

# Southwestern Adventures

## JAMES OHIO PATTIE, 1824-32

*Fur trappers explore the Southwest, rediscover the Grand Canyon and blaze trails into California.*

In 1825 the young James Ohio Pattie with his father, Sylvester Pattie, left Missouri for Santa Fé with Sylvestre Pratte's train. They spent the year trapping the Gila River. Although Americans were forbidden to trap in New Mexico, James Pattie was excluded from the ban for rescuing a former governor's daughter from the feared Comanche.

Late in 1825 James Pattie joined Michel Robideau and a party of 14 French Canadians heading west to the Gila and Colorado rivers. The party was soon beset by Papago Indians near present-day Phoenix. Normally friendly, the Papago left only Robideau, Pattie and one other man alive. Fortunately the three men soon met up with Ewing Young and his party of trappers. These included Tom "Peg Leg" Smith who, up on the Green River in the winter of 1827, amputated his own leg with a butcher knife.

Young's party reached the Mohave villages, previously visited in 1825 by Jedediah Smith, and then by Richard Campbell's party, who had murdered several Mohave and hanged them from trees. Young's men repeated the atrocity after Young declared that the Mohave shot arrows at his bed while he was sleeping. They then crossed the Colorado, going up along the north rim of the Grand Canyon to the Grand River and its sources. They were the first white men to see the Grand Canyon since the Spaniards nearly three centuries before (▶ *page 36* ).

Pattie later claimed that they crossed over the front range of the Rockies along the South Platte, reaching the Big Horn and Yellowstone River and crossing over the Continental Divide into Flathead country. This is a somewhat incredible distance to have traveled in a single season. It is likely that Pattie was confused and that the trek was much shorter. After taking the Grand to its head, they crossed over to the South Platte, then turned south along the Front Range, crossing the mountains westward at La Vela Pass, then heading south to Santa Fé.

In 1830 the Patties made trips to the west coast of Mexico via the Gila River and down the Colorado across the baja deserts into California. But by the time the Patties reached the mission that is now San Diego, Jedediah Smith had already arrived in California. So

had the trapper Richard Campbell who, with his party of 35, had taken a more direct route. In 1830 Pattie and his father were thrown into prison in San Diego by the Spanish. His father died. After James Pattie was released he claimed to have inoculated 22,000 mission Indians and Spanish against smallpox, though the mission population was only 12,851 and the epidemic was measles. Penniless, Pattie traveled back to his home town, Cincinnati, and dictated his story to the writer-clergyman Timothey Flint. It was published in 1831.

By 1829 several routes were regularly traveled across the Southwest to California. Ewing Young and Kit Carson followed the route via Zuñi and the Gila river. Peg Leg Smith led a party down from the Green River. Manuel Armijo followed Escalante's trail of 1776 (▶ *page 126*). He went to California via a crossing north of the Grand Canyon, then via the Virgin River to Las Vegas Meadows, and finally across the Mohave Desert to Cajon Pass. This route was called "The Old Spanish Trail." In 1830 William Wolfskill followed in Armijo's footsteps but blazed a trail south, past present-day Parowan and St George, Utah. Finally, in 1832, David Jackson and 11 men swung far south through present-day Tucson, San Xavier del Bac Mission and along Father Kino's old 18th century trail to California (▶ *page 120*). California was now the magnet for trade with the Mexicans.

Meanwhile, traveling north from Taos in 1824-25, Etienne Provost met William Ashley's party (▶ *page 150*) and was among the first white men to see Utah Lake and Great Salt Lake. If he saw Great Salt Lake in the fall of 1824 then he was the first white man to do so. However this is disputed and it may have been the spring of 1825. Many other bands of trappers out of Taos followed in his footsteps as the San Juan River country became a popular trapping ground on the way to the annual Green River rendezvous.

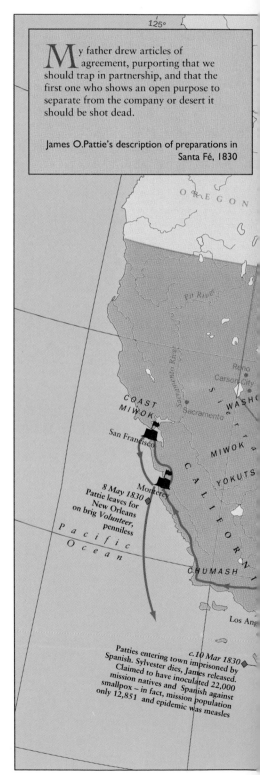

My father drew articles of agreement, purporting that we should trap in partnership, and that the first one who shows an open purpose to separate from the company or desert it should be shot dead.

James O. Pattie's description of preparations in Santa Fé, 1830

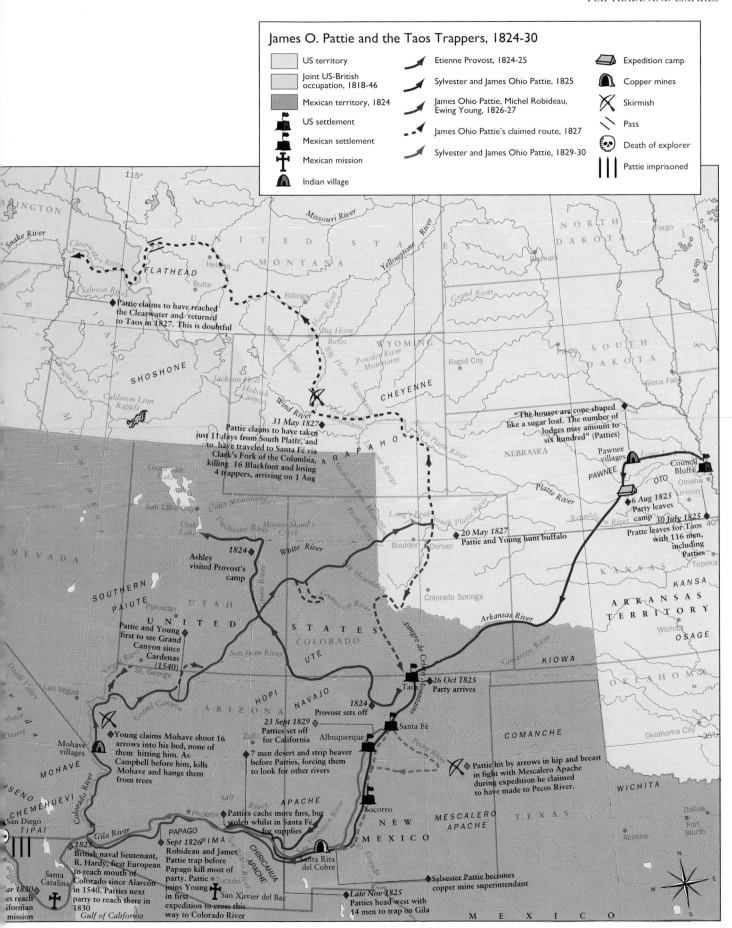

## James O. Pattie and the Taos Trappers, 1824-30

US territory

Joint US-British occupation, 1818-46

Mexican territory, 1824

US settlement

Mexican settlement

Mexican mission

Indian village

Etienne Provost, 1824-25

Sylvester and James Ohio Pattie, 1825

James Ohio Pattie, Michel Robideau, Ewing Young, 1826-27

James Ohio Pattie's claimed route, 1827

Sylvester and James Ohio Pattie, 1829-30

Expedition camp

Copper mines

Skirmish

Pass

Death of explorer

Pattie imprisoned

Pattie claims to have reached the Clearwater and returned to Taos in 1827. This is doubtful

31 May 1827
Pattie claims to have taken just 11 days from South Platte, and to have traveled to Santa Fé via Clark's Fork of the Columbia, killing 16 Blackfoot and losing 4 trappers, arriving on 1 Aug

"The houses are cone-shaped like a sugar loaf. The number of lodges may amount to six hundred" (Patties)

Pawnee villages

Council Bluffs

6 Aug 1825
Party leaves camp

30 July 1825
Pratte leaves for Taos with 116 men, including Patties

1824
Ashley visited Provost's camp

20 May 1827
Pattie and Young hunt buffalo

Pattie and Young first to see Grand Canyon since Cardenas (1540)

26 Oct 1825
Party arrives

Taos

1824
Provost sets off

23 Sept 1829
Patties set off for California

7 men desert and strip beaver before Patties, forcing them to look for other rivers

Albuquerque

Santa Fé

Pattie hit by arrows in hip and breast in fight with Mescalero Apache during expedition he claimed to have made to Pecos River.

Young claims Mohave shoot 16 arrows into his bed, none of them hitting him. As Campbell before him, kills Mohave and hangs them from trees

Mohave villages

Patties cache more furs, but stolen whilst in Santa Fé for supplies

Socorro

1825

British naval lieutenant, R. Hardy, first European to reach mouth of Colorado since Alarcón in 1540. Patties next party to reach there in 1830

Sept 1826
Robideau and James Pattie trap before Papago kill most of party. Pattie joins Young in first expedition to cross this way to Colorado River

San Xavier del Bac

Santa Rita del Cobre

Sylvester Pattie becomes copper mine superintendant

Late Nov 1825
Patties head west with 14 men to trap on Gila

ar 1830
es reach ifornian mission

Santa Catalina

# Spying Out an Emigrant Trail
## THE EXPEDITIONS OF BONNEVILLE AND WALKER, 1832-34

*Under the guise of fur-trading, Bonneville explores Green River country to spy out conditions for emigrants. He sends out Walker, who finds a viable central trail to California.*

In May 1832 Captain Benjamin Louis Eulalie Bonneville set out from Fort Osage, near present-day Kansas City, at the head of a long train of trappers and wagons bound for the heart of the Green River fur country. He had been given a mysterious two-year leave from the army to embark on a fur trade venture that came to be known throughout the West as "Bonneville's Folly."

His route out along the Platte and over South Pass is not important, except that he was the first to take wagons over South Pass, as far as the Green River, thus proving that emigrants would also be able to make the journey. But why Bonneville was allowed to take up fur trading is still unresolved. His real purpose may have been to spy on the British in the Northwest. His twin-towered fort on Horse Creek Fork of the Green River was ideally suited to monitor the activities of British trappers and Indians, or even invading soldiers. It stood athwart the approaches to South Pass, Union Pass, Jackson's Hole, Snake River, Bear River, Humboldt River and the Great Salt Lake.

The idea is not so far fetched. Bonneville was instructed by the War Department to note all aspects of natural history and

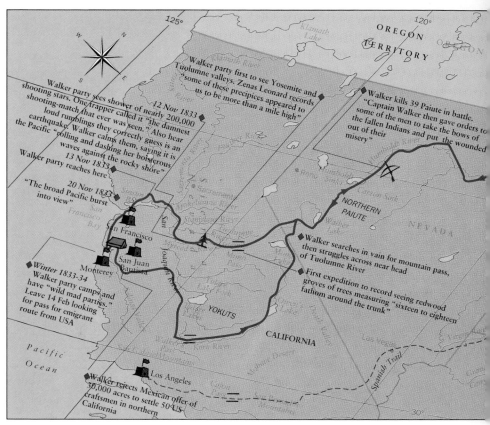

virtually everything about the Indians of the Rocky Mountains, especially their ways of making war. Indeed, General Macomb's orders enjoined Bonneville to collect "every information which you may conceive would be useful to the Government." This was all to be at his own or some mysterious private backer's expense.

By the end of the summer, Bonneville had built his fort and sent parties of trappers to Bear River. He himself moved north and east to Pierre's Hole. He then went into winter camp way up on the Salmon River. When he returned to the 1833 rendezvous at the Green River, he had little to show for his fur trapping enterprise despite the very good men working for him. His rivals scorned, but

*Left: Alfred Miller's portrait of Joseph Rutherford Walker captures the romantic self-image of this ruthless mountain man. His right hand rests on his rifle, and on a gold chain around his neck, he wears a glass or silver container inscribed "Fra Diavolo," after a then-popular opera about an Italian bandit leader.*

Bonneville had another card to play.

In 1833 Bonneville sent mountain man Joseph Rutherford Walker to find a feasible central trail to California. He disguised the mission, saying that Walker was scouting the western shores of the Great Salt Lake. This was perhaps because Walker was likely to travel below the 42nd parallel, thus trespassing on Spanish territory. Zenas Leonard, the clerk attached to the party, inadvertently revealed its true objective. He wrote: "I was anxious to go to the coast of the Pacific, and for that purpose hired with Mr Walker for a certain sum per year."

With California as his true destination, Walker made straight for the Humboldt River, following its great bend southward to the Humboldt Sinks near Mono Lake. Later Bonneville's map would refer to the Sinks as "Battle Lakes." It was there that Walker ordered his men to let fly a withering rifle volley at a large group of Paiute Indians. They were armed with bows and arrows but

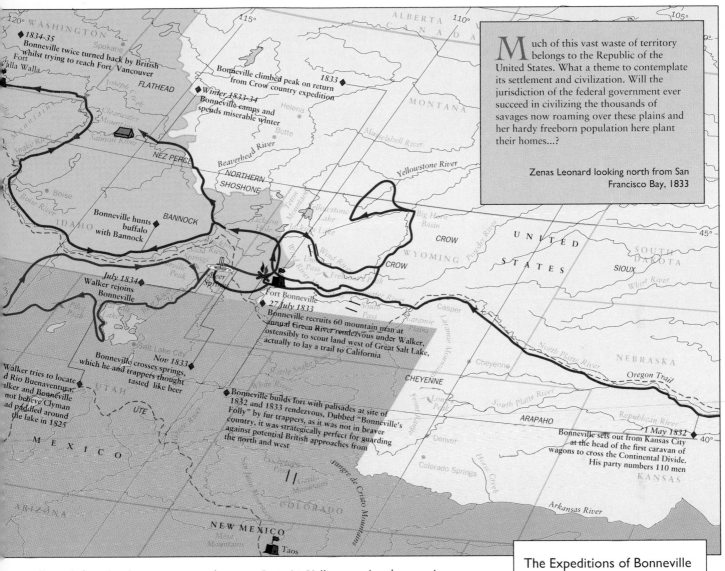

120° WASHINGTON  115°    ALBERTA  110°   CANADA  105°

**1834-35**
Bonneville twice turned back by British whilst trying to reach Fort Vancouver
Fort Walla Walla

Spokane

FLATHEAD

Bonneville climbed peak on return from Crow country expedition  **1833**

**Winter 1833-34**
Bonneville camps and spends miserable winter

Helena

MONTANA

Joseph Creek

Clearwater Mountains

NEZ PERCE

Salmon River

Butte

Beaverhead River

Musselshell River

NORTHERN SHOSHONE

Yellowstone River

Boise

Snake River

IDAHO

Boise River

Bonneville hunts buffalo with Bannock

BANNOCK

Bannock Peak

Soda River

Bear River Springs

Bonneville Peak

**July 1834**
Walker rejoins Bonneville

Bear Springs

Yellowstone Lake

Teton Mountain

Jackson Hole

Jackson Lake

Union Pass

Wind River

Fremont's Peak

Big Horn Basin

Powder River

CROW

CROW

WYOMING

UNITED STATES

SOUTH DAKOTA

SIOUX

White River

45°

Pine Lake

Fort Bonneville
**27 July 1833**
Bonneville recruits 60 mountain man at annual Green River rendezvous under Walker, ostensibly to scout land west of Great Salt Lake, actually to lay a trail to California

Great Plains

Sweetwater River

South Pass

Laramie Mountains

Casper

North Platte River

NEBRASKA

**Nov 1833**
Bonneville crosses springs, which he and trappers thought tasted like beer

Salt Lake City

UTAH

Walker tries to locate d Rio Buenaventura; alker and Bonneville not believe Clyman ad paddled around the lake in 1825

Bear River

UTE

Green River

**Bonneville builds fort with palisades at site of 1832 and 1833 rendezvous. Dubbed "Bonneville's Folly" by fur trappers, as it was not in beaver country, it was strategically perfect for guarding against potential British approaches from the north and west**

CHEYENNE

Fremont Peak

Long Peak

South Platte River

Cheyenne

Oregon Trail

Laramie River

ARAPAHO

Republican River

Denver

MEXICO

Green River

Grand River

Uncompahgre Plateau

ARIZONA

sangre de Cristo Mountains

COLORADO

Colorado Springs

Horse Creek

Arkansas River

KANSAS

**1 May 1832**
Bonneville sets out from Kansas City at the head of the first caravan of wagons to cross the Continental Divide. His party numbers 110 men

40°

NEW MEXICO

West Mountains

Taos

M uch of this vast waste of territory belongs to the Republic of the United States. What a theme to contemplate its settlement and civilization. Will the jurisdiction of the federal government ever succeed in civilizing the thousands of savages now roaming over these plains and her hardy freeborn population here plant their homes...?

Zenas Leonard looking north from San Francisco Bay, 1833

## The Expeditions of Bonneville and Walker, 1832–34

| | |
|---|---|
| | US territory |
| | Joint US-British occupation, 1818–46 |
| | Mexican territory, 1832 |
| | US fort |
| | British fort |
| | Mexican settlement |
| | Bonneville, 1832–34 |
| | Walker, 1833–34 |
| | Rendezvous |
| | Winter camp |
| | Skirmish |
| | Pass |
| | Springs |
| | Redwood forests |

Walker believed they were ready to "overwhelm" his party.

Just where Walker crossed the Sierras into California is disputed. It seems likely that he went up what became known as Walker's River, through Mono Pass and along the divide between the Merced and Tuolome rivers. They were thus the first white men to see the canyon of the Yosemite. The trip was hard but dazzling. First there was the canyon and the giant redwood trees "measuring sixteen to eighteen fathoms around the trunk," then an earthquake and a meteor shower. After coming to the arm of the great ocean at Suisun Bay, they found the beautiful coasts of the Pacific, south of San Francisco, where "they stared in amazement at stranded whales lying like helpless Gullivers washed up on a Lilliputian beach."

Walker's route back was more practicable, though the barren wastes of the Great Basin caused thirst so terrible that they drank the blood of their horses. He moved down the San

Joaquin Valley to what became known as Walker's Pass, a low, easy crossing of the southern end of the Sierras. From there he turned northward in the great silent Basin. On reaching the Humboldt Sinks he again abused and murdered the helpless Diggers. He then followed the Humboldt River, but near old Fort Hall and the main trail at Bear River, branched off overland to the Snake River. At Bonneville's behest, Walker had achieved no mean feat. He had found a practicable emigrant trail to California, signaling the approaching era of Manifest Destiny.

Bonneville was recalled in disgrace and court martialed for overstaying his leave. He told the military court of secret personal instructions from President Andrew Jackson, but the General did not back him up. Whatever orders there had been to extend his leave, they had disappeared from the military records.

# Beyond the Mississippi

## THE SURVEYS OF LIEUTENANT FRÉMONT, 1842-48

*During expeditions dogged by tragedy and political intrigue, Frémont circumnavigates the West and pioneers a new transcontinental route.*

From 1842 until the Civil War, the US Army's Corps of Topographical Engineers conducted what has been termed a "Great Reconnaissance" of the American West. The Corps, accompanied by scientists and artists, sponsored expeditions to promote development and settlement and actively publicized its findings.

John Charles Frémont as a Corps member, had already explored Cherokee country in 1836 and 1837, and accompanied Joseph N. Nicollet, a French-born scientist, on expeditions to the Red Pipestone Quarry in far western Minnesota in 1838-39. He had also led his own survey of the Des Moines River in 1841. Since 1838 Frémont had been son-in-law and protégé of Thomas Hart Benton, a powerful senator from Missouri, who was keen to secure the vast Oregon Territory for the United States.

In 1842 Benton persuaded Congress to provide funds for a Topographical Corps expedition into the Rockies. Frémont arrived in St Louis by the end of May. He headed up the Missouri by steamboat, meeting Kit Carson who would become his fast friend. Frémont journeyed along the Platte on the Oregon Trail and eventually marched his

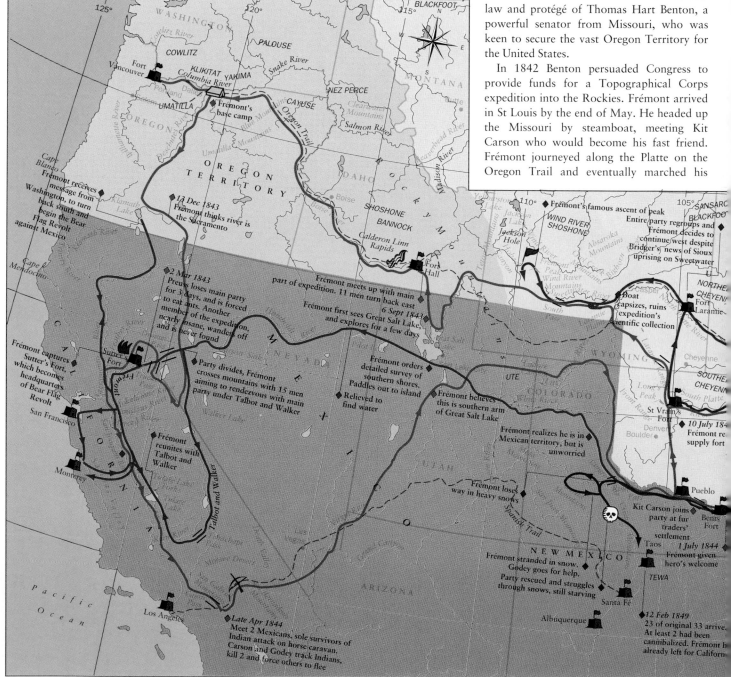

men, mostly French *voyageurs*, through the South Pass and into the Wind River Mountains. Here Frémont paddled all around the lake subsequently named after him, and scaled what he believed to be the Wind River's loftiest peak, and planted a flag emblazoned with an American eagle.

In 1843 Frémont led his men from St Vrain's Fort south to the upper Arkansas. With a picked party of men Frémont crossed the Laramie Plains to the Sweetwater River. In the meantime, the others were following the Sweetwater emigrant route. Beyond the Wasatch Mountains they explored the Great Salt Lake area and then pushed on to the Columbia River and Oregon. From the Dalles, Frémont turned south for California, making one last search for the mythical Buenaventura River, and turned west into the Sierras. For 30 days his men, soon deserted by their frightened native guides, struggled through the deep snows of Truckee Pass until they reached Sutter's Fort.

After a stay in California, Frémont led his men through the San Joaquin Valley and over what they believed to be Walker's Pass (actually Tehachapi Pass) into the Great Basin.

*Right: Drawing of Frémont's expedition in the Rocky Mountains by Edward or Richard Kern. It was reproduced in the publisher's prospectus for Frémont's* Memoirs, *1886.*

From the Las Vegas meadows, Joseph Walker led them east into Colorado's vast meadowlands.

In 1845 Frémont received orders to survey the Red River. Instead, he headed out to California where he helped instigate the Bear Flag Revolt, an action for which he was later court-martialed. He resigned from the army and, in 1848, led the first of two private expeditions to locate a central Pacific railroad route. Both expeditions became disasters. During the first, some of his best men perished in the snows of San Juan Mountains and a few fell victim to cannibalism.

Frémont had proved that no "Rio Buenaventura" ran west from Great Salt Lake and he defined the Great Basin as such. He and his men circumnavigated the whole of the American West making many scientific observations. His cartographer, Charles Preuss drew up a great map of the entire west, as well as a hugely detailed map for emigrants of the Oregon Trail.

I never was so fascinated. I never grew so fast in my life. Every scene and circumstance in the narrative was painted in my mind to last and to last forever... I fancied I could see Frémont's men, hauling the cannon up the savage battlements of the Rocky Mountains, flags in the air, Frémont at the head, waving his sword, his horse neighing wildly in the mountain wind, with unknown and unnamed empires on every hand. It touched my heart when he told how a weary little brown bee tried to make its way from a valley of flowers far below across a spur of snow, where he sat resting for a moment with his men; how the bee rested on his knee till it was strong enough to go on to another field of flowers beyond the snow... I was no longer a boy... now I began to be inflamed with a love for action, adventure, glory, and great deeds away out yonder under the path of the setting sun.

Joaquin Miller, "the Poet of the Sierras," on Frémont's ascent of the Wind River Mountains, 1842

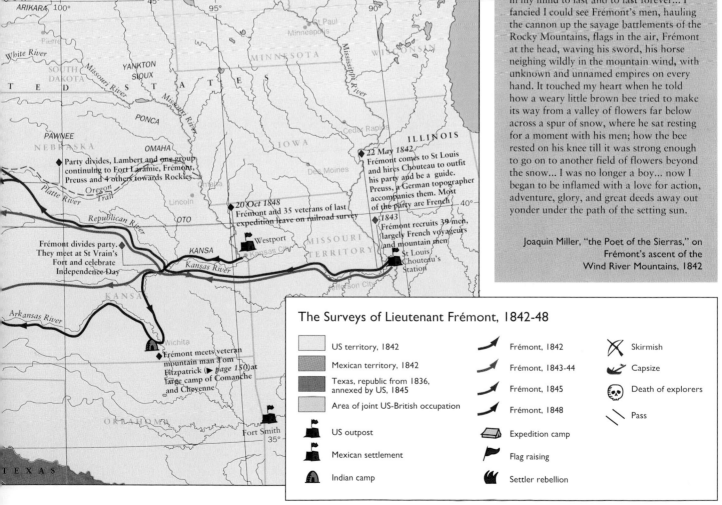

The Surveys of Lieutenant Frémont, 1842-48

| | |
|---|---|
| ☐ US territory, 1842 | ↗ Frémont, 1842 |
| ☐ Mexican territory, 1842 | ↗ Frémont, 1843-44 |
| ☐ Texas, republic from 1836, annexed by US, 1845 | ↗ Frémont, 1845 |
| ☐ Area of joint US-British occupation | ↗ Frémont, 1848 |
| 🏭 US outpost | Expedition camp |
| 🏭 Mexican settlement | Flag raising |
| ⛺ Indian camp | Settler rebellion |
| ✗ Skirmish | |
| Capsize | |
| ☠ Death of explorers | |
| Pass | |

# The Soldier Archeologists

## EMORY'S MEXICAN WAR RECONNAISSANCE, 1846

*Topographer Emory surveys New Mexico,
and finds the awe-inspiring ruined pueblos of
the Pecos and Gila valleys.*

During the Mexican war, the army attached topographical engineers to most of its major field commands. Lieutenant William H. Emory headed the topographical unit that accompanied Colonel Stephen Watts Kearny and his 300 dragoons on a march of conquest to Santa Fé. They then went on to San Diego through southwestern territory whose

> On the hill, before reaching the rancheria, the Pacific opened for the first time to our view, the sight producing strange but agreeable emotions. One of the mountain men who had never seen the ocean before, opened his arms and exclaimed: "Lord there is a great prairie without a tree."
>
> From Emory's account of the expedition's arrival near San Diego, 10 December 1846

*Above: Diamond-back rattlesnakes (crotalus atrox ), found throughout the Southwest. Emory's team recorded and classified masses of fauna and flora, and he included pictures of many of them in his published report .*

geography was only incompletely understood.

Emory, a career military man with strong connections to the Coast Survey and the new Smithsonian Institution, had an avid interest in science. Leaving Lieutenants James W. Abert and William G. Peck behind to map and survey the territory of New Mexico, Kearny rode out of Santa Fé on 25 September 1846. With his topographical corps were two civilians: Norman Bestor, a statistician, and the landscape painter John Mix Stanley (▶ *page 168*). As Kearny and Emory headed down the Rio Grande and west along the

upper Gila River, they found much to occupy them in the field of natural history. Just before Valverde, New Mexico, they met Kit Carson on his way east with news that California had been surrendered to the Americans. Now Kearny sent two-thirds of his men back to Santa Fé. The rest continued west with Kit Carson, who reluctantly agreed to guide them to the Pacific. Along the Gila River, Emory found many interesting ancient ruins and artifacts, which he first believed to be Aztec, but later realized were remains of a distinct native culture that had once flourished there. He identified at least 12 aboriginal towns as having once lined the banks of the Gila. His most important find was the Casa Grande, or Casa Montezuma, its pink sandstone walls still largely standing after 400 years.

From the junction of the Gila and Colorado rivers Kearny's men suffered immeasurably for eight days as they marched through desert on their way to Warner's Ranch, in the foothills of the Sierra Nevada of California. Just east of Warner's Ranch, near the native village of San Pascual, Kearny's troops clashed with Mexican soldiers in a desperate hand-to-hand conflict. Although superior in numbers, the Mexicans, who had been armed mainly with lances, retired from the field first. Nevertheless, the Americans could hardly claim this as a victory: whereas the Mexicans lost only 2 men, 18 Americans were killed and 13 wounded. Kearny himself was badly wounded. Emory had proved himself a hero when he killed the lancer about to finish off his commander. Following the battle, the Army of the West found itself barricaded in what was called Snooks Ranch. On the night of 8 December, Kit Carson, Lieutenant

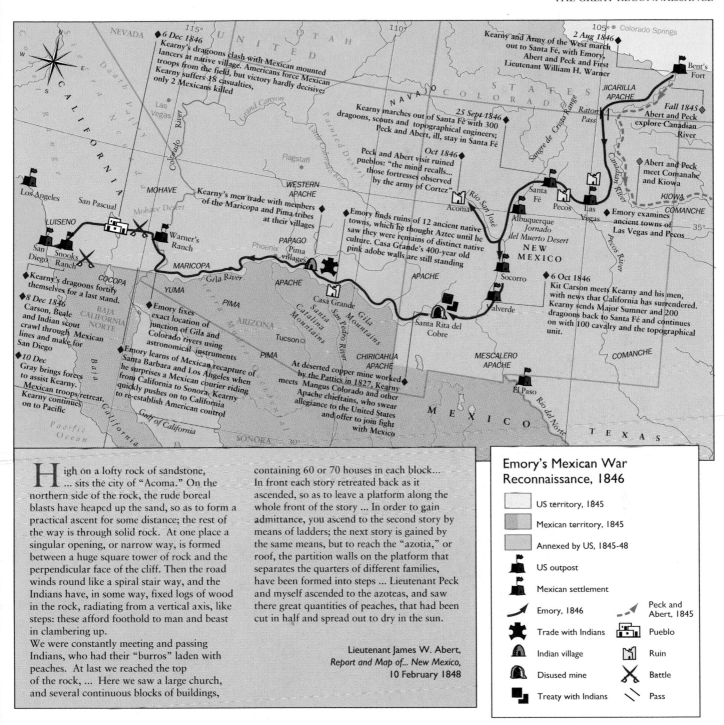

**Map labels (clockwise/geographic):**

NEVADA · UNITED STATES · UTAH · COLORADO · Colorado Springs

6 Dec 1846
Kearny's dragoons clash with Mexican mounted lancers at native village. Americans force Mexican troops from the field, but victory hardly decisive; Kearny suffers 18 casualties, only 2 Mexicans killed

2 Aug 1846
Kearny and Army of the West march out to Santa Fé, with Emory, Abert and Peck and First Lieutenant William H. Warner

Bent's Fort

JICARILLA APACHE

Fall 1845
Abert and Peck explore Canadian River

CALIFORNIA · Sierra Nevada · Death Valley · Las Vegas · Grand Canyon · Painted Desert · NAVAJO · Flagstaff · Little Colorado River · Colorado River

Kearny marches out of Santa Fé with 300 dragoons, scouts and topographical engineers; 25 Sept 1846 Peck and Abert, ill, stay in Santa Fé

Sangre de Cristo Range · Raton Pass · Canadian River

Abert and Peck meet Comanche and Kiowa

KIOWA · COMANCHE

Oct 1846
Peck and Abert visit ruined pueblos: "the mind recalls... those fortresses observed by the army of Cortez"

MOHAVE · Mohave Desert · WESTERN APACHE

Kearny's men trade with members of the Maricopa and Pima tribes at their villages

Los Angeles · San Pascual · Warner's Ranch · LUISENO · San Diego · Snooks Ranch · COCOPA · YUMA · PIMA · MARICOPA · Gila River · Phoenix · PARAGO · Pima villages · APACHE · Santa Catalina Mountains · San Pedro River · Gila Mountains · Casa Grande · Tucson · PIMA · ARIZONA · BAJA CALIFORNIA NORTE · Baja California · Gulf of California · SONORA

Emory finds ruins of 12 ancient native towns, which he thought Aztec until he saw they were remains of distinct native culture. Casa Grande's 400-year old pink adobe walls are still standing

Acoma · Rio San José · Santa Fé · Pecos · Albuquerque · Jornado del Muerto Desert · NEW MEXICO · Las Vegas · Pecos River

Emory examines ancient towns of Las Vegas and Pecos · 35°

Socorro · APACHE

6 Oct 1846
Kit Carson meets Kearny and his men, with news that California has surrendered. Kearny sends Major Sumner and 200 dragoons back to Santa Fé and continues on with 100 cavalry and the topographical unit.

Kearny's dragoons fortify themselves for a last stand.

8 Dec 1846
Carson, Beale and Indian scout crawl through Mexican lines and make for San Diego.

10 Dec
Gray brings forces to assist Kearny. Mexican troops retreat, Kearny continues on to Pacific.

Emory fixes exact location of junction of Gila and Colorado rivers using astronomical instruments

Emory learns of Mexican recapture of Santa Barbara and Los Angeles when he surprises a Mexican courier riding from California to Sonora. Kearny quickly pushes on to California to re-establish American control

At deserted copper mine worked by the Patties in 1827, Kearny meets Mangus Colorado and other Apache chieftains, who swear allegiance to the United States and offer to join fight with Mexico

CHIRICAHUA APACHE · Santa Rita del Cobre · Valverde · MESCALERO APACHE · El Paso · Rio del Norte · COMANCHE · MEXICO · TEXAS · SONORA · 30°

Pacific Ocean

---

High on a lofty rock of sandstone, ... sits the city of "Acoma." On the northern side of the rock, the rude boreal blasts have heaped up the sand, so as to form a practical ascent for some distance; the rest of the way is through solid rock. At one place a singular opening, or narrow way, is formed between a huge square tower of rock and the perpendicular face of the cliff. Then the road winds round like a spiral stair way, and the Indians have, in some way, fixed logs of wood in the rock, radiating from a vertical axis, like steps: these afford foothold to man and beast in clambering up.

We were constantly meeting and passing Indians, who had their "burros" laden with peaches. At last we reached the top of the rock, ... Here we saw a large church, and several continuous blocks of buildings, containing 60 or 70 houses in each block... In front each story retreated back as it ascended, so as to leave a platform along the whole front of the story ... In order to gain admittance, you ascend to the second story by means of ladders; the next story is gained by the same means, but to reach the "azotia," or roof, the partition walls on the platform that separates the quarters of different families, have been formed into steps ... Lieutenant Peck and myself ascended to the azoteas, and saw there great quantities of peaches, that had been cut in half and spread out to dry in the sun.

Lieutenant James W. Abert,
*Report and Map of... New Mexico*,
10 February 1848

### Emory's Mexican War Reconnaissance, 1846

| | |
|---|---|
| | US territory, 1845 |
| | Mexican territory, 1845 |
| | Annexed by US, 1845-48 |
| | US outpost |
| | Mexican settlement |
| | Emory, 1846 |
| | Peck and Abert, 1845 |
| | Trade with Indians |
| | Pueblo |
| | Indian village |
| | Ruin |
| | Disused mine |
| | Battle |
| | Treaty with Indians |
| | Pass |

---

*Left: Giant cactus (cereus giganticus), towering above a group of Indians, near the Gila River. Drawn by Paulus Roetter, and published in Emory's* United States and Mexican Boundary Survey Report *in 1859, giant cacti had only been seen by Indians and plainsmen in Texas, before Emory's march to the Pacific in 1846.*

Edward F. Beale and an Indian scout were able to break through the Mexican lines and make for San Diego. There they recruited reinforcements, 180 sailors and marines who, under the command of Lieutenant A.V.F. Gray, marched to Snooks Ranch and finally overcame the Mexicans. Kearny's army was then able to march on to the Pacific.

Despite the military character of Kearny's expedition, Emory ensured that it fulfilled scientific objectives as well. Upon returning home, he drew the first map to portray southwestern geography accurately. His report also included topographical descriptions, lists of flora and fauna, and careful comments on the area's geology and fossil remains. Perhaps most importantly, his studies of ancient ruins pioneered the study of native ethnology through archeological remains. All in all, Emory managed to turn out a many-sided description of a very interesting and hitherto little understood area of the continent.

# The Ancient Southwest Revealed

## THE SURVEYS OF SIMPSON AND SITGREAVES, 1849-51

*Hidden amid the canyons and mesas of the southwest, US military topographers discover the spectacular ruins of a lost civilization.*

In August 1849 topographical engineer Lieutenant James H. Simpson left Santa Fé, New Mexico, with three topographical assistants. They were part of a punitive expedition against the Navajo, led by Lieutenant Colonel John M. Washington, for their raids on outlying New Mexico settlements.

Simpson marched due west and made a detailed record of the Jemez pueblo on the Rio Grande. The party then crossed the headwaters of the Puerco River, marched through a desert studded with mesas and entered the Chaco Canyon. Leading a detached reconnaissance, Simpson located the ruins of no less than ten ancient and enormous pueblos of the Anasazi, the largest complex of Indian pueblos in North America and the home of a great, lost civilization.

From Chaco Canyon, Washington led his men, including Simpson, to the foothills of the Chuska Mountains. After overcoming a group of Navajo and killing six of them, Washington's artillery moved into Canyon de Chelly, a Navajo stronghold. After a further skirmish with the Navajo. Washington was able to enforce a peace. Simpson then reconnoitred the canyon with an escort of 60 soldiers including the artist Richard Kern. They discovered spectacular prehistoric pueblos (▶ *page opposite*) and on their return march, Simpson studied further ruins in the Canyon Bonito, the village of Zuñi and Inscription Rock, a landmark carved with the names both of Indians and the Spanish conquistadors of 1605 (▶ *page 40*).

The soldiers then marched through the

Puerco Valley's pueblo towns and back to Santa Fé. Simpson reported his spectacular findings to the Corps of Topographical Engineers and, aided by information from mountain man Richard Campbell, advised that a new railroad route might run west from the Rio Grande, past Zuñi and across the Colorado into California.

In summer 1851 Captain Lorenzo Sitgreaves was assigned to assist Colonel Edwin Vose Sumner in his efforts to suppress the Navajo, and was sent to follow up Simpson's suggestion of a southern railroad route. Sitgreaves marched west out of Albuquerque with 50 infantry across present-day Arizona. He was accompanied by an army topographer, Lieutenant John G. Parke, the naturalist Dr S.W. Woodhouse, Richard

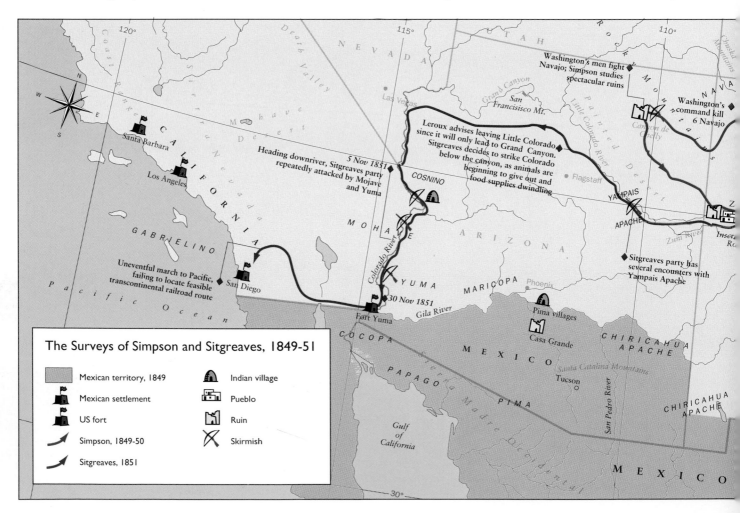

## The Surveys of Simpson and Sitgreaves, 1849-51

- (shaded) Mexican territory, 1849
- Mexican settlement
- US fort
- Simpson, 1849-50
- Sitgreaves, 1851
- Indian village
- Pueblo
- Ruin
- Skirmish

Kern, and a guide, Antoine Leroux.

Heading west in the shadow of the Indians' sacred San Francisco Mountains the party was attacked near the Colorado River by the Cosnino. They were beset by repeated ambushes. Antoine Leroux and another member of the party were wounded, Mojave wounded Dr Woodhouse and Yuma killed one straggler with war clubs. The party struggled into Fort Yuma, and eventually moved on to California.

No satisfactory railroad route to the Pacific was found but Simpson recorded the spectacular pueblo ruins he had encountered, while Sitgreaves produced valuable reports of the Wupatki ruins of Arizona, the village of Zuñi, and of his experiences with Yampais Apache and Cosnino Indians.

We had got about two miles when I came near treading on a rattle snake. I immediately jumped back and struck him on the head with my ramrod and then seized him back of the head. Unfortunately my hold was too long and he throwing round his head struck me on my finger I immediately commenced sucking it and asked for string but they had none and I pulled a buckskin string off the wallet of my compass & got Lieut P to tie it around the finger as quick as possible. I then lanced my finger well with my knife and sent off Ross for some Ammonia. I continued sucking it all the time I was walking when near the Pueblo we were met by Ross and I applied the Ammonia immediately and drank some Whiskey, on getting in the house I took some Ammonia inwardly and commenced drinking brandy. The pain when the snake first struck me was very severe and made me sick at the stomack but this soon passed away. I lanced my finger freely again and held it in warm water and it bled finely then placed it in a cup of Ammonia. They continued giving me Brandy and I was soon unconscious of every thing that was going on. How long I remained in this condition I am unable to say.

Dr Samuel Washington Woodhouse,
17 September 1851

It was somewhat exciting to observe, as we approached the valley of Chelly, the huts of the enemy, one after another, springing up into smoke and flame, and their owners scampering off in flight.

Lleutenant James Hervey Simpson,
Canyon de Chelly, September 1849

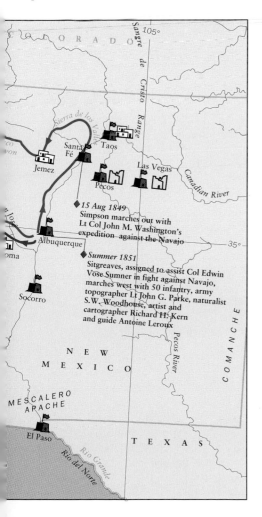

*Right: View of a ruined and ancient pueblo, spectacularly situated beneath an overhanging rock in the Canyon de Chelly. This lithograph, which was widely distributed in the mid-19th century, is based on a drawing made in September 1849 by Richard Kern, the expedition's artist and cartographer. Kern accompanied both Simpson and Sitgreaves and had previously accompanied Frémont on his ill-fated 1848 railroad survey (▶ page 158).*

# Grand Canyon Country

## THE SURVEYS OF IVES AND MACOMB, 1857-59

*The US Army, anticipating a war with the Mormons, sends its first expeditions into the Grand Canyon, in search of new supply routes into the Great Basin.*

*Left: Originally sent to America by the Prussian geographer Alexander von Humboldt, Heinrich Balduin Möllhausen accompanied Ives into the Grand Canyon. With Egloffstein he produced the first popular lithographs of its spectacular landforms.*

> ike the grand canyons of the Colorado, the broad valleys, bounded by high and perpendicular walls belong to a vast system of erosion, and are wholly due to the action of water. Probably nowhere in the world has the action of this agent produced results so surprising both as regards their magnitude and their peculiar character. It is not at all strange that a cause, which has given to what was once immense plain, underlaid by thousands of feet of sedimentary rocks, conformable throughout, a topographical character more complicated than that of any mountain chain; which has made much of it absolutely impassable to man, or to any animal but the winged bird, should be regarded as something out of the course of nature... the outlines of the western part of the North American continent were approximately marked out by areas of shallower water in an almost boundless ocean, but by groups of islands and broad continental surfaces of dry land.
>
> **John Strong Newberry on the formation of the Grand Canyon**

Late in 1857 a topographical engineer, First Lieutenant Joseph Christmas Ives, was sent up the Colorado River to look for a water route to the Great Basin. His party included geologist, Dr John Strong Newberry, topographer, F.W. von Egloffstein, and the artist, Balduin Möllhausen.

On 1 November, at Robinson's Landing, they unloaded the prefabricated metal parts of the paddle steamer USS *Explorer*, which they assembled watched by the crews of other steamers and Cocopa Indians. On 22 December word arrived that the Mormon war had begun. Ives was ordered to assess rapidly the navigability of the Colorado. Ives' pilot, Captain D.C. Robinson, arrived a week later and that night the *Explorer* was launched.

On 8 January they entered Black Canyon, the first of the Colorado's gigantic chasms. When the *Explorer* struck a submerged rock, Ives declared they had reached the Colorado's head of navigation. With two others Ives explored the canyon in a skiff, rowing as far upriver as the Las Vegas Wash. Meantime Mormon spies attempted to persuade the area's Mohave and Paiute to attack Ives' men. This was averted by gifts and diplomacy.

Ives sent half his men back down the river on the *Explorer*. He himself left the river to search for the Mormon Road with Newberry, Egloffstein, Möllhausen, Lieutenant Tipton and 20 soldiers. Two Hualpais guides led the party to the Grand Canyon. In April they reached its floor, near the mouth of Diamond Creek – probably the first white men to enter the canyon. Deserted by the guides, they spent two days exploring the canyon. They followed an Indian trail that led over ledges so narrow that some had to crawl along them. They finally clambered up out of the canyon onto the south rim of the Colorado Plateau.

Early in May, at the Little Colorado River, Ives split up his remaining men again, sending the supply train directly to Fort Defiance. Ives, Newberry, Egloffstein and a few others crossed the Little Colorado in boats made of canvas stretched over wooden frames. They then marched northeast across the Painted Desert to the Hopi pueblos, a peaceful community built on three sacred mesas. Despite warnings from the Hopi, they headed north hoping to reach the Colorado River again. But the desert proved too harsh and they retreated back to the pueblos. The next time they marched east. Although an increasing number of hostile Navajo trailed their party daily, on 23 May they reached Fort Defiance without incident.

Newberry was the first geologist to see the Colorado River's mile-deep canyon and his study of its geological strata greatly expanded knowledge of the formation of the whole continent. Egloffstein invented a map-making technique, still used today, for representing physical features in sculptured relief. Ives' own expedition report was a masterpiece, combining the characteristics of a scientific paper and romantic literature.

Two years later, in 1859, another topographical engineer Captain John M. Macomb led a party into the Colorado River system. Newberry was also part of the expedition. After traveling up the Chama River he crossed the headwaters of the San Juan River and then headed west, exploring Indian ruins in the shadow of Mesa Verde. After a difficult march across the sage plain, Macomb's party became the first white men to view the intricate canyon country around the junction of the Green and Grand rivers. Newberry not only found the first dinosaur bones of the far West, he also devised an early geological concept of the entire plateau .

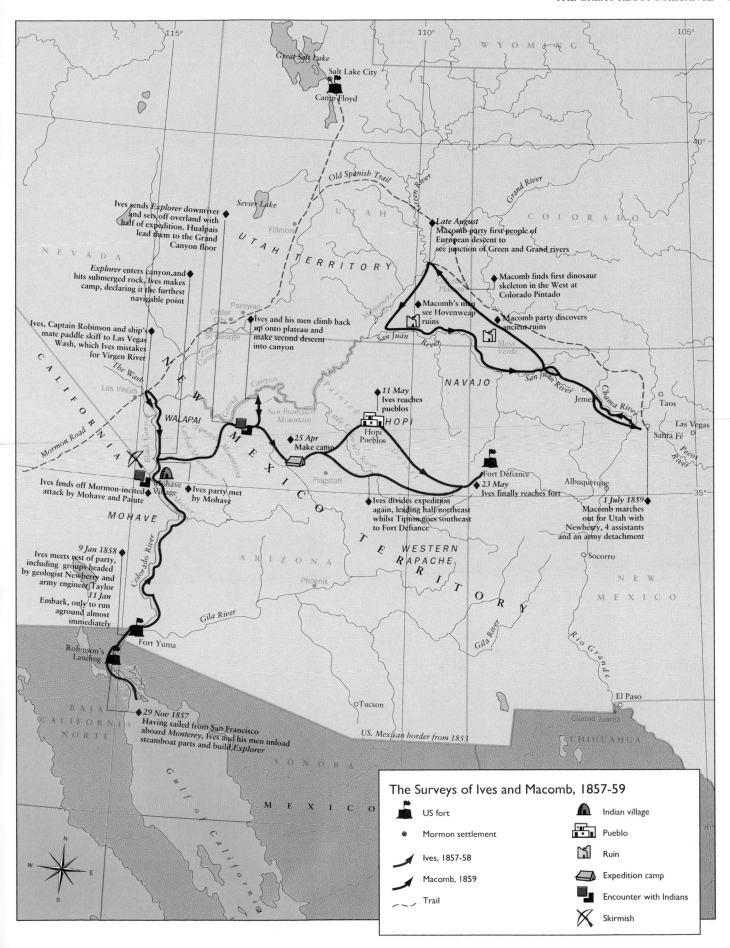

Ives sends *Explorer* downriver and sets off overland with half of expedition. Hualpais lead them to the Grand Canyon floor

*Explorer* enters canyon, and hits submerged rock. Ives makes camp, declaring it the furthest navigable point

Ives, Captain Robinson and ship's mate paddle skiff to Las Vegas Wash, which Ives mistakes for Virgen River

Ives fends off Mormon-incited attack by Mohave and Paiute

9 Jan 1858
Ives meets rest of party, including groups headed by geologist Newberry and army engineer Taylor
11 Jan
Embark, only to run aground almost immediately

29 Nov 1857
Having sailed from San Francisco aboard *Monterey*, Ives and his men unload steamboat parts and build *Explorer*

Ives and his men climb back up onto plateau and make second descent into canyon

Late August
Macomb party first people of European descent to see junction of Green and Grand rivers

Macomb finds first dinosaur skeleton in the West at Colorado Pintado

Macomb's men see Hovenweap ruins

Macomb party discovers ancient ruins

11 May
Ives reaches pueblos

25 Apr
Make camp

Ives party met by Mohave

Ives divides expedition again, leading half northeast whilst Tipton goes southeast to Fort Defiance

23 May
Ives finally reaches fort

1 July 1859
Macomb marches out for Utah with Newberry, 4 assistants and an army detachment

US. Mexican border from 1853

## The Surveys of Ives and Macomb, 1857-59

- US fort
- Mormon settlement
- Ives, 1857-58
- Macomb, 1859
- Trail
- Indian village
- Pueblo
- Ruin
- Expedition camp
- Encounter with Indians
- Skirmish

# The Search for an Iron Trail

## THE GREAT RAILROAD SURVEYS, 1853-55

*The American government spends over $1 million in search of the best railroad route to the Pacific coast. Cities along the Mississippi compete to be its eastern terminus.*

The Great Pacific Railroad Surveys were set up to find "the most economical and practicable" route to the Pacific coast. Giant railroad conventions were held in St Louis, Memphis and New Orleans and after the Pacific Railroad Survey Bill in 1853, expeditions were sent out on three routes west.

The Atlantic and Pacific Railroad Company proposed a railroad west from Vicksburg, along the 32nd parallel. This "southern route" was favored by Secretary of War Jefferson Davis (later president of the Confederate states) since it would spread slavery and enable the South to dominate Congress. Senator Stephen Douglas of Illinois, an investor in the Illinois Central Railroad, favored a northerly route from Lake Superior, Chicago or Cairo, Illinois. Representative J.S. Phelps of Missouri held out for a route west from Springfield, the state capital. Others, from Hannibal and St Joseph, Missouri, favored the Oregon Trail.

Isaac I. Stevens, the new governor of Washington Territory and a former topographical engineer, explored between the 47th and 49th parallels. Lieutenant John W. Gunnison led an expedition along the 38th parallel. Gunnison and his men were killed by Ute. Lieutenant E.G. Beckwith took over and found a route over the Sierras, but his proposal was largely ignored. Lieutenant Amiel Weeks Whipple led a party west along the 35th parallel. When Congress insisted on a "southern" expedition the route was split in two. Lieutenant John G. Parke explored from San Diego to the Rio Grande; Captain John Pope from there to the Pacific. Lieutenant R.S. Williamson headed south from San Francisco and found five passes through the Sierras. He then explored northward to the Columbia with Lieutenant Henry L. Abbott.

The surveys produced a political stalemate. Ironically, Beckwith's route was the most suitable. But it had to be rediscovered by professional railroad men before northern capitalists were able to push through "the Great Central Route." Likewise it was not until a professional engineer investigated "Doc" Strong's route that the Central Pacific Railroad was formed in 1861.

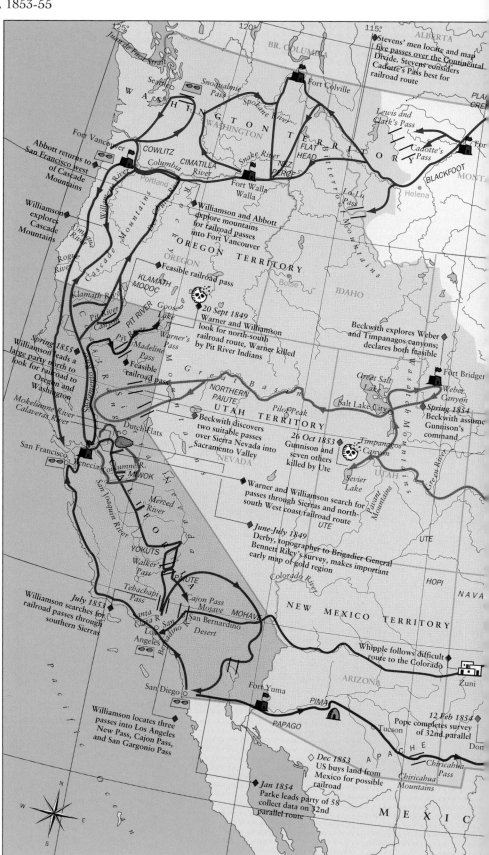

The Great Pacific Railroad
Surveys, 1853-55

Goldfields Survey, 1849

Warner and Williamson, 1849

Stevens, 1853

Gunnison and Beckwith, 1853

Williamson and Parke, 1853

Whipple, 1853

Parke, 1854

Pope, 1854

Williamson and Abbott, 1855

Proposed railroad
starting

Proposed railroad
destination

US fort

Pueblo

Pass

Goldfields

Massacre

Indian
village

The Captain's mule turned with him and plunged down the hill; and having been carried about two hundred yards, he fell from the animal, dead. The guide dismounted and prepared to fire, but finding he could not aim his rifle he succeeded in remounting and retiring down the hill. He died the next morning. The party was thrown into confusion and retreated at once... Cave died before reaching the valley, while Barling... has nearly recovered.

Lieutenant R.S. Williamson on the killing
of Captain W.H. Warner in an ambush
by Pit River Indians

CANADA

SAKATCHEWAN

MANITOBA

BRITISH NORTH AMERICA

ASSINIBOIN

Missouri River

Fort Union

Yellowstone River

Stevens sends small parties of men off on side excursions to cover as much ground as possible. Party reunites at Fort Union

NORTH DAKOTA

Bismark

SIOUX

Duluth

MINNESOTA TERRITORY

OJIBWA

WISCONSIN

St Paul

6 June 1853
Stevens leads party to find transcontinental railroad route between 47th and 49th parallels

SOUTH DAKOTA

Missouri River

UNORGANIZED TERRITORIES

WYOMING

Lake Michigan

Detroit

Cedar Rapids

IOWA

Des Moines

Chicago

ILLINOIS

INDIANA

OHIO

Lake Erie

NEBRASKA

Platte River

Lincoln

Republican River

23 June 1853
Gunnison sets out to find railroad route between 38th and 39th parallels

Grand River

St Joseph

Hannibal

Springfield

St Louis

Louisville

COLORADO

Fort Leavenworth

Jefferson City

unnison

Sangre de Cristo Pass
Cochetopa Pass

San Luis Valley

CHEYENNE

KANSAS

MISSOURI

KENTUCKY

Cairo

TEWA

KIOWA

Canadian River

COMANCHE

14 July 1853
Whipple leads party to explore the 35th parallel

OKLAHOMA

Oklahoma City

Fort Smith

ARKANSAS

Memphis

TENNESSEE

lbuquerque

Whipple's group meets Ives's party, which has orders to accompany them to California

WICHITA

COMANCHE

Red River

Fort Washita

Little Rock

ARKANSAS

Arkansas River

Fort Belknap

NEW MEXICO

Llano Estacado

TEXAS

Pope declares that a railroad can easily be built across Guadalupe Mountains and the Llano Estacado if artesian wells are sunk at strategic points.

ALABAMA

Vicksburg

MISSISSIPPI

Guadalupe Mountains

l Paso

Guadalupe Pass

Rio Grande

Horsehead Crossing

Pecos River

LOUISIANA

Mobile

BILOXI

New Orleans

LIPAN APACHE

# A Topographic Romance

## ARTISTS AND SCIENTISTS OF THE GREAT PACIFIC RAILROAD SURVEYS

*As the cartographers of the Railroad Surveys map the American West, scientists unveil its topography and their artist colleagues record its visual splendors.*

The expeditions of the Great Pacific Railroad Surveys were economically and politically inspired, but they conducted a great reconnaissance of the West. The survey reports filled 13 massive volumes, including an entire volume of maps, panoramas and pictures.

Among these was the first accurate, detailed map of the whole trans-Mississippi West, a great scientific achievement by 27 year old Lieutenant G. K. Warren. One of the important maps of American history, it was a careful composite of the numerous expedition route maps and field notes, as well as previous works by Emory and Preuss. The volume also

included three geological maps. One was by Swiss geologist Jules Marcou, who accompanied Lieutenant Amiel Weeks Whipple on the difficult route between Albuquerque and Los Angeles. A second map by W. P. Blake controverted Marcou's findings. The third geological map, by James Hall of the New York State History Survey, the "dean" of American paleontologists, was based on the work of John Strong Newberry in the Grand Canyon, of F.V. Hayden and Fielding B. Meek, as well as many other topographical engineer expeditions of the period.

Perhaps the most spectacular results of the

Railroad Surveys were the hundreds of drawings, paintings, lithographs, engravings and fold-out panoramas produced by the field artists. Highly romantic in manner, they offered the first comprehensive picture of the West. The best were by F.W. von Eggloffstein, John Mix Stanley and Gustavus Sohon, but many others joined the surveys.

The artist-naturalist Heinrich Balduin von Möllhausen had been a protegé of the great German geographer Alexander von Humboldt. In 1853 Möllhausen was also part of Whipple's expedition. Five years later he and Eggloffstein were recruited by Lieutenant

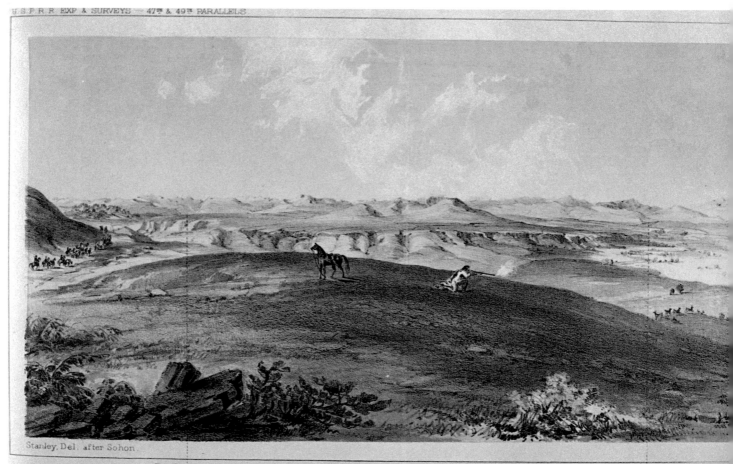

U.S.P.R.R. EXP. & SURVEYS — 47ᵀᴴ & 49ᵀᴴ PARALLELS

Stanley, Del. after Sohon.

Dearborn River.                                    Cadotte's Pass.

MAIN CHAIN OF THE ROCKY MOUNTAINS, AS SEEN FROM THE EAST, — EXTENDING

Joseph Christmas Ives to record his venture into the Grand Canyon (▶ *page 164*). On his return to Germany, Möllhausen wrote many novels based on his American experiences, and would walk around Potsdam dressed as a mountain man.

Artists were by no means immune to the dangers experienced by the other surveyors. Richard H. Kern, a member of the Academy of Natural Sciences in Philadelphia, survived Frémont's disastrous 1848 expedition (▶ *page 158*) and his journey with Simpson and Sitgreaves into the Canyon de Chelly, where he painted the ancient pueblo (▶ *page 162*). But

he was killed by Ute Indians when on Gunnison's 1853 railroad survey – along with Gunnison, botanist Frederick Creuzefeld and five other expedition members.

Extraordinary scientific drawings by

geologists, botanists, zoologists and amateur ethnologists portrayed the thousands of specimens they brought back with them. Their work is also part of the achievement of the Great Pacific Railroad Surveys.

*Below: This panorama of "The Main Chain of the Rocky Mountains, As Seen From the East," combines the work of two of the most gifted artists to work on the railroad surveys. The three-panel, hand-colored foldout lithograph was engraved by John Mix Stanley after a drawing by Gustavus Sohon. It first appeared in Governor Isaac Stevens's General Report (1854).*

*Both men accompanied Stevens on his 1853 survey, which set out from St Paul, Minnesota with orders to find a transcontinental route between the 47th and*

*49th parallels. Stevens thought Cadotte's Pass would provide the most viable route, and along with the Marias Pass, it is clearly labeled on the panorama.*

*Sohon and Stanley could not have seen all the topographical detail they included from any one point. The view is a composite one, put together from a number of sketches, to form a kind of three-dimensional map. This European technique was introduced to the survey by Sohon and brought to perfection by Egglofstein.*

GENERAL REPORT — PLATE LII

Sarony, Major & Knapp, Lith? 449 Broadway NY

Marias Pass

POINT NORTH OF THE MARIAS PASS TO NEAR THE LITTLE BLACKFOOT PASS

# Adventures on the 40th Parallel

## THE SURVEYS OF KING AND WHEELER, 1867-73

*Clarence King, a brilliant young scientist, surveys a vast tract of the American West, Lieutenant George M. Wheeler develops mapping techniques still in use today.*

In 1867 Clarence King, at 25 years old the darling of the scientific establishment, was appointed head of the Geological and Geographical Exploration of the 40th Parallel. With a party of hand-picked civilian scientists, he studied the alkali deserts and rugged mountains of western Nevada. His first season was hard and adventurous and many of his men came down with malaria. High up a peak, King's theodolite was struck by lightning. His right arm and side turned brown for three days.

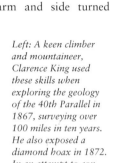

*Left: A keen climber and mountaineer, Clarence King used these skills when exploring the geology of the 40th Parallel in 1867, surveying over 100 miles in ten years. He also exposed a diamond hoax in 1872. In an attempt to con investors, two men had claimed to have found diamonds in a mesa in Colorado. They had in fact secretly "salted" the field with precious stones beforehand. King's exposure of the hoax saved not only the San Francisco Stock Exchange, but thousands of potential investors. He became the toast of San Francisco, and nationally was applauded as a "cool headed man of scientific education."*

That winter King studied Virginia City's Comstock Lode and explored the mine shafts and tunnels of Mount Davidson. Timothy O'Sullivan, perhaps the West's greatest photographer, took the first pictures ever taken down a mine, and King's topographers drew detailed maps, at two miles to the inch.

During winter 1868 James D. Hague began a study of Colorado's silver mines while the main party surveyed the Great Basin. King realized that it was really composed of two ancient glacier-fed lakes, Lake Bonneville and Lake Lahonton, separated by a high mountain-studded plateau.

In 1869-70 King covered the area between the Salt Lake and the Green River, studied the mountains of the Pacific Coast and discovered a glacier at the foot of Mount Shasta, the first located in the USA. Over the next years King extended his survey east to the Front Range of the Rockies, worked the length of the parallel again, and completed his study of the Great Basin's geology.

Although King insisted that geologic change was caused by sudden catastrophes, his survey was perhaps the most sophisticated of his day. He saw to the publication of Arnold Hague's classic work, *The Mining Industry*, in 1870 and uncovered a major diamond hoax in 1872. In 1879 he was made director of the newly-created United States Geological Survey.

Lieutenant George M. Wheeler worked for the United States Geographical Surveys West of the 100th Meridian. Despite grueling experiences Wheeler never matched the flamboyant King. He and his men, including Timothy O'Sullivan who took stark and extraordinary landscape photographs, surveyed and mapped the West beyond the 100th meridian. Although falsely denied by John Wesley Powell and James Terry Gardner, Hayden's cartographer, Wheeler produced the earliest contour maps of the area.

Wheeler's parties explored and re-surveyed in California, Nevada, Utah, Colorado, Idaho, Wyoming, Montana, Nebraska and New Mexico. In 1879 Congress made Wheeler's survey part of the US Geological Survey. Wheeler's quadrant system was later adapted by Powell and remains central to the mapping of the Survey today.

## The Surveys of King and Wheeler, 1867-73

| | |
|---|---|
| ☐ | Area surveyed by King, 1867-73 |
| ☐ | Area surveyed by Wheeler, 1867-72 |
| ⚑ | US fort |
| ⛺ | Base camp |
| ◪ | Expedition winters |
| ☁ | Explorer struck by lightning |
| ↓ | Mines |
| ▲ | Hoax gem strike |
| ⚓ | Boat capsizes |
| ◼ | Rescue |

The route lay for more than 39 miles in light, white, drifting sand, which was traversed between 5 am and 6 pm, the center of the desert being reached about meridian. The stifling heat, great radiation, and constant glare from the sand were almost overpowering, and two of the command succumbed near nightfall, rendering it necessary to pack one man on the back of a mule to the first divide on the route, where a grass sward was reached at the end of the long sandy stretch, while the second, an old and tried mountaineer, became unconscious for more than an hour in nearly the same locality.

Lieutenant George M. Wheeler describes
Death Valley

**1870**
King turns to study of volcanoes of the Pacific Northwest. Climbing Mount Shasta, first to discover active glacier in USA

**3 May 1871**
Wheeler launches survey, sending out 30 men, including two lieutenants, army surgeon, photographer, geologists and newspaper reporter. Split up to reconnoiter area around Nevada's rich mining districts

**King struck by lightning** while using his theodolite in a storm. Expedition had fanned out to survey Virginia City, Truckee and Hot Springs Mountains, and Pyramid Lake; in great heat, most get malaria and are sent to Unionville

**1871**
King's men work out of fort, surveying country between Green and Front Range of Rockies

**Nov 1872**
King makes way to peak just north of Brown's Hole, site of supposed gem strike, and exposes "Great Diamond Hoax"

**1868**
King and party continue survey from Great Basin to Great Salt Lake

**King crawls into a cave after a grizzly bear**

**Late 1867**
King sends most of his men to winter in Carson City, and holes up in Virginia City with the geologist, Gardner, and O'Sullivan, studying Comstock Lode silver mines

**Spring 1869**
King establishes new base camp and sends men out to work through Wasatch and Uinta Mountains and along Green River Divide

**Fall 1871**
King meets Henry Adams, soon his staunchest supporter

**July 1871**
Wheeler leads group into valley, where they suffer sunstroke, lack of water and up to 120°F

**Summer 1873**
One of Wheeler's survey parties, working from Denver, meets party from the Hayden survey (▶ page 178). Surveys overlap throughout summer to ire of Congress

**11 Oct 1871**
Wheeler loses one boat in rapids, with rations, journals, scientific instruments and collections

**18 Oct 1871**
Wheeler and his men finally reach mouth of creek, and meet rescue party

**17 July 1867**
Cavalry escort arrives and meets King and his team of topographers, geologists, a botanist, an ornithologist and a photographer at base camp

**16 Sept 1871**
Wheeler leads group including 14 Mohave to look for head of navigation of Colorado

OREGON
MONTANA
IDAHO
SOUTH DAKOTA
NEBRASKA
NORTHERN PAIUTE
Mount Shasta
Truckee Mountains
Comstock Lode
NEVADA
Virginia City
Carson City
Glendale
Halleck Station
Great Salt Lake
Salt Lake City
Fort Bridger
Brown's Hole
Diamond Peak
SOUTHERN CHEYENNE
WESTERN SHOSHONE
Stillwater Range
Wasatch Mountains
Sevier Lake
Uintah Mountains
Green River
UTAH
UTE
ARAPAHO
COLORADO
ARAPAHO
KANSAS
Coast Range
Sierra Nevada
Death Valley
PAIUTE
Las Vegas
Shinumo Plateau
Grand
Great Basin
Canyon de Chelly
Chaco Canyon
Chuska Mountains
Canyon Bonito
JICARILLA APACHE
UNORGANIZED TERRITORY
Santa Barbara
Mohave Desert
Los Angeles
CALIFORNIA
San Francisco Mountains
Painted Desert
Flagstaff
Little Colorado River
ARIZONA
Puerco River
Zuni River
NAVAJO
Rio San Jose
Taos
Santa Fe
Pecos
Canadian River
UNITED
San Diego
UNITED
YUMA
Colorado River
MARICOPA
Phoenix
STATES
NEW MEXICO
Albuquerque
Socorro
Valverde
COCOPA
Yuma
PAPAGO
WESTERN APACHE
San Pedro River
Gila River
Tucson
CHIRICAHUA APACHE
MESCALERO APACHE
Pecos River
El Paso
Rio Grande
Baja California
Gulf of California
Sierra Madre Occidental
MEXICO
TEXAS
LIPAN APACHE
Pacific Ocean

# The Mysterious Colorado

## THE SURVEYS OF JOHN WESLEY POWELL, 1869-78

*John Wesley Powell leads a Smithsonian expedition down the Colorado River into the Grand Canyon. He then directs a vast survey of this last unknown area of the West.*

In May 1869 Major John Wesley Powell set off down the unknown Colorado River, from Green River City, Wyoming. He led a party of nine men: Powell's brother, Walter, Oramel and Seneca Howland, Bill Dunn, George Bradley, Jack Sumner, Billy Rhodes Hawkins, Andrew Hall and Frank Goodman. There was no scientist in the group, though Powell was a self-taught natural historian.

In four small boats Powell's men plunged

through dramatic canyons and braved stupendous rapids. One boat was lost early on, in a treacherous fall on the Green River, when Oramel Howland failed to see a warning signal from Powell. Later, the one-armed Powell fell from a cliff and had to cling on until he was saved by George Bradley, using his longjohns as a rope. By the end of August the party ran desperately short of rations. Finding themselves faced with the treacherous waters that would become known as Separation Rapids, the Howland brothers and Bill Dunn decided that they had had enough. They climbed out of the canyon and onto the Shivwits Plateau, where they were felled by the arrows of Shivwit Indians. The rest of the party successfully ran the remainder of the canyon and returned to a heroes' welcome.

Powell immediately began to prepare for a second trip, for which he received a federal appropriation and the position of Director of the Geographical and Topographical Survey of the Colorado River. He set out in 1871, and the following year sent a party north beyond the canyon, where they discovered the Escalante, the last unknown river in the United States, and the Henry Mountains, the last unknown range.

Powell developed an interest in the languages of the region, becoming fluent in many of them and compiling over 200 vocabularies. In 1873 Powell was appointed special Indian commissioner by the federal government. He made many proposals about ways of establishing a workable and humane reservation system. In 1874 Captain Clarence Dutton joined the survey staff (▶ *page 174*). In 1879, Powell founded the Bureau of Ethnology, for the study of Indian culture.

Powell's *Report on the Arid Regions of the United States*, published in 1878, advocated the setting up of irrigation co-operatives and the regulation of grazing and farming. His radical ideas were never implemented because of the vested interests of land speculators, water monopolists and cattle ranchers, large and small.

*Left: A photograph of Powell in the Grand Canyon with a Paiute Indian, taken by Jack K. Hillers on the 1873 survey. Formerly a teamster, Hillers was originally employed by Powell as a general laborer and boatman, becoming expedition photographer during the second part of Powell's river journey.*

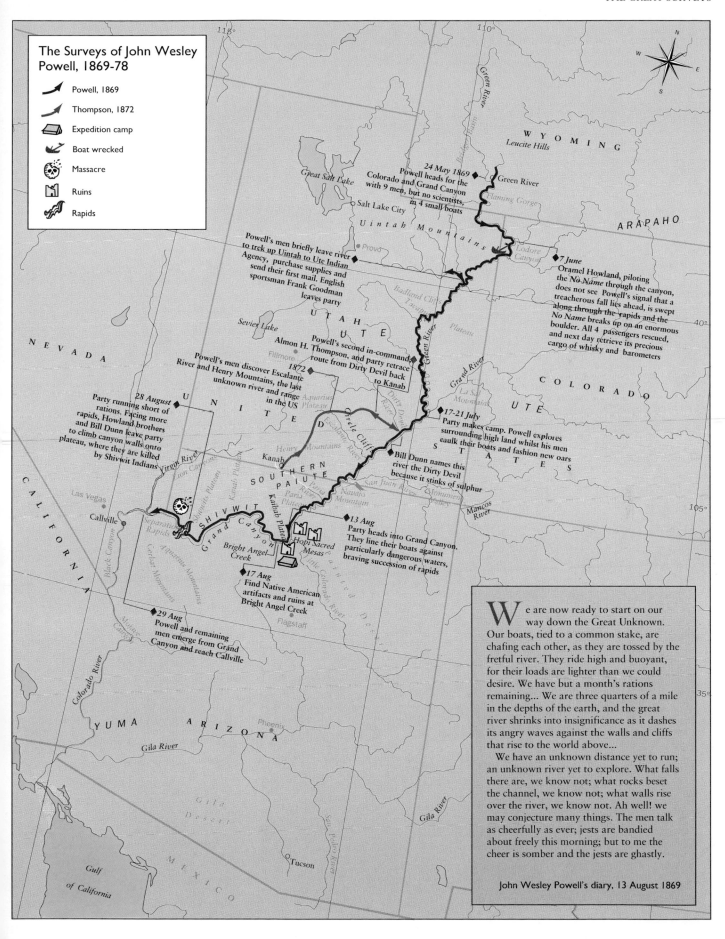

## The Surveys of John Wesley Powell, 1869-78

- Powell, 1869
- Thompson, 1872
- Expedition camp
- Boat wrecked
- Massacre
- Ruins
- Rapids

**24 May 1869**
Powell heads for the Colorado and Grand Canyon with 9 men, but no scientists, in 4 small boats

Powell's men briefly leave river to trek up Uintah to Ute Indian Agency, purchase supplies and send their first mail. English sportsman Frank Goodman leaves party

**1872**
Almon H. Thompson, Powell's second in command, and party retrace route from Dirty Devil back to Kanab

Powell's men discover Escalante River and Henry Mountains, the last unknown river and range in the US

**28 August**
Party running short of rations. Facing more rapids, Howland brothers and Bill Dunn leave party to climb canyon walls onto plateau, where they are killed by Shivwit Indians

**7 June**
Oramel Howland, piloting the *No Name* through the canyon, does not see Powell's signal that a treacherous fall lies ahead, is swept along through the rapids and the *No Name* breaks up on an enormous boulder. All 4 passengers rescued, and next day retrieve its precious cargo of whisky and barometers

**17-21 July**
Party makes camp. Powell explores surrounding high land whilst his men caulk their boats and fashion new oars

Bill Dunn names this river the Dirty Devil because it stinks of sulphur

**13 Aug**
Party heads into Grand Canyon. They line their boats against particularly dangerous waters, braving succession of rapids

**17 Aug**
Find Native American artifacts and ruins at Bright Angel Creek

**29 Aug**
Powell and remaining men emerge from Grand Canyon and reach Callville

Hopi Sacred Mesas

We are now ready to start on our way down the Great Unknown. Our boats, tied to a common stake, are chafing each other, as they are tossed by the fretful river. They ride high and buoyant, for their loads are lighter than we could desire. We have but a month's rations remaining... We are three quarters of a mile in the depths of the earth, and the great river shrinks into insignificance as it dashes its angry waves against the walls and cliffs that rise to the world above...

We have an unknown distance yet to run; an unknown river yet to explore. What falls there are, we know not; what rocks beset the channel, we know not; what walls rise over the river, we know not. Ah well! we may conjecture many things. The men talk as cheerfully as ever; jests are bandied about freely this morning; but to me the cheer is somber and the jests are ghastly.

John Wesley Powell's diary, 13 August 1869

# Into the Grand Canyon

CLARENCE E. DUTTON AND WILLIAM H. HOLMES, 1874-82

*Dutton and Holmes create an unparalleled record of the spectacular landscape of the Grand Canyon.*

Captain Clarence Dutton was a Yale-educated scientist. After serving in the US army in the Civil War, he was assigned to a quiet posting in upstate New York. This gave him the leisure to develop his scientific interests, and he began to correspond with James Hall, the paleontologist and geologist. By 1871, the army had reassigned Dutton to Washington. At the meetings of the Washington Philosophical Society, he met many of the most influential American scientists of the day, including Major John Wesley Powell (▶ *page 172*), who offered him a position on his Survey of the Colorado River in 1874.

In a sense, Dutton's ideas concerning geomorphology were a development of Powell's, but he added a romantic aura and a heightened literary style to Powell's thinking. Among his published works are *The High Plateaus of Utah* (1880) and *The Tertiary History of the Grand Cañon District* (1882), in which he presented his work of 1879 for the United States Geological Survey.

The immense power of the erosion that had created the high plateaus of Utah had been discovered by Dutton's colleague William H. Holmes. A veteran of Hayden's Yellowstone and Colorado surveys (▶ *pages 176–79*), Holmes joined Powell's staff in 1879. He was both an artist and a geologist, and his understanding of the underlying forms of the landscape enabled him to raise topographic art to its highest level. His unique panoramas remain the most accurate visual renditions of the Grand Canyon ever produced.

Clarence Dutton's dramatic word pictures ensured that his meticulous scientific observations were more vivid than those of any geologist of the 19th century, except perhaps his mentor, John Wesley Powell himself. Dutton's romanticism was revealed

in the names he gave to the canyon's prominent features. Vishnu's Temple, for example, reflects the orientalism fashionable in the late 19th century, while American Indian names such as Kaibab Plateau and Toroweays Fault reflect Powell's ethnographic interests.

As Powell and Dutton, together with Grove Karl Gilbert, roamed over and probed the canyon country, they not only developed new skills and knowledge, they came to represent a new kind of explorer. In *The Tertiary History of the Grand Cañon District*, Dutton takes the reader on an exploring expedition over the whole of the canyon country showing how the arid lands of the West had at one time been a vast inland sea punctuated by volcanoes, fracturing and fire. Together with the work of Powell, Dutton's analysis created much of the bases for an understanding of the geological history of the continent.

As the sun draws near the horizon, the great drama of the day begins. Throughout the afternoon the prospect has been gradually growing clearer. The haze has relaxed its steely glare and has changed to a veil of transparent blue. Slowly the myriads of details have come out and the walls are flecked with lines of minute tracery, forming a diaper of light and shade... The promontories come forth from the opposite wall. The sinuous lines of stratification which once seemed meaningless, distorted, and even chaotic, now range themselves into a true perspective of graceful curves, threading the scallop edges of the strata...All things seem to grow in beauty, power, and dimensions. What was grand before has become majestic, the majestic becomes sublime, and, ever expanding and developing, the sublime passes beyond the reach of our faculties and becomes transcendent. The colors have come back. Inherently rich and strong, though not superlative under ordinary lights, they now begin to display an adventitious brilliancy. The western sky is all aflame. The scattered banks of cloud and wavy cirrhus have caught the waning splendor, and shine with orange and crimson. Broad slant beams of yellow light, shot through the glory-rifts, fall on turret and tower, on pinnacled crest and winding ledge, suffusing them with a radiance less fulsome, but akin to that which flames in the western clouds. The summit band is brilliant yellow; the next below is pale rose. But the grand expanse within is a deep, luminous, resplendent red. The climax has now come. The blaze of sunlight poured over an illimitable surface of glowing red is flung back into the gulf, and commingling with the blue haze, turns it into a sea of purple of most imperial hue – so rich, so strong, so pure that it makes the heart ache and the throat tighten. However vast the magnitudes, however majestic the forms, or sumptuous the decoration, it is in these kingly colors that the highest glory of the Grand Cañon is revealed.

Clarence E. Dutton describes Point Sublime in *The Tertiary History of the Grand Cañon District,* 1882

*Left: This panorama, shown in three panels, depicts the Kaibab division of the Grand Canyon, seen from Point Sublime.*

*Created by William H. Holmes, it was one of many published in Clarence Dutton's The Tertiary History of the Grand Cañon District, 1882.*

*To draw these panoramas, Holmes spent hour after hour in the blazing sun of the canyon rim, squinting into a camera lucida. This device uses a prism to reflect the objects in front of it, in such a way that they appear to lie on the artist's paper. They can then be traced to a high level of accuracy.*

*Holmes managed to convey, like no other artist, the vast, scenic magnificence of the Grand Canyon in all its topographical and geological complexity.*

# Yellowstone's Grand Drama

## EXPLORERS OF THE YELLOWSTONE, 1869-71

*The marvels of Yellowstone are greeted with huge public enthusiasm. The army explores the area, and in a spectacular journey Hayden discovers the Upper Geyser Basin.*

After John Colter's discovery of Yellowstone in 1808 (▶ *page 146*), trappers explored parts of the region. But it was yet to be examined by a scientific explorer and in the mid-1860s, the area was still blank on maps. There was a rumor in 1863 that Captain W.W. DeLacy entered what is now the park. But the army's western divisions sent no expedition, despite the clamor of the residents of Virginia City, Helena and Bozeman, Montana. So in summer 1869 three civilians, David E. Folsom, C.W. Cook and a ranch hand named Peterson, set off from Helena to prospect in Yellowstone. At first they remained closed-mouth on the marvels they had seen but in 1870, Folsom sold their story to the Western Monthly Magazine.

Public enthusiasm then ran so high that the army agreed that Lieutenant Gustavus C. Doane and five soldiers should explore the area, with a civilian party led by Nathaniel P. Langford and Montana's surveyor general, General Henry D. Washburn. They reached what is now the park, just west of the Absaroka Mountain, domain of the Crow Indians. A few Crow followed them closely but did not interfere. Once in the Yellowstone they found the wild beauties of the lake, thermal springs, lava flows and steam jets. They reached and named most of the great geysers including "Old Faithful." All except one was convinced that Yellowstone should never serve the purposes of any one individual. It should be a national park.

Two parties explored Yellowstone the following summer. On 11 July Ferdinand V. Hayden, head of the Interior Department's Geographical Surveys of the Territories West of the 100th Meridian, led a group from Ogden, Utah. At Fort Ellis, north of the park area, they found army Captain J.W. Barlow also preparing to lead a party to the headwaters of the Yellowstone.

On 15 July Hayden left Fort Ellis. When Barlow left a day later, he generally followed the route taken by Washburn and Doane. But by traveling south from Yellowstone Lake toward the Upper Snake River, he broke new ground and discovered Heart Lake. Hayden's reconnaissance was more spectacular. From Boettler's Ranch, they marched past the iron-red Cinnabar Mountain and the Devil's Slide and reached Mammoth Hot Springs. After exploring the ravines of Tower Creek, they ascended Mount Washburn, to view the Yellowstone basin and the Tetons. Down in the basin Thomas Moran made dozens of sketches of the Grand Canyon of the Yellowstone, which resulted in his greatest work. W.H. Jackson photographed the Grand Canyon along with Mammoth Hot Springs and the geyser basins. In August Hayden, leading three other men, headed northwest and discovered Upper Geyser Basin.

On his return Hayden joined up with Northern Pacific Railroad interests and lobbied in Washington for the establishment of Yellowstone National Park. N.P. Langford did so too, becoming known as "National Park" Langford.

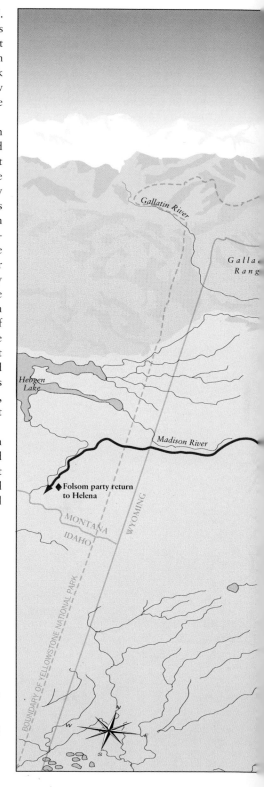

*Left: "The Great Blue Spring, Lower Geyser Basin of the Yellowstone," by Thomas Moran (1876). On settling in the US, the English born artist Moran had decided to "paint as an American, on an American basis." Accompanying Hayden into the Yellowstone, he and photographer William H. Jackson recorded the bizarre and breathtaking topography for an incredulous public.*

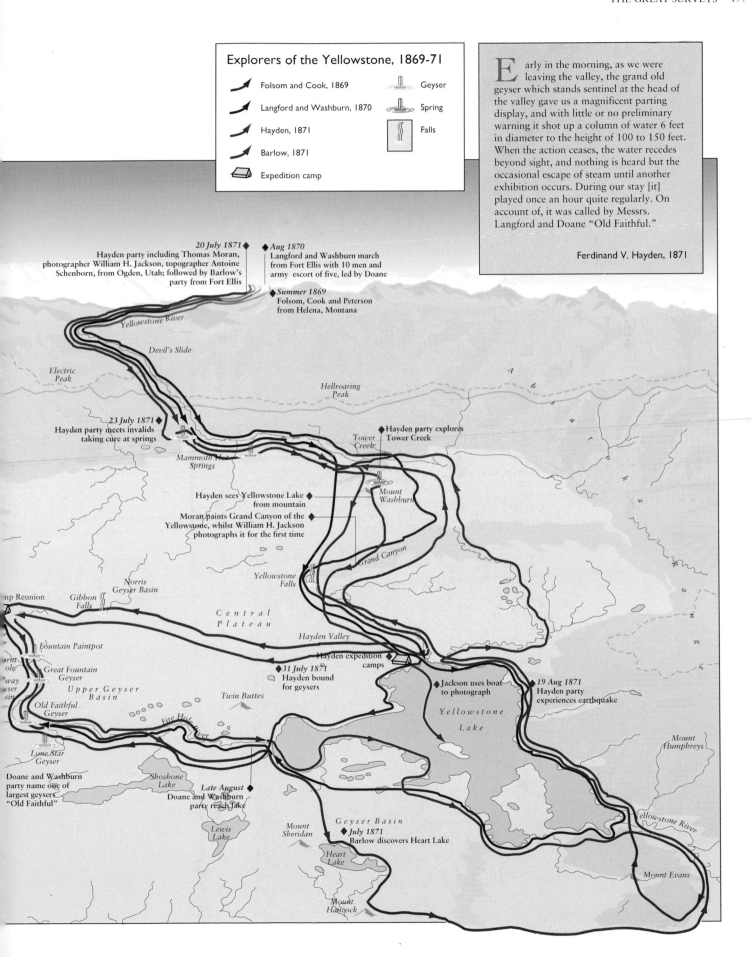

## Explorers of the Yellowstone, 1869-71

- Folsom and Cook, 1869
- Langford and Washburn, 1870
- Hayden, 1871
- Barlow, 1871
- Expedition camp

- Geyser
- Spring
- Falls

Early in the morning, as we were leaving the valley, the grand old geyser which stands sentinel at the head of the valley gave us a magnificent parting display, and with little or no preliminary warning it shot up a column of water 6 feet in diameter to the height of 100 to 150 feet. When the action ceases, the water recedes beyond sight, and nothing is heard but the occasional escape of steam until another exhibition occurs. During our stay [it] played once an hour quite regularly. On account of, it was called by Messrs. Langford and Doane "Old Faithful."

*Ferdinand V. Hayden, 1871*

**20 July 1871**
Hayden party including Thomas Moran, photographer William H. Jackson, topographer Antoine Schenborn, from Ogden, Utah; followed by Barlow's party from Fort Ellis

**Aug 1870**
Langford and Washburn march from Fort Ellis with 10 men and army escort of five, led by Doane

**Summer 1869**
Folsom, Cook and Peterson from Helena, Montana

*Yellowstone River*

*Devil's Slide*

*Electric Peak*

*Hellroaring Peak*

**23 July 1871**
Hayden party meets invalids taking cure at springs

Hayden party explores Tower Creek

*Tower Creek*

*Mammoth Hot Springs*

*Mount Washburn*

Hayden sees Yellowstone Lake from mountain

Moran paints Grand Canyon of the Yellowstone, whilst William H. Jackson photographs it for the first time

*Grand Canyon*

*Norris Geyser Basin*

*Yellowstone Falls*

*Gibbon Falls*

*Camp Reunion*

*Central Plateau*

*Hayden Valley*

*Fountain Paintpot*

*Great Fountain Geyser*

**31 July 1871**
Hayden bound for geysers

Hayden expedition camps

Jackson uses boat to photograph

**19 Aug 1871**
Hayden party experiences earthquake

*Upper Geyser Basin*

*Twin Buttes*

*Yellowstone Lake*

*Old Faithful Geyser*

*Fire Hole River*

*Mount Humphreys*

*Lone Star Geyser*

Doane and Washburn party name one of largest geysers "Old Faithful"

*Shoshone Lake*

**Late August**
Doane and Washburn party reach lake

*Lewis Lake*

*Mount Sheridan*

*Geyser Basin*

**July 1871**
Barlow discovers Heart Lake

*Heart Lake*

*Mount Hancock*

*Yellowstone River*

*Mount Evans*

# Colorado's Wonderlands

## FERDINAND HAYDEN'S SURVEY, 1873-76

*Hayden leads the Interior Department's
Geological Survey of the Territories. He wins
fame as an explorer but faces criticism as a
scientist.*

Ferdinand Vandiveer Hayden, in 1869 appointed survey director of the Interior Department's newly-formed United States Geological Survey of the Territories, considered his primary task was to publicize and promote the West to the American people.

In sponsoring Western exploration, the Interior Department, perhaps even more than the army, sought to open up new lands, in the first place for tourists and later for settlers. In doing so, two of its duties were to assess resources and classify land. In 1869 Hayden explored the mountains of Colorado and New Mexico from Denver to Santa Fe. In 1870 Hayden covered north-eastern Utah and southern Wyoming. He then spent two years in the Yellowstone. During the following years of the survey, 1869-78, he supervised large teams of men in the field.

Like Clarence King (▶ *page 170*) Hayden was a geologist who, as a surgeon during the Civil War, had served in the Union Army.

Thirteen years older than King, Hayden came from a different generation of scientists. His training and influences were American rather than European. They came from John Strong Newberry, who made the first geological study of the Grand Canyon, and James Hall, paleontologist on the early 19th century New York Natural History Survey. Before the Civil War, Hayden had spent several years searching for fossils in the Dakotas, Montana and Wyoming, and he contributed substantially to American geology. With Fielding B. Meek he had assembled the first model of the Cretaceous horizon in the American West. After the war Hayden returned to the Dakotas searching for fossils. Then, in 1867, Hayden ran a federal government survey, county by county, of the resources of the new state of Nebraska. In 1868 he received an appropriation for an expedition to the Rocky Mountains of southern Wyoming.

Between 1873 and 1876, with James Gardner, formerly of the King survey, he led an exhaustive survey of Colorado. The painter Thomas Moran, topographer William H. Holmes and photographer William H. Jackson were important members of the survey. In 1873 Hayden, Jackson and a party discovered the Mount of the Holy Cross, a peak in western Colorado. Jackson's photographs of the snow-filled crevasses in the form of a crucifix proved enormously popular. In 1874 a party led by Jackson and Holmes discovered the ancient ruins of Mancos Canyon near Mesa Verde in Colorado.

Ferdinand V. Hayden gained considerable fame as an explorer through his work with the Survey of the Territories. Through the paintings of Thomas Moran, the photographs of William Henry Jackson, and the panoramas of William H. Holmes (▶ *page 174*), Hayden brought the wonders of the West to the American people.

However during the later years of the survey his work as a scientist came under fire, sometimes unfairly. Unlike Clarence King,

*Left: Hayden's men surveying from the
summit of Silverton Mountain, San Juan
County, Colorado in 1874. The seated man
sketching is probably the artist Holmes; the
photograph is by the survey's photographer,
W.H. Jackson.*

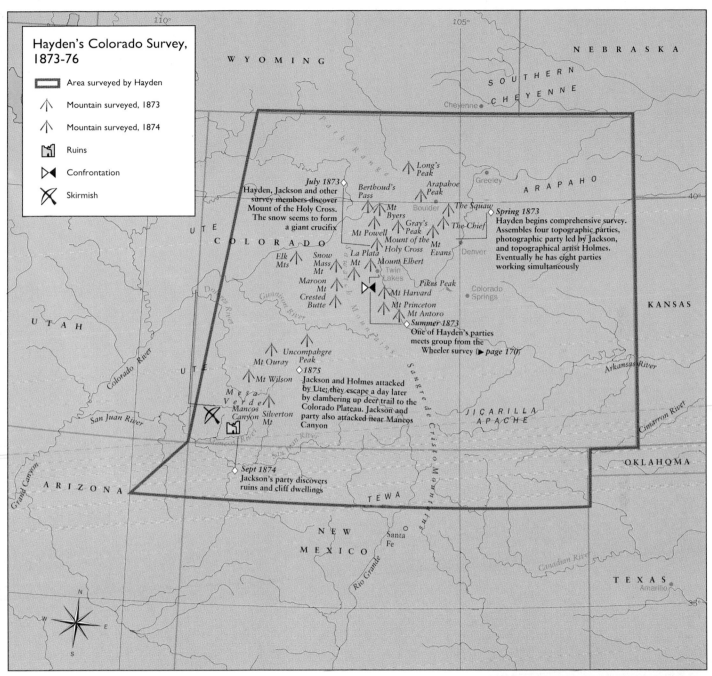

Hayden's Colorado Survey,
1873-76

- ▭  Area surveyed by Hayden
- ⋀  Mountain surveyed, 1873
- ⋀  Mountain surveyed, 1874
- 🏛  Ruins
- ▷◁  Confrontation
- ✕  Skirmish

*July 1873*
Hayden, Jackson and other survey members discover Mount of the Holy Cross. The snow seems to form a giant crucifix

*Spring 1873*
Hayden begins comprehensive survey. Assembles four topographic parties, photographic party led by Jackson, and topographical artist Holmes. Eventually he has eight parties working simultaneously

*Summer 1873*
One of Hayden's parties meets group from the Wheeler survey (▶ page 170)

*1875*
Jackson and Holmes attacked by Utes; they escape a day later by clambering up deer trail to the Colorado Plateau. Jackson and party also attacked near Mancos Canyon

*Sept 1874*
Jackson's party discovers ruins and cliff dwellings

who worked systematically through his data trying to arrive at synthesized theory, Hayden tended to publish data immediately, before fully interpreting it. After 1873, he published a *Bulletin* which included a wide variety of papers by many different scientists. Although in essence it was an important new scientific journal, it received stern criticism from academics who disliked Hayden. Yet he also published the final reports of other scientists which were often proved to be definitive works and major contributions to their respective fields.

Hayden gained fame bringing the Rocky Mountains and the Yellowstone to the attention of Americans. His map of the Yellowstone region which included a far larger tract than just the lake, the geyser basins, and the Grand Canyon. This influenced the US Congress to set aside a larger tract of the Yellowstone than they might have done, for preservation as the nation's first national park.

Just as the sun was sinking below the western walls of the cañon, one of the party descried far up the cliff what appeared to be a house with a square wall and apertures indicating two stories... The discovery... inspired us immediately... to scale the height and explore it... All hands started up, but only two persevered to the end... Up we hauled... boxes containing the camera and chemicals by... long ropes.

William H. Jackson, on his ascent to a Mancos Canyon cliff dwelling, Colorado, 1874

# Part V : The Far North

By 1800, the outline of the North American continent had been explored and mapped; by the 1880s, most of the interior had been surveyed. One frontier remained: the far north. The challenge of this uniquely hostile environment was to tax the resources of governments and individuals of several nations until well into the 20th century.

Ever since John Cabot's 1497 voyage, the dream of a Northwest Passage had lured explorers to the high latitudes of the New World. By the end of the 18th century, this search, and the commercial activities of fur traders, had encompassed Lake Athabasca, Baffin Island and Hudson Bay. But much of the ice-bound wilderness of the Canadian north offered serious climatic impediments to conventional discovery and traditional European settlement.

In the first half of the 19th century, however, a series of remarkable explorers entered a territory larger than Western Europe and opened it to discovery and commerce. Naval expeditions under Ross and Parry made important discoveries in the Arctic archipelago, and John Franklin led two daring expeditions down the Coppermine and Mackenzie rivers to explore the Arctic coast. In the 1830s, George Back and Richard King set out from the Great Slave Lake down the Great Fish River, to find John Ross's naval expedition, which was missing in the Arctic.

Hudson's Bay Company agents also played a major part. In the east, Atkinson and Hendry explored the interior of the Labrador peninsula; to the north, Dease and Simpson charted missing portions of the Arctic coast; while in the west, Robert Campbell and John Bell each discovered a different overland route between the MacKenzie and Yukon drainages, linking the two major river systems of the Canadian North.

Meanwhile the Russians were busy exploring their Alaskan territory. A naval voyage under Otto von Kotzebue probed the northwest coast, while Russian fur-hunters and their creole descendents pushed up the rivers and deep into the interior.

Sir John Franklin's last expedition, which set out from Gravesend in England in May 1845, proved to be one of the 19th century's most publicized tragedies. Its disappearance in the ice-bound channels of the Canadian Arctic gripped the imagination of the public on both sides of the Atlantic, and over the next 25 years, some 50 Land and sea expeditions were sent out to find Franklin or discover his fate. Although these expeditions uncovered a phenomenal amount of new territory, their urgent priority caused them to ignore equally vast areas of the Arctic. By the time Franklin's fate became clear, the task of finding the Northwest Passage had cost the British Admiralty so much money, taken so much time, and killed so many men, that they abandoned the Arctic without actually traversing by ship any of the routes they had discovered.

In 1859 the Hudson's Bay Company's exclusive control over Canada would come up for reconsideration. Many in Britain's government believed that the vast province held more than just opportunities to trade furs. Gold had been found on the Fraser River; and the immense southern prairies might well be prime farmland that would attract European immigrants, blocking any United States expansion northwards. From 1857 to 1859, Lieutenant John Palliser surveyed the southern prairies, tabulating their natural resources, locating passes through the Rockies and mapping large areas never before recorded by geographers. Henry Youle Hinde, meanwhile, analyzed the geology of the region, laying out immigration routes to the Saskatchewan.

The Americans, meanwhile, were taking an increasing interest in Alaska. From 1865 to 1867, the Western Union Telegraph Survey charted the interior; in 1868, W.H. Dall, naturalist with the survey, learned to his delight that the United States had purchased Alaska from the Russians. Despite a series of military expeditions in the 1880s, exploration proceeded slowly until the gold rush years of 1896-98 brought thousands of prospectors and pioneers flooding into Alaska and the Canadian northwest.

In the Arctic, meanwhile, attention had shifted to the North Pole and the "Open Polar Sea" which was then believed to surround it. This was the objective of the final Arctic expedition sponsored by the British Admiralty. Commanded by George Strong Nares, its sledge team came within 399.5 miles of the Pole in May 1876. The next attempts were to be American: the ill-fated journey of Greely, and Robert E. Peary's dogged quest. The honor of completing the northwest passage, meanwhile, fell to a Norwegian, Roald Amundsen, in 1905. Another Norwegian, Otto Sverdrup explored Ellesmere Island, and the Canadians Bernier and Stefansson filled most of the remaining gaps in the map of the far north.

Peary's claim to have reached the Pole in April 1909 is the subject of controversy to this day. He was in no doubt, however, that his goal was the culmination of centuries of North American exploration. In his diary for April 1909, he wrote:

"My work is the finish, the cap and climax, of 300 years of effort, loss of life and expenditure of millions, by some of the best men of the civilized nations of the world, and it has been accomplished with a clean cut dash, spirit, and I believe, thoroughness characteristically American. I am content."

# Russia Meets America

## THE RUSSIANS IN ALASKA, 1790-1863

*During the first half of the 19th century Russian* promyshlenniki *(Siberian fur-hunters) take over the maritime fur trade and explore and settle Alaska.*

During the 1790s the Lebedev-Lastochkin Company dispatched Vasily Ivanov, a hunter, to explore the interior of Alaska. Ivanov appears to have reached the upper Kuskokwim River; a few Russian historians conjecture that he even reached the Yukon.

By 1799 the Russian American Company was chartered to gain a monopoly of the Alaskan trade. From precarious footholds on the coast it depleted the southern fur regions. So the Company gradually shifted north into the unknown heart of Alaska, enslaving hundreds of Aleut, and other tribes and placing them under *promyshlennik* supervision.

In April 1818 Petr Korsakovsky set out to cross the Alaska peninsula and spent two years trading and exploring around Nushagak Bay. Some of his men later took their own expeditions: Afanasy Klimovsky explored the Copper River in 1819; Feodor Kolmakov established the first post north of the Alaska peninsula at New Aleksandr Redoubt; Rodionov, a trader, reached the upper Kuskokwim via the Mulchatna River.

In 1816, on the northern coast of Alaska, Otto von Kotzebue took naturalists and artists to explore what became the Kotzebue Sound. In 1837 Thomas Simpson sailed from Mackenzie Bay to Point Barrow; and sailing from the west in 1838 Aleksandr Kashevarov reached 35 miles east of the point.

During the late 1820s and 1830s the Russian American Company sent a group of Russian creoles, including Klimovsky, Kashevarov, Petr Malakhov and Andrei Glazunov, to the Kronstadt Navigation College near St Petersburg. In the summers of 1829-30 Ivan Vasiliev and the Russian creole Semyon Lukin explored the Tikchik Lakes and upper Kuskokwim drainage, constantly facing down hostile natives. When Vasiliev sailed back to New Aleksandr Redoubt he received 3000 rubles from the company for his zeal in "journeying into America's interior." In 1832 Lukin and Feodor Kolmakov returned to the Kuskokwim, establishing Kolmakov's Redoubt.

In 1833 the Russians founded a post on St Michael Island, a convenient starting point for the Yukon interior. Glazunov and Lukin finally located the Yukon River from there in 1833. They returned a year later, reaching

*Below: A view of the Russian settlement at New Archangel, by F.H. von Kittlitz. A former Russian army officer who had fought in the Napoleonic wars, Kittlitz visited Alaska as as artist and naturalist in 1826. The lithograph shows "the most important and crowded area of the city." An Aleut watches the Russians, on their way to the Orthodox Church, from a rock which, "according to convention ... belongs to the natives."*

Kolmakov's Redoubt, but when Glazunov tried to reach Cook Inlet starvation and cold turned him back.

Malakhov left St Michael in 1838, advancing up the Yukon to the huge Koyukuk River. The following year he built a small blockhouse at Nulato. L.A. Zagoskin also left from St Michael and his travels of 1842-44 provided a rare scientific glimpse of the Alaskan interior.

By the late 1840s the Russians were facing competition from the Hudson's Bay Company. When A.H. Murray founded Fort Yukon in 1847, it served as an advance guard of English exploration (▶ page 194). In 1863 Semyon Lukin's son, Ivan, made a daring journey from Nulato to the new English fort: a symbolic link between Russian and Anglo-American explorers.

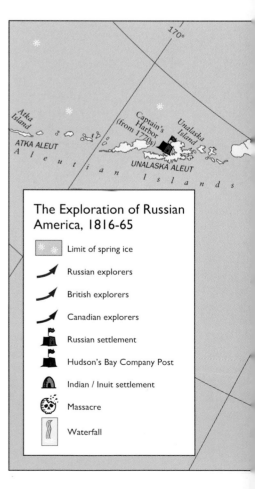

### The Exploration of Russian America, 1816-65

* Limit of spring ice
* Russian explorers
* British explorers
* Canadian explorers
* Russian settlement
* Hudson's Bay Company Post
* Indian / Inuit settlement
* Massacre
* Waterfall

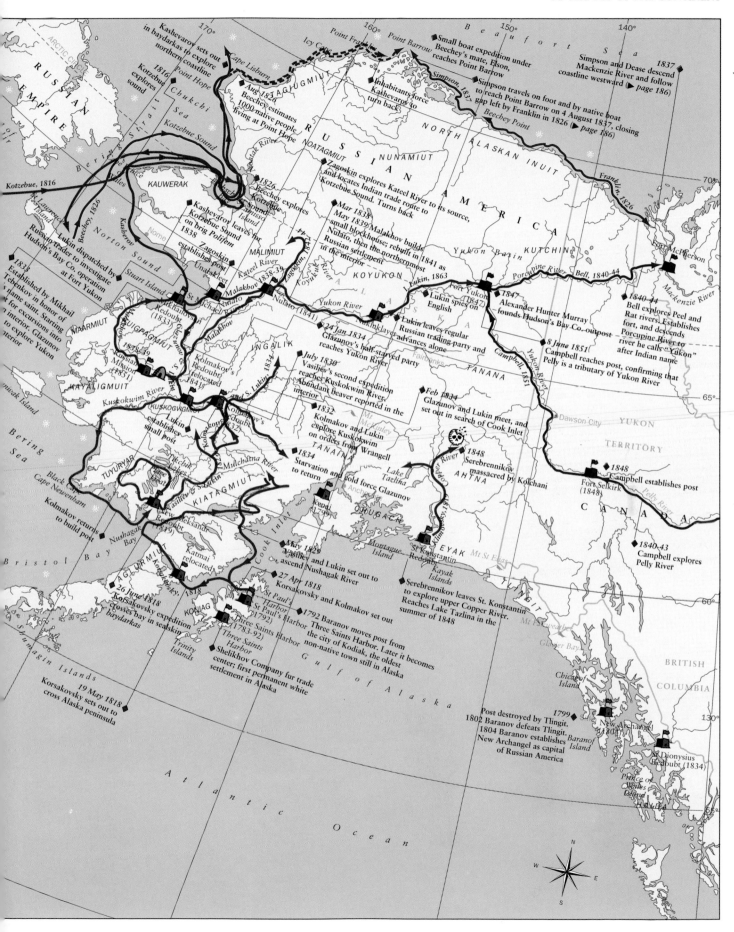

Kashevarov sets out
in baydarkas to explore
northern coastline

1816
Kotzebue
explores
sound

Kotzebue, 1816

Russian trader to investigate
Hudson's Bay Co. operation
at Fort Yukon

1838
Established by Mikhail
Tebenkov in honor of
his name saint. Starting
point for excursions into
the interior. Glazunov
leaves to explore Yukon
interior

Aug 1826
Beechey estimates
1000 native people
living at Point Hope

1826
Beechey explores
Kotzebue Sound

Kashevarov leaves for
Kotzebue Sound on brig Polifem

1838 Zagoskin
establishes post

Kashevaroy leaves for

Beechey, 1826

Lukin dispatched by

Kasheyor
Sound

MALIMIUT

Kateel River 1838-39

Kashevarov to
turn back

Small boat expedition under
Beechey's mate, Elson,
reaches Point Barrow

Inhabitants force
Kashevarov to
turn back

Simpson travels on foot and by native boat
to reach Point Barrow on 4 August 1837, closing
gap left by Franklin in 1826 ( ▶ page 186)

Simpson, 1837

Beechey Point

1837
Simpson and Dease descend
Mackenzie River and follow
coastline westward ( ▶ page 186)

Franklin, 1826

Zagoskin explores Kateel River to its source,
and locates Indian trade route to
Kotzebue Sound. Turns back

Mar 1838
May 1839 Malakhov builds
small blockhouse; rebuilt in 1841 as
Nulato, then the northernmost
Russian settlement
in the interior

Malakhov 1838-39

Nulato (1841)

24 Jan 1834
Glazunov's half-starved party
reaches Yukon River

July 1830
Vasiliev's second expedition
reaches Kuskokwim River.
Abundant beaver reported in the
interior

1832

Kolmakov and Lukin
explore Kuskokwim
on orders from Wrangell

1834
Starvation and cold force
to return

KUSKOGVIGMIUT

Lukin
establishes
small post

Kolmakov's
redoubt
1832

1834
Starvation and cold force Glazunov

Lake
Tazlina

1848
Serebrennikov
massacred by Kolchani

Feb 1834
Glazunov and Lukin meet, and
set out in search of Cook Inlet

Lukin spies on
English

Lukin leaves regular
Russian trading party and
advances alone

Fort Yukon
(1847)

Alexander Hunter Murray
founds Hudson's Bay Co. outpost

Campbell, 1851

8 June 1851
Campbell reaches post, confirming that
Pelly is a tributary of Yukon River

Bell, 1840-44

Porcupine River

Fort McPherson

1840-44
Bell explores Peel and
Rat rivers. Establishes
fort, and descends
Porcupine River to
river he calls "Yukon"
after Indian name

1840-43
Campbell explores
Pelly River

1848
Campbell establishes post

Fort Selkirk
(1848)

Serebrennikov leaves St. Konstantin
to explore upper Copper River.
Reaches Lake Tazlina in the
summer of 1848

May 1829
Vasiliev and Lukin set out to
ascend Nushagak River

27 Apr 1818
Korsakovsky and Kolmakov set out

1792 Baranov moves post from
Three Saints Harbor. Later it becomes
the city of Kodiak, the oldest
non-native town still in Alaska

Shelikhov Company fur trade
center; first permanent white
settlement in Alaska

26 June 1818
Korsakovsky expedition
crosses bay in sealskin
baydarkas

19 May 1818
Korsakovsky sets out to
cross Alaska peninsula

Kolmakov returns
to build post

Russian
Mission
(1851)

Mikhailovskii
(Redoubt)
(1833)

St Michael
Redoubt

Kolmakov's
Redoubt
relocated
1841

Nushagak
Bay

Katmai
relocated

St Paul's
Harbor
(1792)

Three Saints
Harbor
(1783-92)

Trinity
Islands

Shumagin Islands

Post destroyed by Tlingit
1802 Baranov defeats Tlingit
1804 Baranov establishes
New Archangel as capital
of Russian America

1799

New Archangel
(1804)

Baranof
Island

St Dionysius
Redoubt (1834)

Prince of
Wales
Island

BRITISH
COLUMBIA

HAIDA

# The Land God Gave to Cain

## THE EXPLORATION OF THE LABRADOR PENINSULA, 1816-43

*The inhospitable wastes between Hudson Bay and the Atlantic, bypassed as the traders moved west, are finally explored by the Hudson's Bay Company.*

When Jacques Cartier landed on the northern shore of the Gulf of St Lawrence in 1534, he dismissed it as "the land God gave to Cain." This was long taken to apply to the whole vast hinterland of the Labrador peninsula. As late as the beginning of the 19th century, only the coastal fringes and the more important southerly lakes and rivers had been mapped. When the Hudson's Bay Company tried to move inland it encountered formidable obstacles. Individuals could travel light over the frozen landscape in winter, despite the severe weather, but open water was essential for the canoes of the supply brigades. Many of the streams were too low to use in summer, and north of Rupert House there were no white birch trees large and straight enough to provide canoe bark. Traders had to live off the country, and in the north the boulder-strewn surface was carpeted only by lichens and mosses. There was also little reliable information about the Naskapi who occupied the northern interior.

In 1816 and 1818 George Atkinson, a mixed-blood Company servant, explored Great Whale and Little Whale rivers, and in 1820 a more far-ranging journey was carried out by James Clouston, a former school-teacher in the Company's service at Eastmain House. With Naskapi guides and hunters he crossed the central plateau, though he turned back about a hundred miles short of the sea. Clouston realized that the Naskapi were "more independent of European goods than any other Indians whom I have seen," and that the Company would find it difficult to turn them into fur-trappers.

In 1828 William Hendry, accompanied by Atkinson and Indian guides, crossed the peninsula again, and this time reached the mouth of the Koksoak River. Two years later Nicol Finlayson repeated the journey and established Fort Chimo near the sea at Ungava Bay. The little huddle of buildings, a Company factor wrote later, was "surrounded by a country that presents as complete a picture of desolation as can be imagined." It was 600 miles from the nearest

*Below: Explorers in the Labrador peninsula found the rivers broken in many places by rapids. They were obliged to make frequent portages, carrying their canoes overland until they found the next navigable stretch of river.*

*This illustration of a portage on the Moisie River appeared in Henry Youle Hind's Explorations in the Interior of the Labrador Peninsula (1863). It was drawn by his artist brother William, who accompanied him on his 1861 expedition.*

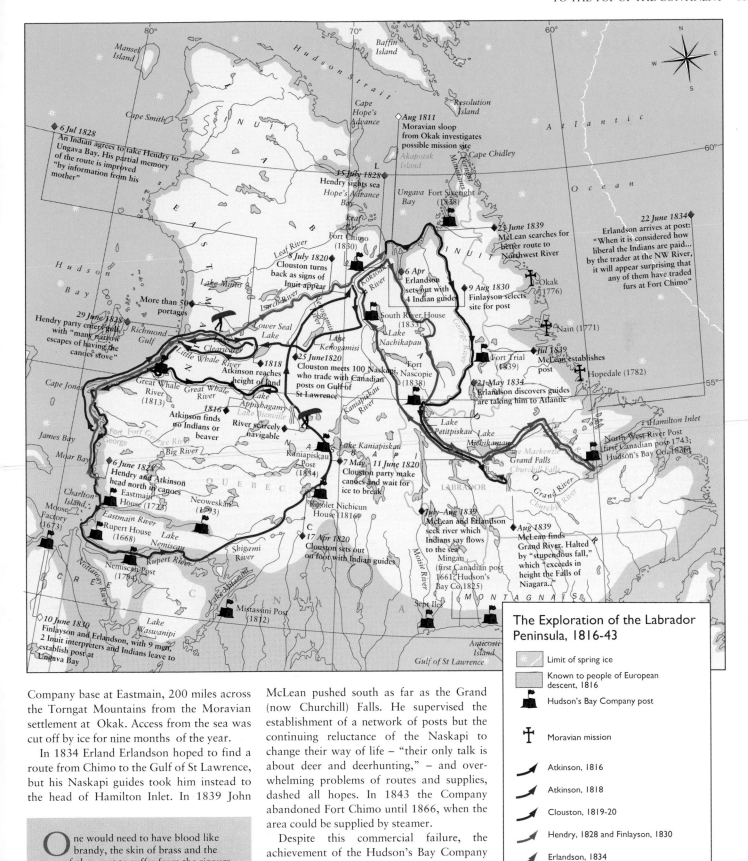

6 Jul 1828
An Indian agrees to take Hendry to Ungava Bay. His partial memory of the route is improved "by information from his mother"

Aug 1811
Moravian sloop from Okak investigates possible mission site

15 July 1828
Hendry sights sea Hope's Advance Bay

22 June 1834
Erlandson arrives at post: "When it is considered how liberal the Indians are paid... by the trader at the NW River, it will appear surprising that any of them have traded furs at Fort Chimo"

More than 50 portages

29 June 1828
Hendry party enters gulf with "many narrow escapes of having the canoes stove"

8 July 1820
Clouston turns back as signs of Inuit appear

6 Apr
Erlandson sets out with 4 Indian guides

9 Aug 1830
Finlayson selects site for post

25 June 1839
McLean searches for better route to Northwest River

Okak (1776)

Nain (1771)

1818
Atkinson reaches height of land

25 June 1820
Clouston meets 100 Naskapi who trade with Canadian posts on Gulf of St Lawrence

Jul 1839
McLean establishes post

Fort Trial (1839)

21 May 1834
Erlandson discovers guides are taking him to Atlantic

Hopedale (1782)

1816
Atkinson finds no Indians or beaver

River scarcely navigable

7 May – 11 June 1820
Clouston party make canoes and wait for ice to break

6 June 1828
Hendry and Atkinson head north in canoes

17 Apr 1820
Clouston sets out on foot with Indian guides

July–Aug 1839
McLean and Erlandson seek river which Indians say flows to the sea

Aug 1839
McLean finds Grand River. Halted by "stupendous fall," which "exceeds in height the Falls of Niagara..."

10 June 1830
Finlayson and Erlandson, with 9 men, 2 Inuit interpreters and Indians leave to establish post at Ungava Bay

Mingan (first Canadian post 1661; Hudson's Bay Co, 1825)

### The Exploration of the Labrador Peninsula, 1816-43

- Limit of spring ice
- Known to people of European descent, 1816
- Hudson's Bay Company post
- Moravian mission
- Atkinson, 1816
- Atkinson, 1818
- Clouston, 1819-20
- Hendry, 1828 and Finlayson, 1830
- Erlandson, 1834
- McLean, 1839
- Portage
- Falls

Company base at Eastmain, 200 miles across the Torngat Mountains from the Moravian settlement at Okak. Access from the sea was cut off by ice for nine months of the year.

In 1834 Erland Erlandson hoped to find a route from Chimo to the Gulf of St Lawrence, but his Naskapi guides took him instead to the head of Hamilton Inlet. In 1839 John McLean pushed south as far as the Grand (now Churchill) Falls. He supervised the establishment of a network of posts but the continuing reluctance of the Naskapi to change their way of life – "their only talk is about deer and deerhunting," – and overwhelming problems of routes and supplies, dashed all hopes. In 1843 the Company abandoned Fort Chimo until 1866, when the area could be supplied by steamer.

Despite this commercial failure, the achievement of the Hudson's Bay Company was considerable. Its traders had mapped most of the main waterways of the Labrador interior, and had established new posts on the lakes of the central plateau.

One would need to have blood like brandy, the skin of brass and the eyes of glass, not to suffer from the rigours of a Labrador winter.

James Mckenzie, 1808

# The Bleak Canadian North

## SEARCHES FOR THE NORTHWEST PASSAGE, 1818-45

*The British map many miles of Arctic
coastline but fail to make the missing link in
the Northwest Passage.*

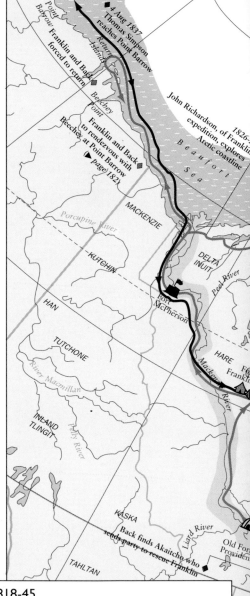

After the Napoleonic wars, the British Royal Navy was left with a large officer corps. In 1818, encouraged by Cook's success (▶ *page 130*), the Admiralty sent out its first naval expedition under John Ross, to investigate three potential openings in Baffin Bay. Ross examined the entrances to Smith Sound and Jones Sound and quickly declared them closed. After sailing into Lancaster Sound, he suddenly turned and headed for home, claiming later that his path had been blocked by mountains. No-one else on board would confirm this.

William Edward Parry, Ross's second-in-command, returned to Lancaster Sound in 1819 and proved that Ross's mountains were an Arctic mirage. He then explored Prince Regent Inlet and headed west into Viscount Melville Sound. Twice he tried to complete a Northwest Passage through McClure Strait but was prevented by ice from Beaufort Sea. Parry's second voyage was less successful. He was unable to force his way through Fury and Hecla Strait, the northern passage out of Foxe Basin. On his third mission, he lost his ship, the *Fury*, before he could explore any new ground.

In 1819 Lieutenant John Franklin was sent out with George Back, John Richardson and Robert Hood. In 1820 Franklin's "British Arctic Land Expedition" established Fort Enterprise and explored from the Coppermine River delta to Melville Sound. Franklin mapped 550 miles of coast but his expedition was prey to starvation, death, murder and cannibalism. In 1825, on a second land expedition led by Franklin, John Richardson and Kendall set out east from the Mackenzie River delta. Franklin and Back turned west to rendezvous with Captain Beechey at Point Barrow, but bad weather caused them to turn back at Return Islands.

In 1829, frustrated by the lack of progress, a philanthropic gin distiller, Felix Booth, sponsored John Ross's second expedition. With his nephew James Clark Ross as second-in-command, Ross sailed down Prince Regent Sound in search of an opening to the west. The two Rosses mapped James Ross Strait and parts of King William Island and in 1831 James Clark Ross located the Magnetic North Pole. The Ross expedition then disappeared in the ice-bound Gulf of Boothia until 1833. On a search financed by public supscription George Back and Dr Richard King reached the Thlew-ee-choh, or "Great Fish River" returning to winter at Fort Reliance. In April 1834 they heard of Ross's return after four winters in the Arctic. In June, after a difficult descent down the Great Fish River, naming Pelly, Garry, and Franklin Lakes along the way, they explored the Arctic coast.

During 1837-38 Peter Dease and Sir Thomas Simpson of the Hudson's Bay Company charted missing portions of the coast from Return Islands to Point Barrow. In 1839 they set out to the coast again, but missed the key to the Northwest Passage, Rae Strait, because it was frozen over. In 1840 another Hudson's Bay Company agent, Robert Campbell, reached the Pelly River (▶ *page 183*). The explorers of the Hudson's Bay Company were comparatively more successful than other explorers, being better adapted to the harsh conditions and developing better relations with their Inuit guides.

By the 1840s a potential Northwest Passage had been mapped along the northern coast of Canada but there was still a missing link between Lancaster Sound and Kent Peninsula. Lobbied by the Royal Geographical Society, in May 1845 the Admiralty again sent out Sir John Franklin. Already 59 years old, Franklin left with 128 men aboard the *Erebus* and the *Terror*. After two months at sea, a group of whaling ships crossed paths with Franklin near the entrance to Lancaster Sound. They were the last Europeans to see him alive (▶ *page 190*).

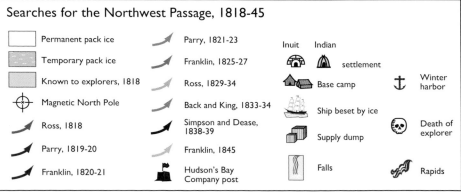

## Searches for the Northwest Passage, 1818-45

| | | |
|---|---|---|
| ☐ Permanent pack ice | ⚓ Parry, 1821-23 | Inuit / Indian |
| ▨ Temporary pack ice | ⚓ Franklin, 1825-27 | 🛖 🛖 settlement |
| ▨ Known to explorers, 1818 | ⚓ Ross, 1829-34 | 🏕 Base camp |
| ⊕ Magnetic North Pole | ⚓ Back and King, 1833-34 | 🚢 Ship beset by ice |
| ⚓ Ross, 1818 | ⚓ Simpson and Dease, 1838-39 | 📦 Supply dump |
| ⚓ Parry, 1819-20 | ⚓ Franklin, 1845 | ≋ Falls |
| ⚓ Franklin, 1820-21 | 🏴 Hudson's Bay Company post | ⚓ Winter harbor / 💀 Death of explorer / ⚡ Rapids |

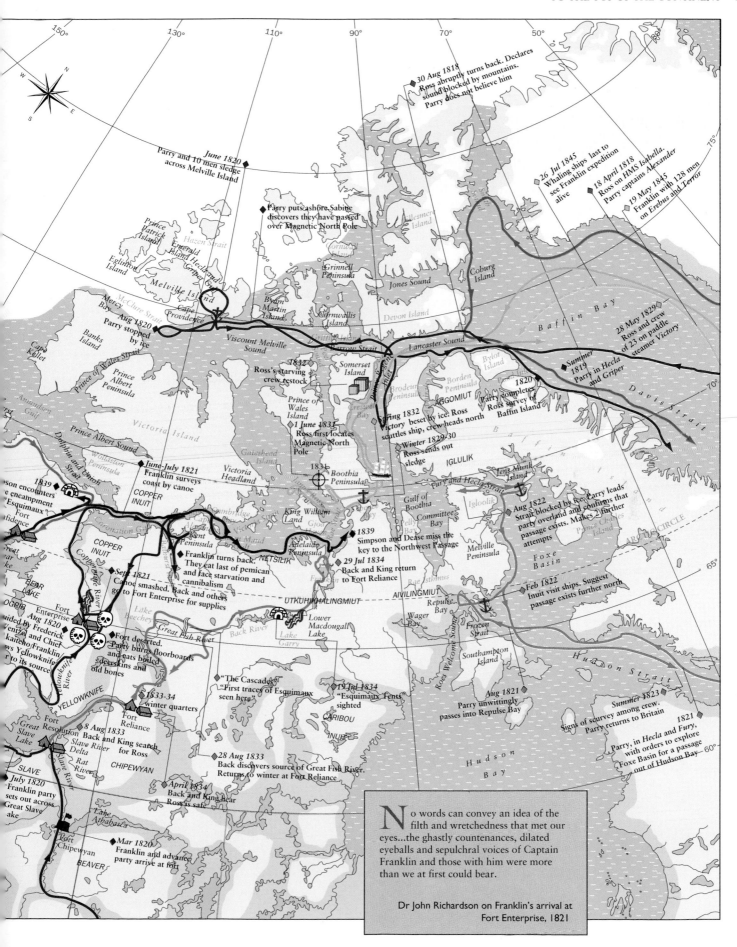

**30 Aug 1818** Ross abruptly turns back. Declares sound blocked by mountains. Parry does not believe him

**26 Jul 1845** last to see Franklin expedition alive

**18 April 1818** Ross on HMS Isabella. Parry captains Alexander

**19 May 1845** Franklin with 128 men on Erebus and Terror

**June 1820** Parry and 10 men sledge across Melville Island

Parry puts ashore. Sabine discovers they have passed over Magnetic North Pole

**28 May 1829** Ross and crew of 23 on paddle steamer Victory

**Aug 1820** Parry stopped by ice

**Summer 1819** Parry in Hecla and Griper

**1832** Ross's starving crew restock

**Spring 1832** Victory beset by ice. Ross scuttles ship, crew heads north

Parry completes Ross survey of Baffin Island

**1 June 1831** Ross first locates Magnetic North Pole

**Winter 1829–30** Ross sends out sledge

**June–July 1821** Franklin surveys coast by canoe

**Aug 1822** Strait blocked by ice. Parry leads party overland and confirms that passage exists. Makes 2 further attempts

**1839** son encounters e encampment "Esquimaux" Fort fidence

**Franklin turns back.** They eat last of pemican and face starvation and cannibalism

**1839** Simpson and Dease miss the key to the Northwest Passage

**29 Jul 1834** Back and King return to Fort Reliance

**Feb 1822** Inuit visit ships. Suggest passage exists further north

**Sept 1821** Canoe smashed. Back and others go to Fort Enterprise for supplies

**Fort deserted.** Party burns floorboards and eats boiled deerskins and old bones

**Aug 1833** ided by Frederick entzel and Chief kaitcho/Franklin ws Yellowknife r to its source

**"The Cascades" "First traces of Esquimaux seen here"**

**19 Jul 1834 "Esquimaux Tents" sighted**

**Aug 1821** Parry unwittingly passes into Repulse Bay

**Summer 1823** Signs of scurvy among crew. Parry returns to Britain

**1833–34** winter quarters

**8 Aug 1833** Back and King search for Ross

**28 Aug 1833** Back discovers source of Great Fish River. Returns to winter at Fort Reliance

**1821** Parry, in Hecla and Fury, with orders to explore Foxe Basin for a passage out of Hudson Bay

**July 1820** Franklin party sets out across Great Slave ake

**April 1834** Back and King hear Ross is safe

**Mar 1820** Franklin and advance party arrive at fort

> **N**o words can convey an idea of the filth and wretchedness that met our eyes...the ghastly countenances, dilated eyeballs and sepulchral voices of Captain Franklin and those with him were more than we at first could bear.
>
> Dr John Richardson on Franklin's arrival at Fort Enterprise, 1821

# Across Canada's Plains and Rockies

## THE SURVEYS OF PALLISER AND HIND, 1857-59

*Palliser and Hind painstakingly chart the last gaps in knowledge of the vast prairielands of southern Canada and the Canadian Rockies.*

In 1856 the Royal Geographical Society in London, through Lieutenant John Palliser, petitioned the Colonial Office to fund a two-year exploration of the wilds of southern Canada: to search out possibilities for European settlement and to block any US plans to expand northward. In 1847 Palliser, once described as "an adventurous, cheerful young Irishman," had already explored up the Missouri River, as far as the 49th parallel, hunting bear and buffalo and witnessing a battle between the Hidatsa and Sioux.

Palliser finally set off in 1857, accompanied by the plant collector Eugene Bourgeau,

magnetic observer Thomas Blakiston, geologist Dr James Hector and astronomer John W. Sullivan. They lacked only an experienced cartographer. They were to cover large areas of southern Canada, below territory previously explored by David Thompson (▶ *page 118*). They also planned to search for passes from the Canadian Rockies to the Columbia River suitable for trading parties and wagon roads, and hoped to find a railroad route through the Rockies and Cascades that would open up a Canadian port to the Pacific.

Palliser's party mapped for the first time the

vast country around the South Saskatchewan River: areas inhabited by warring Assiniboin, Blackfoot and Cree, and mostly vast prairielands covered with buffalo. In the Rocky Mountain region, they found at least four passes, one later used by the Canadian Pacific Railroad. These passes also made it possible to connect western Canada to the rest of the dominion, protecting it from US expansionists.

All year round Palliser's survey expeditions crisscrossed southern Canada. Although most strategic locations had fur trade posts with regular cart or sleigh routes in between, their

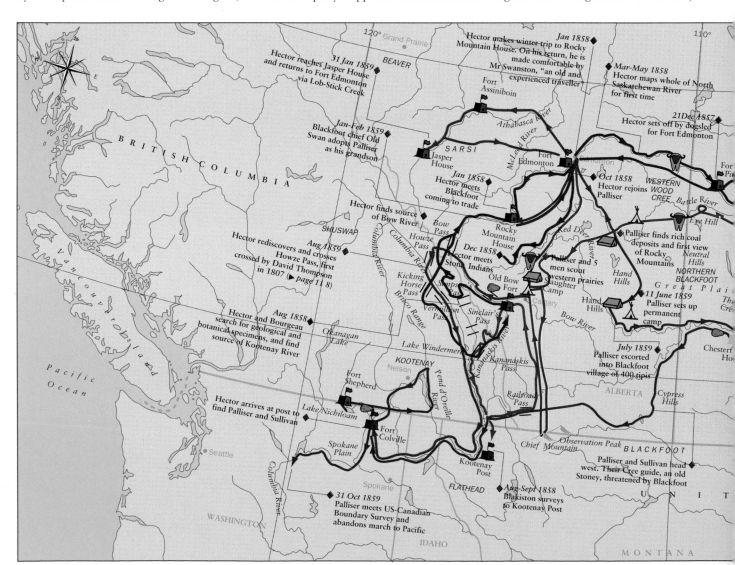

experiences were tough. They dragged carts across prairie and swamp and crossed four passes through the Rockies. Narrowly staving off starvation and in freezing conditions they traveled long distances by dogsled.

Lieutenant Blakiston was the only member of the party to cause difficulty. Unable to get along with his companions he struck out on his own, albeit with some success. Palliser's party was careful to establish good relations with potentially hostile Indians. Aided by Indian guides, they mapped much new territory, and made a thorough investigation of Indian peoples, wildlife, plants, waterways and the US–Canadian frontier. But most of the Rocky Mountain passes had been

traversed much earlier by Thompson, Howze and Sir George Simpson and Palliser did not make any truly new discoveries.

Henry Youle Hind was a professor of chemistry and geology at the University of Toronto and had much in common with the great Prussian geographer, Alexander von Humboldt. He analyzed soils, described the plants, animals, Indian and European peoples of the area and he laid out shorter immigration routes to the Saskatchewan.

Neither Palliser nor Hind was optimistic about the possibilities of agricultural settlement on the great prairies. Palliser's report, published in 1863, tended to see them as much too dangerous for settlers and

ignored the rivers, lakes and woods. Hind concluded that for all the lushness of the plains and river valleys, the prairies themselves had been burned many times and were seriously short of rainfall or rivers. In fact Hind anticipated John Wesley Powell's celebrated report on the arid regions of the USA (▶ *page 172*) by over 20 years.

H aving ascended the slightly elevated ridge we then beheld our game, four or five thousand buffalo....Soon after seeing us the buffalo were in motion at a steady lope, crowding gradually into a thick black mass... the hunters came on at a steady canter increasing with the speed of the buffalo into a hand gallop... We killed seventeen cows.

John Palliser at Slaughter Camp, July 1858

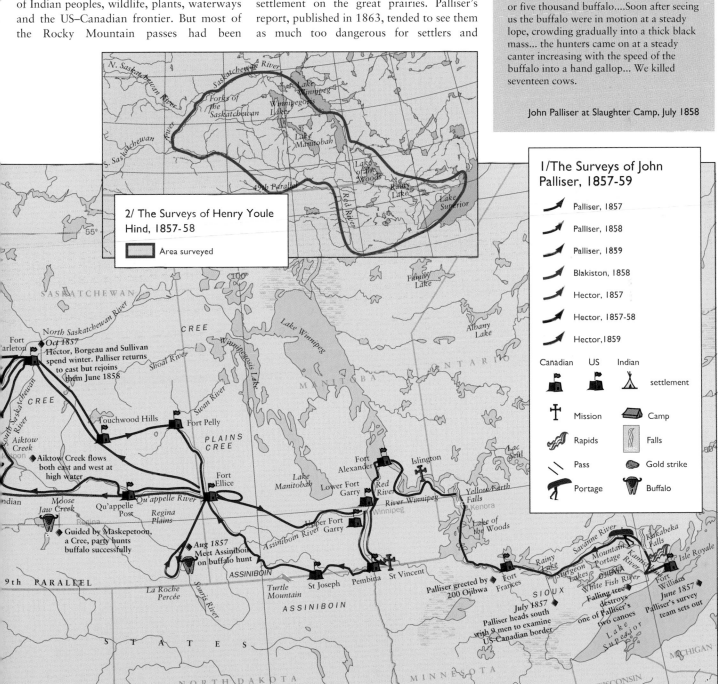

2/ The Surveys of Henry Youle Hind, 1857-58

▭ Area surveyed

1/The Surveys of John Palliser, 1857-59

Palliser, 1857
Palliser, 1858
Palliser, 1859
Blakiston, 1858
Hector, 1857
Hector, 1857-58
Hector, 1859

Canadian    US    Indian

🏰 settlement (Canadian)    🏰 (US)    ⛺ settlement (Indian)

✝ Mission    Camp

Rapids    Falls

Pass    Gold strike

Portage    Buffalo

# Cold and Tragic Shores

## SEARCHES FOR FRANKLIN AND THE NORTHWEST PASSAGE, 1846-1905

*The search for Franklin becomes a cause
célèbre. Much Arctic territory is charted. In
1903-05 Roald Amundsen is the first to cross
the Northwest passage by sea .*

In 1845 when Sir John Franklin left on his last
expedition, he took enough supplies for three
years (▶ *page 186*). There was thus no serious
concern for his expedition until early 1847. At
that point, on the insistence of his wife, Lady
Jane Franklin, and his friend John Ross, the
British Admiralty planned the first rescue
operation. It was to be the first of 50 land and
sea expeditions to search for Franklin and his
crew, the last of which departed in 1878.

In 1848 James Clark Ross retraced
Franklin's route in the *Victory*. On entering
ice-locked Peel Sound he declared it to be
completely impassable and turned back. Since
Franklin had been instructed to use
Wellington Channel as an alternative Ross
instructed the Admiralty to concentrate future
search operations further north. As it was,
Franklin had died the previous year, but Ross

was then turning his back on Franklin's
starving crew in the process of abandoning
their ice-bound ships.

In 1850 six more rescue operations began.
The *Investigator* and *Enterprise*, under the
general command of Richard Collinson, were
instructed to search the coast of Alaska. When
the two ships separated in fog near Cape
Horn, the ambitious Robert McClure by-
passed his commander and reached Banks'
Island by early September. The more cautious
Collinson turned back and spent the winter in
Hong Kong.

The ice carried the *Investigator* halfway up
Prince of Wales Strait, and sledge trips the
following spring confirmed the strait as a
possible route for the Northwest Passage. A
second attempt to sail through the strait
during the summer of 1851 was thwarted by

ice just 25 miles short of Melville Sound.
Collinson meanwhile returned to the area
and, though neither realized this, tagged two
weeks behind McClure until the latter
rounded the top of Banks Island. Ice kept
McClure anchored in Mercy Bay for two
years. When Collinson turned back to explore
the southern coast of Victoria Island, he came
within 40 miles of Franklin's ships.

Dissatisfied with the Admiralty's efforts,
Lady Franklin hired William Kennedy, a
Canadian fur trader, and Joseph-Rene Bellot,
a 25-year-old French sailor, to search south of
Lancaster Sound. In the spring of 1852,
Kennedy and Bellot sledged across Peel Sound
and circled Prince of Wales Island. They
encountered a narrow gorge that separated
Somerset Island from Boothia Peninsula,
which Kennedy named Bellot Strait. It was a

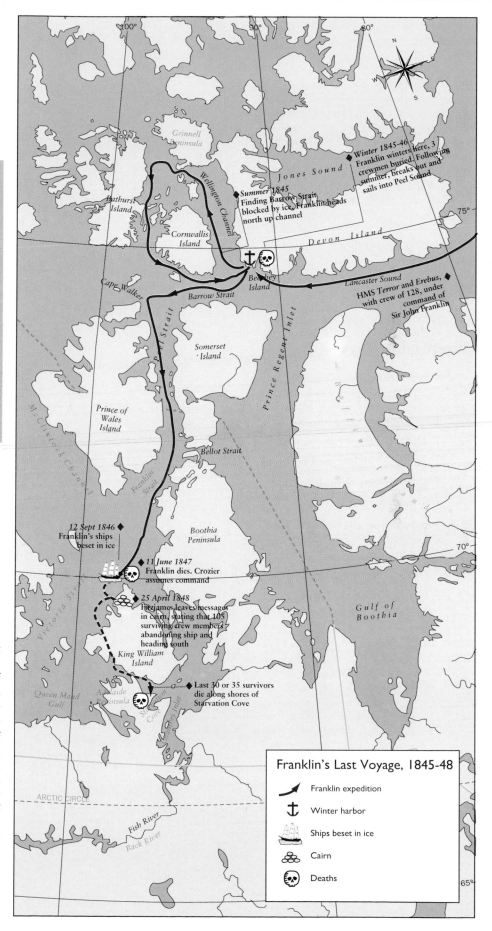

A pril 25th, 1848 – HM's Ships Terror and Erebus were deserted on 22nd April, 5 leagues N.N.W. of this, having been beset since 12th September 1846. The Officers & crew, consisting of 105 souls, under the command of Captain F.R.M Crozier, landed here on Lat. 69° 37' 42" N, long. 98° 41' W. Sir John Franklin died on 11th June 1847; and the total loss by deaths in the Expedition has been to this date 9 officers & 15 men.

(signed) James Fitzjames,
Captain HMS Erebus

and start tomorrow, 26th for Back's Fish River

(signed) F.R.M. Crozier, Captain and Senior Officer

Note discovered by Lt. William Hobson in cairn at Point Victory

Left: The tombstones of three of Franklin's men lie beneath the midnight sun on Beechey Island. The seaman, stoker and Royal Marine died there during the expedition's first winter. The engraving was based on drawings by the explorer Elisha Kent Kane (▶ pages 198-201)

third possible route for the Northwest Passage.

On 15 August 1852 the last and largest of the British Admiralty's search expeditions landed at Beechey Island. The autocratic Sir Edward Belcher led five ships, sending Henry Kellett and Leopold M'Clintock off in two of them to search for Collinson and McClure. In April 1853 Lieutenant Bedford Pim found McClure at Mercy Bay. Belcher meanwhile wintered off the Grinnell Peninsula. After exploring the region by sledge, both arms of the expedition tried to rendezvous at Beechey Island. But Belcher had to abandon all four ships in the summer of 1854. Only the timely arrival of supply ships, the *Phoenix* and the *Talbot*, relieved the over-crowding on Belcher's remaining ship, the *Northstar*.

In 1853 Lady Franklin persuaded Henry

Grinnell to finance a search led by the American ship's surgeon Elisha Kent Kane (▶page 198-201). But the first solid evidence about Franklin's expedition came in 1853 when John Rae interviewed Inuit around Pelly Bay and retrieved articles removed from the ships. Four years later, Lady Franklin sent Francis Leopold M'Clintock to follow up Rae's lead. M'Clintock forced his way to the western end of Bellot Strait, and during the spring of 1859 sent out three search teams. A party led by William Hobson discovered a cairn containing the only message left by Franklin's crew. M'Clintock's men established the final location of Franklin's ships and proved that he had died in 1847. They suggested that none of Franklin's crew of 128 had survived.

The pace of explorations slackened after M'Clintock's expedition confirmed the tragedy of Franklin's last journey. Rival interests had emerged. In particular, in 1867 the United States had purchased Alaska (▶page 194).

In June 1879, American explorer Frederick Schwatka, confirmed M'Clintock's report. Traveling a record 4,000 miles overland by sledge, Schwatka gathered additional artifacts and information about the final days of Franklin's crew. In 1923, Knud Rasmussen, a Norwegian scientist, explored Starvation Cove for the first time and concluded that this was where the last survivors had died. In the mid-1980s, scientists performed autopsies on three of Franklin's crew who had been found frozen and buried on Beechey Island. They concluded that their deaths had not been caused by lead poisoning. No logbooks, journals, or diaries have yet been recovered from that fateful expedition. Nor have the sunken hulls of either of Franklin's ships been located.

When Roald Amundsen set sail from Christiania, Norway, on 16 June 1903, he was fulfilling a childhood ambition to complete what Franklin had failed to accomplish. To gain public support, Amundsen also set out to relocate the Magnetic North Pole. He succeeded in both his goals. Amundsen sailed through Peel Sound and spent two winters in Gjoa Harbor, King William Island. From there he verified that the Magnetic North Pole had shifted 30 miles to the north. The following summer he successfully navigated the last unexplored leg of the Northwest Passage, emerging from Dolphin and Union Strait early August 1905.

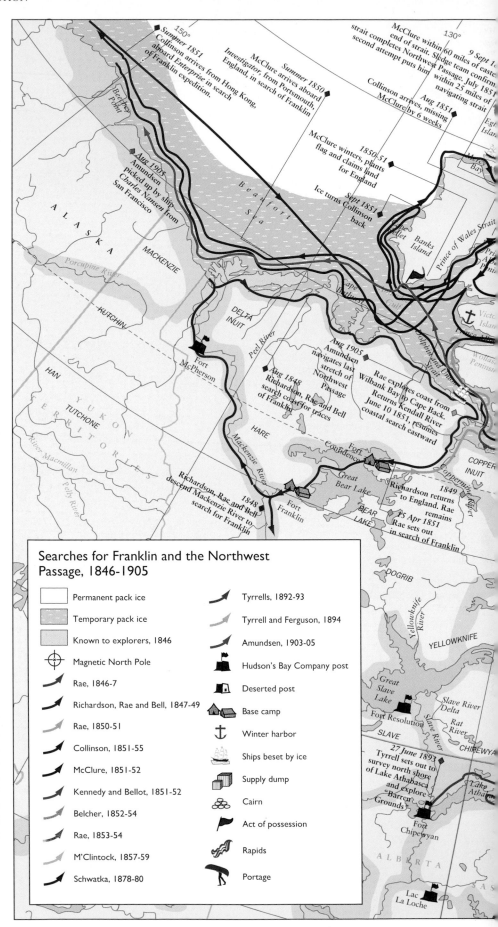

### Searches for Franklin and the Northwest Passage, 1846-1905

- ☐ Permanent pack ice
- ▨ Temporary pack ice
- ▨ Known to explorers, 1846
- ⊕ Magnetic North Pole
- ➤ Rae, 1846-7
- ➤ Richardson, Rae and Bell, 1847-49
- ➤ Rae, 1850-51
- ➤ Collinson, 1851-55
- ➤ McClure, 1851-52
- ➤ Kennedy and Bellot, 1851-52
- ➤ Belcher, 1852-54
- ➤ Rae, 1853-54
- ➤ M'Clintock, 1857-59
- ➤ Schwatka, 1878-80

- ➤ Tyrrells, 1892-93
- ➤ Tyrrell and Ferguson, 1894
- ➤ Amundsen, 1903-05
- 🏭 Hudson's Bay Company post
- 🏠 Deserted post
- 🏘 Base camp
- ⚓ Winter harbor
- ⛵ Ships beset by ice
- 📦 Supply dump
- ⚙ Cairn
- 🚩 Act of possession
- 〰 Rapids
- ⌒ Portage

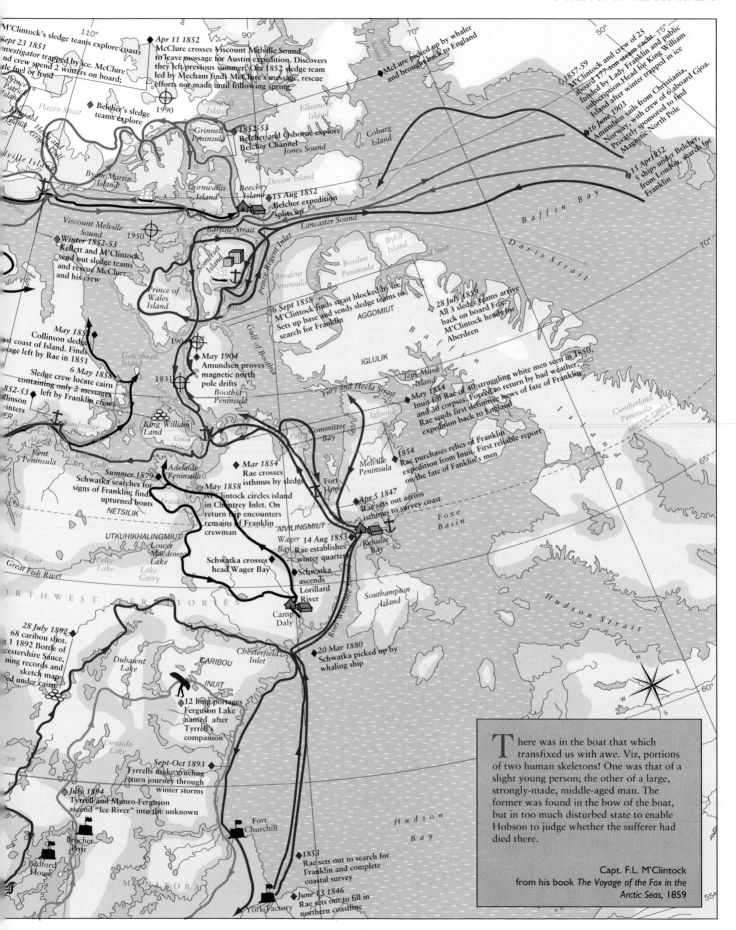

M'Clintock's sledge teams explore coasts

*Apr 11 1852*
McClure crosses Viscount Melville Sound to leave message for Austin expedition. Discovers they left previous summer. Oct 1852 sledge team led by Mecham finds McClure's message, rescue efforts not made until following spring

McClure picked up by whaler and brought back to England

1857-59
M'Clintock and crew of 25 aboard 177-ton steam yacht funded by Lady Franklin and public subscription. Head for King William Island after winter trapped in ice

*investigator trapped by ice. McClure and crew spend 2 winters on board; ...le fuel of food*

Belcher's sledge teams explore

16 June 1903
Amundsen sails from Christiania, Norway, with crew of 6 aboard Gjoa. Privately sponsored to find Magnetic North Pole

1990

Grinnell Peninsula

1852-53
Belcher and Osborne explore Belcher Channel

15 Apr 1852
5 ships under Belcher, from London, search for Franklin

Winter 1852-53
Kellett and M'Clintock send out sledge teams and rescue McClure and his crew

1950

15 Aug 1852
Belcher expedition splits up

*6 Sept 1858*
M'Clintock finds strait blocked by ice. Sets up base and sends sledge teams to search for Franklin

28 July 1859
All 3 sledge teams arrive back on board Fox, M'Clintock heads for Aberdeen

*May 185...*
Collinson sledge
...st coast of Island. Finds
...ssage left by Rae in 1851

1904

*May 1904*
Amundsen proves magnetic north pole drifts

1831

*6 May 1858*
Sledge crew locate cairn containing only 2 messages left by Franklin crew

*May 1854*
Inuit tell Rae of 40 struggling white men seen in 1850, and 30 corpses. Forced to return by bad weather, Rae sends first definitive news of fate of Franklin expedition back to England

1854
Rae purchases relics of Franklin expedition from Inuit. First reliable report on the fate of Franklin's men

*Mar 1854*
Rae crosses isthmus by sledge

Apr 5 1847
Rae sets out across isthmus to survey coast

Summer 1879
Schwatka searches for signs of Franklin; finds upturned boats

*May 1858*
M'Clintock circles island in Chantrey Inlet. On return trip encounters remains of Franklin crewman

Wager 14 Aug 1853
Rae establishes winter quarters

Schwatka crosses head Wager Bay

Schwatka ascends Lorillard River

Camp Daly

28 July 1892
68 caribou shot.
...1 1892 Bottle of
...estershire Sauce,
...ning records and
...sketch map
...ed under cairn

20 Mar 1880
Schwatka picked up by whaling ship

12 long portages Ferguson Lake named after Tyrrell's companion

Sept-Oct 1893
Tyrrells make grueling return journey through winter storms

July 1894
Tyrrell and Munro-Ferguson ascend "Ice River" into the unknown

Fort Churchill

1853
Rae sets out to search for Franklin and complete coastal survey

June 13 1846
Rae sets out to fill in northern coastline

York Factory

There was in the boat that which transfixed us with awe. Viz, portions of two human skeletons! One was that of a slight young person; the other of a large, strongly-made, middle-aged man. The former was found in the bow of the boat, but in too much disturbed state to enable Hobson to judge whether the sufferer had died there.

Capt. F.L. M'Clintock
from his book *The Voyage of the Fox in the Arctic Seas*, 1859

# Seward's Icebox

## US ALASKA AND THE YUKON GOLD RUSH, 1866-98

*The United States buys Alaska from the Russians and slowly begins to explore the vast, little-known territory it has acquired.*

In 1867 Secretary of State William H. Seward persuaded the US government to buy Alaska from the Russians. As with Jefferson's Louisiana purchase more than 60 years earlier, many thought it an act of folly to acquire a vast tract of wild and inhospitable land, and dubbed it "Seward's Icebox."

Since 1865 the Western Union Telegraph Survey had set out to link Eurasia with North America by telegraph, under Robert Kennicott and Colonel Charles Bulkley. Only a few token miles were laid and Kennicott died of a sudden heart attack in 1866, but the survey introduced American explorers to the interior. Frank Ketchum and Michael Lebarge journeyed from Nulato past Fort Yukon to Fort Selkirk. Other survey members, such as William Healey Dall and Frederick Whymper, collected natural history specimens and became experts on Russian America.

On 3 February 1868 Dall learned of the purchase of Alaska. Like the Russians (▶ *page 182*), the Americans set out to exploit their new possession by setting up the Alaska Commercial Company to rival the Hudson's Bay Company. Exploration of the interior was slow, however. In the summer of 1869 Captain Charles Raymond traveled up the Yukon on a paddlewheel steamer and at Fort Yukon calculated that this Hudson's Bay post was within US territory. In the 1870s, the US Army and the Treasury Department's Coast Survey competed over exploration of the area. In 1879 Lieutenant Henry Ray arrived at bleak Point Barrow for a long scientific mission, while John Muir, a naturalist and writer, studied the spectacular Glacier Bay.

During the 1880s the pace of interior discovery quickened. In 1883 the US Army dispatched Frederick Schwatka and George Stoney on major expeditions. Schwatka went up Chilkoot Pass – a major trail in later gold rushes – built a raft at Lake Lindeman, floated down the Yukon and eventually took an Alaska Commercial Company steamer to St Michael. While he covered little new ground, Schwatka's journey, books and lecture tours were an attempt to rouse public interest in Alaska.

From 1883 to 1885 Lieutenant George M. Stoney of the US Navy and Lieutenant John

Cantwell of the Revenue Marine openly competed in their successive travels up the Kobuk River. The US Army was active as well, launching Henry T. Allen's great expedition of 1885. Allen succeeded in penetrating the Copper River drainage where the Russian, Rufus Serebrennikov had failed (▶ *page 182*). By the end of summer 1885 Allen had explored three immense and largely unknown river systems: the Copper, the Tanana, and the Koyukuk. However his daring reconnaissance attracted little fame. That same year S.B. McLenagan explored the source of the Noatak River, and in 1886 Stoney's men accomplished a monumental journey from Point Barrow to Nulato.

During the 1890s, teams of unsung explorers from the US Geological Survey fanned out into the interior to locate the Brooks Range, calculate the height of Mt. McKinley and wonder at the geysers of Katmai Volcano. The gold rushes of 1896-98 brought thousands of prospectors and pioneers into Alaska, many eager to explore new valleys, rivers, and mountains. In little more than a century the Russian pursuit of furs and American pursuit of minerals had opened up a vast area of North America to the glory and greed of exploration and exploitation.

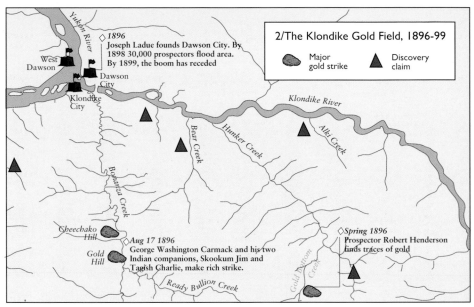

2/The Klondike Gold Field, 1896-99

🥔 Major gold strike   ▲ Discovery claim

◇ *1896*
Joseph Ladue founds Dawson City. By 1898 30,000 prospectors flood area. By 1899, the boom has receded

West Dawson

Dawson City

Klondike City

Cheechako Hill

Gold Hill

◇ *Aug 17 1896*
George Washington Carmack and his two Indian companions, Skookum Jim and Tagish Charlie, make rich strike.

◇ *Spring 1896*
Prospector Robert Henderson finds traces of gold

Klondike River

Bear Creek

Hunker Creek

Alki Creek

Bonanza Creek

Ready Bullion Creek

Gold Bottom Creek

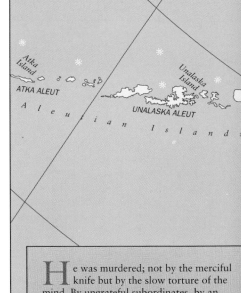

ATKA ALEUT

UNALASKA ALEUT

Atka Island

Unalaska Island

Aleutian Islands

170°

H e was murdered; not by the merciful knife but by the slow torture of the mind. By ungrateful subordinates, by an egotistic and selfish commander, by anxiety to fulfil his commands, while those that gave them were lining their pockets in San Francisco.

William Healey Dall, on hearing of the death of Robert Kennicott in 1866

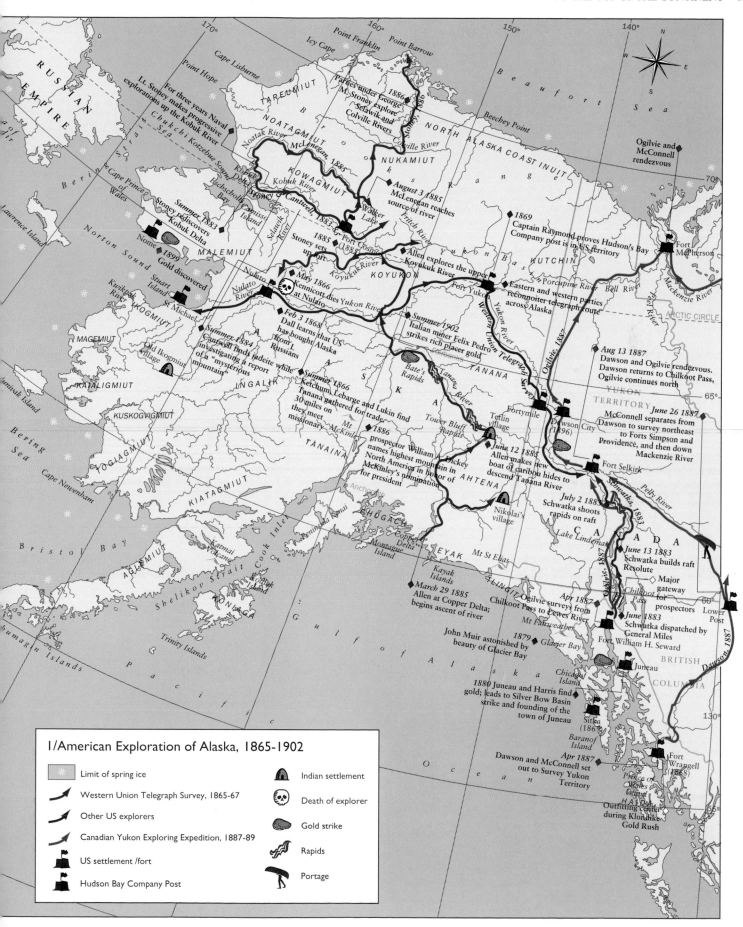

**RUSSIAN EMPIRE**

Point Franklin
Point Barrow
Icy Cape
Point Hope
Cape Lisburne

*Beaufort Sea*

Beechey Point

*B e a u f o r t   S e a*

Ogilvie and
McConnell
rendezvous

1886
Parties under George
M. Stoney explore
Selawik and
Colville Rivers

NORTH ALASKA COAST INUIT

70°

Fort
McPherson

TAREUMIUT

NOATAGMIUT

Noatak River

Colville River

NUKAMIUT

Chukchi Kotzebue Sound Delta
Chukchi Sea

For three years Naval
explorations up the Kobuk River
Lt. Stoney makes progressive

Kobuk River
McLenegan, 1885

Cantwell, 1883-85

Walker
Lake

August 3 1885
McLenegan reaches
source of river

Fitch River

1869
Captain Raymond proves Hudson's
Company post is in US territory

Porcupine River

Bell River

Mackenzie River

ARCTIC CIRCLE

Peel River

KUTCHIN

KOWAGMIUT

Summer 1883
Stoney rediscovers
Kobuk Delta

Nome   1899
Gold discovered

Norton Sound

Selawik River

Stoney sets
up fort

1885 Fort Cosmo
(1885)

Koyukuk River

Allen explores the upper
Koyukuk River

Fort Yukon

Eastern and western parties
reconnoiter telegraph route
across Alaska

Yukon Basin

Western Union Telegraph Survey

Ogilvie, 1887

Aug 13 1887
Dawson and Ogilvie rendezvous.
Dawson returns to Chilkoot Pass,
Ogilvie continues north

65°

June 26 1887
McConnell separates from
Dawson to survey northeast
to Forts Simpson and
Providence, and then down
Mackenzie River

MALEMIUT

Nulato River

Nulato

May 1866
Kennicott dies
at Nulato

Yukon River

KOYUKON

Summer/1902
Italian miner Felix Pedro
strikes rich placer gold

Fairbanks

TANANA

YUKON
TERRITORY

Stuart
Island

St Michael

Feb 3 1868
Dall learns that US
has bought Alaska
from Russians

KUIKPAK
River
IKOGMIUT

Summer 1884
Cantwell finds jadeite while
investigating a report
of a "mysterious
mountain"

Bate's
Rapids

Tanana River

Tetlin
village

Fortymile

Dawson City
(1896)

Schwatka, 1883

Pelly River

Fort Selkirk

MAGEMIUT

Old Ikogmiut
village

KATALIGMIUT

INGALIK

ALASKA

Summer 1866
Ketchum, Lebarge and Lukin find
Tanana gathered for trade.
30 miles on
they meet
missionary

Tower Bluff
Rapids

June 12 1885
Allen makes new
boat of caribou hides to
descend Tanana River

KUSKOGWIGMIUT

Bering
Sea

Cape Newenham

KIATAGMIUT

Mt
McKinley

1886
prospector William
Dickey
names highest mountain in
North America in honor of
McKinley's nomination
for president

AHTENA

Nikolai's
village

July 2 1883
Schwatka shoots
rapids on raft

Lake Lindeman

C A N A D A

TOGIAGMIUT

Katmai
Volcano

Kodiak
Island

Cook Inlet

Anchorage
Kenai Peninsula

CHUGACH

Copper
Delta

EYAK

Mt St Elias

June 13 1883
Schwatka builds raft
Resolute

Chilkoot
Pass

Major
gateway
for
prospectors

60°

Lower
Post

AGLEMIUT

Trinity Islands

Shelikov Strait

KONIAGA

Gulf
of
Alaska

March 29 1885
Allen at Copper Delta;
begins ascent of river

Kayak
Islands

Montague
Island

TLINGIT

Mt Fairweather

Apr 1887
Ogilvie surveys from
Chilkoot Pass to Lewes River

Chilkoot
Pass

June 1883
Schwatka dispatched by
General Miles

Fort
William H. Seward

Dawson, 1887

Bristol Bay

John Muir astonished by
beauty of Glacier Bay

1879
Glacier Bay

Juneau

BRITISH

130°

P a c i f i c

1880 Juneau and Harris find
gold; leads to Silver Bow Basin
strike and founding of the
town of Juneau

Chicago
Island

COLUMBIA

humagan Islands

O c e a n

Dawson and McConnell set
out to Survey Yukon
Territory

Sitka
(1867)

Baranof
Island

Apr 1887
Dawson and McConnell set
out to Survey Yukon
Territory

Fort
Wrangell
(1868)

Prince
of Wales
Island

HAIDA

Outfitting center
during Klondike
Gold Rush

55°

---

## 1/American Exploration of Alaska, 1865-1902

| | |
|---|---|
| ❄ | Limit of spring ice |
| ➤ | Western Union Telegraph Survey, 1865-67 |
| ➤ | Other US explorers |
| ➤ | Canadian Yukon Exploring Expedition, 1887-89 |
| 🏭 | US settlement /fort |
| 🏭 | Hudson Bay Company Post |

| | |
|---|---|
| ⛺ | Indian settlement |
| ☠ | Death of explorer |
| 🥔 | Gold strike |
| 〰 | Rapids |
| 🛶 | Portage |

# The Crown of the Continent

## EXPLORATIONS IN THE ARCTIC ARCHIPELAGO, 1906-18

*Norwegian and Canadian explorers unveil
the world's last unknown landmass – the vast
archipelago of the Canadian Arctic.*

The search for Sir John Franklin (▶ *pages 190-93*) had uncovered much new territory, but equally vast areas of the Arctic had been ignored. By the time Franklin's fate became clear, attention had shifted toward the "Open Polar Sea" and the North Pole. It was not until the 20th century that explorers returned to the Arctic.

The first thorough scientific survey was of the region north of Jones Sound and west of Smith Sound. In 1898 Otto Sverdrup, commander of the Second Norwegian Expedition, planned to take his ship *Fram* around the northern coast of Greenland. But ice in Kane Basin forced him to change his plan and instead he took the opportunity to survey the crown of the northern hemisphere.

Sverdrup, primarily while waiting for the summer tides to clear the ice from Smith Sound, initiated forays into the highlands of Ellesmere Island. His serious work did not begin until he moved his winter quarters into Jones Sound. Then, from his base camp in Harbor Fjord (1899-1900) and Goose Fjord (1900-02), Sverdrup sent out sledge teams. They established the connection between Greely's Fjord and Nansen Sound, discovered the islands of Ellef Ringnes and Amund Ringnes and, in spite of John Ross's claim, proved that Jones Sound was not closed off by "very high mountains." Sverdrup also came within 25 miles of circumnavigating Axel Heiberg, the island he found and named for his sponsor, the Norwegian consul.

The next phase of exploration began as Canada went about annexing the north Arctic islands. Joseph Bernier led a series of four missions to the region for the Canadian Marine and Fisheries Department. The missions carried out a variety of tasks from intensive surveys of unexplored areas to posting fines and planting Canadian flags. In 1906-07 Bernier swept through Lancaster Sound toward the Beaufort Sea, pausing just long enough at each major island to lay Canada's claim upon the soil. When ice prevented him from going farther than the eastern coast of Melville Island, he turned back to claim Victoria and Banks islands in 1908-09. That year the "impassable" McClure Strait was uncharacteristically clear of ice and had his orders allowed it, Bernier

felt confident that he could have completed the Northwest Passage. Instead Bernier finished the season dispensing whaling licences around Navy Board Inlet.

Suddenly aware that an opportunity had been missed, the Canadian government issued new orders to Bernier. In 1910-11, on his third journey, Bernier went immediately to McClure Strait but his opportunity of sailing through the Northwest Passage was lost, it was no longer open. However this third journey accomplished more original scientific work than the first two missions combined. From their winter harbor at Arctic Bay, Bernier dispatched J.E. Lavoi on two long sledge trips to survey the hitherto uncharted Brodeur Peninsula, from Admiralty Inlet to Fury and Hecla Strait. Along the way, a Mr English, the ship's geologist, located a variety of minerals, including significant deposits of sulphur. In 1912-13 on the fourth mission, Bernier explored Gifford Fjord from Foxe Basin to Admiralty Inlet.

Vilhjalmur Stefansson of Canada, an anthropologist who specialized in Arctic peoples, persuaded the Canadian government to sponsor a massive, two-pronged exploration of the region around Victoria Island and Coronation Gulf. In 1914 a trio of ships set out from British Columbia, headed for the Beaufort Sea. An easterly tide of ice separated Stefansson's team from their supply ship *Karluk*, which later sank near Wrangel Island. Undeterred, Stefansson took off across the ice wasteland north of Martin Point, Alaska, with two other men, and succeeded in his main aim – proving that the Beaufort Sea could sustain life. The party survived for three months by augmenting their meagre supplies with seals caught miles away from land.

Stefansson set up winter quarters at Cape Kellett, Banks Island, and from there continued his exploration of the Beaufort Sea and the north Arctic islands. On his long circular treks, he discovered all the remaining northern islands, making links between his own and Sverdrup's findings. He also explored the interior of Victoria Island. Over five years, Stefansson made three journeys across the Beaufort Sea.

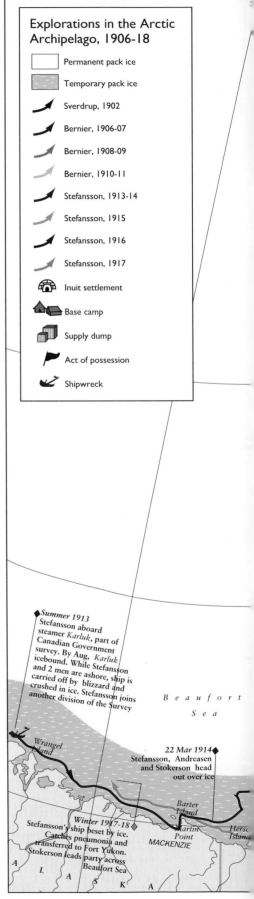

**Explorations in the Arctic Archipelago, 1906-18**

- ☐ Permanent pack ice
- ▨ Temporary pack ice
- Sverdrup, 1902
- Bernier, 1906-07
- Bernier, 1908-09
- Bernier, 1910-11
- Stefansson, 1913-14
- Stefansson, 1915
- Stefansson, 1916
- Stefansson, 1917
- Inuit settlement
- Base camp
- Supply dump
- Act of possession
- Shipwreck

*Summer 1913* Stefansson aboard steamer *Karluk*, part of Canadian Government survey. By Aug, *Karluk* icebound. While Stefansson and 2 men are ashore, ship is carried off by blizzard and crushed in ice. Stefansson joins another division of the Survey

*Beaufort Sea*

Wrangel Island

**22 Mar 1914** Stefansson, Andreasen and Stokerson head out over ice

Barter Island

*Winter 1917-18* Stefansson's ship beset by ice. Catches pneumonia and transferred to Fort Yukon. Stokerson leads party across Beaufort Sea

Martin Point
MACKENZIE

Herschel Island

A L A S K A

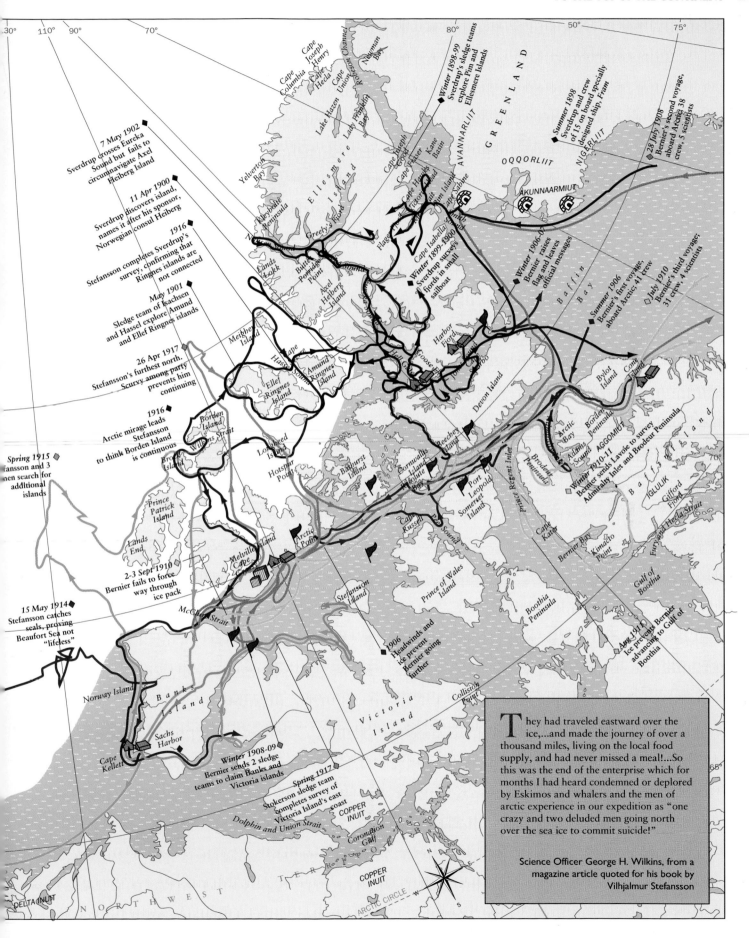

7 May 1902
Sverdrup crosses Eureka
Sound but fails to
circumnavigate Axel
Heiberg Island

11 Apr 1900
Sverdrup discovers island,
names it after his sponsor,
Norwegian consul Heiberg

1916
Stefansson completes Sverdrup's
survey, confirming that
Ringnes islands are
not connected

May 1901
Sledge team of Isachsen
and Hassel explore Amund
and Ellef Ringnes islands

26 Apr 1917
Stefansson's furthest north.
Scurvy among party
prevents him
continuing

1916
Arctic mirage leads
Stefansson
to think Borden Island
is continuous

Spring 1915
Stefansson and 3
men search for
additional
islands

15 May 1914
Stefansson catches
seals, proving
Beaufort Sea not
"lifeless"

2-3 Sept 1910
Bernier fails to force
way through
ice pack

Winter 1908-09
Bernier sends 2 sledge
teams to claim Banks and
Victoria islands

Spring 1917
Stokerson sledge team
completes survey of
Victoria Island's east
coast

1906
Headwinds and
ice prevent
Bernier going
further

Winter 1898-99
Sverdrup's sledge teams
explore Pim and
Ellesmere Islands

Summer 1898
Sverdrup and crew of 15 on board specially
designed ship Fram

28 July 1908
Bernier's second voyage,
aboard Arctic 38
crew, 5 scientists

Winter 1906-07
Bernier raises
flag and leaves
official messages

Summer 1906
Bernier's first voyage,
aboard Arctic, 41 crew

July 1910
Bernier's third voyage,
31 crew, 4 scientists

Winter 1899-1900
Sverdrup surveys
fiords in small
sailboat

Winter 1910-11
Bernier sends Lavoie to survey
Admiralty Inlet and Brodeur Peninsula

Aug 1910
Ice prevents Bernier
advancing to Gulf of
Boothia

They had traveled eastward over the
ice,...and made the journey of over a
thousand miles, living on the local food
supply, and had never missed a meal!...So
this was the end of the enterprise which for
months I had heard condemned or deplored
by Eskimos and whalers and the men of
arctic experience in our expedition as "one
crazy and two deluded men going north
over the sea ice to commit suicide!"

Science Officer George H. Wilkins, from a
magazine article quoted for his book by
Vilhjalmur Stefansson

# The Big Nail

## THE RACE TO THE POLE, 1853-1909

*The dream of an Open Polar Sea is replaced by the lure of the North Pole. Robert Peary may have been first to arrive there but his claim is even now clouded by controversy.*

In spring 1854 Elisha Kent Kane, an American ship's surgeon with a crew of 17, made four futile attempts to find a way to the Open Polar Sea. Like many others he was also searching for survivors from Sir John Franklin's ill-fated journey of 1845 (▶ *page 190-193*).

In June 1854 Kane sent out four of his last six healthy men in an abortive effort to climb the massive Humboldt Glacier. The other two, William Morton and Hans Hendrik, a Greenland Inuit, cut across Peabody Bay to the top of Kane Basin. Early in July they found their path blocked by a steep cliff, Cape Constitution. Morton scrambled up, the first white man to view the northward expanse of ice-free blue water, Kennedy Channel. Convinced it led to the Open Polar Sea, Kane later wrote, "I do not believe there was a man among us who did not long for the means of entering its bright and lonely waters."

Two other Americans were frustrated in their search for the fabled Open Polar Sea. In 1860 Dr Isaac Hayes, surgeon on Kane's 1853 expedition, led a sledge team north along Ellesmere Island. After a month on the ice, Hayes believed he was above 81°N, a position that would have placed him near Lady Franklin Bay. Later explorers calculated that he only reached Cape Joseph Good. In 1871

an eccentric American explorer, Charles Francis Hall, ascended Cape Brevoort and looked across the Lincoln Sea, a sea of solid ice from Cape Joseph Henry to the horizon. Hall died in November 1871, after several weeks of illness. The official claim was that he died from a stroke but a century later, in 1968, an autopsy concluded he had been systematically poisoned by arsenic. Forced to abandon their ship the *Polaris*, some of Hall's crew shuttled between ice floes. They were eventually rescued 2000 miles south, off Newfoundland. Although he did not live to claim his achievement, Hall had effectively closed the book on the Open Polar Sea and confirmed Kane's "American route" as the path to the North Pole.

The British Admiralty's last Arctic expedition left Portsmouth in May 1875, led by George Strong Nares. He stationed the *Discovery* at a base camp at Lady Franklin Bay and continued north in the *Alert* to Cape Sheridan. In 1876 Nares launched three sledge teams. Albert Hastings Markham surpassed Parry's farthest north record of 1827 (▶ *page 186*), only 400 miles from the Pole; Lewis Beaumont reached Sherard Osborn Fiord and claimed a farthest east record; Pelham Aldrich headed north in search of a vantage point for the North Pole itself.

In 1881 the US Army used a scientific expedition to compete with the British. Adolphus Washington Greely, with two dozen men and two Greenland Inuit, established a weather station, Fort Conger, at Lady Franklin Bay. Greely then sent out two of his men, James B. Lockwood and David Brainard, who broke several records for farthest north, east and west, but Greely's expedition is best known for its disastrous end. Though stocked with plenty of supplies, Greely decided to abandon Fort Conger in August 1883 and go in search of emergency supplies at Cape Sabine. Two weeks later the ice encased Greely's four open boats near Cape Hawks and inched them southward. Greely abandoned the boats hoping to reach shore and walk the rest of the way. Halfway across the ice the current abruptly cut them adrift on a mile-wide ice floe. On hitting a stable iceberg the desperate men clambered to

safety and established Camp Clay on the north side of Pim Island. They were rescued nine months later, but only seven men, including Greely, were still alive.

To the American public, Robert Edwin Peary personified the ideal Arctic explorer. A civil engineer with the US Navy, in 1886 Peary took leave from Nicaragua to spend a few months on Greenland's icepack. He returned twice to cross northern Greenland: first in 1892 with a party of six, including Matthew Henson, his personal servant; second in 1895 when, with Henson and Hugh Ross Lee, he nearly lost his life.

The need to reach the North Pole soon became the goal of Peary's life. On his first attempt he was backed by wealthy industrialists of the Peary Arctic Club, but his ship the *Windward* could go no further than Cape d'Urville. While setting up supply depots for the journey during winter 1898-99, Peary had lost most of his toes, but they hauled supplies almost 300 miles to Cape Sheridan. He then set off from a point near Cape Hecla in spring 1902. After two weeks struggling over pressure ridges, he gave up on 21 April. He had surpassed Markham's farthest north of 1876, but failed to exceed either Nansen's record of 1895 or Umberto Cagni's record of 1900.

In spring 1906 Peary launched his second major assault on the North Pole from Cape Columbia. After a month of back-breaking work, the expedition came to a standstill on 26 March, when they ran into a river of open water, the "Big Lead." It was a week before "Big Lead" was covered by new ice. Then Peary, Henson and six Inuit headed for the Pole. On 21 April they had to abandon their goal. According to Peary's unverified calculations, they were 200 miles short of the Pole but had achieved a new all-time record of 87° 06' N.

Peary's third and final expedition departed New York harbor on 6 July 1908. This time the whole world was watching and it was the North Pole or nothing. The *Roosevelt* landed at Floeberg Beach on 5 September 1908 and they began to lay out supply depots. On 28 February 1909 the first team took off across the ice, covering 10 to 15 miles a day. On 1 April Bob Bartlett, Peary's navigator, was

> M y life work is accomplished. The thing which it was intended from the beginning that I should do, the thing which I believed could be done and that I could do, I have done. I have got the North Pole out of my system. After 23 years of effort, hard work, disappointments, hardships, privations, more or less suffering, and some risks, I have won the last great geographical prize...for the credit of the United States, the Service to which I belong, myself and my family. My work is the finish, the cap and climax, of 300 years, loss of life and expenditure of millions, by some of the best men of the civilized nations of the world, and it has been accomplished with a clean cut dash, spirit, and I believe, thoroughness characteristically American. I am content.
>
> **Robert E. Peary's**
> **personal diary for April 1909**

disappointed to be told to turn back to camp. The North Pole was still 153 miles away. Peary, Henson and four Inuit – Egingwah, Seeglo, Ootah and Ooqueah - then made their final assault. Based on progress of the previous five days, Bartlett figured it would take them eight days to reach the Pole. They made it in four. On 6 April 1909 Robert Peary took a reading at Camp Jessup which placed them within three miles of the North Pole. Peary had achieved his dream. Or had he?

When Peary returned to Newfoundland, he was to hear that Frederick Cook had reached the North Pole on 21 April the previous year. A vigorous international dispute arose. Cook's claim was accepted by Denmark but public opinion turned against him when an earlier claim that he had ascended Mount McKinley proved to be fraudulent. And when Cook was unable to produce his original North Pole records, the University of Copenhagen declared his claim "not proved." Until his death in 1940 Cook continued to defend his claim and his honor. Meanwhile, with little scrutiny, the Polar triumph officially passed to Peary.

Until recently most scholars affirmed

Robert Peary as the first person to reach the North Pole, although some claims have been made for Matthew Henson, who was the first to arrive at Camp Jessup. In 1973 American astronomer Dennis Rawlins challenged Peary's unverified astronomical co-ordinates. Although Rawlins' own figures were later shown to be flawed, he had successfully rekindled the controversy.

In September 1988 the National Geographic Society reversed eight decades of support for Peary. They published a report by Wally Herbert, a British Arctic explorer, in which he suggested that the drifting ice pack might have carried Peary 60 miles off course. Also, if Peary had maintained his previous speed, he would have reached only 89° 5' N, over 60 miles short of the Pole. In 1989 scientists tried to determine whether the shadows in Peary's photographs from Camp Jessup matched a Polar position. They were hampered by cloud cover. In 1990 the National Archives released three unpublished "sunny" photographs for examination. The controversy continues.

In 1958 the nuclear submarine USS Nautilus, under the command of William

*Above: Iceberg and sea ice afloat in Melville Bay, northwest Greenland. It was through these waters that Elisha Kent Kane's party, half-dead of starvation, struggled in July and August 1855 on the way back from their unsuccessful search for the Open Polar Sea. They eventually reached the safety of Upernavik, further south along the Greenland coast, where a Spanish ship picked them up.*

Anderson, traveled under the North Pole and James Calvert took the USS Skate under the North Pole the following year. In April 1968 four amateur explorers arrived at the North Pole atop snowmobiles, the first overland expedition to reach the Pole since Peary. Wally Herbert led four men across the Pole in April 1969. Their sled journey of 14 months had been supplied by drops from the air. In May 1968, Ann Bancroft, a Minnesota school teacher, became the first woman to arrive at the North Pole, part of an eight-member team led by Will Steger. Ten days later, Jean-Louis Etienne, a French explorer, reached the same spot using only skis and pulling his own sled. The Japanese explorer Naomi Uemura arrived at the Pole alone and by dogsled in April 1978. They were all airlifted out. It was the age of the machine.

*5 Mar 1909*
Peary held up for 5 days
by "Big Lead"

*26 Mar 1906*
Peary comes to "Big Lead" but unable to cross
*2 Apr 1906*
Peary, Henson and 6 Inuit travel north alone

*28 June 1906*
Peary later claims that
from this cape he saw
"Crocker Land" along
northwest horizon

*6 Mar 1906*
Peary, Henson and
company
depart for North Pole
from Cape Hecla

Peary's
"Crocker
Land"

Cape
Thomas
Hubbard

*3 Apr -25 Jun 1876*
Aldrich leads
six men along coast

*28 Feb -1 Mar 1909*
Peary divides 24 men into
7 teams. Peary brings up rear

*Apr 21 1902*
Peary abandons
first attempt to
reach Pole

Nansen Fiord

Velheron Bay

Grant Land

Nesmith Glacier

Ellesmere Island

Axel Heiberg Island

Greely Fiord

*Summer 1882*
Greely explores Ellesmere
Island interior by sledge

Cape Brainard

*May 1883*
Lockwood, Brainard and Fred
mistake fiord for interior lake

*5 Sept 1908*
Peary's ship *Roosevelt*
arrives at its 1906 base

*11 May 1876*
Markham's farthest
399.5 miles from Pole

*31 Aug 1875*
Nares launches
three sledge teams

Markham
Inlet

Lake
Hazen

*11 Aug 1881*
Greely sets up Fort
Conger weather station,
with supplies for 3 years

Cape
Hecla

Joseph Henry
Cape Sheridan

Lincoln S

Floeberg
Beach

*20 May 1854*
Kane sends Hayes and Godfrey to explore
western shore in unsuccessful search for passage
to Open Polar Sea

Grinnell Land

Agassiz
Glacier

Joseph Good

Cape
Frazer

Ella
Bay

*25 Aug 1875*
*Discovery* made into
base camp. Nares
continues north in *Alert*

Discovery
Harbour

Fort
Conger

Newman Ba

*9 Sept 1883*
Trapped in ice, Greely
abandons steamer and jolly boat.
Haul their goods across ice to
Ellesmere Island but stranded on floe

*28 Sept 1883*
Greely's men escape ice floe.
They suffer starvation,
frostbite and death before
rescue by USS *Bear* in
June 1884

Camp Cla

Cape
Sabine Island

Kennedy Channel

Hall
Basin

Cape
Brevoort

Cape
Bry

1871
Hall's
burial
place

*5 Sept 1906*
Peary from New
City on Roosevelt

187

Charles Francis Hall
farthest nort

Jones Sound

Devon Island

Smith Sound

Renselaer Bay

Etah

Kane
Basin

Cape
Constitution

Washington
Land

Peabody
Bay

*9 Aug 1883*
Greely heads south
in steam launch *Lady
Greely* and 3 small boats

*July 1854*
Morton and Hendrik cut across
bay. Morton climbs cape and
sees ice-free water. This later
convinces Kane that Open Polar
Sea exists

Nyeboe Land

*12 Jun 1881*
Greely and crew of 24
from New York City
aboard steamer
*Proteus*. Picks up 2 Inuit,
Jens and Fred,
at Godhaven

*6 Sept 1853*
Blocked from
further advance,
Kane sets up base camp

Humboldt
Glacier

Natsilivik

*11 May 1855*
Kane and surviving crew
abandon ice-locked *Advance*
and drag two open boats
across ice

*30 May 1853*
Kane from New York
City aboard 144-ton
brig *Advance*, with
crew of 17. Searches
for Franklin and
passage to Open
Polar Sea

*17 June 1855*
Kane expedition reaches
open water

*27 Apr 1854*
Kane stopped by
bad weather

*June 1854*
Four of Kane's men fail to
ascend glacier. Polar bears
destroy their food depots,
so they return to ship

G

R

*29 May 1875*
Nares from
Portsmouth in
command of two
ships, *Alert* and
*Discovery*,
instructed to
sail through Kane
Basin and reach
North Pole by
ship or sledge

*11-18 Jul 1855*
Kane waits out storm

*July-Aug 1855*
Almost starved, Kane and his
men return to Upernavik

Melville
Bay

Metgorite
Island

W        E

N

S

42°

100°

75°

77°

60°

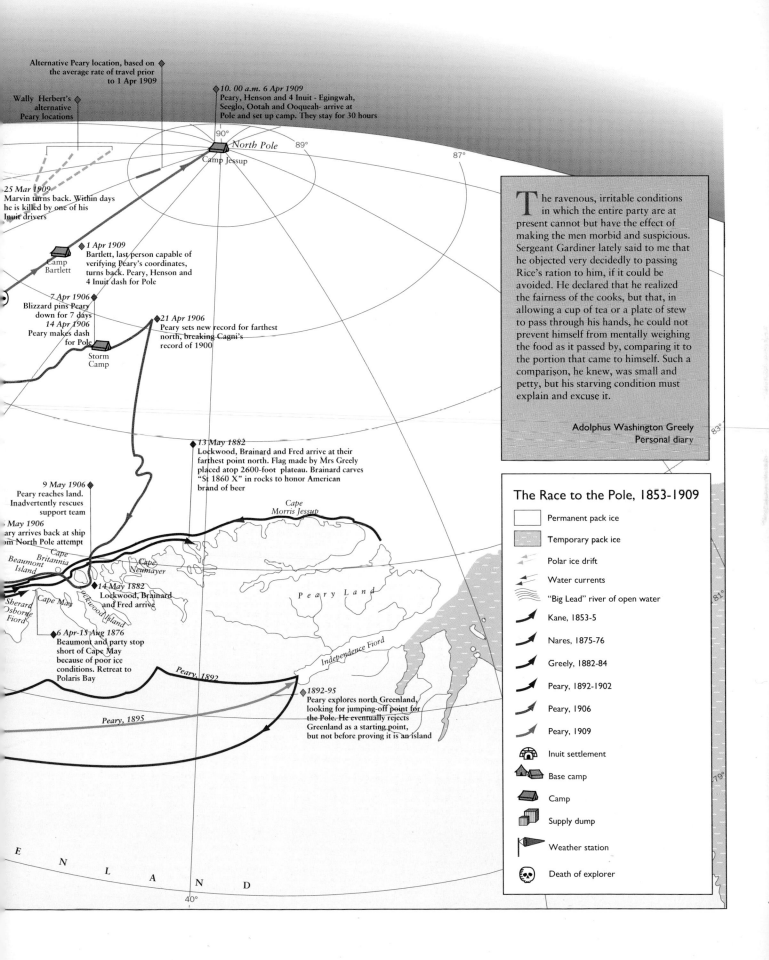

Alternative Peary location, based on
the average rate of travel prior
to 1 Apr 1909

Wally Herbert's
alternative
Peary locations

10. 00 a.m. 6 Apr 1909
Peary, Henson and 4 Inuit - Egingwah,
Seeglo, Ootah and Ooqueah- arrive at
Pole and set up camp. They stay for 30 hours

90°   North Pole   89°   87°
Camp Jessup

25 Mar 1909
Marvin turns back. Within days
he is killed by one of his
Inuit drivers

1 Apr 1909
Bartlett, last person capable of
verifying Peary's coordinates,
turns back. Peary, Henson and
4 Inuit dash for Pole

Camp
Bartlett

7 Apr 1906
Blizzard pins Peary
down for 7 days
14 Apr 1906
Peary makes dash
for Pole

21 Apr 1906
Peary sets new record for farthest
north, breaking Cagni's
record of 1900

Storm
Camp

13 May 1882
Lockwood, Brainard and Fred arrive at their
farthest point north. Flag made by Mrs Greely
placed atop 2600-foot plateau. Brainard carves
"St 1860 X" in rocks to honor American
brand of beer

9 May 1906
Peary reaches land.
Inadvertently rescues
support team

May 1906
ary arrives back at ship
m North Pole attempt

Cape
Britannia
Beaumont
Island

Cape
Neumayer

Cape
Morris Jessup

Peary Land

14 May 1882
Lockwood, Brainard
and Fred arrive

Cape May

Lockwood Island

Sherard
Osborne
Fiord

6 Apr-15 Aug 1876
Beaumont and party stop
short of Cape May
because of poor ice
conditions. Retreat to
Polaris Bay

Independence Fiord

Peary, 1892

1892-95
Peary explores north Greenland,
looking for jumping-off point for
the Pole. He eventually rejects
Greenland as a starting point,
but not before proving it is an island

Peary, 1895

83°

81°

79°

E   N   G   L   A   N   D

40°

The ravenous, irritable conditions
in which the entire party are at
present cannot but have the effect of
making the men morbid and suspicious.
Sergeant Gardiner lately said to me that
he objected very decidedly to passing
Rice's ration to him, if it could be
avoided. He declared that he realized
the fairness of the cooks, but that, in
allowing a cup of tea or a plate of stew
to pass through his hands, he could not
prevent himself from mentally weighing
the food as it passed by, comparing it to
the portion that came to himself. Such a
comparison, he knew, was small and
petty, but his starving condition must
explain and excuse it.

Adolphus Washington Greely
Personal diary

## The Race to the Pole, 1853-1909

Permanent pack ice

Temporary pack ice

Polar ice drift

Water currents

"Big Lead" river of open water

Kane, 1853-5

Nares, 1875-76

Greely, 1882-84

Peary, 1892-1902

Peary, 1906

Peary, 1909

Inuit settlement

Base camp

Camp

Supply dump

Weather station

Death of explorer

# Bibliography

GENERAL AND REFERENCE

Bakeless, John, *The Eyes of Discovery: The Pageant of North America as Seen by the First Explorers*, New York, 1950

Brebner, John B., *The Explorers of North America 1492-1806*, London, 1933

Canada, Surveys and Mapping Branch, *The National Atlas of Canada*, Ottawa, 1982

Cumming, W.P., *The Southeast in Early Maps*, 2nd ed., Chapel Hill, NC, 1962

Cumming, W.P., R.A. Skelton and D.B. Quinn, *The Discovery of North America*, London, 1971

Cumming, W.P., S.E. Hillier, D.B. Quinn and Glyndwr Williams, *The Exploration of North America 1630-1776*, London, 1974

DeVoto, Bernard, *The Course of Empire*, Boston, 1952

*Dictionary of Canadian Biography*, Vols I-XII, Toronto, 1966-90

Garrett, Wilbur, and John Garver, *National Geographic Atlas of North America: Space Age Portrait of a Continent*, Washington, D.C., 1987

Gerlach, Arch C., ed., *The National Atlas of the United States of America*, Washington, D.C., 1970

Harris, R. Cole, ed. *Historical Atlas of Canada, I: From the Beginning to 1800*, Toronto, 1988

Lewis, G. Malcolm "Indian Maps," in C.M. Judd and A.J. Ray eds., *Old Trails and New Directions: Papers of the Third North American Fur Trade Conference*, Toronto, 1980, pp. 9-23

National Geographic Society, *The World of the American Indians*, Washington, D.C., 1974.

Portinario, P., and F. Knirsch, *The Cartography of North America 1500-1800*, New York, 1987

Quinn, D.B., ed. with Alison M. Quinn and Susan Hillier, *New American World*, 5 vols., New York, 1979

Ruggles, Richard I., *A Country so Interesting: The Hudson's Bay Company and Two Centuries of Mapping 1670-1870*, Montreal and Kingston, Ont., 1991

Vorsey, Louis De, "Amerindian Contributions to the Mapping of North America," *Imago Mundi*, XXX, 1978, pp.71-78

Wheat, Carl I., *Mapping the Transmississippi West*, 5 vols., San Francisco, 1957

## Part I: A Continent on the Edge of the World

### THE ATLANTIC COASTS REVEALED

Asher, G.M., ed., *Henry Hudson the Navigator*, London, 1860

Biggar, H.P., ed., *The Voyages of Jacques Cartier*, Ottawa, 1924

Dodge, Ernest, *North-west by Sea*, New York, 1961

Ganong, W.F., ed. T.E. Layng, *Crucial Maps in the Early Cartography and Place-Nomenclature of the Atlantic Coast of Canada*, Toronto, 1964

Hoffman, Bernard G., *Cabot to Cartier: Sources for a Historical Ethnography of Northeastern North America 1497-1550*, Toronto, 1961

Markham, A.H., ed., *The Voyages and Works of John Davis*, London, 1880

Markham, C.R., ed., *The Voyages of William Baffin*, London, 1881

Morison, Samuel Eliot, *The European Discovery of America: The Northern Voyages*, New York, 1971

Neatby, Leslie H., *In Quest of the North West Passage*, London, 1958

Quinn, D.B., *England and the Discovery of America 1481-1620*, London, 1974

Quinn, D.B., *North America from Earliest Discovery to First Settlements*, New York, 1977

Sauer, Carl O., *Sixteenth Century North America: The Land and the People as Seen by the Europeans*, Berkeley and Los Angeles, 1971

Stefansson, Vilhjalmar, *The Three Voyages of Martin Frobisher*, London, 1938

Williamson, J.A., ed., *The Cabot Voyages and Bristol Discovery under Henry VII*, Cambridge, England, 1962

Wroth, Lawrence C., *The Voyages of Giovanni da Verrazzano*, New Haven, Conn. and London, 1970

### THE SPANISH BORDERLANDS

Bannon, John F., *The Spanish Borderlands Frontier 1513-1821*, Albuquerque, New Mex., 1974

Bolton, Herbert E., ed., *Spanish Explorations in the Southwest 1542-1706*, New York, 1916; reprinted 1959

Bolton, Herbert E., *Coronado: Knight of Pueblos and Plains*, Albuquerque, New Mex., 1964

Chapman, Charles E., *A History of California: The Spanish Period*, New York, 1921

Day, A. Grove, *Coronado's Quest*, Berkeley, Calif., 1940

Hallenbeck, Cleve, *Alvar Nuñez Cabeza de Vaca: The Journey and Route of the First European to Cross the Continent of North America*, Glendale, Calif., 1940

Hammond, George P., and A. Rey, eds. *Narratives of the Coronado Expedition 1540-1542*, Albuquerque, New Mex., 1940

Hammond, George P., and A. Rey, *Don Juan de Oñate, Colonizer of New Mexico 1595-1628*, Albuquerque, New Mex., 1953

Hodge, F.W., and T. H. Lewis, eds. *Spanish Explorations in the Southern United States 1528-1543*, New York, 1907; reprinted 1959

Holmes, M.G., *From New Spain by Sea to the Californias 1519-1668*, Glendale, Calif., 1963

Husdon, Charles, and Carmen Chaves Tesser, *The Forgotten Centuries: Indians and Europeans in the American South, 1521-1704*, Athens, Ga., 1992

Jones, Oakah L., *Pueblo Warriors and the Spanish Conquest*, Norman, Okla., 1966

Lowery, Woodbury, *The Spanish Settlements within the Present Limits of the United States 1513-1561*, New York, 1901

Maynard, Theodore, *De Soto and the Conquistadores*, New York, 1930

Mathes, W. Michael, *Vizcaino and Spanish Expansion in the Pacific Ocean 1580-1630*, San Francisco, 1968

Wagner, Henry R., *Spanish Voyages to the Northwest Coast of America in the Sixteenth Century*, San Francisco, 1929; reprinted 1966

Wagner, Henry R., *The Cartography of the Northwest Coast of America to the Year 1800*, Berkeley and Los Angeles, 1937

Wagner, Henry R., "Apocryphal Voyages to the Northwest Coast of America," *Proceedings of the American Antiquarian Society*, N.S., XLI, 1931, pp. 179-234

## Part II: The Opening of a Continent
RUGGED AND LABORIOUS BEGINNINGS

Barbour, Philip L., *The Three Worlds of Captain John Smith*, Boston, Mass., 1964

Barbour, Philip L., ed. *The Jamestown Voyages under the First Charter 1606-1609*, Cambridge, England, 1969

Biggar, H.P., "Jean Ribaut's Discoverye of Terra Florida," *English Historical Review*, XXXII, 1917, pp. 253-70

Biggar, H.P., ed. *Works of Samuel de Champlain*, Toronto, 1922-36

Cell, Gillian T., ed., *Newfoundland Discovered: English Attempts at Colonisation 1610-1630*, London, 1982

Hulton, Paul, ed., *America 1585: The Complete Drawings of John White*, Chapel Hill, NC, 1984

Lanctot, Gustave, *A History of Canada*, vol. I: *From its Origins to the Royal Régime 1663*, Cambridge, Mass., 1963

Lewis, Clifford M., and Albert J. Loomie, *The Spanish Jesuit Mission in Virginia 1570-1572*, Chapel Hill, NC, 1953

Lowery, Woodbury, *The Spanish Settlements within the Present Limits of the United States: Florida 1562-1574*, New York, 1911

Quinn, D.B., ed., *The Voyages and Colonizing Enterprises of Sir Humphrey Gilbert*, London, 1940

Quinn, D.B., *The Roanoke Voyages 1584-1590*, London, 1955

Quinn, D.B., *Set Fair for Roanoke: Voyages and Colonies 1584-1606*, Chapel Hill, NC, 1985

Quinn, D.B., *Explorers and Colonies: America, 1500-1625*, London, 1990. Especially pp.257-284: "The Attempted Colonization of Florida by the French, 1562-1565"; and pp.301-320, "Newfoundland in the Consciousness of Europe in the Sixteenth and Early Seventeenth Centuries"

Rowe, Frederick W., *A History of Newfoundland and Labrador*, Toronto, 1980

Trudel, Marcel, *The Beginnings of New France 1524-1663*, Toronto, 1973

THE QUEST FOR THE WESTERN SEA

Adams, Arthur T., *The Explorations of Pierre Esprit Radisson*, Minneapolis, Minn., 1961

Biggar, H.P., ed., *Works of Samuel de Champlain*, Toronto, 1922-36

Burpee, L.J. *The Search for the Western Sea*, Toronto, 1935

Delanglez, Jean, *Life and Voyages of Louis Jolliet*, Chicago, 1948

Doughty, A.G., and Chester Martin, eds., *The Kelsey Papers*, Ottawa, 1929

Eccles, W.J., *The Canadian Frontier 1534-1760*, New York, 1969

Hamilton, N. Raphael, *Marquette's Explorations: The Narratives Reexamined* Madison, Wisc., 1970

Heidenreich, Conrad E., *Explorations and Mapping of Samuel de Champlain 1603-32*, Monograph no. 17, *Cartographica*, 1976

Nute, G.L., *Caesars of the Wilderness: Médart Chouart, Sieur des Groseilliers and Pierre Esprit Radisson 1618-1710*, New York, 1943

Kellogg, Louise P., ed., *Early Narratives of the Northwest 1634-1699*, New York, 1917; reprinted 1959

Rich, E.E., *The Fur Trade and the Northwest to 1857*, Toronto, 1967

Severin, Timothy, *Explorers of the Mississippi*, London, 1967

Thwaites, Reuben G., ed., *The Jesuit Relations and Allied Documents*, Cleveland, 1896-1901

## Part III: Expanding Frontiers
TO THE MOUNTAINS AND BEYOND

Alvord, Clarence W., and Lee Bidgood, *The First Explorations of the Trans-Allegheny Region 1650-1674*, Cleveland, 1912

Bailey, Kenneth P., "Christopher Gist and the Trans-Allegheny Frontier," *Pacific Historical Review*, XIV, 1945

Bakeless, John, *Daniel Boone*, New York, 1939

Billington, Ray Allen, *Westward Expansion: A History of the American Frontier*, 2nd ed., New York, 1960

Boyd, William K., ed., *William Byrd's Histories of the Dividing Line*, Raleigh, N.C., 1929

Brown, Lloyd A., *Early Maps of the Ohio Valley*, Pittsburgh, 1959

Corkran, David H., *The Creek Frontier 1540-1783*, Norman, Okla., 1967

Crane, Verner W., *The Southern Frontier 1670-1732*, Ann Arbor, Mich., 1929; reprinted 1956

Cumming, William P., ed., *The Discoveries of John Lederer*, Charlottesville, Va. 1958

Cumming, William P., *The Southeast in Early Maps*, 2nd ed. Chapel Hill, NC, 1962

Darlington, William M., ed., *Christopher Gist's Journals*, Pittsburgh, 1893

Gehring, Charles T., and William A. Starna, eds., *A Journey into Mohawk and Oneida Country 1634-35: The Journal of Harmen Meyndertz van den Bogaert*, Syracuse, NY, 1988

Jameson, J.F., ed., *Narratives of New Netherland 1609-1664*, New York, 1909; reprinted 1959

Johnston, J. Stoddard, ed., *First Explorations of Kentucky*, Louisville, 1898

Lawson, John, ( ed. Hugh Lefler), *A New Voyage to Carolina*, Chapel Hill, NC, 1967

Leach, Douglas, *The Northern Colonial Frontier 1607-1763*, New York, 1966

Moore, Alexander, ed., *Nairne's Muskhogean Journals: The 1708 Expedition to the Mississippi River*, Jackson, Miss., 1988

Parker, John. ed., *The Journals of Jonathan Carver and Related Documents 1766-1770*, St Paul, Minn., 1976

Savage, Henry, *Discovering America 1700-1875*, New York, 1979

Thwaites, R.G., ed., *Early Western Travels 1748-1764*, vol. I [Weiser and Croghan] , Cleveland, Ohio, 1904

Wood, Peter H., *et al*, *Powhatan's Mantle*, Lincoln, Neb., 1989. Especially pp. 6-20: Helen H. Tanner, "The Land and Water Communication System of the Southeastern Indians" and pp. 292-343: Gregory A. Waselkov, "Indian maps of the Colonial Southeast"

THE TRANS-MISSISSIPPI WEST

Bannon, John Francis, *The Spanish Borderlands Frontier 1513-1821*, Albuquerque, New Mex., 1970

Burpee, L.J., ed., *Journals and Letters of Pierre Gaultier de Varennes de la Vérendrye and his Sons*, Toronto, 1927

Caruso, John A., *The Mississippi Valley Frontier: The Age of French Exploration and Settlement*, New York, 1966

Crouse, Nellis M., *Lemoyne d'Iberville: Soldier of New France*, Ithaca, NY, 1954

French, B.F., ed., *Historical Collections of Louisiana and Florida*, New York, 1846-53. See vol. I (1846) for explorations of Joutel, Tonty; vol. III (1851) for explorations of La Harpe, Le Sueur, du Tisné

Galloway, Patricia K., ed., *La Salle and his Legacy: Frenchmen and Indians in the Lower Mississippi Valley* , Jackson, Miss. 1982

Hamilton, Raphael N., "The Early Cartography of the Missouri Valley," *American Historical Review*, vol. 39, 1934, pp. 645-62

Hoffman, F.L., ed., *Diary of the Alarcón Expedition into Texas 1718-1719*, Los

Angeles, 1935

Luebke, Frederick C., *et al, Mapping the North American Plains*, Norman, Okla., 1987. Especially ch. 2: Raymond Wood, "Mapping the Missouri River through the Great Plains, 1673-1895"; and ch. 4: G. Malcolm Lewis, "Indian Maps: Their Place in the History of Plains Cartography"

Margry, Pierre, ed., *Découvertes et Établissements des Français dans l'Ouest et dans le Sud de l'Amérique 1614-1754*, Paris, 1879-88. See vol VI, pp.455ff. for abridged journal of Pierre and Paul Mallet, 1739-40

Murphy, E.R., *Henry de Tonty: Fur Trader of the Mississippi*, Baltimore, Md., 1941

Nasatir, A.P., ed., *Before Lewis and Clark: Documents Illustrating the History of the Missouri 1785-1904*, St Louis, Mo., 1952

Norall, Frank, *Bourgmont: Explorer of the Missouri 1698-1725*, Lincoln, Neb., 1989

Pelletier, Monique, "Exploration and Colonisation of Louisiana," *Map Collector*, no. 24, 1983

Reinhartz, Dennis and Colley, Charles C., eds., *The Mapping of the American Southwest*, College Station, Tex., 1987. Especially: David Buisseret, "Spanish and French Mapping of the Gulf of Mexico in the Sixteenth and Seventeenth Centuries"

Weddle, Robert S., *Wilderness Manhunt: The Spanish Search for La Salle*, Austin, Tex., 1973

Weddle, Robert S., ed., *La Salle, the Mississippi and the Gulf*, 1987

Wood, Peter H., "La Salle: Discovery of a Lost Explorer," *American Historical Review*, 89, 1984, pp. 294-323

## Part IV: Ocean to Ocean

THE NORTHERN FUR TRADE

Bliss, Michael, "Conducted Tour," *The Beaver*, vol. 69, 1989, pp.16-24. Alexander Mackenzie's Journey to the Arctic Ocean, 1789

Burpee, L.J., ed., *Journals and Letters of Pierre Gaultier de Varennes de la Vérendrye and his Sons*, Toronto, 1927

Burpee, L.J., ed., "York Factory to the Blackfeet Country," The Journal of Anthony Hendry (Henday) 1754-55, *Proceedings of the Royal Society of Canada*, 3rd series, vol. I, 1907

Burpee, L.J., ed., "An Adventurer from Hudson Bay," The Journal of Matthew Cocking from York Factory to the Blackfeet Country 1772-73, *Proceedings of the Royal Society of Canada*, 3rd series, vol. 2, 1908

Eccles, W.J., *Essays on New France*, Toronto, 1987. Especially pp.50-60: "New

France and the Western Frontier"; and pp. 96-109: "La Mer de l'Ouest: Outpost of Empire"

Glover, Richard, ed., *A Journey from Prince of Wales's Fort in Hudson's Bay to the Northern Ocean... by Samuel Hearne*, Toronto, 1958

Glover, Richard, ed., *David Thompson's Narrative 1784-1812*, Toronto, 1962

Helm, June, "Mattonabbee's Map," *Arctic Anthropology*, 26, 1989, pp. 28-47

Lamb, W. Kaye, ed., *The Letters and Journals of Simon Fraser 1806-1808*, Toronto, 1960

Lamb, W. Kaye, ed., *The Journals and Letters of Sir Alexander Mackenzie*, Cambridge, England, 1970

Lewis, G. Malcolm, "La Grande Rivière et Fleuve de l'Ouest/ The Realities and Reasons behind a Major Mistake in the 18th-Century Geography of North America," *Cartographica*, vol. 28, 1991, pp. 54-87

MacGregor, James G., *Peter Fidler: Canada's Forgotten Surveyor 1769-1822*, Toronto, 1966

Morse, Eric W., *Fur Trade Canoe Routes of Canada*, Ottawa, 1969

Pentland, David H., "Cartographic Concepts of the Northern Algonquian Indians," *The Canadian Cartographer*, XII, 1975, pp. 149-160

Rich, E.E., *The Fur Trade and the Northwest to 1857*, Toronto, 1967

Ross, Eric, *Beyond the River and the Bay*, Toronto, 1970

Tyrrell, J.B., ed., *The Journals of Samuel Hearne and Philip Turnor*, Toronto, 1934

Wagner, Henry R., *Peter Pond, Fur Tracer and Explorer*, New Haven, Conn., 1955

Williams, Glyndwr, *The British Search for the Northwest Passage in the Eighteenth Century*, London, 1962

Williams, Glyndwr, "Captain Coats and the East Main," *The Beaver*, Winter 1963, pp. 4-13

Williams, Glyndwr, "The Puzzle of Anthony Henday's Journal" 1754-55, *The Beaver*, Winter 1978, pp. 40-56

THE PACIFIC NORTHWEST

Beaglehole, J.C., ed., *The Journals of Captain James Cook on his Voyages of Discovery: The Voyage of the* Resolution *and* Discovery *1776-1780*, Cambridge, England, 1967

Beals, Herbert K., ed., *For Honor and Country: The Diary of Bruno de Hezeta*, Portland, Ore., 1985

Beals, Herbert K., ed., *Juan Pérez on the Northwest Coast*, Portland, Ore., 1989

Bolton, Herbert E., ed., *Kino's Historical

Memoir 1683-1711*, Cleveland, Ohio, 1919

Bolton, Herbert E., ed., *Anza's California Expeditions*, Berkeley, Calif., 1930

Bolton, Herbert E., *Pageant in the Wilderness: The Story of the Escalante Expedition to the Interior Basin 1776*, Salt Lake City, Utah, 1950

Cook, Warren L., *Flood Tide of Empire: Spain and the Pacific Northwest 1543-1819*, New Haven, Conn., 1973

Cutter, Donald C., *Malaspina & Galiano: Spanish Voyages to the Northwest Coast 1791 & 1792*, Vancouver, 1991

Fisher, Raymond H., *Bering's Voyages: Whither and Why*, Seattle, Wash., 1977

Fisher, Robin, *Vancouver's Voyage: Charting the Northwest Coast 1791-1795*, Vancouver, 1992

Fisher, Robin, and Hugh Johnston, eds., *Captain James Cook and His Times*, Vancouver, 1979. Especially pp.59-80: Glyndwr Williams, "Myth and Reality: James Cook and the Theoretical Geography of Northwest America;" and pp.99-120, Christon I. Archer, "The Spanish Reaction to Cook's Third Voyage"

Galvin, John, ed., *The First Spanish Entry into San Francisco Bay 1775*, San Francisco, 1971

Golder, Frank A., ed., *Bering's Voyages*, New York, 1925

Inglis, Robin, ed., *Spain and the Pacific Northwest Coast*, Vancouver, 1992

Kendrick, John, ed., *The Voyage of Sutil and Mexicana 1792: The Last Spanish Exploration of the Northwest Coast of America*, Spokane, Wash., 1991

Lamb, W. Kaye, ed., *The Voyage of George Vancouver 1791-1795*, London, 1984

Leighly, J.L., *California as an Island*, San Francisco, 1972

Masterton, James R., and Helen Brower, *Bering's Successors 1745-1780*, Seattle, Wash., 1948

Shalkop, Antoinette, ed., *Exploration in Alaska*, Anchorage, Alas., 1980

Wagner, Henry R., *A Cartography of the Northwest Coast of America to the Year 1800*, Berkeley, Calif., 1937

JEFFERSONIAN PATHFINDERS

Allen, John Logan, *Passage through the Garden: Lewis and Clark and the Image of the American West*, Urbana, Ill., 1974

Banda, Eldon, ed., *The Handbook of Texas*, vol. 3, Austin, Tex., 1952

Bannon, John Francis, *The Spanish Borderlands Frontier 1513-1821*, Albuquerque, New Mex., 1974

Beck, Warren A., and Inez D. Haase, *Historical Atlas of the American West*,

Norman, Okla., 1959

Benson, Maxine, ed., *From Pittsburgh to the Rocky Mountains: Major Stephen Long's Expedition 1819-1820*, Golden, Colo., 1988

Bolton, Herbert Eugene, *Spanish Exploration in the Southwest 1542-1706*, New York, 1916

Bradbury, John, *Travels in the Interior of America in the Years 1809, 1810, and 1811*, Lincoln, Neb., 1986

Coues, Elliott, ed., *The Expeditions of Zebulon Montgomery Pike*, 2 vols., 1895; reprinted New York, 1987

Coues, Elliott, *The Manuscript Journals of Alexander Henry and of David Thompson, 1799-1814*, 2 vols., New York, 1897; reprinted Minneapolis, Minn., 1965

Ferris, Robert, ed., *Lewis and Clark: Historic Places Associated with their Transcontinental Exploration*, Washington, D.C., 1975

Gass, Patrick, *Journals of the Voyages and Travels of a Corps of Discovery under the Command of Capt. Lewis and Capt. Clarke of the Army of the United States*, Philadelphia, 1911

Goetzmann, William H., *Exploration and Empire: The Explorer and the Scientist in the Winning of the American West*, New York, 1967

Irving, Washington, *Astoria or Enterprise Beyond the Rocky Mountains*, 3 vols., London, 1836

Jackson, Donald, ed., *The Journals of Zebulon Montgomery Pike*, 2 vols., Norman, Okla., 1966

John, Elizabeth, A.H., *Storms Brewed in Other Men's Worlds: The Confrontation of Indians, Spanish, and French in the Southwest 1540-1795*, Lincoln, Neb., 1975

Loomis, Noel M., and Abraham P. Nasatir, *Pedro Vial and the Roads to Santa Fé*, Norman, Okla., 1967

Moulton, Gary, ed., *The Journals of Lewis and Clark*, 7 vols., Lincoln, Neb., 1983-91. Especially vol. I: *Atlas of the Lewis and Clark Expedition*

Nasatir, A.B., *Before Lewis and Clark*, 2 vols. n.d., reprinted Lincoln, Neb., 1990

Nasatir, A.B., ed., *Three Years among the Indians and Mexicans*, Philadelphia, 1962

Newcomb, W.W., *The Indians of Texas*, Austin, Tex., 1961; revised ed. 1990

Pike, Zebulon, *An Account of Expeditions to the Sources of the Mississippi and through the Western Parts of Louisiana to the Sources of the Arkansaw, Kans, La Platte, and Pierre Juan Rivers, Performed by Order of the Government of the United States During the Years 1805, 1806, and 1807, and a Tour Through the Interior Parts of New Spain when Conducted through their Provinces by Order of the Captain-General in the year 1807*, Philadelphia, 1810

Rollins, Phillip Ashton, ed., *The Discovery of the Oregon Trail: Robert Stuart's Narrative of his Overland Trip Eastward from Astoria in 1812-13*, New York, 1935

Ronda, James, *Astoria and Empire*, Lincoln, Neb., 1990

Ronda, James, *Lewis and Clark among the Indians*, Lincoln, Neb., 1988

Wagner, Henry R., Charles Camp and Robert Becker, *The Plains and the Rockies: A Critical Bibliography of Exploration, Adventure and Travel in the American West 1800-1865*, San Francisco, 1982

Webb, Walter, ed., *The Handbook of Texas*, 2 vols., Austin, Tex., 1952

Weber, David, ed., *Albert Pike: Prose Sketches and Poems Written in the Western Country*, College Station, Tex., 1987

Wheat, Carl I., *Mapping the Transmississippi West*, 6 vols., San Francisco, 1960

FUR TRADE AND EMPIRES

Batman, Richard, *James Pattie's West: The Dream and the Reality*, Norman, Okla., 1984

Brooks, George R., ed., *The Southwest Expeditions of Jedediah S. Smith: His Personal Account of the Journey to California 1826-1827*, Lincoln, Neb., 1989

Camp, Charles L., ed., *James Clyman, Frontiersman*, Portland, Ore., 1960

Chittenden, Hiram M., *A History of the Fur Trade of the Far West*, 2 vols., New York, 1902; reprinted Stanford, Calif., 1954

Cline, Gloria G., *Peter Skene Ogden and the Hudson's Bay Co.*, Norman, Okla., 1974

Cline, Gloria G., *Exploring the Great Basin*, Norman, Okla., 1963

Clokey, Richard M., *William H. Ashley: Enterprise and Politics in the Trans-Mississippi West*, Norman, Okla., 1980

Dale, Harrison C., ed., *The Ashley-Smith Explorations and the Discovery of a Central Route to the Pacific*, California, 1941

Flores, Dan L., ed., *Journal of an Indian Trader: Anthony Glass and the Texas Trading Frontier, 1790-1818*, College Station, Tex., 1985

Gilbert, Bill, *Westering Man: The Life of Joseph Walker*, Norman, Okla., 1983

Goetzmann, William H., *The Mountain Man*, New York, 1978

Goetzmann, William H., ed., James Ohio Pattie and Timothy Flint, *The Personal Narrative of James Ohio Pattie*, 1905; reprinted Lincoln, Neb., 1984

Guild, Thelma S., and Harvey L. Carter, *Kit Carson: A Pattern for Heroes*, Lincoln, Neb., 1984

Hafen, Leroy R., *Mountain Men and the Fur Trade of the Far West*, 10 vols. Especially vols. 6 and 8, 1965

Harris, Burton, *The Original History of John Colter: His Years in the Rocky Mountains*, New York, 1952; reprinted Basin, Wyo., 1977

Irving, Washington, *The Adventures of Captain Bonneville, U.S.A., in the Rocky Mountains and the Far West*, 2 vols., New York, 1849

Loomis, Noel M., and Abraham P. Nasatir, *Pedro Vial and the Roads to Santa Fé*, Norman, Okla., 1967

Morgan, Dale L., *Jedediah Smith and the Opening of the West*, Indianapolis, Ind., 1953; reprinted Lincoln, Neb., 1964

Newman, Peter C., *Caesars of the Wilderness*, 3 vols., Markham, Ont., 1985; especially vol. 2

Oglesby, Richard, *Manuel Lisa and the Opening of the Missouri Fur Trade*, Norman, Okla., 1963

Quaife, Milo M., ed., *Kit Carson's Autobiography*, Lincoln, Neb., 1966

Sullivan, Maurice, ed., *The Travels of Jedediah Smith*, Santa Ana, Calif., 1934

*The Trail Blazers*, New York, Time-Life Books, 1973

Todd, Edgeley W., ed., *The Adventures of Captain Bonneville*, Norman, Okla. 1961

Townsend, John K., *Across the Rockies to the Columbia*, Philadelphia, 1839; reprinted Lincoln, Neb., 1963

Vestal, Stanley, *Joe Meek: The Merry Mountain Man*, Lincoln, Neb., 1963

Webber, David J., ed., David H. Coyner, *The Lost Trappers: A Collection of Interesting Scenes and Events in the Rocky Mountains*, Norman, Okla., 1970

Webber, David J., *The Taos Trappers*, Norman, Okla., 1968

THE GREAT RECONNAISSANCE

Abbott, Henry L., " Report upon Explorations for a Railroad Route from the Sacramento Valley to the Columbia River," *Pacific Railroad Reports*, vol. 6

Bender, Averam B., "Government Explorations in the Territory of New Mexico, 1846-1859," *New Mexico Historical Review*, vol. IX, 1934, pp. 12-13

Bender, Averam B., "Opening Routes across West Texas, 1848-1850," *Southwestern Historical Quarterly*, vol. XXXVII, 1933-34, p.119

Brandon, William, *The Men and the Mountain*, New York, 1955

Carvalho, S.N., *Incidents of Travel and Adventure in the Far West with Colonel Frémont's Last Expedition*, Philadelphia, 1954

Cooke, Philip St George, W.H.C. Whiting and Francis X. Aubrey, *Exploring Southwestern Trails 1846-1854*, Glendale, Calif., 1938

Emory, William H., "Notes of a Military Reconnaissance from Fort Leavenworth in Missouri to San Diego in California, Including Parts of the Arkansas, Del Norte, and Gila Rivers," 30th Cong., 1st sess., *Sen. Exec. Doc. 7*, 1848

Emory, William H., "Report on the United States and Mexican Boundary Survey," 34th Cong., 1st sess., *H.R. Exec. Doc. 135*, 1857

Frémont, John C., *Memoirs of My Life*, Chicago and New York, 1887

Frémont, John C., *Report of the Exploring Expedition to the Rocky Mountains in the Year 1842, and to Oregon and California in the years 1843-44*, Buffalo, NY, 1851

Frémont, John C., *Report on an Exploration of the Country Lying between the Missouri River and the Rocky mountains on the line of the Kansas and Great Platte Rivers*, Buffalo, NY, 1851

Garber, Paul N., *The Gadsden Treaty*, Philadelphia, 1923, pp. 11-12

Garrard, Lewis H., *Wah-to-yah and the Taos Trail*, Norman, Okla. 1955

Goetzmann, William H., *Army Exploration in the American West, 1803-1863*, New Haven, Conn., 1959

Goetzmann, William H., *Exploration and Empire: The Explorer and the Scientist in the Winning of the American West*, New York, 1967

Goetzmann, William H., *Exploring the American West 1803-1879*, Washington, D.C., 1982

Goetzmann, William H., *New Lands, New Men: America and the Second Great Age of Discovery*, New York, 1986

Gudde, Erwin G., and Elisabeth K. Gudde, eds., *Exploring with Frémont*, Norman, Okla.,1958

Hafen, Le Roy, *Frémont's Fourth Expedition*, 1960

Harney, W.H., "Report of the Battle of Blue Water," 34th Cong., 1st sess., *H.R. Exec. Doc. I*, 1855-56

Henry, John Frazier, *Early Maritime Artists of the Pacific Northwest Coast, 1741-1841*, Seattle, Wash., 1984

Hine, Robert, *Edward Kern and American Expansion*, New Haven, Conn., 1962

Humphreys, A.A., and G.K. Warren, "An Examination by Direction of the Hon. Jefferson Davis, Sec. of War of the Reports of Explorations for Railroad Routes from the Mississippi to the Pacific, made under the Orders of the War Department in 1853-54...," 33rd Cong., 1st sess., *H.R. Exec, Doc. 129*, 1855

Humphreys, Col. Andrew A., "Report of the Office of the Pacific Railroad Explorations and Surveys, Nov. 29, 1856," 34th Cong., 3rd sess., *H.R. Exec. Doc. I*, 1856-57, p. 212

Ives, Lt. J.C. "Report upon the Colorado River of the West," 36th Cong., 1st sess., *H.R. Exec. Doc., 90*, 1861

Jackson, Donald, and Mary Lee Spence, eds., *The Expeditions of John Charles Frémont*, 3 vols., Urbana, Ill., 1970

Kearny, Stephen W., "Report of a Summer Campaign to the Rocky Mountains...in 1845," 29th Cong., 1st sess., *Sen. Exec. Doc. I*, 1846, pp.221ff.

Macomb, Capt. John, *Report of the Exploring Expedition from Santa Fé, New mexico, to the Junction of the Green and Grand Rivers of the Great Colorado of the West in 1859*, Washington, D.C., US Engineer Dept., 1876

Madsen, Brigham D., ed., *Exploring the Great Salt Lake: The Stansbury Expedition of 1949-50*, Salt Lake City, Utah, 1989

Marcy, Capt. Randolph B., and Capt. George McClellan,*Exploration of the Red River of Louisiana in the Year 1852*, Washington, D.C., 1853

Marcy, Randolph B., "Report of a Route from Fort Smith to Santa Fé," 31st Cong., 1st sess., *Sen. Exec. Doc. 64*, 1850

Möllhausen, Baldwin, *Diary of a Journey from the Mississippi to the Coasts of the Pacific with a United States Government Expedition*, trans. Mrs Percy Sinnett, 2 vols., London, 1858

Mullan, John, "Report and Map of Capt. John Mullan, United States Army, of his Operations while Engaged in the Construction of a Military Road from Fort Walla Walla, on the Columbia River, to Fort Benton, on the Missouri River," 37th Cong., 3rd sess., *Sen. Exec. Doc., 43*, 1863

Mumey, Nolie, *John Williams Gunnison*, Denver, Colo., 1955

Preuss, Charles, *Topographical map of the Road from Missouri to Oregon... in VII Sections... from the Field Notes and Journal of Captain John C. Frémont*, Washington, D.C., 1846

Raynolds, William F., "Report on the Exploration of the Yellowstone and the Country drained by that River," 40th Cong., 2nd sess., *Sen. Exec. Doc. 77*, 1868

Reinhartz, Dennis, and Charles C. Colley, *The Mapping of the American Southwest*, College Station, Tex., 1987

*Reports of Explorations and Surveys to Ascertain the Most Practicable and Economical Route for a Railroad from the Mississippi River to the Pacific Ocean*, 12 vols. in 13, Washington, D.C., 1855-1861

Rolle, Andrew, *John Charles Frémont: Character as Destiny*, Norman, Okla., 1991

Savage, Henry,*Discovering America 1700-1875*, New York, 1979

Settle, Raymond W., ed., *The March of the Mounted Riflemen from Fort Leavenworth to Fort Vancouver, May to October, 1849*, Lincoln, Neb., 1989

Simpson, J.H., "Journal of a Military Reconnaissance from Santa Fé, New Mexico to the Navajo Country Made with the Troops under Command of Brevet Lieutenant Colonel John M. Washington, Chief of the Ninth Military Department and Governor of New Mexico," 31st Cong., 1st sess., *Sen. Exec. Doc. 64*, 1850, pp. 55-168

Simpson, James H., "Report and Map of the Route from Fort Smith, Arkansas, to Santa Fé, New Mexico," 31st Cong., 1st sess., *Sen. Exec. Doc. 12*, 1850

Simpson, James H., *Report of Explorations Across the Great Basin of the Territory of Utah for a Direct Wagon-Route from Camp Floyd to Genoa, in Carson Valley in 1859*, Washington, D.C., 1876

Sitgreaves, Lorenzo, "Report of an Expedition down to the Zuñi and Colorado Rivers," 32nd Cong., 2nd sess., *Sen. Exec. Doc. 59*, 1853

Smith, W.F., "Report... of Routes from San Antonio to El Paso," 31st Cong., 1st sess., *Sen. Exec. Doc. 64*, 1850

Stansbury, Capt. Howard, *Exploration and Survey of the Valley of the Great Salt Lake of Utah*, Philadelphia, 1852

Warren, G.K., "Explorations in the Dacota Country in the Year 1855," 34th Cong., 1st sess., *Sen Exec. Doc. 76*, 1856

Warren, G.K., "Journal," Warren Papers, MS, New York State Library, Albany, NY

Warren, G.K. *Preliminary Report of Explorations in Nebraska and Dakota in the Years 1855-56-57*, Washington, D.C., 1875

Williamson, Robert S., "Report of a Reconnaissance of a Route through the Sierra Nevadas by the Upper Sacramento," 31st Cong., 1st sess., pt. II, *Sen. Exec. Doc. 47*, 1849-50, p.17

Williamson, Robert S., "Report of

Exploration in California for Railroad Routes to Connect with the Routes near the 35th and 32nd Parallels of North Latitude," *Pacific Railroad Reports*, vol. V, pp. 41-43

Woodhouse, Dr S.W., "Journals," MS, Philadelphia Academy of Natural Sciences

Ylarrequi, José S., *Datos de los trabjos astronomicos y topograficos dispuestos en forma de diario...*, Mexico, 1850, p.12. See also "Diario del Genl. Pedro Garcia Conde sobre los limites de las dos California... En relacion con los trabjos astronomicos y topograficos," MS, Archives del Ministerio de Relaciones Exteriores, Mexico City

THE GREAT SURVEYS

Bartlett, Richard A., *Great Surveys of the American West*, Norman, Okla., 1962

Dutton, Clarence E., *The Tertiary History of the Grand Cañon District with Atlas*, Washington, D.C., 1851; facsimile reprint, Santa Barbara and Salt Lake City, 1977

Goetzmann, William H., *Exploration and Empire: The Explorer and the Scientist in the Winning of the American West*, New York, 1967

Haines, Aubrey L., *The Yellowstone Story: A History of Our First National Park*, 2 vols., Yellowstone Library and Museum Association, 1977

Hayden, Ferdinand V., *Annual Reports of the US Geological and Geographical Survey of the Territory*, 12 vols, Washington, D.C., 1867-78

Jones, Capt. William A., *Report upon the Reconnaissance of Northwestern Wyoming including Yellowstone National Park, Made in the Summer of 1873*, Washington, D.C., 1875

King, Clarence, *Systematic Geology*, Washington, D.C., 1878

Powell, John W., *Report on the Lands of the Arid Regions of the United States*, Washington, D.C., 1878; reprinted New York, 1961

Powell, John W., *The Report of the Colorado River and its Canyons*, 1895; reprinted 1967

Schmeckebier, Lawrence F., *Catalogue and Index of the Publications of the Hayden, King, Powell and Wheeler Surveys*, Washington, D.C., 1904

Stegner, Wallace, *Beyond the Hundredth Meridian: John Wesley Powell and the Second Opening of the West*, Boston, 1953

Wheat, Carl I., and Dale L. Moran, *Jedediah Smith and his Maps of the American West*, San Francisco, Calif., 1954

Wheeler, Lt. George M., *Preliminary Report: Exploration in Nevada and Arizona*, Washington, D.C., 1871

Wheeler, Lt. George M., *US Geographical Surveys West of the 100th Meridian: Reports*, 7 vols., Washington, D.C., 1876-1879

Wilkins, Thurman, *Clarence King: A Biography*, Albuquerque, New Mex., 1988, revised and enlarged edition

**Part V: The Far North**

TO THE TOP OF THE CONTINENT

Allen, Henry T., *Report of an Expedition to the Copper, Tanana and Koyukuk Rivers in the Territory of Alaska in the Year 1885*, Washington, D.C., 1887

Back, Sir George, *Narrative of the Arctic Land Expedition to the Mouth of the Great Fish River...*, London, 1836

Bernier, Capt. J.E., *Report on the Dominion of Canada Government Expedition to the Arctic Islands and Hudson Strait on Board the DGS* Arctic, Ottawa, 1910

Berton, Pierre, *Klondike Fever*, Toronto, 1972, revised edition

Berton, Pierre, *The Arctic Grail: The Quest for the North West Passage and the North Pole*, New York, 1988

Cameron, Ian, *To the Farthest Ends of the Earth, 150 Years of World Exploration by the Royal Geographical Society*, New York, 1980

Chauncey, C. Loomis, *Weird and Tragic Shores: The Story of Charles Francis Hall, Explorer*, New York, 1971

Chevigny, Hector, *Russian America: The Great Alaskan Venture, 1741-1867*, New York, 1965

Cooke, Alan, and Clive Holland, *The Exploration of Northern Canada 500-1920: A Chronology*, Toronto, 1978

Corner, George W., *Doctor Kane of the Arctic Seas*, Philadelphia, 1972

Dall, William Healy, *Alaska and its Resources*, Boston, Mass., 1870

Dawson, George M., *Report on an Exploration on the Yukon District, N.W.T. and Adjacent Northern Portion of British Columbia*, Ottawa, 1898

Fairley, T.C., ed., *Sverdrup's Arctic Adventures*, 1959

Federova, Svetlana G., *The Russian Population in Alaska and California, Late 18th Century - 1867*, Kingston, Ont., 1973

Gibson, James R., *Imperial Russia in Frontier America*, New York, 1976

Gutteridge, Leonard F., *Icebound: The Jeanette Expedition's Quest for the North Pole*, Annapolis, Md., 1986

Herschel, Sir John F.W., ed., *Admiralty Manual of Scientific Enquiry*, London, 1851; reprinted Kent, England, 1974

Hind, Henry Youle, *Narrative of the*

*Canadian Red River Exploring Expedition of 1857 and of the Assiniboin and Saskatchewan Exploring Expedition of 1858*, Edmonton, Alb., 1971

Kane, Elisha Kent, *Artcic Explorations in the years 1853, '54, '55*, 2 vols., Philadelphia, 1856

Karamanski, Theodore J., *Fur Trade and Exploration: Opening the Far Northwest, 1821-1852*, Norman, Okla., 1983

Lopez, Barry, *Arctic Dreams*, New York, 1986

Mirsky, Jeanette, *To the Arctic: The Story of Northern Exploration from Earliest Times to the Present*, 2 vols in 1, Edmonton, Alb., 1971

Muir, John, *Travels in Alaska*, New York, 1915

Neatby, L.H., *Conquest of the Last Frontier*, Toronto, 1966

Neatby, L.H., *In Quest of the Northwest Passage*, New York, 1958; reprinted 1962

Newman, Peter C., *Caesars of the Wilderness: The Story of the Hudson's Bay Co.*, 2 vols. Markham, Ont., 1985

Peary, Robert E., *The North Pole: Its Discovery in 1909 under the Auspices of the Peary Arctic Club*, New York, 1910; reprinted 1986

Schwatka, Frederick, *Along Alaska's Great River*, London 1883

Schwatka, Frederick, *Compilation of Narratives of Exploration in Alaska*, Washington, D.C., 1900

Sherwood, Morgan B., *The Exploration of Alaska, 1865-1900*, New Haven, Conn., 1965

Smith, Barbara Sweetland, and Redmond J. Barnett, eds., *Russian America: The Forgotten Frontier*, Tacoma, Wash., 1990

Spry, Irene M., *The Palliser Expedition: An Account of John Palliser's British North America Expedition 1857-60*, Toronto, 1963

Spry, Irene M., ed., *The Papers of the Palliser Expedition, 1857-1860*, Toronto, 1968

Stanley, George F.G., ed., *John Henry Lefroy, in Search of the Magnetic North*, Toronto, 1955

Starr, S. Frederick, ed., *Russia's American Colony*, Durham, NC, 1987

Stefansson, Vilhjalmur, *The Friendly Arctic: The Story of Five Years in Polar Regions*, New York, 1925

Thompson, David, ed., *Joseph Burr Tyrrell: A Narrative of his Explorations*, n.d.

Thomson, Don W., *Man and Meridians: The History of Surveying and Mapping in Canada*, 2 vols., Ottawa, 1966

Tikhmenev, P.A., *A History of the Russian-American Company*, trans. and ed. by R.A.

Pierce and A.S. Donnelly, Seattle, Wash.,
   1978
Tomkins, Stuart R., *Alaska: Promyshlennik
   and Sourdough*, Norman, Okla., 1945
Van Stone, James W., ed., *Russian
   Exploration in Southwest Alaska: The
   Travel Journals of Petr Korsakovskiy
   (1818) and Ivan Ya. Vasilev (1829)*,
   Fairbanks, Alas., 1988
Webb, Melody, *The Last Frontier: A History
   of the Yukon Basin of Canada and Alaska*,
   Albuquerque, New Mex., 1985
Weems, John E., *Peary: The Explorer and the
   Man*, New York, 1967
Wilson, Clifford A., *Campbell of the Yukon*,
   Toronto, 1970
Wright, Allen A., *Prelude to Bonanza: The
   Discovery and Exploration of the Yukon*,
   Victoria, 1976
Wright, Theon, *The Big Nail: The Story of
   the Cook-Peary Feud*, New York, 1970
Zaslow, Morris, *The Northward Expansion
   of Canada, 1914-1967*, vol. 17, *The
   Canadian Centenary Series*, Toronto, 1988
Zaslow, Morris, *The Opening of the
   Canadian North, 1870-1914*, vol. 16, *The
   Canadian Centenary Series*, Toronto, 1971

# Index

The index includes only those places which are annotated on the maps, have a keyed symbol, or are mentioned in the text. Names added for locational purposes are not indexed. Variant spellings are given in brackets, and separately cross-referenced.

The index also includes personal and other proper names mentioned in the text or annotations. References to names occurring only in the text are distinguished by t after the page number. Numbers in bold indicate a main entry. Modern place names are indicated by the inclusion of country or state abbreviations after the entry.

Abbreviations
a/f *alternative form*
Dut. *Dutch*
Eng. *English*
form. *formerly*
Fr. *French*
Ind. *Indian*
Sp. *Spanish*
tr. *transitory*

# Acknowledgements

20   Detail of south wall of Greenway Chapel, Tiverton Church, Devon, England. Photo by A.F. Kersting.
22   Suit of armor of a Spanish Man at Arms. M13 A.J. 1941. Fitzwilliam Museum, Cambridge, England.
24   Detail from map, "The Vatican Verrazano," Biblioteca Apostolica Vaticana, Rome.
28   John White drawing of a "Skirmish." Courtesy of the Department of Prints and Drawings, British Museum: No. P.S. 172482.
30   Jens Munk at Port Churchill. Woodcut from Munk's *Navigatio Septentrionalis*, Copenhagen, 1624. Det Kongelige Bibliotek, Copenhagen, Denmark.

  Baffin Chart. Add Ms 12206 fol 5-6. *True relation of his fourth voyage for the Discovery of the North-west passage in the year 1615. A coloured chart of the ship's course between the latitude 61° 66°.* By permission of the British Library.
32   "Prickly Pear," from *Florilegium Renovatum et Auctum*, Francofurti 1641. By permission of the British Library.
34   De Soto engraving from Theodori de Bry, *America* Part V. National Maritime Museum, Greenwich, England.
36   "Indians defending a town," drawing by Diego Muñoz Camargo. Glasgow University Library, Scotland. MS Hunter 242 f 317r.

  Sikyatki ceramic, Arizona, 16th century. Clay and paint. Dept. of Anthropology, Smithsonian Institution, Washington, D.C. Photo no. 155690.
38   Juan de Martinez of Messina. Detail of one of 18 "very curious geographical charts elegantly drawn on vellum in colors and gilded," 1578. By permission of the British Library. Harleian, 3450 No. 10.
40   Map by Cornelius de Jode. Courtesy Ayer Collection, Newberry Library, Chicago, Illinois. No. 135 J9 1593. Vol. 1 fol. 11 - 12.

  Inscription at El Morro, New Mexico by Juan de Oñate. Photo by Jerry Jacka.
46   Jacques Le Moyne de Morgues, illustration of Fort Caroline, engraved and published by Theodori de Bry in *America* Part II, plate IX, 1598. National Maritime Museum, Greenwich, England.
48   John White drawing of Indian in war paint. Courtesy of the Department of Prints

and Drawings, British Museum: 53A.
50   Map by Nicolas de Fer, "La Peche des Mourues," 1698. Courtesy of the National Archives of Canada, Ottawa.
52   Engraving of first building in Québec. Champlain's *Voyages de Sieur de Champlain* 1613. By permission of the British Library.

  Portable lead inkwell and clay pipe, c. 1624. Courtesy of the Ministry of Cultural Affairs. Québec, Canada.
54   Map by Adriaen Block, 1614. From the Algemeen Rijsarchiefdienst, General State Archives, Dept of Maps and Drawings, The Hague, Netherlands. (VEL 520).
56   The Powhatan Mantle, Woodlands Algonquin, Ashmolean Museum, Oxford, England. 1685. B.205.

  John Smith's map of Virginia engraved by William Hole and published in *A Map of Virginia*, Oxford, 1612. By permission of the British Library.
58   "Champlain with his allies the Algonkians, Hurons and Montagnais, met their enemies the Iroquois on 29 July 1609." *Voyages de Sieur de Champlain*, Paris 1612. By permission of the British Library.

  Montagnais Indians, from *Voyages de Sieur de Champlain*, Paris 1612. By permission of the British Library.
60   Canoes from the Codex Canadiensis. Pen and ink drawing attributed to Louis Nicolas. Thomas Gilcrease Institute of American History and Art, Tulsa, Oklahoma.

  Manuscrit de Père Chauchetière. Pen and ink drawing, "Les six premiers sauvages de la Prairie viennent d'Onneiout." Archives départementales de la Gironde, France.
62   Map drawn by Père Jacques Marquette, 1673. From the Archives de la Compagnie de Jésus, St Jérome, Québec. Canada.
64   Niagara Falls after a drawing by Louis Hennepin from *Nouvelle Découverte d'un trés Grand Pays*, Paris 1697. By permission of the British Library.
66   Portrait of Charles II of England from the original charter of the Hudson's Bay Company. Provincial Archives of Manitoba, Winnipeg, Canada.

  Beaver from the Codex Canadiensis. Pen and ink drawing attributed to Louis Nicolas. Thomas Gilcrease Institute of American History and Art, Tulsa, Oklahoma.

68   Engraving of buffalo from *A Discovery of a Vaste Country in America* by Louis Hennepin, London, 1698. Photo: C. Schüler, Codex Photographic Archive, London.
72   Dutch trade gun, Flemish knife and Venetian glass bead, 17th century, found on Iroquois village site. Museum of the North American Fur Trade, Chadron, Nebraska.
76   Tuscarora Indian tribunal. Pen and wash drawing by Franz Louis Michel, 1711. Burgerbibliothek, Bern, Switzerland.
78   Rawlinson Copperplate no. 29 of Virginia. Courtesy of the Bodleian Library, Oxford, England.

  "The Parrot of Carolina," hand-colored engraving by Mark Catesby FRS, and published in *The Natural History of Carolina*, London, 1731. By permission of the British Library.

  Frontispiece from William Gardiner, *Practical Surveying Improved*, London, 1737. By permission of the British Library.
82   Wampum belt, c.1700. Royal Ontario Museum, Toronto. No. ROM HD 6364/2B.
84   J.R. Lewis, engraving of Daniel Boone. Missouri Historical Society, St Louis, Missouri. No. POR-B-11.

  Beaver trap said to have belonged to Daniel Boone. West Virginia State Museum, Charleston. Photo by M. Keller.
86   Engraving of waterfall from Jonathan Carver, *Travels through the Interior Parts of North America in the Years 1766, 1767 and 1768 etc.* Dublin, 1779. By permission of the British Library.
88   Drawing of a calumet by Minet. Pen and ink drawing over pencil. National Archives of Canada, Ottawa. No. MG, B 19.
90   L'Archévêque and Grollet's painting of ship on parchment with message, 1684-85. Archivo General de Indias, Seville, Spain.
92   Le Buteaux, "View of the camp of Biloxi," 1720. Newberry Library, Chicago, Illinois. No. Ayer MS map 147.
94   Illustration from M. Le Page du Pratz, *Histoire de la Louisiane*, Paris, 1758. By permission of the British Library.
96   La Verendrye, lead plate. Robinson Museum, South Dakota State Historical Society, Pierre, South Dakota. No. 80.125.
98   Ramón de Murillo, pen and ink and watercolor of a leatherjacket soldier. Archivo

General de Indias, Seville, Spain.
**104** Beaver Pool. Engraving from the Baron Lahotan, Lord Lieutenant of the French Colony, *New Voyages to North America, Giving Full Account of the Customs, Commerce, Religion and Strange Opinions of the Savages of that Country,* London, 1703, Vol II. By permission of the British Library.
**106** Engraving of Inuit from *A Voyage to Hudson's Bay by the* Dobbs, Galley *and* California *in the Years 1746-1747 for Discovering a North West Passage,* by Henry Ellis, Gent. Agent for the Proprietors in the said Expedition, London, 1748. By permission of the British Library.
**108** Engraving of canoes from Samuel Hearne, *A Journey from the Prince of Wales's Fort in Hudson's Bay to the Northern Ocean - Undertaken by Order of the Hudson's Bay Company for the Discovery of Copper Mines and a North west Passage etc. in the years 1769-1772,* London, 1797. By permission of the British Library.
**110** James Isham, plan of York Fort, c.1750. Hudson's Bay Company Archives, Winnipeg, Canada. G.2/5.
**112** "A Winter View in the Athapuscow Lake," January 1772. In Samuel Hearne, *A Journey ... (op. cit., 108).* By permission of the British Library.
**114** James Webber, pen and ink and wash drawings of "The Indian Dwellings of Western Slopes of the Rockies." By permission of the British Library.
**118** Robert Irvine, watercolor of Fort William, c.1812. Hudson's Bay Company Archives, Winnipeg, Manitoba, Canada.
**123** Engraving of sea otter, from Georg W. Steller, *Auafuhrliche Beschraburg* 1753. By permission of the British Library.

Aleut woman from Unalaska 1767. From an atlas of drawings by M. D. Levashov. Photo. by A.F. Golder. University of Washington Libraries, Seattle. F.M-25.
**124** Map by Pedro Font of San Francisco Bay. By permission of the British Library. Add Ms 17,651 fol 9.

Jose Cardero, watercolor drawing of La Mision del Carmelo de Monterey. Bancroft Library, Honeyman Collection, University of California, Catalog No. 615 fig. 622.
**126** Map by Manuel Agustin Mascaro. "Plano general de la mision y Pueblo de Arispe" 1780. By permission of the British Library. MS 17661.
**128** Jose Cardero, drawing of Pira y Sepulcros de la Familia del Actual Nakau en Puerto de Mulgrave. Museo Navale, Madrid.
**130** James Webber, pen and wash drawing of the Resolution and canoes in Prince William Sound, 1778. By permission of the

British Library. Add 15514 fol 10.
**132** Jose Cardero, watercolor of "Panoramica de la entrada al puerto de Nootka." Museo de America, Madrid. Collection Bouza tomo I-12 No Inv. 2..270.
**136** Page from the Field Notes of William Clark for 17-20 January 1804, showing Clark's drawing for the Keelboat. Yale collection of Western Americana, Beinecke Rare Book and Manuscript Library, New Haven, Connecticut.
**140** George Catlin, "Comanches giving the arrows to the Medecine Rock." Oil on canvas. National Museum of American Art/Art Resource. Smithsonian Institute, Washington, D.C.
**144** L. Clarke, aquatint engraving after Samuel Seymour. Frontispiece to *Account of an Expedition from Pittsburgh to the Rocky Mountains, performed in the years 1819-1820,* London, 1823. By permission of the British Library.
**146** Carl Bodmer, watercolor of Piegan Blackfeet Man, NA 148. Joslyn Art Museum, Omaha, Nebraska.
**148** James Madison Alden, watercolor of the Kootenay river. Sketch no. 40, *Landscape views of the area along the North west boundary, 1857-62.* National Archives and Records Administration Cartographic and Architectural Branch, Washington, D.C.
**150** Alfred Jacob Miller, pencil and watercolor of Green River Camp and Rendezvous. Yale Collection of Western Americana, Beinecke Rare Book and Manuscript Library, New Haven, Connecticut.
**156** Alfred Jacob Miller, watercolor portrait of Captain Joseph Reddeford Walker. Joslyn Art Museum, Omaha, Nebraska.THE GREAT
**158** Engraving called "Natural Obelisks" from a drawing by Edward or Richard Kern made during Frémont's journey through the Rocky Mountains, 1848-49. The Huntington Library, San Marino, California.
**160** Two illustrations from *Report of the United States and Mexican Boundary Survey* made under the direction of the Secretary of the Interior by William H. Emory. Vol II. Washington, 1859. 34th Congress, 1st Session. Cactacea of the Boundary, by George Engelmann. View along the Gila, Cereus Giganteus, drawn by Paulus Roetter and engraved by James D. Smillie. Reptiles of the Boundary, Crotalus Atrox. By permission of the British Library.
**162** Richard Kern, wash drawing of "Ruins of an Old Pueblo," Academy of Natural Sciences of Philadelphia, Philadelphia.
**164** Heinrich Balduin Mollhausen, colored engraving entitled "Schluten im Hoch-

Plateau und Aussicht" from *Reisen in die Felsengebirge Nord Amerikas.* By permission of the British Library.
**168** John Mix Stanley after Private Gustavus Sohon, hand-colored lithograph of the Main Chain of the Rocky Mountains, from I.I. Stephens's survey report on the 47th Parallel. Yale Collection of Western Americana, Beinecke Rare Book and Manuscript Library, New Haven, Connecticut.
**170** Photo. of Clarence King mountaineering, by Timothy O'Sullivan. Bancroft Library, University of California.
**172** John Wesley Powell with a Paiute Indian. Photo. Department of the Interior, US Geological Survey, Reston, Virginia.
**174** William H. Holmes, "Panorama from Point Sublime" from Clarence Dutton, *The Tertiary History of the Grand Cañon District,* 1882. Department of the Interior, US Geological Survey, Reston, Virginia.
**176** Thomas Moran's chromolithograph of The Great Blue Spring, Lower Geyser Basin of the Yellowstone, Thomas Gilcrease Institute of American Art, Tulsa, Oklahoma.
**178** Members of the Hayden Survey team surveying from Point Sublime. Photo by Timothy O'Sullivan. Department of the Interior, US Geological Survey, Reston, Virginia.
**182** Lithograph after a drawing by Alexandre Postels of the Russian colony at Novo Arkhangelsk, 1827. From *Voyage autour du Monde fait par ordre de sa Majesté l'Empereur Nicolas I.* By permission of the British Museum.
**184** William G.R. Hind, "Portage on the Moisie River." Oil on board painted while on the expedition to Labrador, 1861. J. Ross Robertson Collection. Metropolitan Toronto Reference Library, Ontario, Canada.
**190** The tombstones of three of Franklin's men on Beechey Island. Engraving based on a sketch by Elisha Kent Kane in 1850. Courtesy New York Public Library.
**196** Icebergs and sea ice, Melville Bay, 1991. Photo: Bryan and Cherry Alexander, Sturminster Newton, Dorset, England.

**Additional acknowledgements:**
Special thanks are due to: Vivien Hart, Pere Joseph Cossette SJ, Carole Thibault and Michel Brassard, George Miles, Henry Spall, Felicia G. Pickering, Charles E. Hanson Jr., the staff of Royal Geographical Society Libraries.